CONSTRUCTING INTELLECTUAL PROPERTY

What is 'intellectual property'? This book examines the way in which this important area of law is constructed by the legal system. It argues that intellectual property is a body of rules, created by the legal system, that regulates the documented forms of abstract objects, which are also defined into existence by the legal system. Intellectual property law thus constructs its own objects of regulation, and it does so through the application of a collection of core concepts. By analyzing the metaphysical structure of intellectual property law and the concepts the legal system uses to construct 'intellectual property', this book sheds new light on the nature of this fascinating area of law. It explains anomalies between social and intellectual property uses of concepts such as authorship – here dubbed 'creatorship' – and originality, and it helps to explain the role of intellectual property from a structural (rather than the traditional normative) perspective.

Dr. Alexandra George is a Senior Lecturer in Law at the University of New South Wales, Australia. She is the editor of the book *Globalization and Intellectual Property* (2006), and her works have been published in numerous journals, including *Oxford Journal of Legal Studies*, *Res Publica*, *Archiv für Rechts- und Sozialphilosophie*, *Santa Clara Journal of International Law*, *UTS Law Review*, *Journal of Brand Management*, and *Sydney Law Review*. Her main areas of scholarly interest are the applied legal philosophy of intellectual property, globalization, and international intellectual property law and policy, as well as issues concerning copyright piracy and trademark counterfeiting.

Constructing Intellectual Property

Alexandra George
University of New South Wales

CAMBRIDGE
UNIVERSITY PRESS

CAMBRIDGE UNIVERSITY PRESS
Cambridge, New York, Melbourne, Madrid, Cape Town,
Singapore, São Paulo, Delhi, Mexico City

Cambridge University Press
32 Avenue of the Americas, New York NY 10013-2473, USA

Published in the United States of America by Cambridge University Press, New York

www.cambridge.org
Information on this title: www.cambridge.org/9781107691773

First published 2012
First paperback edition 2013

A catalogue record for this publication is available from the British Library

Library of Congress Cataloguing in Publication Data
George, Alexandra.
Constructing intellectual property / Alexandra George.
p. cm.
Includes bibliographical references and index.
ISBN 978-1-107-01461-9 (hardback)
1. Intellectual property – Philosophy. I. Title.
K1401.G46 2012
346.04′8–dc23 2011030302

ISBN 978-1-107-01461-9 Hardback
ISBN 978-1-107-69177-3 Paperback

To my parents,

Charles and Elizabeth George

Brief Contents

Contents

Figures

Acknowledgements

The debts I have incurred in writing this book are numerous and deep. I would here like to thank all of those people who have assisted me.

Infinite thanks to my family and friends for being unwavering in their support for me. I appreciate it more than I can express.

My sincere thanks to Derek Jones, Dave Lexton, and Jeff Duckett, who acted with kindness, selflessness, and honour to combat gross injustice.

I am greatly indebted to Chris Birch SC, Ralph Melano, Dennis Patterson, Matt Rimmer, Daniel Stoljar, Wojciech Sadurski, and Tom Campbell for their support and feedback on drafts of this work. Thank you also to Lionel Bently and Roger Shiner for helpful comments on an early draft chapter, to all of those who offered suggestions on papers that became parts of the work, and to Cambridge University Press's insightful and supportive anonymous reviewers.

Tremendous thanks to John Berger at Cambridge University Press. Thank you also to David Jou and the copy editor, Mary Becker, and to Bindu and the team at NewGen Publishing for their careful editorial work.

Thank you also to Tony Antoniou, Bruce Ayling, Philip Baker QC, Linda and Graham Christian, Susanna and Dicky Clymo, Monika and John Cutts, Graham Dutfield, Brendan Edgeworth, Richard Gallifant, John Gardner, Tibor Gold, Paul Gwynne, Jose and Jim Harris, Patsy Hay, Paul Huehnergard, Andrew Karney, Dimity Kingsford-Smith, Nicola Lacey, Bruce Landesman, Kathleen Mastrogiacomo, Margaret McKercher,

James Rigney, Leon Trakman, Michael Williams, and Alex Ziegert, for their kindness, friendship, advice, feedback, mentoring, and encouragement along the way.

Above all, to my parents, who invested so much in my education and supported so many years of my studies, and to my grandparents, who always encouraged and believed in me, I will be eternally grateful.

Of course, any errors, oversights, or omissions are mine alone, and entirely my responsibility.

Authorities

CONVENTIONS AND TREATIES

Agreement on Technical Cooperation between ISO and CEN (1991); passed as ISO Council resolution 18/1990 and CEN General Assembly resolution 3/1990

Agreement on Trade Related Aspects of Intellectual Property Rights (1984)

Australia–United States Free Trade Agreement (1994)

Berne Convention for the Protection of Literary and Artistic Works of 9 September 1886, completed in Paris on 4 May 1896 (as revised and amended)

Convention on the Control and Marking of Articles of Precious Metals (1972)

Convention Establishing the World Intellectual Property Organization (1967)

General Agreement on Tariffs and Trade (1947)

Nice Agreement Concerning the International Classification of Goods and Services for the Purposes of the Registration of Marks (1957)

Paris Convention for the Protection of Industrial Property of March 20, 1883 (as revised and amended)

Universal Copyright Convention (1952)

Universal Declaration of Human Rights (1948) (UN)

STATUTES AND CASES ORGANIZED BY JURISDICTION

AUSTRALIA

Statutes and Regulations:

Brands Act 1918 (Qld)
Brands Regulation 1998 (Qld)
Copyright Act 1968 (Cth)
Copyright Amendment Act 1984 (Cth)
Copyright Amendment (Moral Rights) Act 2000 (Cth)
Crimes Act 1900 (NSW)
Interpretation of Legislation Act 1984 (Victoria)
Patent Act 1990 (Cth)
Road Safety (Traffic Management) Regulations 2009 (Victoria)
Trade Marks Act 1995 (Cth)
Trade Practices Act 1974 (Cth)
US Free Trade Agreement Implementation Act 2004 (Cth)

Cases:

Apple Computer Inc v Computer Edge Pty Ltd (1983) 50 ALR 581
Doodeward v Spence (1908) 6 CLR 406
Federal Commissioner of Taxation v United Aircraft Corp (1943) 68 CLR 525
IceTV Pty Ltd v Nine Network Australia Pty Ltd (2009) 239 CLR 458
Nine Network Australia Pty Ltd v IceTV Pty Ltd [2007] FCA 1172
John Bulun Bulun & Anor v R & T Textiles Pty Ltd (1998) IPR 51
Opposition by Claude Ruiz Picasso to registration of trade mark application 754587(42) – PIZZA PICASSO PIZZAS OF ART and device – filed in the name of Robyn Thomas (7 September 2001), available at the IP Australia website: http://www.ipaustralia.gov.au/pdfs/trademarks/hearings/754587.pdf [accessed 10 May 2010]
Prior v Lansdowne Press Pty Ltd (1975) 12 ALR 685
R v Jagamara (Unreported, Northern Territory Supreme Court, 28 May 1984)
Rescare Ltd v Anaesthetic Supplies Pty Ltd (1992) 25 IPR 119

Row Weeder Pty Ltd v Nielsen (1998) IPR 400

Shell Co of Australia Ltd v Rohm & Haas Co (1949) 78 CLR 601

Smith Kline & French Laboratories (Australia) Ltd v Secretary, Department of Community Services and Health (1990) 17 IPR 545

Taco Co (Aust) v Taco Bell (1982) 42 AR 177

Universal City Studios v Zeccola (1982) 46 ALR 189; 67 FLR 225

Victoria Park Racing and Recreation Grounds Company Limited v Taylor (1937) 58 CLR 479

EUROPEAN UNION

Directives and Regulations:

The Convention for the Protection of Human Rights and Fundamental Freedoms (1950) (Council of Europe)

Council Directive 93/98/EEC of 29 October 1993 Harmonizing the Term of Protection of Copyright and Certain Related Rights, Official Journal L 290, 24/11/1993 P. 0009–0013

Council Regulation (EC) No. 207/2009 of 26 February 2009 on the Community Trade Mark

European Court of Justice Cases:

Canon Kabushiki Kaisha v MGM [1999] EPC 117

Lloyd Schuhfabrik Meyer & Co GmbH v Klisjen Handel BV [2000] FSR 77

Ralf Sieckmann v Deutsches Patent-und Markenamt [2003] ETMR 466

Reckitt & Colman Products v Borden Inc [1990] All ER 873

Sabel BV v Puma AG, Rudolf Dassler Sport [1998] RPC 199

Sieckmann v Deutsches Patent-und Markenamt [2003] RPC 38

UNITED KINGDOM

Statutes and Regulations:

An Act Declaring the Rights and Liberties of the Subject and Settling the Succession of the Crown 1689

Adventure Activities Licensing Regulation 2004

Copyright Act 1709, 8 Anne c.19

Copyright Act 1775

Copyright Act 1911, s.22

Copyright, Designs and Patents Act 1988

Duration of Copyright and Rights in Performances Regulations 1995 (Statutory Instrument 1995, No. 3297)

Hallmarking Act 1973

Patent Law Amendment Act 1852 (15 & 16 Vict. c.83)

Patents Act 1835 (5 & 6 Will. 4 c.83)

Patents Act 1886 (49 & 50 Vict. c.37)

Patents Act 1902 (2 Edw. 7 c.53)

Patents Act 1949 (12, 13 & 14 Geo. 6 c.87)

Patents Act 1977

Patents and Designs Act 1907 (& Edw. 7 c.29)

Patents and Designs Act 1919 (9 & 10 Geo. 5 c.80)

Patents and Designs Act 1932 (22 & 23 Geo. 5 c.32)

Patents and Designs (Convention) Act 1928 (18 Geo. 5 c.3)

Patents, Designs and Trade Marks Act 1883 (46 & 47 Vict. c.57)

*Patents, Designs and Trade Marks Act*1885 (48 & 49 Vict. c.63)

Registered Designs Rules 1995 (SI 1995/2912 and SI 2001/3950)

Statute of Anne, 8 Anne, ch.19 (1710)

Statute of Monopolies 1623 (21 Jac. 1 c.3)

Theft Act 1968

Trade Mark Registration Act 1875 (38 & 39 Vict. c.91)

Trade Marks Act 1994

Cases:

Arsenal Football Club Plc v Reed [2001] RPC 46

Ashdown v Telegraph Group Ltd (2001) 3 WLR 1368

Ashmore v Douglas Horne [1987] FSR 533

BBC v Talksport [2001] FSR 53

Clothworkers of Ipswich Case Godbolt, tit. 351, p. 25; reported (1653) 78 ER 147

Criminal Clothing Ltd v Aytan's Manufacturing (UK) Ltd [2005] EWHC 1303

Darcy v Allin, 77 Eng. Rep. 1260 (Queen's Bench, 1602)

Designers Guild v Williams [2000] 1 WLR 2416.
Donoghue v Allied Newspapers Limited (1938) Ch. 106
Exxon Corporation v Exxon Insurance Consultants International [1982] 1 Ch. 119
Francis Day and Hunter v 20th Century Fox [1940] AC 112
Hyde Park Residence Ltd v Yelland [2000] Ch. 14; EMLR 363
Lion Laboratories v Evans [1985] QM 525
MacMillan v Cooper (1924) 40 TLR 186
Philips v Remington (1998) RPC 283
Powell v Birmingham Vinegar [1897] 14 RPC 720
Reddaway v Banham [1896] AC 199
Redwood Music v Chappell [1982] RPC 109
University of London Press Ltd v University Tutorial Press Ltd [1916] 2 Ch. 601
Walter v Lane (1900) AC 539
Warnink v Townend [1979] AC 731
Wood v Boosey (1868) LR 3 QB 223
ZYX Music GmbH v King [1995] 3 All ER 1

UNITED STATES

Statutes:

Constitution of the United States of America
Copyright Act 1976; Pub. L. 94–553; 90 Stat. 2541 (1976) (17 U.S.C. §§ 101–810) (amending 44 U.S.C. §§ 505 & 2113; 18 U.S.C. § 2318)
Copyright Term Extension Act 1998; S 505, Pub. L. 105–298, 11 Stat. 2827 (1998) (amending 17 U.S.C. §§301–304)
Declaration of Independence (4 July 1776)
Digital Millennium Copyright Act 1998 Pub. L. 105–304.112 Stat. 2860 (1998)
Food and Agricultural Code, s.20661–20672 (California)
Lanham (Trademark) Act 15 USCA §1051–1127 (2000)
Omnibus Trade and Competitiveness Act 1988

Cases:

Bridgeman Art Library v Corel Corp., 36 F. Supp. 2d 191 (S.D.N.Y. 1999)

Burrow-Giles Lithographic Co. v Sarony, 111 U.S. 53 (1884)

Calhoun v Lillenas Publishing, Civ. Nos. 01-11413, 01–11415 (11th Circuit, 2002)

Campbell v Acuff-Rose Music, 510 U.S. 569 (1994)

CDN Inc. v Kapes, 197 F.3d 1256, 1261 (9th Circuit, 1999)

Dallas Cowboys Cheerleaders, Inc. v. Pussycat Cinema, Ltd., 604 F.2d 200 at 2005 (2d Cir. 1979)

Diamond v Chakrabarty, 447 U.S.303 (1980)

Durham Industries, Inc. v Tomy Corp., 630 F.2d 905 (2nd Circuit, 1980)

Emerson v Davies, 8 F.Cas 615 at 619 (CCD Mass, 1845)

Ets-Hokin v Skyy Spirits Inc., 225 F.3d 1068 (9th Circuit, 2000)

Feist Publications, Inc. v Rural Telephone Service Co. (1991) 499 U.S.340

Folsom v Marsh, 9 F.Cas. 342 (Circuit Court of Massachusetts, Oct Term 1841)

Gracen v Bradford Exchange, 698 F.2d 300 (7th Circuit, 1983)

Harper & Row Publishers, Inc. v Nation Enters., 471 U.S. 539, 556 (1985)

Herman v Youngstown Car Manufacturing Co., 191 F. 579, 112 CCA 185 (6th Cir. 1911)

Jacobellis v Ohio (1964), 378 US 184

Mattel, Inc v MCA Records, 28 F.Supp. 2d 1120 (C D California, 1998), *affirmed* 296 F.3d 894 (9th Circuit, 2002)

Moore v Regents of University of California 215 Cal.App.3d 709 (1988); *affirmed* in part, reversed in part, 51 Cal.3d 120, 793 P.2d 479 (1990)

Panduit Corp v Stahlin Bros Fibre Works Inc, 575 F.2d 1152 at 1159, 197 USPQ (BNA) 726 (6th Circuit, 1978)

Ringling Bros.-Barnum & Bailey Combined Shows, Inc. v. Utah Div. of Travel Dev., 170 F.3d 449 at 459 (4th Cir. 1999)

OTHER JURISDICTIONS

Zimbabwe:

Armorial Bearings, Names, Uniforms and Badges Act [Acts 12/1971, 40/1977, 29/1981 (s.59), 7/198, 22/2001 (s.4); S.I. 490/1981 (s.3)], Ch. 10:01

Abbreviations

ACCC	Australian Competition and Consumer Commission
AWI	Australian Wool Innovation Limited
Berne Convention	*Berne Convention for the Protection of Literary and Artistic Works* (1886)
BSI	National Standards Body (UK), formerly known as the British Standards Institution
CEN	European Committee for Standardization
Cth	Commonwealth of Australia
CTM	Community Trade Mark (EU)
IAAO	International Association of Assay Offices
IPC	Intellectual Property Committee
IPRs	intellectual property rights
ISO	International Organization for Standardization
NIAAA	National Indigenous Arts Advocacy Agency
Nice Convention	*Nice Agreement Concerning the International Classification of Goods and Services for the Purposes of the Registration of Marks* (1957)
NSW	New South Wales, Australia
Paris Convention	*Paris Convention for the Protection of Industrial Property* (1883)
Qld	Queensland, Australia

Sonny Bono Copyright Term Extension Act	*Copyright Term Extension Act* (1998) (US)
TCEs	traditional cultural expressions
TK	traditional knowledge
TRIPS Agreement	*Agreement on Trade Related Aspects of Intellectual Property* (1994)
USPTO	United States Patent and Trademark Office
Vienna Agreement	*Agreement on Technical Cooperation between ISO and CEN* (1991)
WIPO	World Intellectual Property Organization
WIPO Convention	*Convention Establishing the World Intellectual Property Organization* (1967)
WTO	World Trade Organization

1 Introduction

INTELLECTUAL PROPERTY LAWS REGULATE ACCESS TO AND/or the use of ideational objects such as ideas, information, knowledge, and symbols. Many of the most valuable assets of the world's largest corporations lie in their intellectual property portfolios: the trademarks of Coca Cola, Nike, and Ford are some obvious examples of the value of corporations being tied to their intellectual property rights. The copyright holdings of publishers, movie studios, and software developers such as Penguin, Warner Bros., and Microsoft, respectively, offer further examples. The value of patents on inventions, some of which are owned by agricultural, pharmaceutical, and biotechnology companies, is also immense. With so much depending on the nature of intellectual property laws, the stakes are high and questioning of these laws can be met coolly by those with vested interests in preserving the status quo or improving the benefits they can reap from the existing system. With so much vested in the contemporary system, much law-making in this area rests on implicit and explicit assumptions that 'intellectual property' – the objects of regulation by intellectual property laws – exists independently of the law and exists in pre-legal forms that are then registered and/or regulated by the law. This book challenges such suppositions.

In an environment in which massive sums of money are dependent on the continuation of expectations created by existing intellectual property laws, those who do challenge assumptions underpinning the status quo are often branded 'radical' and accused of trying to undermine the system. That is not the aim of this volume. This book is an explanatory attempt from within the intellectual property system. Using references found within the jurisprudence of intellectual property and the broader jurisprudence on which intellectual property rests, it seeks to clarify what 'intellectual property' is, or is not, how it is structured, its characteristics, and the conditions in which intellectual propertization occurs and thrives. This study seeks to explain intellectual property, not to undermine it.

Framing the backdrop for analysis throughout the volume, this opening chapter begins with a fairy tale to demonstrate or remind us that things are not always what they seem, and to make the point – a point that is often forgotten in discussions about intellectual property law – that the law does not have to be the way that it is. It could almost always be better. The approach taken here is that to question and discuss the law and our ways of thinking about it is not subversive. Rather, it is constructive and likely, eventually, to bring about improvements in the consistency and coherence of those laws.

1.1. An Intellectual Property Fairy Tale

Once upon a time there was a vain emperor who loved fashion and new clothes. His kingdom was joyful and festive, and the palace regularly organized carnivals in which the emperor would parade to show off his latest outfits. People flocked from all over the world to visit this happy place.

One day two swindlers arrived in the kingdom. They pretended to be weavers and boasted that they could create the finest, most beautiful and delicate cloth that anyone had ever imagined. Their gorgeous colours and patterns, they said, were exceptional, and their fabric was featherlight. They heightened curiosity and concern by explaining that garments made from their material possessed the amazing quality of being invisible to anyone who had secretly broken the law.

'What splendid cloth,' thought the emperor. 'If I wore an outfit made of this material, I could distinguish the honest people from the criminals and I would know which people were unfit for their jobs. I must commission the weavers to make some of this cloth for me immediately.' And he paid a large advance to the swindlers so that they could start working on a suit for him straightaway.

The swindlers set up their looms and pretended to weave busily. They asked for silk and the most precious gold thread, and they seemed to be working at the looms until late into the night.

'I wonder how my outfit is coming along?' the emperor thought. But he felt uneasy when he recalled that those who had broken the law would not be able to see it (because sometimes he was not really sure that he completely knew what the law meant himself). The emperor decided to send his most loyal, trusted, and highly skilled minister to check on the weavers' progress.

The old minister went into the room where the swindlers sat working. He looked towards them and blinked. He could see nothing on the looms. 'Oh, no!' His heart raced. 'Am I really a law-breaker? I should never have thought so, but why can't I see the cloth? I must not let anybody know. Can it be possible that I have broken the law and am not fit for my office? Nobody must realize that I am unable to see the cloth.'

'How pretty! It is exceedingly beautiful,' commented the poor man. 'What a lovely pattern and brilliant colours. I will tell the emperor that I like this cloth very much.'

The two swindlers looked delighted and told him how they had chosen the luminescent colours to weave into the fabric's striking pattern. The old minister listened attentively, anxious to report everything about the cloth back to the emperor accurately.

Some days later the emperor sent a trusted judge to see if the cloth was nearly finished. Like the senior minister, he gazed anxiously at the looms where the precious fabric was supposed to be. His heart sank as he realized he could not see the material.

'Isn't it beautiful?' asked the swindlers.

'Perhaps I am really not smart enough to understand the law properly, which is why the cloth is invisible to me. Could it be that I am not fit for my important job?' thought the judge, who had sometimes marvelled at his own success. 'Everyone says I am so competent and clever, but is it possible that I really do not deserve this position?' He turned to the swindlers and praised the cloth, resolving not to let anybody know what had happened.

'Oh, it is excellent,' gushed the judge when he went back to the emperor. 'You'll be amazed by the stunning fabric those weavers are creating for you.'

Everybody in the kingdom talked excitedly about the marvellous cloth. The emperor grew impatient to see it for himself, and he eventually plucked up the courage to visit the two clever swindlers. They still appeared to be working hard.

'Isn't it magnificent?' exclaimed the two officers who had previously been to inspect the cloth and who now accompanied the emperor. 'Come closer and see the shimmering colours, Your Majesty.' They pointed enthusiastically at the empty looms, each imagining that he alone could not see the cloth.

The emperor moved closer. 'What is this?' he thought with a sense of panic. 'Why can't I see it? No, no. This is terrible! Surely I have not done something illegal. How could *I* have broken the law? Am I unfit to be emperor? There will be a revolution if people find out.'

He smiled at the weavers and nodded contentedly as he looked at the empty loom. 'I am pleased,' the emperor said finally.

All his attendants looked and looked. Not one of them wanted to admit to the others that he could not see anything on the looms, so they all praised the fabric and urged the emperor to wear the wonderful new clothes at a great pageant. Everybody seemed to be so delighted that the emperor appointed the two swindlers Imperial Court Weavers.

At last the swindlers announced the suit was ready. The emperor undressed, and the swindlers pretended to drape him in the new garments, piece by piece. The emperor turned slowly before the mirror, looking at himself from every side.

'They look wonderful!' affirmed the courtiers. 'What a beautiful pattern! And how well everything fits! It really is a fine suit of clothes!'

The master of ceremonies announced that the procession was ready to begin. The chamberlains each pretended to hold the emperor's train in their hands, anxious that others might realize they could not see anything.

The emperor marched in the procession under the regal canopy, and everyone in the street or peering from windows exclaimed, 'Indeed, the new suit is incomparable! How elegant! What a fabulous train!' Admitting that they could see nothing would have been tantamount to proclaiming themselves criminals, so the pretence was perpetuated. The emperor's clothes had never been so greatly admired: 'How wonderful! Absolutely gorgeous!' everybody agreed.

'But he has nothing on at all,' said a little child at last.

'Goodness gracious! Listen to the voice of an innocent child,' his father gasped. People whispered to each other what the child had said, and realization raced through the crowd. 'But he has nothing on at all,' everyone cried.

That made a deep impression upon the emperor, as he thought they were right.

'Remain dignified!' the emperor told himself sternly. 'I must stay calm, keep smiling and waving, and pretend nothing is wrong.' Behind him, the emperor's chamberlains walked with ever greater dignity, as though they still believed they were carrying a train.[1]

AND SO IT IS WITH INTELLECTUAL PROPERTY?

In many respects, Hans Christian Andersen's fairy tale about the emperor's new clothes reads like a metaphor for intellectual property.[2]

[1] Adapted from various translations of Hans Christian Andersen, 'The Emperor's New Suit', *Fairy Tales of Hans Christian Andersen* (1837). Danish author Andersen lived in Europe from 1805 to 1875, so his story is no longer covered by copyright law in the United Kingdom, the United States, the European Union, or Australia. It is therefore in the 'public domain' (see discussion in Chapter 4, §4.2.5.b, for an explanation of this concept) and can be freely used and/or adapted by anyone.

[2] This analogy between the 'Emperor's New Clothes' and intellectual property was presented at the First Annual Intellectual Property and Communications Law and Policy

The term 'intellectual property' means different things to different people,[3] but most conceptions include explicit or implicit reference to a legally regulated, artificially created monopoly over intangible objects of communication, such as ideas, information, knowledge, and symbols.

The unquestioning way in which many societies have accepted the introduction of intellectual property laws – and a particular version of intellectual property that has been presented to them as a fait accompli – shares a key similarity with the story of the emperor's new clothes. Many people believed that the emperor's new clothes had a physical existence independent of what society believed about the outfit, but in fact the emperor's new clothes were merely a figment of the collective imagination. Likewise, many people believe that intellectual property has a physical existence that is independent of what society believes about it and that this necessitates its regulation. This book suggests, instead, that intellectual property exists only after it has been brought into being by law, and it too is therefore a figment of the collective imagination.

The analogy is not perfect. The main distinction between the alleged new clothes worn by the emperor and objects of regulation by intellectual property law is that the former is – to use terminology that will be explained in Chapter 3 – an 'ideational object'[4] only. The clothes have no tangible form in which they could be perceived by others. By contrast, objects of regulation by intellectual property law characteristically require fixation in a 'documented form'[5] before rights attach to them.

Another difference between intellectual property and the emperor's new clothes is that no law mandated compliance with the myth of the

Scholars Roundtable, Michigan State University–DCL College of Law, 20–21 February 2004. My thanks to the participants at that conference for their insightful comments on and discussion of this topic.

[3] For an analysis of these meanings, see the discussion in Chapter 2. For an analysis of the metaphysics of intellectual property, see Chapter 3.

[4] See Chapter 3, §3.2.2.

[5] See Chapter 3, §3.2.3.

emperor's new clothes, whereas the prescriptions of intellectual property laws demand recognition of the intellectual property objects they create and compliance with the rules that regulate human behaviour with respect to those objects.

The myth of the existence of the emperor's new clothes was also propagated by swindlers whose goal was to deceive. It would be stretching the analogy a little too far to suggest that the law of intellectual property was created by swindlers engaged in a conspiracy to deceive, although it is probably uncontroversial to observe that the development of intellectual property has been driven by those with vested interests.[6]

Like all analogies, that between intellectual property and the emperor's new clothes thus has limitations, but it nonetheless provides an accessible introduction to – and method of provoking critical thought about – some of the more complex philosophical ideas contained in the pages that follow.

1.2. Drawing Analogies and Questioning Assumptions

Every day we make numerous assumptions about how society functions. We unquestioningly accept statements made by those in positions of authority and unthinkingly conform to social norms that guide our thoughts and behaviour. This is a part of human nature and it is part of the human condition. It is neither positive nor negative, but it is worthy of attention for what it can tell us about the operation of particular societies and the processes by which intellectual propertization has evolved. The following pages use the analogy of the 'Emperor's New Clothes' to help identify and unpack some common social beliefs and assumptions about the nature of intellectual property.

[6] See Chapter 2, §2.1.1.c.

1.2.1. Assumptions About the Existence of Intellectual Property

When an 'expert' (albeit one with a vested interest) convincingly maintains that the emperor's new clothes exist and take a particular form, other people – some gullible, others doubting their own judgement and/or with their own interests to protect – go along with the charade that the garments do in fact exist in this form.

Similarly, when someone with a vested interest talks convincingly about intellectual property as though it exists as a pre-legal object, it can be easy for others also to imagine it exists as such. Although they cannot perceive it with their five senses (sight, sound, smell, touch, and taste), they accept or pretend that intellectual property is akin to something with a physical or 'real' existence.[7] They suppose or conceive that there is such a thing as intellectual property that lies out there in the world waiting to be discovered and regulated. They receive mental images of what the things regulated by intellectual property laws are like, or they reflect upon the consequences of those laws being applied. Like all ideas, information, and knowledge that exist when they 'materialize' in human minds, intellectual property thus acquires an imagined existence.[8] These imaginary objects are then regulated by law.

[7] 'Existence' is used here to denote physical or 'real' existence, ie, existence as a tangible object that can be perceived by the human senses. For a summary of the philosophical discussion of 'existence', see S. G. Williams, 'Existence', in Jaegwon Kim and Ernest Sosa (eds.), *A Companion to Metaphysics* (Oxford: Blackwell, 1995) at 145–150. Physical or 'real' existence will be distinguished later from existence as a 'non-existent object'.

[8] 'Imagination' is used here in a sense described in Michael Tye, 'Image/Imagination', in Jaegwon Kim and Ernest Sosa (eds.), *A Companion to Metaphysics* (Oxford: Blackwell, 1995) at 234–235, ie, the power to imagine (form a mental image); reflect in words; suppose; conceive. Jim Baggott, *A Beginner's Guide to Reality* (London: Penguin, 2005) explains: 'With imagination we can see things that do not yet exist. We can anticipate things we haven't experienced. We can envisage a future yet to come. We can plan' (at 17), and 'We now live within a reality that has become a complete invention of our postmodern urban, industrial society and media culture. To some it has become a dream world, a hyperreality, no longer based on anything identifiably real' (at 19). 'Hyperreality' is a concept used by Jean Baudrillard; see generally Jean Baudrillard, *Simulacra and Simulation* (Ann Arbor: University of Michigan Press, 1981). It refers

Intellectual property is created by law and regulated by law, and in this way it differs from objects that are not imaginary but have pre-existing physical forms that influence the manner in which they are controlled and that allow them to be defined by reference to tangible properties. While objects of regulation by intellectual property law must generally attach to a physical object,[9] it is not the physical object that is the object of regulation (ie, it is not the physical object that is the 'intellectual property object'). The intellectual property object remains an imaginary thing, even though it is evidenced by a proximation in the tangible object. There is no way of knowing whether two people who turn their minds to the intellectual property object are envisaging identical things. Perhaps each imagines a slightly different impression of the same thing. Yet, from a legal perspective, both are quite possibly imagining accurately the same object that is being regulated by intellectual property law. To the extent that 'existence' denotes physical existence, intellectual property objects are non-existent objects. However, to the extent that intellectual property laws define into existence the non-existent objects that they then regulate in the context of their connection to tangible objects, and to the extent that regulation of human behaviour towards these tangible objects has physical consequences, 'intellectual property' is very real.

1.2.2. Assumptions About the Authority of 'Intellectual Property'

Someone authoritative describes the patterns and colours in the emperor's imaginary new clothes. Nobody wants to appear to have secretly broken the law, and there is a human inclination to conform rather than challenge a dominant view.[10] Few people are content to be shunned or ostracized, or

to a simulation or imperfect representation of physical or behavioural reality that no longer resembles that reality. It is a result of media or other representations of 'reality' that distort fact. See discussion in Baggott, above at 14.

[9] See Chapter 3, §3.2.3.

[10] A famous demonstration of this came with the Asch conformity experiments, in which a social psychologist tested the tendency of people to conform when confronted with a majority opinion that conflicted with their own. College students in the United States

to suffer prosecution, persecution, or damage to their career, and the social tendency is therefore for all to pretend they can see the emperor's outfit.

When someone authoritative describes what she or he thinks the things controlled by intellectual property laws are like or should be like, there can be a similar social tendency – particularly among those with vested interests – to assume or pretend that these things have an objectively identifiable character.[11] The emperor has nothing on at all, and his clothes are a figment of the social imagination. They are thoughts or mental images that have not been given a physical or material form external to the mind/brain of the thinker: they are real only in the sense that they are thought to be real and in the ways in which this triggers real effects as people respond to them.[12] The manner in which the population behaves towards the idea[13] that the emperor is wearing a new suit reflects the norms that society has built around the regulation of ideas, information,

were asked to compare lines drawn on a card and indicate which two lines were of the same length. When others in the room gave the wrong answer because they had been secretly briefed to do so, an unsuspecting subject tended to also give the wrong answer more than a third of the time. The tendency was less pronounced when at least one other person gave the correct answer. See S. E. Asch, 'Opinions and Social Pressure' (1955) 193:5 *Scientific American* 31–35.

Hogan describes this as 'rational acquiescence', which he defines as 'consent to the status quo based on an understanding of the physical, economic, or emotional harm one might suffer for rebellion.' See Patrick Colm Hogan, *The Culture of Conformism: Understanding Social Consent* (Durham, NC: Duke University Press, 2001) at 13.

[11] For psychological theory about obedience to authority, see Thomas Blass (ed.), *Obedience to Authority: Current Perspectives on the Milgram Paradigm* (London: Lawrence Erlbaum, 2000), especially conclusions drawn from an experiment at 204–210.

[12] The idea that something is real if it is perceived as such finds popular recital in quotes such as Douglas Adams's 'Everything you see or hear or experience in any way at all is specific to you. You create a universe by perceiving it, so everything in the universe you perceive is specific to you' (Douglas Adams, *Mostly Harmless* [New York: Ballantine, 1992], chap. 9). The quote frequently attributed to Pablo Picasso –'Everything you can imagine is real' – suggests a similar theme. These views capture the belief that humans react to their subjective perceptions of reality rather than to an objective reality, and those perceptions thus have 'real' effects.

[13] For a summary of uses of the concept of an 'idea' in philosophical thought, see M. B. Bolton, 'Idea', in Jaegwon Kim and Ernest Sosa (eds.), *A Companion to Metaphysics* (Oxford: Blackwell, 1995) at 225–227.

symbols, and knowledge, and the same holds true for the way in which people react to intellectual property laws.

1.2.3. Compliance with Assumptions and Social Norms

Someone declares that those who cannot see the emperor's new clothes are secret law-breakers, and it becomes the accepted wisdom that this is the way things are. Anyone who challenges this view risks being accused of undermining the legal system.

Someone declares the rules of intellectual property law and these rules become received precedents, with those who break the laws suffering legal penalties, and those who voice fear that the premises are questionable tending to be branded stupid, incompetent, or seditious.[14] A similar result can sometimes even be achieved simply by advocating new intellectual property norms sufficiently strongly, with dissenters being dismissed as 'immoral' or 'unethical', regardless of what the content of those laws may be.[15]

'Shunning' is a tried and tested strategy of leaders who marginalize and discredit dissidents and other free-thinking 'threats' to a regime by branding them mad, unreasonable, or subversive, and by relegating them to psychiatric wards, mental asylums, and prisons.[16] Psychiatrist Thomas

[14] For example, consumers who do not understand intellectual property law or who do not buy 'authentic' objects of intellectual property when they can purchase identical or adequate copies (ie, unauthorized 'fakes') more cheaply are accused of supporting organized crime. The following statement is from the Internet website of the Merthyr Tydfil County Borough Council Trading Standards Service, a government office in Wales: 'The damage [counterfeiting] causes is far reaching in today's society.... Terrorism, drug dealing and other underworld activities are often linked in and make money from the supply of counterfeit items. By buying counterfeits you are indirectly supporting these criminals [*sic*] activities': http://www.merthyr.gov.uk/tradingstandards/services_contents.html (accessed 25 May 2006).

[15] See, eg, Jessica Litman's discussion of attendees feeling marginalized at conferences where others may not share their views: Jessica Litman, 'The Politics of Intellectual Property' (2009) 27 *Cardozo Arts and Entertainment Law Journal* 313–320.

[16] See, eg, Kim Murphy, 'Speak Out? Are You Crazy?' (30 May 2006) *Los Angeles Times*: 'In a throwback to Soviet times, Russians who cross the powerful are increasingly

Szasz is probably better known for some of his rather extreme and controversial statements, but the following observation about the nature of criminality and mental illness seems to describe a truism:

> [I]ndividuals do not exist in nature labelled as criminals or mentally ill; what do exist are persons who violate social norms and who are then categorized in various ways. When masses of men, especially the pillars of society, automatically prejudge rule violators as heretics, witches, or mental patients, then we witness one of the most fundamental social mechanisms by means of which groups secure the cohesion of their members – namely, scapegoating.[17]

It is thus not surprising that people often perceive, pretend to perceive, and even question their perceptive responses if they do not actually perceive, the same things that those around them seem to be perceiving.[18] Those who wish to propound a certain belief need merely to project a perception that everyone – or even 'a' or a 'rational' or an 'ethical' or a 'moral', 'reasonable', or [add just about any positive adjective] person – holds this belief in order to help solidify public opinion behind it.

In such conditions, characterizing critics of intellectual property laws as irrational, immoral, unjust, a threat to the fabric of society, or lacking an understanding of its nuances is arguably not so different from saying that those who cannot see the emperor's new clothes are necessarily law-breakers. Engendering fear of ridicule, reprisal, or shunning is an effective method of generating self-censorship and stifling criticism, as is instilling fear of legal repercussions. Persuading – intentionally or otherwise – someone not to behave in a certain way with respect to ideas,

hustled into mental asylums, rights activists say'; Joseph Kahn, 'Sane Chinese Put in Asylum, Doctors Say' (16 March 2006) *New York Times*: 'Dutch psychiatrists have determined that a prominent Chinese dissident who spent 13 years in a police-run psychiatric institution in Beijing did not have mental problems that would justify his incarceration, two human rights groups said Thursday.'

[17] Thomas Szasz, *Insanity: The Idea and Its Consequences* (New York: Wiley, 1987) at 119–120.

[18] See, eg, the findings of the Asch conformity experiments at §1.2.2 and above n. 10.

information, knowledge, or communicative symbols (such as language, logos, or images) for fear of repercussions is also to harness the *chilling effect*.[19]

The result is that the emperor's new clothes become a 'fact' of life. It is normal and conventional for people in the emperor's kingdom to accept that his wonderful clothes do in fact exist, even if they cannot see or perceive them themselves. It is even expected that such a belief will be held. In this sense, the emperor's clothes hold a status similar to that held by sorcery or religion in some societies.

[19] This term stems from First Amendment jurisprudence in the United States and is widely used in literature and cases concerning defamation law. When the media claim that fear of legal repercussions is deterring them from publishing material that would be of public interest, the law is described as having a 'chilling' effect. As one commentator explains: 'Administrative censorship and court injunctions prevent publication in an immediate and straightforward manner. In contrast, the threat of a criminal prosecution or a civil action for damages may deter the media from publishing a story, even though if a prosecution (or action) were brought, the press (or other media outlet) would be able to defend the action.' See Eric Barendt, Laurence Lustgarten, Kenneth Norrie, and Hugh Stephenson, *Libel and the Media: The Chilling Effect* (New York: Oxford University Press, 1997) at 190. The effect, as noted by Frederick Shauer, 'Social Foundations of the Law of Defamation: A Comparative Analysis' (1980) 1 *Journal of Media Law and Practice* 3–23 at 11, is that the media organization may be fearful of publishing material that may lead to a defamation action, so it self-censors. This inevitably heightens the risk that some factually accurate material will not be published because, for example, the source insists on anonymity or because the media outlet fears the cost of defending its publication in court. See Lois G. Forer, *A Chilling Effect: The Mounting Threat of Libel and Invasion of Privacy Actions to the First Amendment* (New York: W. W. Norton, 1987) at 16–17 for a discussion of this effect in practice.

Intellectual property laws that are too strong or vague can have a comparable effect. See, eg, Derek J. Schaffner, 'The Digital Millennium Copyright Act: Overextension of Copyright Protection and the Unintended Chilling Effects on Fair Use, Free Speech and Innovation' (2004) 14 *Cornell Journal of Law and Public Policy* 145–169, arguing that the enactment of the US *Digital Millennium Copyright Act* in 1998 precipitated many cases yielding unpredictable results, causing uncertainty, and thus leading to a 'chilling effect', and Ronald Gaither, 'The Chilling Effect of Section 506: The Battle over Digital Sampling in Rap Music' (2001) 3 *Vanderbilt Journal of Entertainment Law & Practice* 195, arguing that the US Copyright Act is too vague to allow artists, lawyers, or the courts to determine whether or not a criminal act of infringement has occurred when samples are taken from one piece of rap music and used in another.

Similarly, the existence of intellectual property has become an increasingly standard and customarily held belief. Although the nature of intellectual property might not be widely understood, and although many of the professionals who would most be expected to understand it find some of its details unclear or artificial,[20] it has become a familiar and accepted part of society. As Jessica Litman observes, 'Years of thinking within the peculiarly counterintuitive constraints of copyright law have a way of mangling one's mind and distorting one's imagination until more prosaic ways of seeing the world simply seem *wrong*.'[21]

While the analogy between the emperor's new clothes and intellectual property does eventually break down (there are, as already noted, structural and substantive differences between complying with a norm founded on belief and one founded in law, and there was no physical link between the fiction of the emperor's new clothes and the social belief in it, whereas intellectual property laws typically rely on a 'tangible' or 'material form' of the idea being regulated), the old fable nonetheless serves as a heuristic introduction to some of the issues addressed in this book.

The goal of this introduction – and of this book more generally – is not to express hostility towards intellectual property, either as a theoretical construct or as the practical working of that construct in the legal system and society, but to suggest that intellectual property is not necessarily what it might at first appear or be assumed to be. As such, the analogy introduces some of the questions and concepts that this book sets out to explore.

[20] David Vaver noted this persuasively in his March 2006 keynote address at the Meredith Memorial Lectures, McGill Law School. This has been published as David Vaver, 'Does the Public Understand Intellectual Property Law? Do Lawyers?' *University of Oxford Faculty of Law Legal Studies Research Paper Series*, Working Paper No. 23/2006 (May 2006).

[21] Jessica Litman, *Digital Copyright* (Amherst, NY: Prometheus, 2001) at 192.

1.3. Exploring the Nature of Intellectual Property

The fundamental research area within which this book falls is: How can legal philosophy explain 'intellectual property'? More specifically, such research asks: How is 'intellectual property' constructed within the legal system?

The exploration of this research question is approached with the use of techniques of applied legal philosophy to examine and test the hypothesis that intellectual property is a conceptual legal construct that is itself composed of other conceptual legal constructs, such as 'creatorship' and 'originality'. If, as this hypothesis implies, intellectual property is constructed within the legal system to allow for the regulation of certain conceptually delineated imaginary things (herein termed 'intellectual property objects'), usually evidenced in 'documented forms', to which rights have been applied, how does this occur?

1.4. Structure of This Book

This volume begins in the present chapter by highlighting the difficulty of knowing what 'intellectual property' refers to, despite its being a powerful and widely used term. The weaknesses of existing methods of defining 'intellectual property' are then surveyed in Chapter 2. Chapters 3 and 4 propose a new theoretical approach to the analysis of intellectual property law that concentrates on the way in which intellectual property doctrines are constructed. Chapter 5 tests that approach against empirical examples of intellectual property–like doctrines, noting both its strengths and deficiencies. Chapter 6 then offers conclusions and suggestions for further potentially fruitful research in the area.

1.4.1. Overview of the Argument

The analogy between the emperor's new clothes and intellectual property provides a backdrop for the analysis that follows. That analysis seeks to offer a deeper explanation of intellectual property than is normally found in the introductory 'definitional' sections of textbooks and monographs addressing other aspects of intellectual property laws' operation and consequences. Rather than glossing over definitional difficulties and relying upon the explanations – generally normative justifications – of intellectual property that are commonly found in the literature, this book commences with an investigation of intellectual property's structure, the language of intellectual property, and the ways in which those responsible for making and influencing the law (governments, judges, and stakeholders such as proprietors of large intellectual property portfolios) use the language of intellectual property to create and expand the discursive possibilities offered by the sphere of intellectual property, often to advantage chosen interests.

This volume then proposes an alternative way of defining 'intellectual property'. It sets out intellectual property's metaphysical structure, suggesting how intellectual property is made, what its common constitutive elements are, and how these elements relate to one another. It then proceeds to test the conclusions from the previous chapters (conclusions that are based on analysis of the classic intellectual property doctrines of copyright, trademark, and patent and design law) against intellectual property–like laws and regulations, reaching the subsequent conclusion that the metaphysics of intellectual property gives only a partial explanation of its form. A more complete understanding of intellectual propertization and the objects that intellectual property law regulates can arguably be obtained by examining the metaphysical structure of intellectual property objects in the context in which they are developed. At this point, considering political and normative justifications relied upon during the process of intellectual propertization can add contextual depth and help to produce a more textured understanding of the subject.

The conclusion synthesizes the findings and provides suggestions for future research.

1.4.2. Introduction

This opening chapter sets the scene for the more complex discussion that follows throughout the book. An adaptation of the familiar fairy tale the 'Emperor's New Clothes' is offered as an analogy in which the public's trust or pretence that the clothes actually exist (even if they cannot themselves perceive them and do not know exactly what they look like) parallels the assumptions made by many people that objects of intellectual property laws exist prior to the laws that regulate them. The hypothesis is posited that, like the emperor's new clothes, objects of intellectual property regulation exist only in human consciousness and imagination, although their effects may be very real.

In other words, the present chapter suggests that, while many people behave as though intellectual property objects exist as natural objects, in fact these objects are creations of intellectual property law. They have no existence as 'intellectual property' apart from the law that creates and sustains them. The main purpose of this chapter is therefore to lay out the hypothesis that intellectual property is a human construct. This will be explained further in Chapters 2 and 3, and sets the backdrop against which an analysis of the nature of 'intellectual property' will be conducted throughout this book. The rest of the present chapter outlines the route that this discussion will take, why it is important, and the context in which it occurs.

1.4.3. What Is 'Intellectual Property'? (Chapter 2)

Chapter 2 suggests that 'intellectual property' is a term that lacks a straightforward or commonly agreed-upon meaning but that is nonetheless symbolically, politically, and rhetorically powerful. It is commonly defined in ways that serve the purpose of the definer but that fail to explain what intellectual property *is*, and this may be because it does not have a simple or generally agreed-upon definition that people can draw on. Rather, it is a contested concept. Its meaning is obscure and debatable, and conclusions depend on the subjective understanding of those using the term in a particular context.

A variety of the ways in which 'intellectual property' is defined within the law is then surveyed and analysed. These include definition by enumeration, definition as a type of 'property', stipulative definition, and intuitive definition. Each of these is found to have practical utility but to lack intellectual rigour.

The chapter concludes that 'intellectual property' is a contested concept that is of great practical and symbolic importance but whose meaning is ambiguous and uncertain. A better method of defining the term is needed if this concept is to be understood as more than a 'floating signifier' that means different things to different people.

1.4.4. *The Metaphysics of Intellectual Property (Chapter 3)*

Given that, as Chapter 2 demonstrates, the usual definitions of 'intellectual property' fail to elicit more than a superficial or instrumental definition, Chapter 3 takes an alternative philosophical approach to explore what 'intellectual property' is. Drawing on techniques of metaphysical analysis, this chapter seeks to identify typical features of the legal doctrines that are usually classified as 'intellectual property'. It concludes that common core criteria for a finding of 'intellectual propertyness' are that an ideational object has been evidenced in a documented form and its scope has been defined through application of the related concepts of 'creatorship' and 'originality'. 'Rights' are then associated with the object. As such, intellectual property objects are legal constructs whose objects of regulation are created and sustained through the use of performative utterances.

1.4.5. *Intellectual Property's Core Criteria (Chapter 4)*

Four core conceptual criteria having been identified in the preceding chapter, Chapter 4 explores the nature of these features and the way in which they work together to construct 'intellectual property'. It also examines intellectual property's 'rights'.

While 'intellectual property' and its constituent doctrines, concepts, and rights may be susceptible to seemingly endless redefinition, the analysis in this chapter explains how several core conceptual criteria and rights can be identified in the traditional forms of those doctrines classically regarded as 'intellectual property'. In one way or another, each intellectual property doctrine arguably constructs its objects of regulation ('intellectual property objects') by defining ideational objects with the requisite degree of original documented form as 'intellectual property objects' and affording the creator of these objects monopoly rights ('intellectual property rights') to exploit them. Together, these concepts and rights form core structural criteria that are arguably common across doctrines commonly referred to as 'intellectual property'. This suggests that the term 'intellectual property' does imply some essential structural criteria, albeit criteria that vary in the forms in which they are found in doctrines and their importance within those doctrines.

This chapter also demonstrates that the conceptual criteria – such as 'creatorship' and 'originality' – that are used by intellectual property laws to define intellectual property's object of regulation are legal constructs. This is evidenced by how greatly they can vary from the ordinary social meanings given to the words 'creator', 'author' (copyright law's version of creatorship), and 'originality' in various contexts. As ordinary meanings reflect the ways in which the underlying ideational objects and documented forms that give rise to intellectual property objects are created in society, the constructed legal meaning (and resulting legal regulation) can diverge from the ways in which the ideational objects that underlie intellectual property objects are actually created in society. Nonetheless, intellectual property laws have become entrenched and robust forms of legal regulation throughout much of the world. The more their peculiarly legal terminology is repeated, the more it becomes ingrained and normal, even when its terms' meanings deviate from the meanings of the same words in common usage in other contexts.

1.4.6. 'Family Resemblance' and Intellectual Property (Chapter 5)

The conclusion that intellectual property doctrines are characterized by the core criteria and rights identified in the preceding chapters raises questions about whether every legal doctrine or regulatory regime bearing these features qualifies as 'intellectual property'. It can quickly be concluded that they do not.

This chapter surveys some of the areas of law that display similarities to intellectual property law but are not regarded as such by international treaties, by governmental intellectual property authorities, or in most of the academic literature.

It concludes that some of these intellectual property–like doctrines (as exemplified by indigenous intellectual property–like objects, even in the absence of explicit 'intellectual property' regimes) lack one or more of the core criteria identified in previous chapters. To this extent, analysis of these non–intellectual property doctrines supports the earlier conclusions that criteria such as 'creatorship' and 'originality' are necessary for the recognition of a doctrine within intellectual property's immediate family. This suggests that the framework set out earlier in the book does indeed add explanatory force to the nature of 'intellectual property'.

Other intellectual property–like doctrines are arguably more like the ancestors or extended family of intellectual property. They were the legal precursors to modern intellectual property doctrines and, even where they live on today, they are replicated by classic intellectual property doctrines.

Depending on one's perspective, these doctrines may or may not support the conclusion that the framework laid out in Chapters 3 and 4 establishes a skeletal structure of intellectual property doctrines. On the one hand, each of these non–intellectual property doctrines arguably has an intellectual property equivalent. Their non–intellectual property status could therefore be explained by the conclusion that they have indeed been intellectual propertized, but that they have also retained a pre–intellectual property form to maintain traditions or for additional regulatory authority. On the other hand, it could be argued that their structural similarities to intellectual property doctrines should have led to their being identified as 'intellectual property', and intellectual property law's failure to do so indicates that something more than the structure laid out in Chapters 3 and 4 is needed to provide an explanation for the division.

The chapter closes with a suggestion that something more can be found to explain this apparent anomaly. Adopting H. L. A. Hart's suggestion that concepts are best understood when their role is examined in context, the chapter concludes that intellectual property is ultimately an historical artefact that is driven by political will. It suggests that, given structural conditions in which the core criteria are present, perhaps the best explanation of why some intellectual property–like doctrines and regulatory systems are excluded from the 'intellectual property' definition has less to do with doctrinal content or jurisprudential consistency, and more to do with political imperatives and agendas at various points in time. Where the political will exists to intellectual propertize objects that have previously fallen outside intellectual property's scope, the core criteria will be employed to create intellectual property objects to which rights can be attached. Appropriate normative justifications for intellectual property may be selected at this point to validate such law-making activity.

Thus, when the core criteria are applied in a favourable socio-economic environment, intellectual propertization is more likely to occur. Mere application of the core criteria is insufficient to trigger intellectual propertization by the legal system in the absence of political will. This explains inconsistencies such as non–intellectual propertization of a doctrine even when all the conditions would point to its being intellectual propertized, or intellectual propertization of an object that would seem to lack one of the core criteria.

1.4.7. Concluding Remarks (Chapter 6)

A brief concluding chapter reiterates the line of argument made throughout the volume. It recaps the main themes addressed, noting in particular the importance of obtaining a definition of intellectual property that indicates its nature; the constructed and autopoietic nature of intellectual property; the metaphysical structure that typifies intellectual property doctrines and their objects of regulation; the core concepts used as tools to build that structure; and the context – including the political context, which may include reference to normative justifications for intellectual propertization – that influences whether intellectual propertization of an object or regulation, or of a doctrine of law, occurs. Together, these themes combine to build a theory that helps to define and explain 'intellectual property' on the basis of metaphysical characteristics.

Chapter 6 also offers closing comments, tying the conclusions reached to recommendations as to how this research may be fruitfully extended and applied in future studies. It suggests that the argument proposed in this volume may ultimately help to enrich normative and political discussions about intellectual propertization.

1.5. Scope of Analysis in This Book

The research having thus been mapped and foreshadowed, all that remains before embarking on the substance of the research itself is a small housekeeping matter – that is, delineating the scope of the study to be undertaken in this book.

When such a large and ambitious research project as 'explaining intellectual property law' is undertaken, the risk is that one will be accused of claiming more than one can deliver. The ambition is clearly not to offer a definitive explanation of everything about intellectual property law, or even everything about the philosophy of intellectual property law (indeed, such a suggestion would be farcical). Thus, explicit choices have to be made about what is to be included and what must be left out. The following comments outline the decisions that were made about where to set the boundaries of the research and how to narrow its focus.

In particular, choices had to be made about the following issues:

- the location of this research in the vast body of literature concerning intellectual property law;
- the areas of intellectual property law to be covered by this book and the examples to be used;
- the jurisdictions covered by analysis in this study; and
- the nature of the audience to whom this book is addressed.

It is hoped that explaining these choices will help to manage the reader's expectations about what this book covers and seeks to achieve. Thus, each is addressed in turn.

1.5.1. Locating This Research

This study has been written in the tradition of 'applied legal philosophy'. It adopts a theoretical approach to the study of intellectual property law, which is grounded in knowledge of the principles of various intellectual property doctrines (most notably, copyright, trademark, and design and patent law) and which draws on techniques of philosophical analysis to develop a systematic, theoretical analysis of the ways in which those doctrines are constructed and operate. It then tests this theory against intellectual property–like doctrines that are not generally considered to qualify as 'intellectual property', and it draws conclusions. As such, it takes a theoretical approach to the issue of intellectual propertization.

There are many ways of theorizing about intellectual property law. Discussions about intellectual property law and theory often take normative approaches that centre on the nature and strength of justifications for intellectual property doctrines. Indeed, it is probably fair to say that the dominant approach to explaining intellectual propertization that is found in the existing literature is normative. That is, it explores the norms that intellectual property law creates, the theoretical justifications for these principles, the political imperatives that drive such norm-making, and the interests protected by the law as a result of these policy decisions. This area of theoretical investigation has been well covered by others and is outside the scope of the current book. Except where relevant to the contested nature of 'intellectual property' and conclusions about how the law arose in its contemporary forms,[22] normative and political explanations will not be examined. To assist the reader, an overview of these explanations (along with references for reading in the area) is offered in an appendix at the end of the book.

Rather than exploring the 'normative' or political, this book places its focus on the 'descriptive' and the 'analytical'.[23] That is, it examines the structure, content, and context of empirical intellectual property laws and attempts to describe and explain these, as opposed to focusing on the justificatory political or norm-making reasons that have triggered intellectual propertization.[24] The focus herein is thus on the preliminary issues of what 'intellectual property' refers to and how it is made.

1.5.2. Intellectual Property Doctrines and Examples Considered

The department of intellectual property law[25] is large and diverse. Covering all of intellectual property's constituent doctrines in sufficient

[22] In particular, Chapter 2 makes reference to some normative and political arguments in its outline of the 'realpolitik' of contemporary intellectual property law-making.

[23] For a discussion about the difference between an analytic approach (as distinct from 'analytic philosophy') and a normative approach, see Katharina Sobota, 'Don't Mention the Norm' (1991) IV:10 *International Journal for the Semiotics of Law* 45–60, especially 46–47 and 59–60. This article approaches the distinction in the context of explaining the difference between an 'analytic rhetoric' analysis of law and a normative analysis of law.

[24] For a discussion of the distinction between normative and descriptive legal analysis, see Roger A. Shiner, 'Law and Its Normativity', in Dennis Patterson (ed.), *A Companion to Philosophy of Law and Legal Theory* (Oxford: Wiley-Blackwell, 2010), 417–445: 'It is commonplace to distinguish between the normative and the descriptive. Descriptions state facts: norms guide action, tell us what to do. It is equally commonplace to note that laws are norms' (at 417).

[25] As discussed in Chapter 2, §2.2.1.a, 'departments of law' is a term coined by Ronald Dworkin to describe the various areas or doctrines into which the legal system is

detail would be beyond the scope of any book. Among the choices that thus had to be made about what to include and exclude was a decision about which intellectual property doctrines to focus on and base central conclusions upon.

Herein lay a chicken and egg conundrum. If the purpose of the research is to explain the nature of intellectual property law by, among other means, looking at the way it is defined, then to choose particular 'intellectual property' doctrines is almost to pre-judge the conclusions in some respects. However, without adopting some prior notion of what 'intellectual property' refers to, there could be no starting point for the discussion.

The volume therefore takes a pragmatic approach – which it later criticizes[26] – that begins with the premise that 'intellectual property', in a practical sense, includes the doctrines discussed as such in international intellectual property treaties and administered by national intellectual property bureaucracies (such as IP Australia and the UK Intellectual Property Office).

A study in the tradition of applied legal philosophy must necessarily draw on empirical bodies of law. In this context, the book's main doctrinal focus is on the classic forms of the central doctrines of copyright, patent, design, and trademark law, whose 'intellectual propertyness' is rarely questioned. Even if queries might be raised about the proper placement and boundaries of these doctrines within the department of intellectual property,[27] there are few who would seriously dispute their nature as contemporary 'intellectual property' doctrines. They are therefore referred to throughout the volume as intellectual property's 'classic' doctrines. To adopt the familial analogy used in Chapter 5,[28] these are

compartmentalized. See Ronald Dworkin, *Law's Empire* (London: Fontana Press, 1986) at 251.

26 See Chapter 2, §2.2.1.

27 See, eg, Orit Fischman Afori, 'Reconceptualizing Property in Designs' (2008) 25 *Cardozo Arts and Entertainment Law Journal* 1106–1178, discussing the scope of design law vis-à-vis copyright and patent law in the United States.

28 See Chapter 5.

the nuclear family of the department of intellectual property, with which non–intellectual property doctrines are compared.

Within these classic intellectual property doctrines that have been selected as the foundation for the analysis in this book, the discussion draws primarily on traditional and fundamental principles of copyright, patent, design, and trademark law. These have been chosen because they are the central tenets of those doctrines, upon which newer developments (and sometimes deviations) have been built.

The examples used from time to time have been chosen because they are thought to be quite representative in their context. An example may, for instance, be representative of the way copyright law works in many jurisdictions (as opposed, eg, to the way it works in just the United Kingdom, United States, or Australia). Or an example may be representative of the way in which intellectual property doctrines function generally. The significance of each example should be clear from its context.

1.5.3. Jurisdictional Focus

The volume has an Anglo-American, common law focus. That is, it is situated in the context of the laws of several English-speaking jurisdictions: the United Kingdom, the United States, and Australia. These are the areas that most of the examples are drawn from, and the majority of examples are taken from Australian and UK law.

It might have become unwieldy and possibly confusing to draw regularly from many jurisdictions. In particular, slight differences in the ways in which various countries apply common standards might have distracted the discussion from the broader outlook needed if generalizations were to be drawn, trends were to be discovered, and hypotheses were to be made.

The choice was therefore made to focus on the expression of intellectual property laws (and, by implicit extension, the way in which these comply with internationally mandated standards) in Australian and UK law. This choice primarily reflects the fact that the book was written while the author was based in the United Kingdom and Australia, and the author thus has a more extensive knowledge of the law of these jurisdictions. Some US examples are also offered, reflecting the significance of US law in contemporary global intellectual propertization. In line with this focus, the literature drawn on throughout the volume is predominantly English-language material in the common law tradition.

It should be noted that the common law focus in this volume does not reflect a lack of interest in civil law jurisdictions. Indeed, valid questions arise as to whether the theory proposed in this book is relevant and/or applicable to the intellectual property traditions of civil law jurisdictions.

Due to the convergence of civil and common law traditions in intellectual property treaty-making for well over one hundred years, and the importance that international treaties have had on the principles underlying intellectual property law throughout much of the world,[29] it seems likely that the hypotheses proposed and the conclusions drawn throughout the book would be similarly applicable in civil law jurisdictions. Preliminary conversations with civil law jurists would tend to confirm this impression, but it is ultimately an issue whose assessment the author must leave to others more expert in civil law jurisdictions' intellectual property laws and their practical implementation.

1.5.4. Audience

As this book follows an 'applied legal philosophy' tradition, it is written for an audience that understands law generally, and intellectual property law in particular, and that is also schooled in legal philosophy and legal theory. Its focus is theoretical, not doctrinal or 'black letter', and its conclusions are largely philosophical in nature.

[29] The *Berne Convention for the Protection of Literary and Artistic Works* (1886), the *Paris Convention for the Protection of Industrial Property* (1883), and the World Trade Organization's *Agreement on Trade Related Aspects of Intellectual Property* (1994) are particularly notable in this respect.

To an intellectual property practitioner with little or no interest in legal philosophy, the discussion herein may seem a little abstract. To a pure philosopher, it may seem to be too subjectively influenced by empirical concerns. The study aims to cover the middle ground between these two extremes, offering a theoretical approach to explain the internal structure and construction of an important area of law. It is hoped that it will thus be of interest not only to lawyers and philosophers, but also to those from other disciplines and backgrounds who are affected by intellectual property laws' reach.

1.6. Investigating the Fairy Tale

Historically, the purpose of fairy tales such as the 'Emperor's New Clothes' has not simply been to entertain. Like fables and legends, many fairy tales are educationally loaded. Such stories teach social norms and morals by helping to instil and reinforce certain values in listeners.

Intended for both adults and children, fairy tales employ a combination of literary devices such as humour, intrigue, wonder, adventure, mystery, action, magic, suspense, emotion, the portrayal of human relations and poetic justice, and a sense of both the familiar and the new.[30] While entertaining the listener, fairy tales traditionally appeal to a person's sense of right and wrong. Passed down through generations, they operate as a gentle method of inculcating in listeners a community's norms.[31]

[30] Techniques used in this literary genre are discussed by Laura Fry Kready, *A Study of Fairy Tales* (Forgotten Books, 2008; originally published 1916) at 14–21.

[31] Jack David Zipes, *Fairy Tale as Myth/Myth as Fairy Tale* (Lexington: University Press of Kentucky, 1994). Discussing the development of the genre, Zipes comments that 'groups of writers, particularly aristocratic woman.... gathered in salons during the seventeenth century and created the conditions for the rise of the fairy tale. They set the groundwork for the institutionalisation of the fairy tale as a "proper" genre intended first for educated adult audiences and only later for children who were to be educated according to a code of *civilité* that was being elaborated in the seventeenth and eighteenth centuries' (at 18).

Just as fairy tales establish behavioural norms, so too does law. Just as the authors of fairy tales use specific literary devices to construct their stories, law-makers use specific techniques to construct intellectual property's objects of regulation. This book concerns itself not with the justice or otherwise of the norms contained in those laws, or with the reasons they came about, but with how and in what form they came to exist. It is concerned not with whether those norms are right or wrong, but with the mechanics of their construction and reproduction. With a better understanding of these preliminary issues, normative and political discussions of intellectual property law should in turn be enhanced.

2 The Difficulty of Defining 'Intellectual Property'

BEFORE THE LAW IS USED TO REGULATE SOMETHING, THE scope and nature of the object of its regulation must be determined. Hence, statutes often commence with a glossary of definitions, and legal analysis usually begins with a statement of its objects. However, this is not so easy with respect to 'intellectual property'.

'Intellectual property' lacks a straightforward meaning and does not have a simple or generally agreed upon definition. Instead, it is an essentially contested concept that is given a variety of definitions and that consistently defies attempts to provide accessible but enlightening insight as to its meaning. The awkward question of what 'intellectual property' really means is often sidestepped, with the term used as a vague reference to an ill-defined – or perhaps even an undefined – idea.

This chapter considers various conceptions of 'intellectual property', surveying several common methods that are employed by those attempting to define or explain what the term means. These can be summarized as definition by enumeration, stipulation, allusion to 'property', and intuition. It will be seen that none of these approaches provides an explanation that adequately elucidates the meaning of 'intellectual property'. Each provides a definition that has a practical or symbolic purpose in some circumstances, but none distinguishes the body of rules from the object of regulation. None addresses the disjuncture between the object of intellectual property regulation and the ideational object that inspires it. As a consequence, none satisfactorily describes what is meant by 'intellectual property'. The discussion in this chapter points to flaws in these types of approaches and raises questions about whether 'intellectual property' does indeed have a fixed and settled meaning.

2.1. The Importance of Defining 'Intellectual Property'

The difficulties associated with defining 'intellectual property' are well recognized. The term does not describe an easily identifiable object, emotion, belief, or behaviour, and there is no single checklist of criteria that can be used to identify whether or not something is 'intellectual property'. 'Intellectual property' is instead an umbrella term that refers to a diverse collection of rules and the objects with respect to which they regulate human behaviour. These are generally understood to be grouped together in doctrines such as copyright, trademark, and patent law, but without further investigation into the nature of those areas of law, reference to intellectual property's constituent doctrines sheds little light on the meaning of the term per se.

Whether or not something is regarded as 'intellectual property' is a result of deciding whether it falls within one of the doctrines that is commonly considered to be intellectual property, but whether a doctrine is or is not considered to be intellectual property is a matter of customary consensus that is reflected in – or driven by – statements of law. What informs and precipitates such consensus-building?

Some doctrines are conventionally considered to be clear-cut examples of intellectual property: copyright, trademark,[1] patent, and design law fall into this category. Others are subject to debate: misappropriation,

[1] Note, however, that not everyone agrees that trademarks should be regarded as (intellectual) property. See the discussion of differences of opinion on this topic in

competition or 'unfair competition' law, rights to control the use of persona (such as 'publicity rights' in the United States),[2] and the law of confidential information and trade secrets are examples of this group.[3]

The distinguishing features or 'criteria' that determine whether the various doctrines are or are not considered to be 'intellectual property' are not immediately obvious and are often couched in vague terms. A typical example is found in a handbook about intellectual property edited by the World Intellectual Property Organization (WIPO), which begins: 'Very broadly, intellectual property means the legal rights which result from intellectual activity in the industrial, scientific, literary, and artistic fields.'[4] However, some legal doctrines that are not traditionally viewed as intellectual property would fit within this sort of definition,[5] and it could exclude others that are generally deemed to be intellectual property or that are thought of as intellectual property even if they are not recognized as legal rights.[6]

Frank I. Schechter, *The Historical Foundations of the Law Relating to Trade-Mark Law* (Union, NJ: Lawbook Exchange, 1999; originally published New York: Columbia University Press, 1925) at 5–6.

2 For a discussion of celebrity identity – the ideational object protected by publicity rights – as property, see Kirsten J. Anker, 'Possessing Star Qualities: Celebrity Identity as Property' (2002) 11 *Griffith Law Review* 147–168.

3 For examples of consideration about whether these are really 'intellectual property', see, eg, Diane Leenheer Zimmerman, 'Fitting Publicity Rights into Intellectual Property and Free Speech Theory: Sam, You Made the Pants Too Long!' (2000) 10 *DePaul-LCA Journal of Art and Entertainment Law* 283–314 at 306; and Scott M. Kline and Matthew C. Floyd, 'Managing Confidential Relationships in Intellectual Property Transactions: Use Restrictions, Residual Knowledge Clauses, and Trade Secrets' (2006) 25 *Review of Litigation* 311–348.

4 World Intellectual Property Organization, *Introduction to Intellectual Property Theory and Practice* (London: Kluwer Law International, 1997) at 3, ¶1.1.

5 Examples include rights arising from the operation of areas of law such as contract, tort, and criminal law.

6 Examples include doctrines that have been unrecognized, or that were traditionally unrecognized (prior to watershed developments such as the Agreement on Trade Related Aspects of Intellectual Property in 1994), such as traditional knowledge and moral rights. See discussion in Chapter 5. They also include the products of intellectual activity that are not covered by intellectual property laws, such as body language or thoughts that are expressed ephemerally but are not captured in a material form. See discussion in Chapter 4, §4.2.2.

Such a definition gives no insight into why certain activities are recognized as legal rights, while other actions resulting from similar intellectual activity are not. Simply listing the legal doctrines that are thought to fall under the intellectual property umbrella but offering no explanation of what criterion it is that gives these doctrines an intellectual property identity does not explain what is unique about intellectual property. It does not explain what sets intellectual property apart from other areas of law. Describing motivations for the creation of intellectual property laws and the application of intellectual property rights to particular objects – a process that can be referred to as 'intellectual propertization' – does allow important insight into this area of law, but it does not explain what the term 'intellectual property' actually means. As will become clearer throughout this volume, it is extremely difficult to explain the nature of 'intellectual property' or offer a clear definition of the term. Slogan-like definitions are not likely to be adequate, yet many of the definitions or explanations that are offered for 'intellectual property' are of this nature.

Several intellectual property scholars have proposed more theoretical definitions that try to extract an intrinsic criterion that unites and is identifiable in all of the intellectual property law's component doctrines. Peter Drahos, for example, has suggested that 'intellectual property rights are rule-governed privileges that regulate the ownership and exploitation of abstract objects in many fields of human activity.'[7] Another example is Wendy Gordon's description of intellectual property as a family of doctrines that controls patterns of valuable intangibles that are monopolized by another person.[8] The definitions proposed by Drahos and Gordon both contain important insights that inform the discussion that follows. They are probably accurate descriptions of features that help set intellectual property apart from other areas of law,

[7] Peter Drahos, *A Philosophy of Intellectual Property* (Aldershot: Ashgate, 1996) at 5.

[8] Wendy J. Gordon, 'Intellectual Property Law', in Peter Cane and Mark Tushnet (eds.), *Oxford Handbook of Legal Studies* (Oxford: Oxford University Press, 2003), 617–646 at 618.

and each is useful in its context. However, taken in isolation, theoretical definitions of this type do not provide a clear picture of what the term 'intellectual property' refers to. Someone completely unfamiliar with the notion of intellectual property would no doubt be little wiser after being offered a more theoretical definition of the type proposed by Drahos and Gordon. So, while such explanations do capture important features of intellectual property and thus offer useful insights into its nature, they do not negate the need for the question: What is 'intellectual property'?

With the term 'intellectual property' characterized by such uncertainty, it is perhaps tempting to disregard the expression as one that is used loosely and in a variety of contexts but that is of little consequence unless used in conjunction with legal details of one of its constituent doctrines. The temptation is to concentrate instead on the way in which those constituent doctrines operate. This shifts the focus from the terminology of the law to its practice, and raises the question of whether it really matters whether or not an area of the law is regarded as 'intellectual property'.

Would it not be more intellectually honest to disregard the imprecise term 'intellectual property' and instead direct attention to the legal significance of discrete doctrines such as copyright, publicity rights, and passing off, regardless of whether or not they are also considered to be constituents of 'intellectual property'? This may be a pragmatic approach, and to sidestep the term 'intellectual property' in favour of a focus on its constituent doctrines does avoid clouding discussions with a term that may sound impressive but whose meaning is uncertain. However, to do so is also to underestimate the rhetorical consequence of a term whose political importance is pervasive and about which useful insights can be drawn by examining the way in which it is used in language. To do so is to step backwards to times when attention to the laws now commonly classified as 'intellectual property' was largely the doctrinal, black-letter approach of practitioners, and when little scholarly attention was paid to the field.

Such an approach examined the operation of intellectual property law within the legal system rather than as a part of societies that are influenced by (and influence) politics, the economy, and culture. This was an unduly narrow approach and, as Rosemary Coombe has noted:

> There has been too little consideration of the *cultural* nature of the actual forms that intellectual property laws protect, the social and historical contexts in which cultural proprietorship is (or is not) assumed, or the manner in which these rights are (or are not) exercised and enforced to intervene in everyday struggles over meaning.[9]

Coombe makes an important point. As a social institution that helps to order behaviour within a society, law (including intellectual property law) must constantly define – and refine – its definitions of the people and objects it regulates. It is therefore valuable to consider exactly what is meant when the term 'intellectual property' is used by legal practitioners and others. Such uses are symptomatic of the socio-economic trends that have led to the creation of legal rights and obligations with respect to the use of ideas, information and knowledge, and the regulation of such objects can have pervasive social and cultural consequences.

2.1.1. The Symbolic Strength of 'Intellectual Property'

'Intellectual property' is a powerful term: appealing for rights to behave in certain ways on the basis of intellectual property claims can be an effective strategic tool for increasing one's wealth and ability to influence cultural development. If 'power' involves being able to persuade others to behave in ways they would not otherwise do,[10] 'intellectual property' seems to have the ability to garner power. This has propelled intellectual property centre stage in many and varied contexts, such as discussions about international trade, employment rights, academic freedom, biodiversity, and the protection of indigenous cultures. Yet some

[9] Rosemary J. Coombe, *The Cultural Life of Intellectual Properties: Authorship, Appropriation, and the Law* (Durham, NC: Duke University Press, 1998) at 7.

[10] See discussion of 'power' in Robert A. Dahl, *Modern Political Analysis* (Englewood Cliffs, NJ: Prentice-Hall International, 1984) at 23ff.

commentators have identified a superficial symbolism in 'intellectual property' and, because of its concurrent power and imprecision, would like to see the term abandoned altogether.

2.1.1.a A Case for Abandoning 'Intellectual Property'?

A prominent critic of the term 'intellectual property' is Richard Stallman, founder of the GNU Project to develop free operating system software for computers.[11] Stallman argues that references to 'intellectual property' systematically distort and confuse discussions about law and policy in relation to doctrines such as copyright and patent. He says that 'its use was and is promoted by those who gain from this confusion'.[12] He thus recommends expunging the term from language,[13] observing that 'intellectual property' is a catchall phrase that is used to unite disparate laws under a single banner and so imply that intellectual property's various doctrines are each instances of a common principle and that each operates in the same way. 'Nothing,' he claims, 'could be further from the case.'[14]

Stallman's recommended solution is to stop using the term 'intellectual property', to rename the World Intellectual Property Organization (WIPO), and to treat doctrines such as copyright, trademark, and patent law as separate areas of law that should be regarded independently of

[11] The GNU Manifesto, written by Richard Stallman in 1985 when he launched the GNU Project, states: 'I have decided to put together a sufficient body of free software so that I will be able to get along without any software that is not free.... GNU is not in the public domain. Everyone will be permitted to modify and redistribute GNU, but no distributor will be allowed to restrict its further redistribution. That is to say, proprietary modifications will not be allowed. I want to make sure that all versions of GNU remain free.... I am asking computer manufacturers for donations of machines and money. I'm asking individuals for donations of programs and work'; http://www.gnu.org/gnu/manifesto.html [accessed 8 December 2008]. See, generally, discussions by Richard Stallman in Joshua Gay (ed.), *Free Software, Free Society: Selected Essays of Richard M. Stallman* (Boston: GNU Press, 2002).

[12] Richard M. Stallman, 'Did You Say "Intellectual Property"? It's a Seductive Mirage' (2004), http://www.gnu.org/philosophy/not-ipr.xhtml [accessed 5 September 2006].

[13] Ibid.

[14] Ibid.

one another.[15] However, 'intellectual property' is well entrenched in the language of law, business, and international politics alike, and its demise does not seem imminent. It is not merely a linguistic term but also a powerful concept. Abandoning the term 'intellectual property', or changing its name, would arguably fail to redress its weaknesses. It would also risk falling into the trap of effectively failing to see the wood for the trees if attention were to be focused on individual doctrines rather than on their cumulative effects. Important insights can be obtained through analysis of both intellectual property generally and its constituent doctrines specifically. So, for those interested in understanding this vaguely defined area of law, neglecting consideration of either level would be counterproductive.

To abandon the term 'intellectual property' would be to try to shift attitudes and perceptions by tinkering with language, much as Stallman argues self-interested proponents of intellectual propertization have done by adopting and entrenching the term in society's popular and legal psyches. In theory, this may be an effective method of modifying socio-legal attitudes about the nature and strength of the law concerning copyright, patents, trademarks, and so on. Similar tactics have been successfully applied to advance certain teleological ends in other contexts, such as when socially marginalized communities appropriate epithets commonly used against them. When such terms are adopted as symbols of community pride and spirit, they can capture the power of a word, disempower the offence in it, desensitize those targeted with the epithet, and ultimately shift the popular meaning of the former insult.[16] However, while this may sometimes be a useful strategy for changing attitudes, it is questionable how effective it would be in practice for intentionally deleting or phasing out a deeply entrenched and practically useful legal

[15] Ibid.

[16] See, eg, discussion in Robin Brontsema, 'A Queer Revolution: Reconceptualizing the Debate over Linguistic Reclamation' (2004) 17 *Colorado Research in Linguistics*, http://www.colorado.edu/ling/CRIL/Volume17_Issue1/paper_BRONTSEMA.pdf. [online journal, accessed 3 October 2006].

concept from society's collective consciousness (especially when the term is very popular in some politically powerful quarters).

Despite its imprecision, the term has practical utility because it describes a concept or 'idea' of intellectual property that is relevant to discussions about many areas of legal, social, and economic policy. As Debora J. Halbert observes:

> Perhaps the most disturbing thing about having to use the idea of intellectual property is that there is no viable alternative term in our modern world that can be used to describe creative and innovative work besides describing it as someone's property.... Ultimately, while I am very critical of the idea of intellectual property and would like to seek alternatives, I find myself using the term because alternatives are scarce and it is easy to use intellectual property to lump together very disparate things. However ... even the words we choose need to be examined and perhaps rethought.[17]

Halbert's recommendation that we examine and rethink a term that automatically implies 'property' in creative and innovative works is arguably wiser than the alternative proposal to abandon the term 'intellectual property' altogether. Confronting the connotations and assumptions of the term head on is likely to be a far more powerful strategy for demonstrating its weaknesses and the entrenched interests that it protects than trying to simply abandon or suppress use of the term and what it represents.

Even if Stallman's proposed adjustment to language is intended as an antidote to those who modify the meaning of traditional legal concepts in their quest for further intellectual propertization,[18] it also sidesteps

[17] Debora J. Halbert, *Resisting Intellectual Property* (London: Routledge, 2005) at 11.

[18] An example might be the use of the word 'theft' in relation to copyright piracy and trademark counterfeiting cases. The UK *Theft Act* 1968, s.1(1) stated, 'A person is guilty of theft, if he dishonestly appropriates property belonging to another with the intention of permanently depriving the other of it,' and it was therefore ill suited for application in copyright and trademark cases, as the objects of regulation (eg, literary or artistic works, or commercial signs) could be infinitely reproduced without depriving the copyright or trademark holder of his, her, or its original property. The loss to the intellectual

fundamentally important jurisprudential questions about why the term 'intellectual property' has been so powerful. Even if it were possible to remove 'intellectual property' from use in popular and legal language, this seems unlikely to happen in the near future. No matter how much one might sympathize with Stallman's frustration about use of the term 'intellectual property', its demise does not seem imminent. A fruitful alternative is to recognize and address the symbolic power of 'intellectual property'.

2.1.1.b Confronting the Charisma of 'Intellectual Property'

Mark Lemley identifies several reasons for the popularity of the term 'intellectual property', including its 'sexiness' and the glamorous images it conjures, and its ability to unite disparate legal doctrines.[19] He notes that it builds a link to the 'rich and venerable legal and academic tradition of property law' and, flowing from that, it tacitly encourages an allusion to be drawn between 'intellectual property' and the legal and philosophical justifications for tangible property. This streamlines the importation of the justifications for tangible 'property' into the rules of 'intellectual property',[20] even though the subject matter and application[21] of the two departments of law can be distinguished in many ways.

property proprietor in such cases was the potential for profiting from the application of an artificial monopoly, but this was a different sort of loss than that incurred when one is permanently deprived of one's property. The use of the term 'theft' in relation to objects of intellectual property rights thus required a redefinition of the term.

For a discussion of the rhetorical use of the word 'theft' in the context of intellectual property law, see Patricia Loughlan, '"You Wouldn't Steal a Car ...": Intellectual Property and the Language of Theft' (2007) 29 *European Intellectual Property Review* 401–405.

Another discussion of the use of the 'language of stealing' in intellectual property discourse can be found in William St. Clair, 'Metaphors of Intellectual Property', in Ronan Deazley, Martin Kretschmer, and Lionel Bently (eds.), *Privilege and Property: Essays on the History of Copyright* (Cambridge: Open Book, 2010), 369–395 at 387–391. St. Clair notes that this metaphor has been adopted by 'both sides' (at 389).

[19] Mark A. Lemley, 'Property, Intellectual Property, and Free Riding' (2004–2005) 83 *Texas Law Review* 1031–1076 at 1034.

[20] Ibid. at 1035.

[21] See, eg, James Bessen and Michael J. Meurer, *Patent Failure: How Judges, Bureaucrats, and Lawyers Put Innovators at Risk* (Princeton, NJ: Princeton University Press, 2008).

The importation of the principles applied to tangible property is frequently observed in calls for new intellectual property doctrines or expanded rights within existing doctrines and, as will be examined later in this chapter,[22] 'intellectual property' is often defined in terms of 'property'. This tactic has great symbolic force, and 'intellectual property' seems to occupy the most headlines and attract the greatest public interest when it comes in the form of passionate pleas from celebrity authors, songwriters and performers who want increased 'property' rights over their compositions. For example, singer Cliff Richard's argument that UK performers should have extended royalties on old recordings 'as a sort of pension fund'[23] is echoed by others with vested interests.

'It's just not right. It is thieving. They give me a heating allowance but they are going to take my royalties away,' complained guitarist Joe Brown, as some of his copyright material neared the end of its existing fifty-year period of protection.[24] Ian Anderson, a musician in the rock band Jethro Tull opines similarly: 'Of course, for Pink Floyd, Elton John,

Bessen and Meurer argue in chaps. 3 and 4 that patent law differs from tangible property because, inter alia, they are implemented in different ways.

[22] See §2.2.2.

[23] Referred to by Don Foster, Member of Parliament, in a House of Commons debate about the United Kingdom's *Gowers Review* of intellectual property, and cited in *Hansard* (17 May 2006), Column 332WH. See http://www.publications.parliament.uk/pa/cm200506/cmhansrd/cm060517/halltext/60517h0061.htm [accessed 19 September 2006]. See also 'Cliff Richard Calls for Music Copyright Change' (19 April 2006) *Reuters*. James Chapman, 'Holidaying Blair in Conflict of Interest over Copyright Law' (30 July 2006) *Mail on Sunday* (UK), http://www.mailonsunday.co.uk/pages/live/articles/news/news.html?in_article_id=398339&in_page_id=1770 [accessed 19 September 2006], highlights the political importance of such campaigns: 'Tony Blair's fondness for "freebie" holidays was again in the spotlight last night as it emerged he singled out Sir Cliff Richard's campaign to change Britain's copyright laws as a priority. The singer, who has given Blair and his family free use of his £3 million villa in Barbados for the past three years, has been lobbying the Government to extend the period for which he can earn royalties on his work.... Last night the revelation that Mr Blair has taken up Sir Cliff's campaign prompted accusations that he may have breached ministerial rules.' (Note that Blair was the UK Prime Minister at the time.)

[24] Quoted in Hugh Davis, 'Old Rockers Band Together to Keep Royalties Coming in from their Hits' (29 March 2006) *The Telegraph* (UK), http://www.telegraph.co.uk/news/main.jhtml?xml=/news/2006/03/29/nroyal29.xm [accessed 19 September 2006].

Rod Stewart – and I'm not short of a few bob – this may not be a problem, but the unsung heroes of the 1950s depend on royalties to pay heating and nursing home bills.'[25] Leaving aside the artificial links drawn here between copyright and social welfare or pension funds,[26] this example indicates the effectiveness with which such campaigns can harness the authority of celebrity and (either explicitly or implicitly) the symbolic power of 'property' claims – claims that are central to the philosophical values on which liberal democratic societies are founded and based (and by which they distinguish themselves from, for example, communist regimes) – to create powerful rhetoric. It is far more emotive and symbolically powerful to personalize an argument by portraying the expiry of a copyright period as a confiscation of a much-loved celebrity's property than simply as the conclusion of a temporary legal privilege.

Celebrities' cries for intellectual propertization can be very effective. For example, in 1998 the US Congress passed the *Sonny Bono Copyright Term Extension Act*,[27] extending copyright terms by twenty years (from fifty to seventy years after the death of the author) following emotive arguments by congresswoman Mary Bono and others with vested interests. Mary Bono happened also to be the widow of Sonny Bono, actor, singer and congressman, and she claimed that her late husband had 'wanted the term of copyright protection to last forever.'[28] Richard Posner, scholar and judge of the US Court of Appeals for the Seventh Circuit, has criticized the statute in the following terms:

[25] Ibid.

[26] The two are fundamentally different to the extent that copyright is private property arising due to the efforts of a particular author, which may or may not bear fruit in the form of royalties, depending on demand for the work in the market. By contrast, public welfare is granted by the state for certain purposes, such as to cover living costs during retirement or following disablement, which may or may not be qualified by criteria such as means testing.

[27] Also referred to colloquially as the *Mickey Mouse Protection Act*.

[28] Recorded at 144 Cong. Rec. H9946–01, H9952 (daily ed., 7 October 1998). For reference to this aspect of the legislation's history, see Mark Rose, 'Copyright and Its Metaphors' (2002) *UCLA Law Review* 1 at 1; and Dan Hunter, 'Culture War' (2005) *Texas Law Review* 1105–1136 at 1120.

> It is a statute with an absurd history. It became a sentimental favorite because Sonny Bono – who was killed in a skiing accident – was reported to have said that: "copyright should be forever." If copyright should be forever, well, just adding twenty years is not an issue. The real pressure for the extension came initially from the descendants – relatives, heirs, and so on – of George and Ira Gershwin and other very successful composers/writers of popular music in the twenties and thirties, whose copyrights were about to expire, and later from the Walt Disney Corporation, which was facing the imminent expiration of the Mickey Mouse copyright. So there was a lot of pressure behind the law, and it was passed.[29]

The passage of the bill into law surely reflects the power of symbolic arguments about rights over intellectual property. Once the power of emotional attachments to a society's celebrities – real and fictional, human and animated – was harnessed, the charm and charisma of intellectual property started to reflect that of the sentimental objects with which it was associated.[30]

2.1.1.c The Realpolitik of Intellectual Property

Posner's mention of the Walt Disney Corporation alludes to a related and extremely successful strategy employed by corporations and industry bodies to bring about widespread and pervasive changes in the law, including new intellectual property doctrines or expanded rights within existing doctrines.

The interested parties that fall within this group often predict terrible social consequences in the absence of such amendments. For example, the industry groups that represent pharmaceutical companies have long argued

[29] Richard A. Posner, 'Do We Have Too Many Intellectual Property Rights?' (2005) *Marquette Intellectual Property Law Review* 173–185 at 181 (presented as the 'Eighth Annual Honorable Helen Wilson Nies Memorial Lecture in Intellectual Property Law', Marquette University Law School, 28 March 2005).

[30] For example, a film star becomes synonymous with her or his intellectual property rights. Hence, to deprive the star of any of those rights may be perceived by fans as damaging or harming the star.

that extended patent terms and increased rights over their patented formulations are necessary in order to recoup the money necessary to invest in further research and development (often referred to as 'R & D') into new medicines. Funding of scientific research is a complex matter that includes wider issues such as government-funded research grants, and the transfer of developments by university-employed scientists into commercially viable products. Examination of these issues is beyond the scope of the current discussion.[31] Suffice to say here that, while there is clear merit in the argument that income generated by patents can be reinvested in research and development into new and improved medicines, the nuances are difficult to report accurately in 'sound bites'. Simplistic sound bites can nonetheless be extremely powerful. For example, the president of the US pharmaceutical industry's trade association told a radio interviewer: 'Believe me ... if you reduce the R & D that this industry is able to provide, it's going to harm my kids and it's going to harm those millions of other Americans who have life-threatening conditions.'[32] Commenting on the strategies embodied in such a tactic, Marica Angell describes this sort of claim as 'a kind of blackmail'.[33]

Lobbying for the acceptance of a message that harnesses the symbolic power that has come to be associated with 'intellectual property' can be a very effective strategy, and it is not confined to single industries or jurisdictions. For example, the 1994 *Agreement on Trade Related Aspects of Intellectual Property* (TRIPS) of the World Trade Organization (WTO) – arguably the most comprehensive and pervasive intellectual property

[31] See the discussion of these issues in the appendix of this book.

[32] Alan F. Holmer, president of the Pharmaceutical Research and Manufacturers of America, quoted in Marcia Angell, *The Truth About the Drug Companies: How They Deceive Us and What to Do About It* (New York: Random House, 2005) at 38. This statement was reportedly made in an interview about proposed price controls on medicines in the United States, but the comment would apply equally to any factor that could negatively influence pharmaceutical companies' profits, such as a diminution of (or even a refusal to expand) rights that would reduce potential patent royalties.

[33] Angell, above n. 32 at 37: 'Implicit in this claim is a kind of blackmail: If you want drug companies to keep turning out life-saving drugs, you will gratefully pay whatever they charge. Otherwise, you may wake up one morning and find there are no more new drugs.'

treaty to date – resulted from an organized campaign of lobbying begun by US-based companies rich in intellectual property assets. Their interests lay in being able to enforce those rights in the United States and abroad, and they garnered the support of local and foreign government and industry bodies with compatible interests.

TRIPS came about after the chief executive officers of Bristol-Myers, CBS, DuPont, General Electric, General Motors, Hewlett-Packard, IBM, Johnson & Johnson, Merck, Monsanto and Pfizer joined forces to form the Intellectual Property Committee (IPC).[34] This industry organization lobbied the US Chamber of Commerce and industry groups within the United States, arguing that it would be in the national interest to link intellectual property issues to international trade negotiations. IPC's members persuaded industry counterparts in Europe and Japan to lobby their own governments with the same message,[35] and a loose grouping of diverse industries and nations united behind a perception of the common good of targeting foreign free-riders who failed to respect their intellectual property interests.[36]

Despite vocal opposition from a group of developing nations, the strategy succeeded. The Japanese government and the European Union quickly joined the US government in calling for globally strong minimum standards of intellectual property worldwide that would be linked to trade issues and, by consolidating their political might, supporters of the campaign were able to precipitate TRIPS. The political manoeuvrings that culminated in this outcome were intricate,[37] and the inclusion

[34] Susan K. Sell, 'Industry Strategies for Intellectual Property and Trade: The Quest for TRIPS, and Post-TRIPS Strategies' (2002) 10 *Cardozo Journal of International and Comparative Law* 79–108 at 81–98. See also Vandana Shiva, *Plunder or Protect? Understanding Intellectual Property Rights* (London: Zed, 2001) at 94–98.

[35] Ibid. at 91–92.

[36] Carlos Alberto Primo Braga, 'The Economics of Intellectual Property Rights and the GATT: A View from the South' (1989) 22 *Vanderbilt Journal of Transnational Law* 243–264 at 245.

[37] See Alexandra George (ed.), *Globalization and Intellectual Property* (Aldershot: Ashgate, 2006), for several articles addressing this topic. See also Peter Drahos, *Information Feudalism: Who Owns the Knowledge Economy?* (London:

of the term 'intellectual property' in the Agreement's title is symbolically significant as it reinforces the impression that 'intellectual property' is a coherent object and that it has an inherent relationship with trade.[38]

Such uses of the term tend to implicitly portray intellectual property as something that has a prior existence to the law and one separate from it. By depicting 'intellectual property' as something that exists separately from the law by which it is enforced in society, they bypass normative consideration of whether it should exist at all and, if so, in what form. When this occurs – whether as a result of sloppy reasoning or an intellectual sleight of hand – attention shifts from questions of what intellectual property is to whether and how it should be regulated. The usually unspoken assumption in such discussions seems to be that 'intellectual property' is a term that describes an object to which 'intellectual property rights' (often referred to as IPRs) can be attached. The question for law-makers becomes: Should intellectual property rights be attached to the intellectual property object? And, if so, which ones? However, all this tends to neglect the prior question of what intellectual property *is* and how to identify objects to which intellectual property rights will be applied.

Rather than focusing on the substance of what they would like to have legal rights over, to control or profit from, those who call for the regulation of *their* intellectual property tend to make a moral claim: they claim a moral entitlement to a pre-existing substance that they would like to be covered by legal regulation. To cast this as a claim to 'intellectual property' is to implicitly align their claims with the usual jurisprudential justifications that are given for intellectual propertization.[39] However, by

Earthscan, 2002); John Braithwaite and Peter Drahos, *Global Business Regulation* (Cambridge: Cambridge University Press, 2000), chap. 24 at 564–577; and Susan K. Sell, *Power and Ideas: North–South Politics of Intellectual Property and Antitrust* (Albany: State University of New York Press, 1998).

[38] This view is contested. See, eg, Shiva, above n. 34 at 95, arguing that 'TRIPs is weighted against basic needs and survival and in favour of trade', thus positing a distinction between these. Shiva suggests that TRIPS represents the imposition of the trade-related values and interests of multi-national corporations on the world's diverse societies and cultures (at 96).

[39] See the appendix of this book for an overview of these justifications.

referring to 'intellectual property' in this way, they are not making a claim to any particular object, or to a right to control a particular object unless the term 'intellectual property' clearly refers to a specific object or thing. Many would contend that it does not and that the concept of 'intellectual property' is a relatively recent development whose modern origins can be traced from specific legal systems.

2.1.2. The Growth of the Idea of 'Intellectual Property'

The emergence of intellectual property as a distinct department of law did not begin until the mid–nineteenth century. Brad Sherman and Lionel Bently comment:

> It is often assumed that intellectual property law is a timeless, almost ahistorical, area of law that has always existed, but if we look at the way the law was understood at the time, we see that one of the notable features of the period was that up until the middle part of the nineteenth century there was no Law of Copyright, Patents, Designs or Trademarks, and certainly no Intellectual Property Law (at least as it is perceived today).[40]

Indeed, the development of modern ideas about intellectual property during this period was characterized by disagreement about the organization of this area of law, and the contemporary taxonomy of intellectual property and its doctrines did not arise until sometime later. Sherman and Bently explain that it was generally agreed that there was a category of laws that rewarded creative mental labour with property rights, but that 'no one model or image had yet come to dominate as the accurate representation of the law.'[41] The result was a lack of consensus and a consequent variability that could be observed in the diverse arrangements made with respect to textbooks and libraries, legal and administrative

[40] Brad Sherman and Lionel Bently, *The Making of Modern Intellectual Property Law: The British Experience, 1760–1911* (Cambridge: Cambridge University Press, 1999) at 95 (note omitted).

[41] Ibid. at 96.

categories, the use of relevant language and concepts, and the choice of which subject matter became objects of 'intellectual property' rights.[42] It took some time before terms such as 'industrial property' and 'literary and artistic property' gave way and their subject matter converged into 'intellectual property'.

A product of the Industrial Revolution, the term 'industrial property' was enshrined as a description for patent and trademark law in the *Paris Convention for the Protection of Industrial Property* (1883). It originally included 'patents, industrial designs, trade marks and trade names'[43] and, in its latest iteration, has come to extend to patents, utility models, industrial designs, trademarks, service marks, trade names, indications of source or appellations of origin, and the repression of unfair competition.[44] It now applies to industry, commerce, agricultural and extractive industries, and to all manufactured or natural products, such as wines, grain, tobacco leaf, fruit, cattle, minerals, mineral waters, beer, flowers, and flour.[45]

Meanwhile, notions that are familiar to modern copyright law fell within the vaguer category of 'literary and artistic works' in the *Berne Convention for the Protection of Literary and Artistic Works* (1886). 'Literary and artistic works' originally included

> [b]ooks, pamphlets, and all other writings; dramatic or dramatico-musical works, musical compositions with or without words; works of drawing, painting, sculpture and engraving; lithographs; illustrations, geographical charts; plans, sketches, and plastic works relative to geography, topography, architecture, or science in general; in fact, every production whatsoever in the literary, scientific, or artistic domain which can be published by any mode of impression or reproduction.[46]

[42] Ibid.

[43] Art. 2 of the *Paris Convention for the Protection of Industrial Property* (20 March 1883).

[44] Art. 1(2–4) of the *Paris Convention for the Protection of Industrial Property* (as amended, 28 September 1979).

[45] Ibid.

[46] Art. 4 of the *Berne Convention for the Protection of Literary and Artistic Works* (9 September 1886).

It now extends to

> every production in the literary, scientific and artistic domain, whatever may be the mode or form of its expression, such as books, pamphlets and other writings; lectures, addresses, sermons and other works of the same nature; dramatic or dramatico-musical works; choreographic works and entertainments in dumb show; musical compositions with or without words; cinematographic works to which are assimilated works expressed by a process analogous to cinematography; works of drawing, painting, architecture, sculpture, engraving and lithography; photographic works to which are assimilated works expressed by a process analogous to photography; works of applied art; illustrations, maps, plans, sketches and three-dimensional works relative to geography, topography, architecture or science.[47]

As the scope of these doctrines expanded and their practical and political importance grew, institutions were established to administer them. Key among these is the World Intellectual Property Organization, and Mark Lemley argues that the term 'intellectual property' came into vogue only after the creation of this institution in 1967.[48]

This historical fact is not usually highlighted by those who use the term 'intellectual property'. After all, however it came about, it exists now and, for the most part, that is what matters in practice and politically. In a sense, the history became largely irrelevant for practical and political purposes once a hegemonic taxonomy of intellectual property had been established. Thus, the relatively recent genesis of the term seems to fade into insignificance in, for example, submissions calling for the expansion or stricter enforcement of intellectual property laws. Such claims tend to focus on contemporary interests and conditions rather than the historical development of 'intellectual property' as a department of law or term of art. This is only to be expected when the historical development of 'intellectual property' could also be inconvenient to

[47] Art. 2(1) of the *Berne Convention for the Protection of Literary and Artistic Works* (as amended, 28 September 1979).

[48] Lemley, above n. 19 at 1033.

those calling for new and greater recognition and regulation of intangible material over which they would like to exercise rights. A review of the historical origins and development of the term reinforces the sense that 'intellectual property' is a relatively recent and ill-defined expression whose meaning is confusingly uncertain. However, drawing attention to this is less likely to win friends and influence people to support intellectual propertization than is appealing to property language that implies that intellectual property has a fixed meaning and dates from time immemorial.

2.1.3. Conclusion

The failure to meaningfully define 'intellectual property' is typical of discussions about intellectual property policy. Without a clear definition of what is being discussed, it is perhaps not surprising that many discussions about 'intellectual property' seem to 'talk past each other'.[49]

In a world in which the term 'intellectual property' is used to attract attention, summarize moral arguments, focus concentration, and persuade (sometimes in a heavy-handed manner) law-makers to change policy relating to matters as diverse as scientific research, arts funding, industrial innovation, international trade, policing, border controls, education and literacy, preservation of cultural heritage, protection of ethnic identity, health, the provision of medicines and methods of medical treatment, and ways of communicating within and between societies, it is worrying that the term is used so loosely. The social consequences of political discussions about 'intellectual property' can be dramatic, yet it is not always clear exactly what is being spoken about.

So what does 'intellectual property' mean? With so much riding on an understanding of this term, defining it clearly is a far from trivial matter.

[49] Brian Bix, *Jurisprudence: Theory and Context* (London: Sweet & Maxwell, 1999) at 12.

2.2. Common Methods of Defining 'Intellectual Property'

Even when attempts are made to define what is meant by the term 'intellectual property', the findings are generally unsatisfactory. There are many techniques by which a legal definition of a term can be obtained. Classic examples include establishing exhaustive tests for what falls under the label, referring to the etymology of the term, explaining the intended use of the term in any particular context, or explaining why the term is politically important or philosophically interesting.[50] Yet definitions of intellectual property are typically superficial. These can be easily called into question or can themselves require further definition before they become at all informative. This can arguably be explained by the manner in which such definitions are composed.

The type of definition explicitly or implicitly offered usually reflects the reasons for the discussion, which are likely to be descriptive, evaluative, prescriptive, or a combination of these.[51] As the methodology adopted in the task of defining 'intellectual property' influences the explanation that results, it is important to consider how various definitional techniques operate, so that this can be overtly acknowledged. The purpose of this section is therefore to provide an overview of some of the techniques commonly employed to define 'intellectual property'.

The following pages outline several frequently used approaches to defining intellectual property, namely:

- intellectual property is the enumerated sum of its legal doctrines;
- intellectual property is the enumerated sum of the objects it regulates;
- intellectual property is a type of 'property';
- intellectual property is whatever the law stipulates it to be; and
- intellectual property is whatever it is intuitively felt to be.

[50] Bix summarizes these four types of definitional technique in ibid. at 27.

[51] Ibid. at 17.

These approaches are not mutually exclusive and they are probably not exhaustive. They operate on different levels and they sometimes overlap, but they have been separated (somewhat artificially at times) in the current discussion for ease of examination. The following survey gives examples of how each type of definition of intellectual property is used in practice, and it comments on the sort of insight that each type of definition offers about the nature of intellectual property.

To foreshadow the conclusions of this chapter: Each of these definitions serves a practical purpose, which may be functional (eg, useful for the day-the-day practice of intellectual property law) or political. In serving these functions, each also plays a self-reinforcing role in promoting the evolution and importance of intellectual property law. However, each of the techniques surveyed here also produces largely empty definitions that tell us little or nothing about the content or function of 'intellectual property' or the law that creates and regulates it. As will become apparent, these approaches are parts of a functional legal system for classifying and standardizing intellectual property, but they shed little light on what constitutes the 'intellectual property' that is being regulated in this way.

2.2.1. Definition by Enumeration

Definition by enumeration – which may also be described as 'extensional definition'[52] – occurs when a definition contains a list of things that constitute the object being defined. The list of components may be representative or it may be exhaustive. However, even when a complete list is offered, definition by enumeration lacks a description of the 'criterion' that explains what those constituents have in common. Definition by enumeration is thus missing the factor that would enable someone unfamiliar with the subject to determine whether or not something is an instance of the object being defined.

[52] Drahos, above n. 7 at 4.

Definition by enumeration is very common in discussions about intellectual property law, where it tends to take one of two forms. It either treats intellectual property as the sum of its constituent legal doctrines or treats it as the sum of its objects of regulation. Neither type of enumerated definition of 'intellectual property' tends to be particularly helpful in shedding light on the nature of intellectual property.

2.2.1.a Intellectual Property as the Enumerated Sum of Its Legal Doctrines

'Departments of law' is a term coined by Ronald Dworkin to describe the various areas or doctrines into which the legal system is compartmentalized.[53] The term 'doctrine' is often used similarly. For the purposes of the current discussion, 'intellectual property' can be considered to be a department of law (along with contract law, tort law, administrative law, constitutional law, and so on), while its sub-categories, such as copyright, patent and trademark law, can be considered to be intellectual property's constituent doctrines.

The sort of enumerative approach that treats 'intellectual property' as the sum of its legal doctrines involves being able to identify when a rule found in an intellectual property doctrine (ie, a legal doctrine that is already commonly acknowledged to be an intellectual property doctrine) is the appropriate legal principle to apply in a given set of circumstances. That is, is the class of object being regulated correctly classified within one of the legal doctrines that is commonly understood to be 'intellectual property'?

Definition by enumeration assumes the pre-existence of categories into which objects are sorted. This is not philosophically rigorous, and it is therefore a pragmatic approach to legal definition that depends on the existence of earlier determinations about what does or does not fall within a legal department or doctrine. It is therefore of little assistance in determining whether something should be classified as intellectual

[53] Ronald Dworkin, *Law's Empire* (London: Fontana Press, 1986) at 251.

property in the first place. Its value lies in determining what falls within already established intellectual property doctrines.

In Anglo-American approaches to legal training, students are taught to 'think like a lawyer'. Martin Krygier describes this as 'learning the idiom of activity of a tradition' and speculates that this is perhaps the only important thing that law schools do begin to teach.[54] In the context of lawyers learning the idiom of activity – at least in jurisdictions following common law traditions – this arguably means becoming adept in the law's prevailing interpretive traditions, such as statutory interpretation and application of the doctrine of precedent.[55] However, before employing those interpretative tools in a given case, lawyers must be able to identify the relevant legal department within whose ambit a fact situation might fall and within which certain types of legal rules that apply to certain types of factual situation are collected. Lawyers thus have the preliminary task of determining whether a legal problem involves a doctrine that falls within the department of tort, contract, administrative law, or intellectual property law, and so on.

Once the appropriate legal department is (or departments are) identified, the correct departmental and doctrinal rules can be applied. Hugh Collins has discussed this in relation to the department of contract law, explaining that the rules of contract law determine which facts will be considered to be relevant to the legal outcome and which will be extraneous. A lawyer or judge can then apply the rules that structure the department – which Collins describes as the 'operational rules of the subsystem' – to the relevant facts in order to determine what the legal consequences will be.[56]

This perspective follows Hans Kelsen in portraying law as a scheme of interpretation[57] in which legal departments and doctrines are the

[54] Martin Krygier, 'Thinking Like a Lawyer', in Wojciech Sadurski (ed.), *Ethical Dimensions of Legal Theory* (Amsterdam: Rodolpi, 1991), 67–90 at 70.

[55] Ibid. See, eg, Krygier's discussion of interpretive techniques in ibid. at 71–75.

[56] Hugh Collins, *Regulating Contracts* (Oxford: Oxford University Press, 1999) at 42.

[57] Hans Kelsen, *Introduction to the Problems of Legal Theory* (Oxford: Clarendon Press, 1992) at 4.

organizational categories. 'Intellectual property' is a departmental term under which certain legal doctrines are collected, and it is part of a lawyer's repertoire of skills to be able to determine whether or not an object or type of behaviour falls within the ambit regulated by an existing doctrine within a given jurisdiction. This is done by applying the doctrinal rules. However, correctly identifying that copyright is a doctrine of intellectual property law is not particularly helpful if the relevant rules of copyright law cannot be appropriately applied. It is the rules of intellectual property's constituent doctrines that are important, rather than the name of the overarching department that is used for organizational convenience. For example, it is of little use to identify a piece of material as being covered by intellectual property law unless one can explain which doctrine it is regulated by and can discuss consequences arising from the conclusion. Saying that something is 'intellectual property' means little without explaining what sort of intellectual property (eg, a trademark or registered design), and explaining what sort of thing that object of intellectual property is, and what consequences arise from that conclusion. Thus, enumerative use of the term requires a constant reductive analysis if it is to be of any assistance in explaining what 'intellectual property' means.

The problem with this form of enumerative definition is that it focuses on the organizational structure of the law but tells us nothing about the *content* of a department or why a legal problem should be classified within it. It thus leaves unanswered a number of fundamental questions. What are the characteristics of the legal problem that make it fall within a particular organizational category? And what are the characteristics of doctrines such as copyright, patent, and trademarks that lead to their being categorized as doctrines of the organizational department of intellectual property? For answers to these sorts of questions, it is necessary to look to a different sort of enumeration, or perhaps even a different sort of definition or explanation of 'intellectual property' altogether.

2.2.1.b Intellectual Property as the Enumerated Sum of Its Objects of Regulation

A common, and perhaps even the standard, method of defining 'intellectual property' is another type of definition by enumeration. This version offers an inventory of intellectual property's doctrines and the objects and rules that fall within them. It attempts to define by categorizing content, implicitly suggesting that intellectual property is the sum of its ingredients but not explaining why those ingredients have been chosen. This definitional method creates a taxonomy of intellectual property by trying to classify objects under the headings it has nominated. It is therefore a 'micro-version' of the definition by enumeration approach because it focuses on the smaller parts that contribute to the whole, but it also has the flaw of failing to nominate an accompanying 'criterion' to explain why its components should be grouped together in the same category.

This version of the definition by enumeration approach is in many ways similar to the version described earlier. While the previous approach focuses on the departments and doctrines that are considered to be intellectual property, thus classifying intellectual property by its overall appearance, an alternative enumerative approach infers a focus on intellectual property's component parts.

An analogy could be made between a definition by enumeration approach to 'intellectual property' and the same approach used to define a 'car'. Defining intellectual property as the sum of its legal doctrines is equivalent in many ways to defining a car by its overall appearance. For example, a car is a rectangular mechanical construction on wheels for transporting people. Treating intellectual property as the sum of its objects of regulation is like cataloguing all of a car's parts: the chassis, the doors, the windows, the engine and its components, and so on. Both types of description indicate the object, but neither offers the full picture. Neither provides a more than superficial definition of either a 'car' or 'intellectual property'.

Definition by enumeration can be effective to the extent that it provides a framework within which lawyers can categorize behaviours and things into the legal boxes that are required to regulate rights and obligations, and to embark on litigation by articulating a cause of action. From this perspective, it is an adequate, serviceable method of defining 'intellectual property', its component doctrines, and the component rules in legal practice. However, definition by enumeration does not capture the essential characteristics that lead to these behaviours or things being categorized as intellectual property in the first place, and it is of little assistance when the identity of the objects regulated by intellectual property laws, and the sorts of rules used to regulate them, keep changing.[58] In this sense it is inadequate, as it provides no basis for determining whether or not something should in fact be defined within the rubric of 'intellectual property'.

In other words, the common approach of defining 'intellectual property' as the enumerated sum of its objects of regulation may be a satisfactory tool for practitioners to work with once the term 'intellectual property' has already been applied to an object. However, it does not assist in determining *whether* it should be applied to the object in the first place, because it does not tell us what 'intellectual property' is or what it comprises. A definition by enumeration approach is therefore more likely to be useful as a method of working with intellectual property law at a practical legal level than as a way of understanding what the term 'intellectual property' really implies. It is a workable method of grouping objects into pre-established legal categories, but it is not as helpful when it comes to establishing or determining the nature of those categories in the first place. It is nonetheless an extremely common method of explaining intellectual property, as the following examples demonstrate.

[58] Jeremy Waldron has identified an equivalent problem in relation to defining 'private property'. See Jeremy Waldron, *The Right to Private Property* (Oxford: Clarendon Press, 1988) at 28.

Textbooks and the very organizations that are responsible for organizing intellectual property laws typically employ an enumerative technique for defining intellectual property. Such definitions catalogue the sorts of things affected by intellectual property law and hint at what these might comprise, but they do not elucidate the essence of intellectual property. They do not tell us what 'intellectual property' is or what binds its constituent doctrines together.

For example, IP Australia, a governmental organization responsible for administering intellectual property law in that jurisdiction, explains intellectual property as follows:

> **Intellectual property** represents the property of your mind or intellect. It can be an invention, trade mark, original design or the practical application of a good idea. In business terms, this means your proprietary knowledge – a key component of success in business today. It is often the edge which sets successful companies apart and as world markets become increasingly competitive, protecting your intellectual property becomes essential. Confidential information (also referred to as trade secrets), patents, registered designs, trade marks, copyright, circuit layout rights and plant breeder's rights are all legally classified as IP rights.[59]

This definition is hardly illuminating. 'The property of your mind or intellect': what does that mean? It would seem to suggest that any thought, idea or object of communication becomes intellectual property, yet a core tenet of copyright law is that it does not confer rights over ideas. The definition then falls back on an enumerated list of objects of regulation and component doctrines. Not only does IP Australia's definition of intellectual property imply legal rights that are broader than are actually offered by Australian intellectual property laws and international intellectual property treaties, but its reference to a list of intellectual property's constituents is also misleadingly superficial. Each of the terms in the

[59] IP Australia website: http://www.ipaustralia.gov.au/ip/index.shtml [accessed 19 January 2004].

given list would need further clarification to contribute meaningfully to the overall definition, and the list does not shed light on what it is that determines why something will or will not be categorized as intellectual property. This definition is therefore quite unenlightening, but it is also typical of definitions offered in an attempt to explain the term 'intellectual property'.

Even international treaties that govern intellectual property can be obtuse in this way. According to the WIPO's definition of 'intellectual property':

> [it] shall include the rights relating to:
>
> - literary, artistic and scientific works,
> - performances of performing artists, phonograms, and broadcasts,
> - inventions in all fields of human endeavor,
> - scientific discoveries,
> - industrial designs,
> - trademarks, service marks, and commercial names and designations,
> - protection against unfair competition, and all other rights resulting from intellectual activity in the industrial, scientific, literary or artistic fields.[60]

It is another list lacking substance. It is inclusive, not exhaustive, and it is so vague that the ordinary meaning of its wording suggests more than is actually regulated by intellectual property laws. Like that of IP Australia, WIPO's definition lists an open-ended litany of the constituent documents of 'intellectual property', each of which requires further legal definition if it is to be meaningful. It is another definition of 'intellectual property' that is itself in need of definition.

This tendency towards the opaque is also found in the WTO's *TRIPS Agreement*'s definition of 'intellectual property', which suffers from the same weakness as that of WIPO. The *TRIPS Agreement* lists intellectual property's constituent doctrines as follows:

[60] Definitions clause of the *Convention Establishing the World Intellectual Property Organization* (*WIPO Convention* (1967), Art 2, ¶viii).

> For the purposes of this Agreement, the term "intellectual property" refers to all categories of intellectual property that are the subject of Sections 1 through 7 of Part II, which include copyright and related rights, trademarks, geographical indications, industrial designs, patents, layout designs of integrated circuits, and protection of undisclosed information.[61]

The *TRIPS Agreement* elucidates the meaning of some of these doctrines,[62] but it leaves the definition of others to characterizations awarded by separate agreements such as the *Berne Convention*,[63] while the scope and meaning of yet other intellectual property doctrines are determined by the domestic law of signatory countries. Defined in this way, the meaning of 'intellectual property' is clearly not static: it is the name attached to an inventory of terms whose meanings vary from jurisdiction to jurisdiction, change every time a new doctrine is added or an old doctrine is abandoned and shift every time one of its doctrines is loosened or strengthened. Zheng Chengsi has observed that 'know-how', 'folklore',

[61] *TRIPS Agreement*, Part I, Art. 1(2).

[62] See, eg, Sec. 2, Trademarks, Art. 15(1): Protectable Subject Matter: 'Any sign, or any combination of signs, capable of distinguishing the goods or services of one undertaking from those of other undertakings, shall be capable of constituting a trademark. Such signs, in particular words including personal names, letters, numerals, figurative elements and combinations of colours as well as any combination of such signs, shall be eligible for registration as trademarks. Where signs are not inherently capable of distinguishing the relevant goods or services, Members may make registrability depend on distinctiveness acquired through use. Members may require, as a condition of registration, that signs be visually perceptible.'

[63] See, eg, Art. 2(1) of the *Berne Convention for the Protection of Literary and Artistic Works* (Paris Text, 1971): 'The expression "literary and artistic works" shall include every production in the literary, scientific and artistic domain, whatever may be the mode or form of its expression, such as books, pamphlets and other writings; lectures, addresses, sermons and other works of the same nature; dramatic or dramatico-musical works; choreographic works and entertainments in dumb show; musical compositions with or without words; cinematographic works to which are assimilated works expressed by a process analogous to cinematography; works of drawing, painting, architecture, sculpture, engraving and lithography; photographic works to which are assimilated works expressed by a process analogous to photography; works of applied art; illustrations, maps, plans, sketches and three-dimensional works relative to geography, topography, architecture or science.'

and 'personal data protection' were added to the realms of 'intellectual property' during the 1980s, thus altering the existing implication of the term,[64] and has argued that the new doctrines and rights should instead be referred to as 'information property' in order to safeguard the traditional meaning of 'intellectual property'. Regardless of whether one agrees that changing the terminology would save the meaning of 'intellectual property', which is arguably contested and uncertain anyway, the point is well made about the flexibility and questionable utility of a term whose meaning keeps shifting.

Apart from its failure to capture the essence of intellectual property, a distinct problem with the potentially endlessly reductionist enumerative method of defining intellectual property is that it provides a definition composed of other legal definitions, and these definitions are built entirely on a pyramid of interdependent concepts rather than on words that are generally agreed to refer to specific types of behaviour, emotions, or objects. This is not a materialist claim that the meaning of words can never be fully knowable unless they refer to tangible objects, but an argument that a lack of agreement about the determinative criteria of 'intellectual property' makes enumerative definitions of the term both dogmatic and unverifiable against objective measures.

This is a well-recognized problem when one is attempting to define concepts. The essential disputability of conceptual meaning stems from the abstract nature of concepts that can be defined only by reference to other concepts or definitions. The difficulty of building legal definitions on concepts is aptly described by Robert Moles:

> When we talk of the description of a concept, the position is different in this important aspect – the object being described does not exist in an area where we could, even in principle, have an equal right of access to check the particular observations which make up the description. They are what we might call 'mental phenomena'. We

[64] Zheng Chengsi, 'Intellectual Property and Information Property' (1989) 9 *European Intellectual Property Review* 327–329 at 328.

> cannot, as we can with the other class of descriptions in the observational field, have access to the objects of description independently of the other's statements about them. Here, it is the statements contained in the description which 'constitute' the concept.... It is for this reason that conceptual analysis depends on setting out the conceptual system being employed by way of definition.[65]

The weakness of enumerative definitional techniques is that they do not set out this conceptual system. So even if one understands how the statements contained in the description of intellectual property (eg, statements about 'copyright', 'literary, dramatic, musical or artistic work', 'patents', 'trademarks' 'passing off', 'confidential information', and so on) operate in practice, it still leaves the question begging: What *is* intellectual property?

2.2.2. Defining Intellectual Property as a Type of 'Property'

One method by which some commentators address the difficulty of explaining what intellectual property actually *is* rather than just enumerating instances of it is to define it as a 'type of property'. Indeed, the very label 'intellectual *property*' suggests this conclusion. Thus, intellectual property is frequently defined as 'property' in an intangible object, and a recurrent theme permeating attempts to define 'intellectual property' involves allusions to the concept of 'property'. It is common to see 'intellectual property' or its doctrines likened to the pre-existing legal department of 'property' law, followed by an attempt to explain why it is or is not 'property'.[66] A typical way of doing this is first to define 'property', or at least to nominate characteristics that are typical of property, and then to show that intellectual property does or does not fit within the given definition.

[65] Robert N. Moles, *Definition and Rule in Legal Theory: A Reassessment of H. L. A. Hart and the Positivist Tradition* (Oxford: Basil Blackwell, 1987) at 24.

[66] See, eg, David Westfall and David Landau, 'Publicity Rights as Property Rights' (2005) 23 *Cardozo Arts and Entertainment Law Journal* 71–123.

D. F. Libling used an 'intellectual property is a type of property' approach when he argued that the right to exploit the commercial value of a tangible or intangible entity is property if it is the result of the expenditure of time, effort, and money by the person claiming title.[67] R. J. Roberts followed the same path when contending that information is not property because property is characterized by its inherent scarcity, and that information is thus the antithesis of property because it is capable of universal possession.[68] And Frank Easterbrook adopted this course when he offered the opposing view that, because intellectual property rights impose no more of a monopoly than other sorts of property rights, 'intellectual property is still property' and the law should treat physical and intangible property identically.[69] Stephen Carter continued the trend even when warning that it might be inconsequential whether or not intellectual property is property in the same sense that other property is property: '[W]hether intellectual property (whatever that is) is property (whatever that is) is the same sense that other things are property (whatever that is).'[70] More recently, James Bessen and Michael Meurer's analysis of whether patents should really be categorized as property compares property-like features of patent law with features of the law of tangible property,[71] and concludes that doctrinal similarity can obscure differences in economic performance arising from differences in implementation.[72] Each of these examples considers whether intellectual property is

[67] D. F. Libling, 'The Concept of Property: Property in Intangibles' (1978) 94 *Law Quarterly Review* 538. Note the similarity between this argument and that of the 'Lockean' perspective, which proposes that 'property' (including intellectual property) arises as a result of mixing one's labour (or time or money) with something found in the state of nature. For a discussion of the Lockean analysis, see Drahos, above n. 7 at 47–54.

[68] R. J. Roberts, 'Is Information Property?' (1987) 3 *Intellectual Property Journal* 209 at 209–210.

[69] Frank H. Easterbrook, 'Intellectual Property Is Still Property' (1990) 13 *Harvard Journal of Law and Public Policy* 108–118 at 113 and 118.

[70] Stephen L. Carter, 'Does It Matter Whether Intellectual Property Is Property?' (1993) 68 *Chicago-Kent Law Review* 715 at 715.

[71] Bessen and Meurer, above n. 21 at 6.

[72] Ibid. at 8.

an intangible form of 'property', but in each case the conclusion also rests on the prior definition given to the concept of 'property'.

Not all commentators welcome this approach. Debora Halbert identifies the core difficulty of defining intellectual property as 'property' when she comments:

> To discuss this topic it is inevitable that one uses the language of rights and property, and this, I would argue, is part of the problem. In many ways, then, it is important to dig into the roots of the logic of the property system itself.[73]

The problem that Halbert alludes to is that the nature of the prior definition of 'property' is itself extremely variable and highly contested.[74]

'Property' is a concept that is notoriously difficult to define. Disagreement over what the term 'property' means results in its sometimes being used in a manner that is both philosophically and legally ambiguous. 'Property' means different things in different contexts. Does it refer to an object? Does it refer to rights? Is it a system? Or is it a conceptual abstraction that encompasses each of these elements? If the last, how should it be described? Jeremy Waldron observes that many writers have argued that property is a concept which defies definition,[75] and Jim Harris cautions that '[d]eductions from purportedly universal definitions of the word "property" are to be deplored.'[76] *Essentially contested concepts* are those ideas or concepts for which it is impossible to identify a single, clearly definable general use of the term that can be held up as the correct or standard use,[77] and 'property' falls squarely into this category. Perhaps Francis Philbrick was correct when suggesting

[73] Halbert, above n. 17 at 11.

[74] See, eg, discussion of this issue in Alexandra George, 'The Difficulty of Defining "Property"' (2005) 25 *Oxford Journal of Legal Studies* 793–813 at 793.

[75] Waldron, above n. 58 at 26ff.

[76] J. W. Harris, *Property and Justice* (Oxford: Oxford University Press, 1996) at 12.

[77] See W. B. Gallie, 'Essentially Contested Concepts', in Max Black (ed.), *The Importance of Language* (Englewood Cliffs, NJ: Prentice Hall, 1962) at 121–146; first published in (1956) 56 *Proceedings of the Aristotelian Society* 167.

that 'what is property may depend upon the action that is dependent upon the answer.'[78]

The difficulties are compounded when it comes to capturing the essence of 'intellectual property'.[79] If we are in disagreement about – or unclear as to – the meaning of 'property', how can 'intellectual property is a type of property' be any less opaque? With the nature of 'property' itself so disputed, simply adding 'intellectual' to the property equation does little to clarify the definition: it suggests an intangible (ie, non-physical) or imaginary (ie, located in the individual or collective mind) form of whatever is implied by the term 'property'. The result is an intensely flexible, and consequently a very vague outcome in which intellectual property can be virtually any incorporeal thing that its definer wants it to be.

A definition of intellectual property as an intangible form of property thus fails to describe clearly what the term refers to. It tells us little more than that the law can be called on to enforce rights over something intangible. However, it does not indicate which intangibles will be treated as property, which criteria will be used to determine which intangibles are to be treated as property, what that treatment will entail (ie, which rights will attach to that property) or why. As Laura Underkuffler points out, 'If all legal rights are property, then property – as a legally cognizable idea, at least – has no particular importance.'[80]

[78] Francis S. Philbrick, 'Changing Conceptions of Property Law' (1938) 86 *University of Pennsylvania Law Review* 691–732 at 694.

[79] See, eg, J. W. Carter, Patricia Lane, Gregory J. Tolhurst, and Elisabeth M. Peden, *Helmore Commercial Law and Personal Property in New South Wales* (Sydney: Law Book Company, 1992, 10th ed.) at 13: 'Since there is no minimal condition, the presence of which is essential for possession, there has been an attempt to analyse the various legal decisions in an attempt to describe the con[cept]. Similarly, the concept of ownership, although involving standard incidents such as the right to possess, the right to sue and manage etc., has been found to possess no single essential or fundamental incident.'

[80] Laura S. Underkuffler, *The Idea of Property: Its Meaning and Power* (Oxford: Oxford University Press, 2003) at 12.

The effect of this sort of definitional technique is therefore to turn 'intellectual property' into an impossibly broad term, which makes 'intellectual property' largely meaningless. All sorts of things might meet the description of an 'intangible form of property', even if not all of these things would generally be considered by intellectual property professionals (such as lawyers, judges, and other law-makers, trademark and patent attorneys, and portfolio managers) to be intellectual property. For example, contracts and human rights could both be described as intangible types of property, but neither would generally be considered to fall within the meaning of 'intellectual property'.

Contracts – promises or agreements that are intended to be legally binding – are intangible (albeit often evidenced in writing) and are legally enforceable. Contracts may be treated by the courts as 'property'[81] that can, for example, be bought or sold. But is 'contract law' an intellectual property doctrine?[82] The intuitive answer is no, but it is more difficult to say why not if 'intellectual property' is defined inclusively as 'intangible property'.

What about human rights? Are human rights intellectual property? Human rights are arguably intangible and many are legally enforceable.

[81] See, eg, D. Bradley Pettit, 'Can an Attorney Defer Recognition of a Fee Income in a Case *Involving* a Structured Settlement?' (1996) 70 *Florida Bar Journal* 36 (noting that under US law relating to the transfer of a life insurance contract, retirement income contract, endowment contract, or other contract providing life insurance protection, only the cash surrender value of the contract is considered to be property); Blake Rohrbacher, 'More Equal Than Others: Defending Property-Contract Parity in Bankruptcy' (2005) 114 *Yale Law Journal* 1099 at 1112 (observing that, under US law, 'an interest in a contract that has "value" and is "contingent at the time of filing and not payable" until termination is property of the estate'); and Susannah L. Baker, 'It's All Fun and Games Until Somebody Declares Bankruptcy: A Debtor's Right to Season Ticket Holder Status' (1997) 14 *Emory Bankruptcy Developments Journal* 182 (noting that, under US law, unexpired contracts are considered property of the estate in bankruptcy).

[82] The text of the written form of a contract may indeed be covered by copyright law and, in this sense, may be regarded as intellectual property. However, the question being considered here is whether contract law, as a department of law, is a doctrine of intellectual property law.

Some commentators have described human rights as 'property'.[83] But human rights are not generally considered to be 'intellectual property'.[84] Why not?

The answer is arguably that something beyond *'intangible' 'property'* needs to be added before a useful definition can be given of intellectual property.[85] This is again a call for a criterion to determine what constitutes 'intellectual property', and this criterion must arguably be concerned with the content of intellectual property. Its identification requires recourse to an alternative definitional technique.

2.2.3. Stipulative Definition

In Lewis Carroll's classic children's story *Through the Looking Glass*, the heroine, Alice, travels through a mythical dream world where everything seems topsy-turvy and confused. Along the way, Alice meets an anthropomorphized egg sitting on a wall, with whom she proceeds to discuss semantics. '"When *I* use a word", Humpty Dumpty said, in a rather scornful tone, "it means just what I choose it to mean – neither more nor less."'[86] Perplexed, Alice queries: 'The question is ... whether you *can* make words mean so many different things.'[87] It is a question that could also be asked of those who define 'intellectual property' using a stipulative technique. For it is not only Humpty Dumpty who is partial to stipulative definition; the technique is also a very popular tool of law-makers, and it is common in intellectual property law.[88]

[83] See, eg, C. B. Macpherson, 'Human Rights as Property Rights' (1977) 24 *Dissent* 72–77.

[84] For example, they do not appear in enumerated definitions of 'intellectual property', such as the definitions considered earlier or found in international intellectual property treaties. Human rights treaties similarly fail to describe human rights as intellectual property rights.

[85] See also reference to intellectual property from a 'property' perspective in the context of a discussion of intellectual property's core criteria, Chapter 4, §4.3.2.

[86] Lewis Carroll, *Through the Looking-Glass*, in *The Complete Works of Lewis Carroll* (London: Nonesuch Press, 1939) at 196.

[87] Ibid.

[88] It is also used in property law and theory more generally. See discussion of this point in Harris, above n. 76, chap. 9 at 139ff.

From a more academic perspective, the stipulative definitional approach can be described as

> the explicit and selfconscious setting up of the meaning-relation between some word and some object, the act of assigning an object to a name (or a name to an object), not the act of recording an already existing assignment.[89]

The essential characteristic of stipulative definition is the 'deliberate, arbitrary, selfconscious choice of a name for a certain thing, or of a thing for a certain name.'[90] According to this method, 'intellectual property' is whatever law-makers stipulate it to be.

Stipulative definition occurs, for example, when the subject matter regulated by intellectual property law's doctrines become 'property' – however that may be defined (and regardless of the difficulties with the approach already outlined) – simply because the law stipulates that that is what they are. Thus, *Berne Convention* signatories devise legislation to protect copyright works, and that legislation might define copyright as property: the UK *Copyright, Designs and Patents Act* 1988 defines copyright as 'a property right',[91] while US copyright law says, 'The ownership of copyright may ... be bequeathed by will or pass as personal property by the applicable laws of intestate succession.'[92] The same holds true for many of intellectual property's other doctrines in various jurisdictions. The Australian *Trade Marks Act* 1995 says that '[a] registered trade mark is personal property',[93] and according to the UK *Trade Marks Act* 1994, '[a] registered trademark is a property right'.[94] The UK *Patents Act* 1977

[89] Richard Robinson, *Definition* (Oxford: Clarendon Press, 1968) at 59.

[90] Ibid. at 60.

[91] *Copyright, Designs and Patents Act* 1988 (UK), s.1(1).

[92] 17 USC 201 – Copyright, 'Ownership of copyright' ¶(a) and ¶(d)(1).

[93] *Trade Marks Act* 1995 (Aust.), s.21(a).

[94] *Trade Marks Act* 1994 (UK), s.2(1). It is interesting to note the wording of this provision: a trademark is a property right. The analysis offered earlier would suggest that the trademark is actually the substance – or property – to which rights attach, which is the approach taken in the Australian trademark example (ibid).

states that '[a]ny patent or application for a patent is personal property',[95] the Australian *Patent Act* 1990 holds that '[t]he exclusive rights are private property',[96] and the US patent statute similarly declares that '[s]ubject to the provisions of this title, patents shall have the attributes of personal property.'[97] In other examples, the 'property' delineations of intellectual property's doctrines can be found in case law. For instance, US courts have noted a plaintiff's property interest in a trademark,[98] but sometimes intellectual property is stipulated by courts not to be property at all.[99] In each case, whether an intellectual property doctrine confers 'property' rights depends on whether the law-makers have stipulated that it will do so.

However, stipulating that *x* is *y* is different from explaining the nature of *x*. It does not, in itself, tell us about the characteristics of *x* or *y*. It may have practical utility in context, but in itself it is of little assistance in determining the nature of the object being defined. This is nicely illustrated by the UK law that defines 'skiing' as 'sliding over snow or ice on skis, skates, sledges or similar equipment', thus including ice hockey, figure skating, bobsledding and snowboarding in its definition.[100] For the purpose of regulating 'adventure activities' in the United Kingdom, ice skating and other ice-related activities are legally stipulated to be 'skiing'; this may have practical utility, but it does not explain much about the nature of skiing as an activity. It would be a misleading place to look if someone with no knowledge of the term 'skiing' wanted to understand its usual meaning. Similarly, stipulating that a particular object or legal doctrine is

[95] *Patents Act* 1977 (UK), s.30(1).

[96] *Patent Act* 1990 (Aust.), s.13(2). Note that the 'rights' – rather than the substance – are deemed to be the property in this example.

[97] 35 USC 261 Patents.

[98] See *Dallas Cowboys Cheerleaders, Inc. v. Pussycat Cinema, Ltd.*, 604 F.2d 200 at 2005 (2d Cir. 1979): 'Plaintiff's trademark is in the nature of a property right.'

[99] See, eg, *Ringling Bros.-Barnum & Bailey Combined Shows, Inc. v. Utah Div. of Travel Dev.*, 170 F.3d 449 at 459 (4th Cir. 1999): '[W]e simply cannot believe that, as a general proposition, Congress could have intended, without making its intention to do so perfectly clear, to create property rights in gross, unlimited in time (via injunction), even in "famous" trademarks.'

[100] *Adventure Activities Licensing Regulations* 2004 (UK), s.2.

'intellectual property' may have practical utility in the day-to-day operation of the law (eg, to explain what sorts of cases are dealt with by the intellectual property division of a court or law firm or to indicate whether something is 'property' that can be sold or bequeathed), but it is not of much help in clarifying what 'intellectual property' actually is or means.

It can be argued that stipulative definitions of abstract objects – such as intellectual property – are necessarily arbitrary because 'there cannot be any one right way to divide up social reality.'[101] This may be so, but stipulative definitions are often driven by pragmatic decisions about the purpose of the definition rather than the inherent characteristics of the object or behaviour being defined, so it is not surprising if they do not contribute to our understanding of the nature of intellectual property or help to determine whether or not something is (or should be) classified as intellectual property.

2.2.4. Intuitive Definition and Intangibility

Definition by intuition is arguably even less precise and useful than the definitional techniques addressed previously for determining what constitutes 'intellectual property'. It relies on nothing more than feelings about what intellectual property consists of, yet it is implicit in many discussions about intellectual property. This tendency sometimes arises when new intellectual property–like doctrines are being spoken about (such as 'publicity rights' in the United States[102] or a doctrine giving monopoly rights over fact compilations[103]), and it sometimes arises when it is being considered whether proposed rights are of an intellectual property–like nature.[104]

[101] Bix, above n. 49 at 18.

[102] See, eg, Alice Haemmerli, 'Whose Who? The Case for a Kantian Right of Publicity' (1999) 49 *Duke Law Journal* 383–492 at 421–422, arguing that image is 'like intellectual property', and publicity rights are like copyright.

[103] See, eg, Jessica Litman, 'After Feist' (1992) 17 *Dayton Law Review* 607–616 at 607 (noting enthusiasm to create sui generis legislation to allow copyright-like monopolies over databases and other compilations of facts).

[104] See, eg, Shawn K. Baldwin, '"To Promote the Progress of Science and Useful Arts": A Role for Federal Regulation of Intellectual Property as Collateral' (1995) 143 *University*

A famous example of 'intuitive definition' in practice is found in the 1964 US Supreme Court case of *Jacobellis v Ohio*,[105] concerning obscenity law. It is not an intellectual property example, but it provides a vivid illustration of the weaknesses of this definitional technique. The question before the Court was whether a motion picture was obscene and therefore not entitled to the constitutional protection of free expression contained in the First and Fourteenth Amendments. Justice Stewart delivered a single-paragraph opinion, stating that protection under the First and Fourteenth Amendments was constitutionally limited to 'hard-core pornography'. He concluded:

> I shall not today attempt further to define the kinds of material I understand to be embraced within that shorthand description; and perhaps I could never succeed in intelligibly doing so. But I know it when I see it, and the motion picture involved in this case is not that.[106]

'I know it when I see it' has become a catch-cry for the practice of definition by intuition.[107]

The fuzziness of this sort of approach is neatly captured by K. W. Wedderburn's reference to an analogous technique in relation to

of Pennsylvania Law Review 1701–1738 at 1703 (arguing that the adoption of a certain approach to the regulation of security interests in intellectual property would also fail to recognize the distinctive nature of intellectual property); Susy Frankel, 'WTO Application of "the Customary Rules of Interpretation of Public International Law" to Intellectual Property' (2006) 46 *Virginia Journal of International Law* 365–432 at 391–392 (arguing that the *TRIPS Agreement* has not abandoned traditional justifications for intellectual property law); J. H. Reichman, 'Electronic Information Tools: The Outer Edge of World Intellectual Property Law' (1992) 17 *Dayton Law Review* 797–838 at 819 (arguing that it would be socially undesirable to allow patent-like restraints, which could not be explained in terms of traditional intellectual property justifications, on trade on computer-generated productions and the outputs of artificial intelligence machines).

105 *Jacobellis v Ohio* (1964), 378 US 184.

106 Ibid. at §197.

107 For a discussion of the 'I know it when I see it' approach applied to US copyright law, see James H. Carter, 'They Know It When They See it: Copyright and Aesthetics in the Second Circuit' (1991) 65 *St. John's Law Review* 773–794.

employment law. Discussing the difference between an employee and a contractor, Wedderburn suggests 'the elephant test'– that is, an employee is like an elephant, 'an animal too difficult to define but easy to recognise when you see it.'[108] In effect, if the animal looks like an elephant, walks like an elephant and smells like an elephant, conclude that it is an elephant.[109]

Using analogous reasoning, would it be safe to say that, if something looks like intellectual property, it must be intellectual property? This seems to be the assumption inherent in cases that define something as 'intellectual property' because it resembles other instances of intellectual property. If something looks like intellectual property (whatever that abstract thing looks like), it is likely to be regulated by intellectual property law.

This approach is particularly common with respect to new sui generis categories of intellectual property such as moral rights, plant-variety types, geographical indications and publicity rights. It also seems to be a self-fulfilling prophecy: if an intuitive analogy can be drawn between a

[108] K. W. Wedderburn, *The Worker and the Law* (Harmondsworth: Penguin, 1986) at 116. Quoted in W. B. Creighton, W. J. Ford and R. J. Mitchell, *Labour Law: Text and Materials* (Sydney: Law Book Company, 1993) at 91. As this book was about to be printed, a decision was handed down in the UK intellectual property case *Lucasfilm Limited and others v Ainsworth and another* [2011] UKSC 39. At para. 47, the Court criticized intuitive definitional methods: 'We would uphold the judgments below very largely for the reasons that they give. But (at the risk of appearing humourless) we are not enthusiastic about the "elephant test" in para [77] of the Court of Appeal's judgment ("knowing one when you see it"). Any zoologist has no difficulty in recognising an elephant on sight, and most could no doubt also give a clear and accurate description of its essential identifying features. By contrast a judge, even one very experienced in intellectual property matters, does not have some special power of divination which leads instantly to an infallible conclusion, and no judge would claim to have such a power. The judge reads and hears the evidence (often including expert evidence), reads and listens to the advocates' submissions, and takes what the Court of Appeal rightly called a multifactorial approach.'

[109] A similar example can be found in the evidence of a London accountant who was asked in 1819 by the Committee on the Resumption of Cash Payments to explain 'a pound'. He answered, 'I find it difficult to explain it, but every gentleman in England knows it.... It is something which has existed in this country for eight hundred years – three hundred years before the introduction of gold.' Quoted in Charles Proctor, *Mann on the Legal Aspect of Money* (Oxford: Oxford University Press, 2005) at 8, ¶604.

new discovery or legal right and pre-existing intellectual property principles, it is likely to be called intellectual property and justified on the basis that it *is* 'intellectual property'. But, again, what does intellectual property look like? Intuition is an awkward enough strategy for clarifying and defining tangible objects. How much more problematic must it be when applied to concepts (such as 'hard-core pornography' or 'intellectual property')? How useful could such a technique be for those trying to identify or classify intangible objects with respect to which there is nothing to be seen (or smelt, touched, tasted, or heard, for that matter)?

Even in cases involving tangible objects, intuitive definition can easily lead to error. For example, an uninformed observer who sees a hedgehog and an echidna (or spiny anteater) could, on the basis of intuitive definition, conclude that the two animals are from the same or closely related species. Both are spiny, both have long, thin snouts with which to forage for food, both have four short legs and are therefore close to the ground, both hibernate during cold weather, both are solitary animals, and both curl into prickly balls to protect themselves against predators. However, hedgehogs are mammals from the sub-family that scientists call 'Erinaceinae', and they are native to Europe, Asia, and Africa, whereas echidnas are monotremes from the family Tachyglossidae and are native to the islands of Australia and New Guinea. The similarities between hedgehogs and echidnas are superficial and are probably the result of what scientists call 'convergent evolution'. In other words, they occurred because the animals evolved over time as they independently adapted to similar but distinct ecologies and environments. They might look similar, but the animals are quite different biologically. This is, for example, evident from their reproductive characteristics. Echidnas lay eggs, which they then incubate in a pouch. After hatching, the baby echidnas gradually develop spikes during their first two months of life. By contrast, hedgehogs gestate inside their mother, and their soft spikes harden several hours after these little 'hoglets' are born. Depending on which characteristics the observer sees and considers to be relevant or important, the intuitive definitional technique may or may not lead to a conclusion that hedgehogs and echidnas are alike.

The same risks apply to intellectual property. Depending on what the definer perceives and considers to be relevant and important, an object may or may not be thought to be intellectual property, but a different viewpoint could produce a different result. Depending on which characteristics the observer sees, the intuitive definitional technique may or may not lead to a conclusion that a legal situation is about intellectual property. The observer applying the intuitive definitional technique may or may not reach the conclusion that two different doctrines – such as copyright and publicity rights – should both be classified as intellectual property. Different people have different perceptions and their intuitive conclusions vary accordingly. Thus, the intuitive approach may or may not be an effective method of determining what should be considered 'intellectual property'. It is 'hit and miss', and it is unsystematic; it does not engender consistency.

Obviously the distinctions given between hedgehogs and echidnas are based on an established scientific classification system that has its own internal rules and that could have been constructed differently. A different system would produce different definitions. However, law and science are similar to the extent that each hosts its own body of internally consistent classification rules that have been devised by people. In order for the legal system to operate and know which social conditions are addressed by which laws, it is necessary to have definitional rules and to know how to classify according to those rules. Intuitive definition does not provide sufficient information about the rules that make up the system to explain what the subject matter of the definition is, or whether its various objects fit.

Despite its flaws, intuitive definition is surprisingly commonplace in law. It can be used to resolve ambiguities,[110] and Brian Bix suggests it is used when 'the intuitions reflect some truth about social phenomena, some truth we understand at the intuitive level but not yet (or not yet

[110] See, eg, M. B. W. Sinclair, 'Plugs, Holes, Filters, and Goals: An Analysis of Legislative Attitudes' (1996) 41 *New York Law School Law Review* 237–284 at 256. Sinclair provides a clear example of this through the stipulative definition of 'good faith' given in US law.

clearly) at an articulate level.'[111] Perhaps this is why intuitive definition is relatively commonplace in intellectual property law, where the meaning of 'intellectual property' itself remains so unsettled. This does, however, compound the problem of the term's opacity.

Moreover, intuitive definitional approaches seem alarmingly unfocused when the very similarity that is identified between the laws is the intangibility of the subject matter. The lack of physical existence of the intangible objects being directly or indirectly regulated[112] by the law means that strong analogies can be drawn between quite diverse intangible objects, especially when the boundaries defining these intangible objects are contested. It means that any law that regulates an ideational object (such as an idea or a piece of information or knowledge) could conceivably be likened to any other law that regulates an ideational object and that all ideational objects could then be lumped under the overarching term 'intellectual property'. Examples might be a 'corporation', 'contract', 'legal tender', such as cash or coinage, or 'human rights', each of which is arguably an intangible object that has been constructed – like intellectual property – by operation of the legal system, yet none of which is generally considered to fall within the definition of 'intellectual property'.

Wendy Gordon notes the vice inherent in using 'intangible' or 'intellectual' as a unifying concept, observing that 'the term "intellectual property" is drastically overbroad, for virtually any interest can be conceived of as a "valuable intangible".'[113] She suggests:

> Perhaps it would be better to say that the 'intellectual' component can be either in the mode of creation, or in the way that product is used.... However, although that approach to definition has the merit of embracing more IP doctrines, it has the vice of over-breadth. All

[111] Bix, above n. 49 at 22.

[112] This distinction rests on the debate about whether 'property' refers to the thing that is the property or the property rights people have in relation to the thing. If the former, the law directly regulates the thing itself. If the latter, the law indirectly regulates the thing by regulating human behaviour with respect to it.

[113] Gordon, above n. 8 at 618.

> things can be invested with meaning, and even the most physical of values may depend on knowledge (e.g. water increases in value once we know that water is for drinking). If 'intellectual' refers to the fact that some aspect of creation, distribution, or use employs the mental faculty, virtually nothing would be excluded.[114]

Gordon thus identifies the key flaw in using 'intangibility' as the criterion driving definition by intuition or, indeed, as the criterion central to any other definitional techniques. Taken to extremes, the result of identifying 'intangibility' as the common criteria that is inherent in instances of intellectual property and that unites intellectual property doctrines could be the inclusion of a potentially infinite array of incorporeal objects within this category. If intangibility is boundless, the abstract objects it contains could be endless. The likely effect is that the scope of intellectual property law would be ever-expanding, ultimately overbroadening the term and making it essentially meaningless.

This risk is particularly real if a key characteristic of intellectual property is intuitively thought to be its intangibility and an intuitive method of definition is being used. While such an approach allows the number of objects that fall within 'intellectual property' to multiply, it leaves us little or no wiser as to what intellectual property is. Intuitive definition is therefore a very problematic approach to apply if a clear meaning is sought for 'intellectual property'. It provides little idea about the nature of 'intellectual property's' objects of regulation or rights, and it leaves unanswered the question: What – beyond an intangible object that is regulated by law – are the characteristics that lead to something being classified as 'intellectual property'? And, therefore, what *is* intellectual property?

2.3. The Inadequacy of Common Definitional Methods

Several interesting conclusions can be drawn from the preceding discussion.

[114] Ibid. at 618–619.

First, it is clear that 'intellectual property' is a symbolically important term that refers to a series of legal doctrines whose modern genesis can be traced to the time of the Industrial Revolution, and the term itself has come into vogue relatively recently. A range of doctrines has since been consolidated under the name 'intellectual property', and the use of that term has grown exponentially since the inception of the WIPO in the 1960s. A consequence is that around 85 percent of the world's population is now required to comply with national intellectual property laws that, due mainly to the requirement to harmonize domestic laws to comply with the WTO's *TRIPS Agreement*, are now reasonably uniform worldwide.[115] The symbolic and practical power of 'intellectual property' thus seems indisputable.

Second, the meaning of this powerful term 'intellectual property' is less than certain. Definitional techniques that attempt to describe what 'intellectual property' means by enumerating some or all of its constituent doctrines or objects fail to explain why those constituents qualify as 'intellectual property'. They tend to offer only a superficial notion of what 'intellectual property' refers to, and they are prone to failure when their lack of a unifying criterion leaves an enumerated definition inadequate as a reference for determining whether or not an object or doctrine is, in fact, intellectual property. Definitional techniques that seek to define intellectual property by stipulating what the term means are similarly uninformative. This category includes those definitions that stipulate that intellectual property refers to property in intangible objects without elucidating its other characteristics. While they might provide information about how the term is used in a particular context, their utility is arguably limited to practical applications of existing rules rather than clarifying why those rules have been applied to particular doctrines or objects. This may be their intended function, but it is not helpful for explaining what 'intellectual property' *is*.

[115] Alexandra George, 'The (In)justice of Globalisation by Intellectual Propertisation' (2007) 93 *Archiv für Rechts- und Sozialphilosophie* 17–31 at 23.

Such definitional techniques are therefore inadequate when one is seeking to obtain an intellectually rigorous explanation of what 'intellectual property' means. The superficiality of the definitions they produce may not prevent them from being useful for the specific applications for which they are intended, but this confirms the view (mentioned at the outset of this discussion) that the type of definition offered will usually reflect the reasons for which it is being offered. For scholars interested in the nature of intellectual property law, the sorts of definitions just outlined are thus interesting despite their flaws. Although they do not explain clearly what intellectual property means, they do lend insight into the interests being invoked by those who use such a definition. Brian Bix argues that it is helpful to pay attention to the usage of a term – rather than just its formal or accepted definition – because the way in which it is used reveals interesting truths.[116] For example, those who list a particular object in an enumerated definition of intellectual property may have an interest in doing so, or their choice may reflect a particular prejudice of the individual responsible for the classification. Likewise, it might be argued that stipulative definitions are arbitrary, but those who supply arbitrary definitions do so to further a purpose. As Claire Kramsch has noted:

> Linguistic signs do not signify in a social vacuum. Sign-making and sign-interpreting practices are motivated by the need and desire of users to influence people, act upon them or even only to make sense of the world around them.... The linguistic sign is therefore a motivated sign.[117]

Understanding this can be informative for anyone trying to understand the term 'intellectual property' and the reasons for its use.

However, understanding the reasons for intellectual propertization is different from – and should logically be subsequent to – understanding the nature of intellectual property. The common definitional techniques summarized earlier arguably provide inadequate answers to the question,

[116] Bix, above n. 49 at 19.

[117] Claire Kramsch, *Language and Culture* (Oxford: Oxford University Press, 1998) at 21.

what *is* intellectual property? The superficial responses they afford seem to do little to explain the nature of intellectual property.

Or do they? Perhaps they are not as unhelpful as they might initially appear. The lack of meaning identified by the definitions surveyed invokes the possibility that 'intellectual property' might be what some semioticians refer to as an 'empty signifier' or 'floating signifier'. Daniel Chandler describes such a term as one that has

> a vague, highly variable, unspecifiable or non-existent signified. Such signifiers mean different things to different people: they may stand for many or even *any* signifieds; they may mean whatever their interpreters what them to mean. In such a state of radical disconnection between signifier and signified, a sign only means that it means.[118]

This is akin to the aforementioned suggestion that 'intellectual property' may be an essentially contested concept, and it suggests that searching for an inherent meaning for the term is unlikely to be fruitful. Perhaps even to search for a simple omnipresent criterion in intellectual property is to embark on an impossible quest. If so, a more sophisticated approach is needed if 'intellectual property' is to be understood as anything more than a collection of signifiers that are alienated from their signifieds and that therefore have little meaning outside the particular contexts in which they are used. Chapter 3 suggests such an approach.

[118] Daniel Chandler, *Semiotics: The Basics* (London: Routledge, 2002) at 74.

3 The Metaphysics of Intellectual Property

THE CONCLUSION THAT 'INTELLECTUAL PROPERTY' LACKS a readily identifiable meaning, and the possibility that it is the sort of term known as an 'essentially contested concept' or an 'empty/floating signifier', necessitate a search for an alternative definition if we are to obtain a meaningful understanding of what intellectual property is.

Examining its constitution and drawing inferences about the way in which it operates might offer insight. The obvious preliminary task of identifying the elements that constitute intellectual property is awkward when it is not clear what 'intellectual property' is, but this problem can be surmounted in the first instance by concentrating on the common characteristics of the classic doctrines that seem to attract little controversy concerning their status as 'intellectual property' and that are recognized as 'intellectual property' by the World Intellectual Property Organization: copyright, patent, and trademark law.[1] Within these doctrines, the traditional elements for establishing

[1] However, note that even the identity of intellectual property law's 'core' doctrines is sometimes challenged. See, eg, Richard Posner, 'Do We Have Too Many Intellectual Property Rights?' (2005) 9 *Marquette Intellectual Property Law Review* 173 at 174: '[A]ctually I do not regard trademarks as intellectual property. They are identifiers. They are compact ways of identifying the source of a product and they do not create any right beyond the right to have an unambiguous identifier of your goods so that consumers are not confused.'

subsistence in copyright law or registrability in patent and trademark law are arguably the most useful to examine for commonalities. These traditional elements form the foundations on which the modern legal doctrines have developed and to which new or alternative elements have sometimes been added, particularly in response to commercial or technological developments. Such elements are the core features of intellectual property doctrines.

By applying metaphysical analytical tools to these classic doctrines – where 'metaphysical' is broadly construed to include methodologies from a range of philosophical, jurisprudential, and critical schools of thought – this chapter considers how society constructs law generally, and intellectual property law in particular. It examines how intellectual property law's doctrines construct their own objects of regulation, which can be distinguished from the ideational objects and their documented forms that are important for discerning and distinguishing between what is and is not regulated by intellectual property laws. The extent to which these components of intellectual property can be considered to be brute or institutional facts is explored in order to help explain how society constructs and internalizes intellectual property law and its objects. So too are the processes by which this construction comes about. In this way, this chapter starts to indicate ways in which the essentially contested concept or empty/floating signifier of 'intellectual property' can be imbued with meaning by those who use it.

3.1. From Description to Constitution

If 'intellectual property' is difficult to define and if any characterization arrived at through the use of standard techniques of legal or descriptive definition is likely to be unsatisfactory and contentious,[2] a more

[2] See, generally, Chapter 2.

sophisticated approach to understanding 'intellectual property' is arguably needed.

This is particularly important when the definition is to be used as the basis for policy discussions and decisions, rather than simply for the routine application of existing legal tenets. When expounded upon in cases in which no existing rule indicates what the outcome should be – the sorts of circumstances that Ronald Dworkin refers to as 'hard cases'[3] – definitions can themselves become determinative in the making of policy. In such situations, and particularly when the objects of regulation can constitute valuable assets whose regulation can have striking social effects, the meaning attributed to or understood by the term 'intellectual property' is obviously significant. This significance is no weaker if 'intellectual property' is determined to be an essentially contested concept or a floating/empty signifier[4] with multiple and shifting meanings.

The sorts of common approaches to the definition of 'intellectual property' surveyed in the preceding chapter produce superficial outcomes that provide some guidance about what is meant when the term is used but explain little about its more fundamental meaning and implications. Without further investigations into what types of objects are regulated by copyright, trademark, and patent law, for example, most of the standard definitions of 'intellectual property' remain largely meaningless. It is not sufficient to say that the objects are 'intellectual', 'intangible', 'incorporeal', 'imaginary', or 'inchoate', or that they are 'property rights'. Many objects fit these descriptions, but not all are regarded or recognized as intellectual property. Such definitional attempts leave begging the question: What is distinctive about 'intellectual property'? What is its distinguishing criterion? The possibility that intellectual property might be an essentially contested concept or floating/empty signifier simply complicates matters.

One way of investigating beneath the surface of 'intellectual property' may be to shift away from the sorts of enumerative, stipulative, and

[3] Ronald Dworkin, *Taking Rights Seriously* (London: Duckworth, 1978) at 83.
[4] See Chapter 2, §2.3.

intuitive techniques of legal definition surveyed in the preceding chapter, which tend not to enquire beyond whatever definition is provided by the relevant source of law and which thus produce superficial definitions. An option is to instead adopt analytical techniques more common to metaphysical analysis.[5]

Broadly speaking, metaphysics is the branch of philosophy that is concerned with being and knowing: 'the ultimate nature of what exists'.[6] To ask a metaphysical question about something is to ask, what *is* it? In other words, what is its nature? What is its structure? How is it constituted? Key metaphysical questions about intellectual property could include: Does intellectual property exist? And if so, what is intellectual property? What are its elements? What constitutes it? And how?

While some may question the utility of asking whether something as commonly accepted as intellectual property exists or what it is, the obvious and pervasive impact of intellectual property law in modern society prompts unrelenting questions about the nature of the objects regulated by intellectual property laws. This makes broad metaphysical analysis very valuable, as it offers a method of looking behind cursory explanations.

The applicability of this sort of philosophical analysis to intellectual property's doctrines was noted by a US judge as early in its development as the mid–nineteenth century. In a decision concerning the unauthorized copying of several hundred pages of written text, Justice Story observed:

> Patents and copyrights approach, nearer to any other class of cases belonging to forensic discussions, to what may be called the metaphysics of the law, where the distinctions are, or at least may be, very subtle and refined, and, sometimes, almost evanescent.[7]

[5] I note that another author, Paul Goldstein, has also used the term 'metaphysics' in relation to intellectual property law. His approach is very different from that offered here. See Paul Goldstein, *Copyright's Highway: The Law and Lore of Copyright from Gutenberg to the Celestial Jukebox* (New York: Hill & Wang, 1994), chap.1. Goldstein uses the chapter to introduce intellectual property's doctrines and concepts, and to distinguish copyright from patents, trademarks, and the public domain.

[6] Bryan Magee, *The Story of Philosophy* (London: Dorling Kindersley, 1998) at 229.

[7] *Folsom v Marsh*, 9 F.Cas. 342 (Circuit Court of Massachusetts, Oct Term 1841), per Story, Circuit Justice.

The subtleties, complexities, and evanescence identified in this opinion extend beyond considerations of distinctions within patent and copyright law to the very heart of what the subject matter of copyright and patent is. They go, as Justice Story implicitly noted, to the metaphysics – the elemental nature and constitution – of intellectual property law and the objects that it creates.

The following discussion explores various ways of analyzing the metaphysical meaning of 'intellectual property'. To do so it borrows from a range of classical and critical theoretical, philosophical, and jurisprudential techniques. Rather than adopt the tools or methodology of any particular school of thought, the analysis offered in this chapter uses ideas from a number of disciplines to explore what is intended and meant by use of the term 'intellectual property'.

A preliminary step in this task is to consider the argument that 'intellectual property' is a product of society rather than a naturally occurring object.

3.2. Law as a Social Construct

Law can be described as a 'social construct'. However, this term carries baggage and its use can be contentious. The politics of the terminology are thus addressed at the outset so that the intended use of this wording is clear.

Ian Hacking has suggested that the phrase 'social construction' has a signalling effect: to adopt it is to 'deem yourself rather radical', whereas one declares oneself to be 'rational, reasonable and respectable' by condemning the term.[8] The use of social constructionist analysis in the current discussion should not be decoded or interpreted in this manner: those who contend that ownership of intellectual property is a natural right will probably find it radical, while those who have noted the historical contingency and development of intellectual property law might

[8] Ian Hacking, *The Social Construction of What?* (Cambridge, MA: Harvard University Press, 2000) at vii.

find it rather trite.[9] The argument offered here is arguably rational and reasonable, though no doubt some readers will disagree with it. Whether it is considered respectable or radical will depend on one's viewpoint. In any event, the use of social constructionist analysis in this discussion is intended to be value neutral:[10] the aim is to use it to analyse (philosophically, if not scientifically) the nature of intellectual property law, not to make a political argument.[11]

Law – including intellectual property law – is a product of human activity. Law does not pre-exist society or operate independently of society; it is constructed by society and it operates within society.[12] It is historically

[9] For an historical analysis that demonstrates the social contingency of intellectual property law see, eg, Brad Sherman and Lionel Bently, *The Making of Modern Intellectual Property Law: The British Experience, 1760–1911* (Cambridge: Cambridge University Press, 1999).

[10] I note that Jessica Litman criticizes those scholars (of copyright law) who try to take an 'objective' position, writing: '[T]he kind of article I find most difficult to respect is the piece that casts itself, implausibly, as the sole occupant of the middle ground, usually by mischaracterizing or caricaturing the scholarship it paints as extremist on either side. So, I'm not suggesting that we'd all write better articles if we started to think nonpartisan thoughts.' See Jessica Litman, 'The Politics of Intellectual Property' (2009) 27 *Cardozo Arts and Entertainment Law Journal* 313–320 at 319. My attempt here *is* to avoid value-laden normative arguments about intellectual propertization, focusing instead on what happens – metaphysically – when intellectual property laws are made.

[11] It is acknowledged that all analysis is unavoidably coloured by the perspective from which it is conducted. A criticism often levelled at those who use social constructionist tools is the lack of self-awareness of the social context that influences their own analysis. For example, I comment elsewhere that social constructionists 'have also been chastised for omitting to acknowledge that their analyses are unavoidably embodied in their authors' viewpoints and for failing to indicate the social context and perspectives from which their observations are made.' Alexandra George, 'The Difficulty of Defining "Property" ' (2005) 25 *Oxford Journal of Legal Studies* 793–813 at 803–804. Similarly, see Mike Michael, 'A Paradigm Shift? Connections with Other Critiques of Social Constructionism', in David J. Nightingale and John Crosby (eds.), *Social Constructionist Psychology: A Critical Analysis of Theory and Practice* (Birmingham: Open University Press, 1999) at 53–54. To make my reasoning – and any assumptions or prejudices that colour it – as transparent as possible, this chapter records in some detail the step-by-step analysis used to reach conclusions. Illustrations provide additional assistance.

[12] Note that some natural lawyers would argue that, as legal standards are devised by humans, they derive from human nature and therefore follow a pattern of natural law

and culturally specific, and these are characteristics that it shares with other socially constructed beliefs and social institutions.[13] Law is a system by which society regulates human behaviour, and it is informed by knowledge that is itself sustained by social processes and that informs social actions. Social constructs are not innate but are dependent on society for their existence, and the legal system is a clear example of this phenomenon.

The rules that make up law's various legal departments – such as tort, contract, administrative law, constitutional law, criminal law, family law, and intellectual property law – are also social constructs. They are doctrines put in place by the legal system, and the behaviours they prescribe or proscribe are enforced by it. These rules regulate the ways in which humans behave towards one another (including the ways they behave within institutional constructs, such as government departments, and the ways they may treat people) and with respect to things. Thus, law is a mechanism of social control.[14] With variable degrees of success in achieving its stated goals in different contexts, the legal system regulates the way in which people conduct themselves within a society, and it is a product of that society.

Laws have no inherently necessary form. This may seem to be self-evident, a truism that needs no further explanation. Yet arguments about intellectual property law often make flawed assumptions about the form or substance of legal doctrines – as though these were objects that could be found in a state of nature – and it is thus useful to emphasize the socially constructed nature of law.

that is independent of a particular society and derives from moral standards that are inherent in human nature. For explanations of such viewpoints see, generally, Robert P. George, *In Defense of Natural Law* (Oxford: Clarendon Press, 1999), and in relation to property rights, Stephen Buckle, *Natural Law and the Theory of Property: Grotius to Hume* (Oxford: Clarendon Press, 1991).

[13] Vivien Burr, *An Introduction to Social Constructionism* (London: Routledge, 1995) at 3–5 and discussion in her following chapters.

[14] This is a core tenet of much sociological jurisprudence. See, eg, Roscoe Pound, *Social Control Through Law* (New Haven, CT: Transaction, 1942).

Although similar laws may be found in quite diverse communities, and the content of laws may be influenced by international treaties and agreements, law is socially specific and laws can change over time. This is the case with intellectual property law, but the principle is perhaps more clearly introduced and illustrated by a less complicated example, such as the law concerning adultery (ie, the law concerning voluntary sexual intercourse between a married person and someone other than his or her spouse), which differs dramatically among jurisdictions. Adultery is illegal in, for example, Switzerland, Greece, Taiwan, and Uganda, but not Britain or Australia. It is a crime punishable by death in some societies, such as Iran and others enforcing strict Sharia (Islamic) law. It was historically not a punishable offence for men to commit adultery in some traditional societies, and it was an ordinary way of life in others. Laws regulating adulterous behaviour are therefore many and varied, and they are affected by other social and legal norms such as culturally specific rules, religious doctrines, and laws governing marriage. While some groups believe particular rules are 'right' and should apply to all peoples, there is no innate or universal law regarding adultery, and the regulation of this form of human behaviour provides a vivid example of how socially contingent law is.

This characteristic of social contingency is not unique to the law concerning behaviour in marriage. Equally lucid examples of laws that differ greatly among jurisdictions are those stating whether and when it is legal to drink alcohol, smoke marijuana, travel in a car without wearing a seatbelt, break a promise, and so on. Laws that structure the form and workings of social institutions such as parliaments, courts, and companies are similarly diverse. Observe, for example, the difference in structure between the constitutional legal frameworks of a totalitarian and a democratic government, or between a monarchic and a republican state. Observe also how one set of laws can be replaced by another at the whim of law-makers when a regime change occurs as a result of democratic processes, revolution, or foreign occupation. In this sense, all law – intellectual property law included – is socially and historically specific.

Intellectual property law is like other departments of law in this respect. Its rules have no intrinsic or naturally obligatory form, as can be illustrated by innumerable comparative and historical examples. For instance, early English trademark laws applied to signs registered with respect to goods but, after amendments in 1994, trademark protection in the United Kingdom was extended to allow marks also to be registered with respect to services.[15] The law in this case responded to changing commercial contexts rather than to any natural form. Another example is Malaysian patent law, which has reflected historical and political change rather than natural law. Patent law developed at different rates in different parts of Malaysia due to the country's former colonial status. Patent laws were introduced into the Malay states with British colonization, but different states were administered by different imperial offices and were therefore subject to a variety of diverse patent laws during the colonial period. Following the formation of the Federation of Malaya in 1948, the different state patent laws were consolidated.[16] These state laws had clearly been contingent on their political and economic contexts at particular points in time rather than adhering to any inherent principle of intellectual property law, and they provide another example of the socially constructed nature of intellectual property laws.

Law – including intellectual property law – is thus a social construct. This is not a good or a bad thing; it is merely an observation about the world. Understanding this is a helpful step towards understanding the nature of intellectual property law and the objects it regulates, and that in turn is important for obtaining an understanding of why some ideational objects become objects of intellectual property laws while others do not.

[15] See, eg, Tom Blackett, *Trademarks* (London: Macmillan Press, 1998) at 7.

[16] Lim Heng Gee, 'A Study of the Historical Development of the Malaysian Patent System', in Alison Firth (ed.), *The Prehistory and Development of Intellectual Property Systems* (London: Sweet & Maxwell, 1997) at 81–121.

3.3. Intellectual Property as an Institutional Fact

Intellectual property law is not only a social construct. Like all law, it is also an institutional fact.[17]

Institutional facts are the socially constructed aspects of culture and society that exist solely within human institutions. They are distinguished from *brute facts*, which are facts whose existence does not depend on a human institution.[18] These terms were coined by philosopher John Searle, who wrote:

> Years ago I baptized some of the facts dependent on human agreement as 'institutional facts', in contrast to noninstitutional, or 'brute' facts. Institutional facts are so called because they require human institutions for their existence.... Brute facts require no human institutions for their existence.[19]

A common example used by Searle and other commentators to illustrate the distinction between brute and institutional facts is money. A paper note (such as a one-dollar bill) consists of a piece of paper and value. The piece of paper is a brute fact because, once a fibrous cellulose pulp has been turned into an object that we identify as paper, that object exists regardless of whether it is recognized as currency by a monetary system. Its physical nature can be established by means of scientific experiments. By contrast, the monetary note's value is an institutional fact because it can be

[17] For a classic discussion of law's status as an institutional fact, see Neil MacCormick, 'Law as Institutional Fact', in Neil MacCormick and Ota Weinberger, *An Institutional Theory of Law: New Approaches to Legal Positivism* (Dordrecht: D. Reidel, 1986) 49–76.

[18] John R. Searle, *The Construction of Social Reality* (London: Penguin, 1996) at 27. Searle notes that, even though brute facts require the institution of language to describe them, they exist independently of that language.

[19] Ibid. at 2ff. Note, however, that brute facts are interpreted through human institutional frameworks (such as language), thus leading to the possibility of different interpretations of a single brute fact. See, eg, Richard Rorty, "Texts and Lumps", in *Objectivity, Relativism and Truth: Philosophical Papers*, Vol. 1 (Cambridge: Cambridge University Press, 1991) 78–92 at 80–84.

ascertained only by reference to the relevant society's monetary institutions. Take away those institutions and the note becomes valueless, except perhaps as a cultural artefact. Anything that, like the note's value, lacks physical form and exists only by virtue of social consensus (tacit or otherwise) and within human institutions constitutes an institutional fact. Law is one example; intellectual property law and the objects that it creates are others.

Intellectual property is an institutional fact that, like the value of a monetary note, can be distinguished from the brute-fact tangible objects with which it is associated. Just as a monetary system creates the institutional framework that gives a bank note its meaning and value as currency, the legal system – in particular, the department of intellectual property law and its constituent doctrines – creates the institutional framework that gives objects their meaning and value as intellectual property. Just as a bank note is a tangible or documented form that represents a particular value, the documented forms required by intellectual property's various doctrines represent intellectual property objects that acquire value by virtue of this status. The bank note and the documented forms are brute facts. The note's monetary value and the documented form's object of intellectual property regulation are institutional facts.

The nature of intellectual property as an institutional fact is illustrated graphically in Figure 3A, which indicates how the social construction and institutionalization of objects of intellectual property can be explained in terms of brute and institutional facts. These principles apply equally to the different intellectual property doctrines, such as copyright, patent, and trademark law, and are outlined in the pages that follow. The elements that combine to form the institution of intellectual property are key features that help explain how intellectual propertization occurs. Each is examined in turn.

3.3.1. The Nature of Intellectual Property 'Law'

Intellectual property is a product of law, and it is dependent on that law for its existence. However, intellectual property objects are different

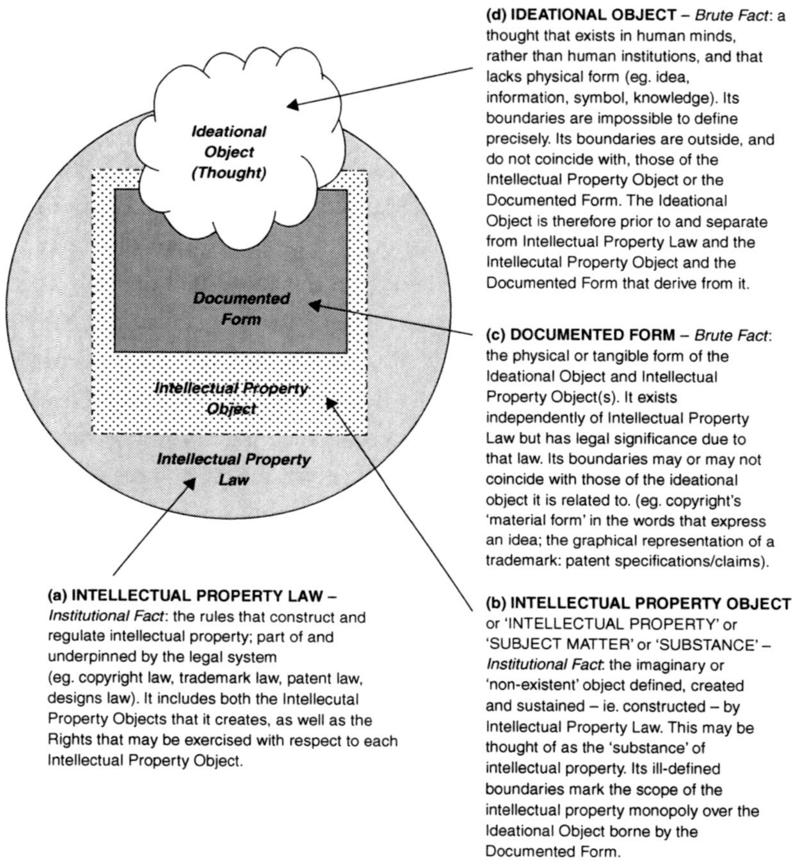

Figure 3A. The Construction of Intellectual Property as an Institutional Fact

from the legal rules – the *intellectual property law* – that define and regulate them. It is the law, labelled (a) in Figure 3A, that creates intellectual property's metaphysical distinctions. These are distinctions between the intellectual property objects themselves, the ideational objects that inspire and are incorporated into the intellectual property objects, and the physical objects (documented forms) associated with intellectual property.

3.3.2. The Nature of Intellectual Property's Physical Object: The 'Documented Form'

The physical object that is associated with intellectual property is something like a painting on canvas, a poet's written words, a built invention, or a record of the series of steps to be performed to bring about an inventive result. It is the tangible evidence of the existence of an ideational object that underpins the intellectual property object. It may be thought of as the *documented form* of the intellectual property object, and it is labelled (c) in Figure 3A. Examples include copyright law's requirement of a 'material form', trademark law's 'graphical representation' in the United Kingdom or 'depiction of the mark' in the United States, and patent law's 'specifications'.

The documented form is a brute fact: it is created by people but, once brought into being, it exists regardless of whether or not a society has implemented an intellectual property law and regardless of whether there is some other institution that affects the way it is used. A painting and a built invention are examples of documented forms that, like the paper in the monetary note example, are brought into being by humans. Once this occurs, these objects exist independently of whether people are thinking about them or whether there is social agreement about their nature or structural composition. Human interpretations of them might change, as might the labels that humans apply to them. However, once created by humans, the documented form of an object of intellectual property exists independently of these interpretations and labels, and it is therefore a brute fact.

3.3.3. The Nature of Intellectual Property's 'Ideational Object'

Whilst an object of intellectual property is usually defined in terms of a documented form, its boundaries will not necessarily coincide with those of the physical object with which it is associated. For example, copyright in a poem is not limited to the words used in the poetic formulation (the documented form) that they are given in that particular verse. A poet can draw on all sorts of ideas, emotions, and literary allusions when expressing thoughts. The thoughts conveyed are *ideational objects*, which are labelled (d) in Figure 3A, and these are not monopolized under copyright law. The same principle is evident in other intellectual property doctrines.

Of all the intellectual property doctrines, copyright law is arguably the most explicit in its rejection of the notion of awarding property rights over an idea. A foundational tenet of the doctrine is that copyright awards a temporary monopoly over an expression of the idea rather than the underlying idea itself. For example, Article 9(2) of the WTO's *TRIPS Agreement* states, 'Copyright protection shall extend to expressions and not to ideas, procedures, methods of operation or mathematical concepts as such.' This is known in copyright theory as the 'idea–expression dichotomy',[20] and it is replicated in many national intellectual property laws.[21] As a result of the idea–expression dichotomy, the poet's

[20] For explanations and discussions of copyright's idea–expression dichotomy, see John K. Halvey, 'A Rose by Any Other Name: Computer Programs and the Idea–Expression Distinction' (1985) 34 *Emory Law Journal* 741–776; Edward Samuels, 'The Idea–Expression Dichotomy in Copyright Law' (1989) 56 *Tennessee Law Review* 321–463; Alfred C. Yen, 'A First Amendment Perspective on the Idea/Expression Dichotomy and Copyright in a Work's "Total Concept and Feel"' (1989) 38 *Emory Law Journal* 393–436; Amaury Cruz, 'What's the Big Idea Behind the Idea–Expression Dichotomy? Modern Ramifications of the Tree of Porphyry in Copyright Law' (1990) 18 *Florida State University Law Review* 221–250; Jon O. Newman, 'New Lyrics for an Old Melody: The Idea/Expression Dichotomy in the Computer Age' (1999) 17 *Cardozo Arts and Entertainment Law Journal* 691–703; Richard H. Jones, 'The Myth of the Idea/Expression Dichotomy in Copyright Law' (1990) 10:3 *Pace Law Review* 551–607.

[21] See references to and explanations of this distinction in the case law of various jurisdictions. For example, in the United States, see *Harper & Row Publishers, Inc. v Nation Enters.*, 471 U.S. 539, 556 (1985) ('copyright's idea/expression dichotomy "strike[s] a definitional balance between the First Amendment and the Copyright Act by permitting free communication of facts while still protecting an author's expression" '); in the United Kingdom, see *Donoghue v Allied Newspapers Limited* (1938) Ch. 106 (copyright is owned by 'the person who has clothed the idea in form, whether by means of a picture, a play or a book'); and in Australia, see *Victoria Park Racing and Recreation Grounds Company Limited v Taylor* (1937) 58 CLR 479 at 498, per Latham

ideational object may relate, for example, to 'the pain of unrequited love', 'the monotony and terror of trench warfare', 'the ecstasy of success', or some other thought or emotion that can be interpreted and expressed in endless ways. These ideational objects are distinct from the tangible forms in which instances of them are documented, and – as will be seen – they are also different from the intangible objects over which intellectual property law awards rights. This pattern is replicated in various ways in other intellectual property doctrines.

3.3.4. The Nature of the 'Intellectual Property Object'

Ideational objects are therefore associated with, but usually do not coincide exactly with, the *object of intellectual property*. This object is perhaps most commonly described simply as the 'intellectual property', a shorthand form of 'the object of regulation by the intellectual property law'. The terms 'intellectual property object', the 'subject matter', and the 'substance' of intellectual property can also be used synonymously. The intellectual property object is the part of the thought that is defined and protected by intellectual property law. It is labelled (b) in Figure 3A.

Copyright law again offers an easily understood example. For instance, in the case of a poem in the United Kingdom (whose copyright law on this point is quite typical of contemporary international standards), the object of intellectual property will formally be a 'literary work' that is expressed in writing,[22] is original,[23] and was created by an 'author' with a

CJ ('The law of copyright does not operate to give any person an exclusive right to state or to describe particular facts. A person cannot by first announcing that a man fell off a bus or that a particular horse won a race prevent other people from stating those facts. The Copyright Act 1912–1935 gives protection only to "original literary dramatic musical and artistic work". What the law of copyright protects is some originality in the expression of thought' [internal references omitted]).

[22] *University of London Press Ltd v University Tutorial Press Ltd* [1916] 2 Ch. 601 at 608, per Peterson J.

[23] *Copyright, Designs and Patents Act* 1988, s.1(1).

required 'qualifying factor' (ie, specified connection) to the jurisdiction in which copyright is claimed.[24] In practice, this means that a legal monopoly to copy some or most of the words of the poem is awarded to the copyright proprietor. If others who are aware of the poem wish to express the same thoughts – communicate the same ideational objects – without infringing the proprietor's copyright, they must do so in such a way that they do not copy the earlier work.[25] That is, they must do so in an original manner:

> The word 'original' does not in this connection mean that the work must be the expression of original or inventive thought. Copyright Acts are not concerned with the originality of ideas, but with the expression of thought, and, in the case of literary work, with the expression of thought in print or writing. The originality which is required relates to the expression of the thought. But the Act does not require that the expression must be in an original or novel form, but that the work must not be copied from another work – that it should originate from the author.[26]

[24] Ibid., ss.153–155. The 'qualifying factor' may also be referred to as the 'connecting factor'.

[25] *University of London Press Ltd v University Tutorial Press Ltd*, above n. 22 at 610, per Peterson J. The 'doctrine of independent creation' provides that an identical or substantively similar work does not infringe copyright in an earlier work if it has been independently created (ie, its creation has not involved copying of the earlier work). However, if the second creator had access to the earlier work, this defence may be difficult to prove. See, eg, *Calhoun v Lillenas Publishing*, Civ. Nos. 01-11413, 01-11415, Eleventh Circuit 2002, a case concerning application of the rule to music in the United States. Thus, a work may attract copyright if it has been created independently, even if it is identical – or nearly identical – to an existing work.

There are also situations in which copies of a work may be used without permission and without infringing copyright. Examples include uses that fall under the doctrines of 'fair use' (in the United States) or 'fair dealing' (in jurisdictions including Australia and the United Kingdom), such as the quotation of works for the purposes of criticism, review, or reporting the news.

[26] *University of London Press Ltd v University Tutorial Press Ltd*, above n. 22 at 608–609, per Peterson J.

This assessment of originality is qualitative rather than quantitative,[27] and it includes all parts of the copyright-protected literary work that are not trivial, valueless, and insignificant.[28]

Patent law provides a similar distinction between the ideational object and the intellectual property object that derives from it. For the inventor seeking to utilize the rights conferred by patent registration, the object of protection will be information about the technical features of the invention, such as the specifications of a particular water pump (a 'product' patent) or the steps required to manufacture a specific medication that reduces pain (a 'process' patent). The intellectual property object is therefore likely to be much narrower than the ideational object. The ideational object would include accrued information that is already known in society and that is not covered by the patent monopoly, such as commonly known data about components and tools that would help a person construct the invention.

The same general traits can be observed in other intellectual property doctrines and, in each case, the intellectual property object may be thought of as a particular interpretation or instance of the ideational object.

The intellectual property object is, in effect, a legal delineation of the part of the ideational object over which intellectual property law provides a monopoly. It is almost always broader than its related documented form, which may therefore be thought of as an incomplete depiction of its scope (it is necessarily incomplete until compared with pre-existing documented forms against which its originality may be assessed).[29]

A comparable analysis has been made, albeit in a different context, in a discussion of John Searle's defence of realism and criticisms of 'perspectivism' (also known as 'relativism', which is the view that there is no absolute truth and all 'truth' is relative to culture, time, place, and other social variables). William Hirstein comments perceptively:

[27] *Designers Guild v Williams* [2000] 1 *WLR* 2416 at 2426, per Lord Millett.

[28] Ibid. at 2418, per Lord Bingham.

[29] See also the discussion of the concept of originality in Chapter 4, §4.2.5.

> As long as the representation and the represented world are different things, there will be properties of the represented world not captured by the representation.... So representations only capture certain properties of the represented things, leaving out an indefinite number of other properties which the things possess. Incompleteness does not imply inaccuracy however. The ontologically objective thing out there has whatever properties it has.[30]

An analogy could be drawn between this and the distinction between the documented form and the intellectual property object, whereby the documented form is the 'representation' and the intellectual property object is the 'represented world'. However, the difference is perhaps that the represented physical world has objectively discernible boundaries that can serve also as convenient definitional boundaries, whereas the intellectual property object's boundaries are never entirely known, are infinitely redefinable and are often dependent on assessments with respect to the scope of other existing or potential intellectual property objects.

3.3.5. The Intellectual Property Object as an Institutional Fact

The documented form – that is, the physical or tangible object – associated with the intellectual property object may be different from the ideational object. Indeed, rarely are they exactly the same.[31] In most cases it would

[30] William Hirstein, *On Searle* (Belmont, CA: Wadsworth, Thompson Learning, 2001) at 71.

[31] An example of a rare instance in which this situation may arise is when the expression *is* the idea. An illustration of this is found in the 'merger doctrine' of US copyright law. A judgement of the Court of Appeals for the Ninth Circuit explains: 'Under the merger doctrine, courts will not protect a copyrighted work from infringement if the idea underlying the copyrighted work can be expressed in only one way, lest there be a monopoly on the underlying idea.... In such an instance, it is said that the work's idea and expression "merge." ' *Ets-Hokin v Skyy Spirits Inc.*, 225 F.3d 1068 (9th Cir. 2000), at 1082 per McKeown J, citing *CDN Inc. v Kapes*, 197 F.3d 1256, 1261 (9th Cir. 1999). The doctrine is discussed in more detail in Scott Abrahamson, 'Seen One, Seen Them All? Making Sense of the Copyright Merger Doctrine' (1998) 45 *UCLA Law Review* 1125–1166.

not be possible to discover an exact correlation of the boundaries between the intellectual property object and the documented form because of the ever-present difficulties involved in trying to determine where the edges of the intellectual property object lie.

The documented form is likewise different from the intellectual property object with which it comes to be associated and to which the legal right to monopolize the intellectual property object attaches. The intellectual property object is related to pre-existing ideational objects (ie, thoughts) that it cloaks or replicates, but it is different from them. The pre-existing ideational objects are arguably brute facts, albeit mental ones that cannot be accessed other than via the mediation of human communication. They are constructed by humans, but because they exist independently of human institutions they are brute facts rather than institutional facts. Pre-existing ideational objects have either no clearly discernible boundaries or boundaries that are imprecise and flexible, while the intellectual property object (ie, a thought with which intellectual property rights will be associated through the intermediary of a documented form) has only the boundaries that are defined by law. These can often be difficult to identify in practice, but they are theoretically knowable through the application of established legal principles.

In contrast to the documented form with which it is associated, an intellectual property object is an institutional fact: it has been defined into existence when law-makers have drawn up intellectual property law, and its actuality is only within and because of intellectual property law's status as a department of the legal system. As noted previously, the intellectual property law that creates the intellectual property object is also an institutional fact as its existence depends on the operation of the

The Pulitzer Prize–winning photograph by Associated Press photographer Huyn Cong ('Nick') Út of a nine-year-old Vietnamese girl (Phan Thị Kim Phúc) running naked from a napalm attack on 8 June 1972 is a famous example of an 'expression' whose idea – a digest of the horror of war and the suffering of civilians, especially children (and particularly in the context of the Vietnam War) – could not be so graphically captured in words. The picture became an iconic symbol for the peace movement in the United States, which opposed the Vietnam War.

legal system, a human institution. Both the documented form of the intellectual property object and the stated law are 'facts' – albeit of different kinds: 'brute' and 'institutional', respectively – because at any given moment they have a static existence. They might change over time, which might be as a result of human intervention (eg, if part of a painting is cut off, or if part of an invention is replaced by a different component, or if a section of the law is amended), and this could alter their status within the legal department of intellectual property law. Nonetheless, at any particular point, one can identify the facticity of the intellectual property object by observing human reactions to it, or can identify the existing intellectual property law by using the established principles of legal reasoning that apply to the relevant legal system. Human perceptions and interpretations of these facts may vary but, so long as the interpretative rules are agreed upon, these objects can be investigated and scientifically repeatable results can be produced to describe the content and nature of both the intellectual property law and the objects it has constructed.[32]

In discussions of the meaning of 'intellectual property' and attempts to understand what the term implies, it is significant to comprehend that intellectual property objects are institutional facts, not pre-existing brute facts (as the language of some claimants would seem to assume). The upshot of this conclusion is that intellectual property objects take exactly the form that they are awarded by intellectual property laws, which themselves take the form awarded by law-makers involved in reaching teleologically driven policy decisions. Thus, a change in the law can lead to a change in the form of an intellectual property object or a potential intellectual property object (which is an intellectual property object that theoretically exists because the law could be called upon to enforce rights with respect to it, even though its boundaries have not yet been formally

[32] This follows the argument in Richard Rorty's essay 'Texts and Lumps', above n. 19 at 78–92. Rorty notes: 'Facts are hybrid entities; that is, the causes of the assertibility of sentences include both physical stimuli and our antecedent choice of response to such stimuli. To say we must have respect for facts is just to say that we must, if we are to play a certain language game, play by the rules' (at 81).

delineated).[33] The institutional fact of an intellectual property object comes into existence only at the point at which the intellectual property object is constructed through the operation of law, though it might not be identified until the point at which its scope comes to be determined because a dispute has arisen. Until they are fused into the brute fact of a documented form and pinned down by legal pronouncements, the brute facts that are the ideas, information and knowledge are ideational objects swirling within society, but the parts that constitute intellectual property's institutional facts remain undefined.

3.4. Intellectual Property's Institutional Facts in Practice

The distinctions outlined in the preceding pages are somewhat abstract, yet they have very tangible effects as they are arguably the elements that make up the various doctrines that fall within the legal department known as 'intellectual property law'. These elements are the building blocks that constitute intellectual property law and its objects of regulation. To the extent that they are abstract, they simply reflect the intangible nature of *intellectual* property. They may be abstract and intangible, socially constructed institutional facts, but they have very real consequences. This is perhaps best illustrated by empirical examples from a couple of intellectual property doctrines.

Drawing on actual court decisions that are quite representative of how intellectual property doctrines function, Figures 3B and 3C offer

[33] For example, the copyright object comes into existence when the brute fact 'material form' to which it attaches is created under pre-specified conditions (eg, 'a work' created by 'an author' who is a 'qualified person' in the jurisdiction, or first published in the jurisdiction, and so on). Even if the proprietor's rights with respect to the copyright object are never enforced, that work – as defined by copyright law – is nonetheless a potential object of copyright regulation because the laws *could* be enforced with respect to the object. This potential for enforceability arguably deters third persons from infringing the copyright proprietor's rights, so a value of copyright laws that could be enforced can be that they have the effect of 'enforcement' without the laws ever actually having to be enforced.

practical examples of the distinctions between the ideational object, its documented form for the purposes of establishing a legally enforceable intellectual property monopoly, and the scope of the relevant intellectual property object. These cases came about due to dissension over the point at which the boundary was drawn between an ideational object and intellectual property objects – in colloquial terms: 'Where does mine end and yours begin? And have you used some of mine without permission?' – culminating in litigation. The location of the boundary determines who can claim, control, and profit from intellectual property rights, and disagreement between interested parties sometimes means that this can be determined only by a court.[34]

3.4.1. A Copyright Example

Using an example from the case of *Campbell v Acuff-Rose Music*,[35] which was decided before the US Supreme Court in 1994, Figure 3B offers a graphic illustration of the difference between the documented form and the scope of the monopoly attracted by the intellectual property object in a copyright case.

'Oh, Pretty Woman' was a hit song in the mid-1960s. Written by Roy Orbison and William Dees in 1964, the rock ballad tells the story of a lonely man who watches wistfully as an attractive woman passes him on the street. He sings about her loveliness, wishing that she would stop and talk to him, dreaming that she would stay with him, and eventually realizing part of his fantasy when she turns and walks back in his direction. The song hit No.1 on the music charts, sold more than 7 million copies (and more copies in its first ten days of release than any previous

[34] A similar argument is made in Peter Drahos, *A Philosophy of Intellectual Property* (Aldershot: Ashgate, 1996) at 153, where he argues: 'We have opted for the view that abstract objects are fictional entities, albeit highly useful ones.... [W]ithin law they form the basis of identity judgements, judgements that ultimately determine who has access to vital capital resources.'

[35] *Campbell v Acuff-Rose Music*, 510 U.S. 569 (1994).

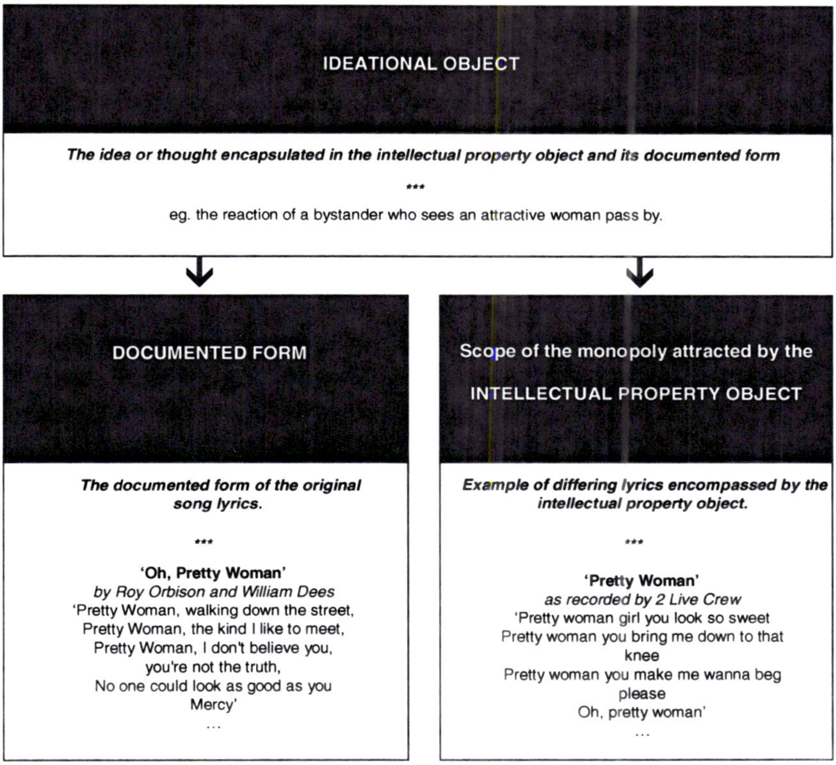

Figure 3B. ***Campbell v Acuff-Rose Music*** **(1994):**

Illustrating the distinction and relationship between an ideational object, its documented form, and the scope of the monopoly it attracts (ie. the intellectual property object) under copyright law (US)

45 rpm single) and was eventually added to the Grammy Hall of Fame. Copyright in the lyrics was assigned to Acuff-Rose Music, Inc.

In 1989 Luther R. Campbell wrote a song called 'Pretty Woman', which in some ways resembled the earlier hit as it too spoke of a bystander's reaction to seeing an attractive woman. Figure 3B illustrates how the opening verses of both songs express the same ideational object.[36] The documented form of 'Oh, Pretty Woman' had established parameters

[36] The lyrics are quoted from Appendices A and B of Justice Souter's opinion in ibid.

against which later creations would be judged. Taking elements from the original work, Campbell had used a technique known as 'sampling' that is common to the rap, hip-hop, and R&B genres.[37] In doing so, he took a portion or 'sample' of one song and reused it as an element of another, thus transforming the documented form of the ideational object of a man's thoughts about a woman's appearance into a recognizably related – though substantively quite different – song. Campbell's lyrics were evocative of 'Oh, Pretty Woman' (as was the associated melody, which sampled a distinctive bass riff from the original music), but they simultaneously deviated from the original ballad's story and tone.

Campbell's song – performed and recorded by his rap group, 2 Live Crew – was somewhat less reverent than the original. For example, rather than expressing adulation of the pretty woman, the rap version advised: 'Big hairy woman you need to shave that stuff' and 'Bald headed woman you know your hair could look nice'. Rather than mimicking the original version's joyful ending:

[37] As these musical styles have evolved, 'sampling' has become an issue of much discussion and debate in copyright law, not least because of the cultural implications involved. See, eg, E. Scott Johnson, 'Protecting Distinctive Sounds: The Challenge of Digital Sampling (1987) 2 *Journal of Law & Technology* 273; Randy S. Kravis, 'Does a Song by Any Other Name Still Sound as Sweet? Digital Sampling and Its Copyright Implications' (1993) 43 *American University Law Review* 231–276; Henry Self, 'Digital Sampling: A Cultural Perspective' (2002) 9 *UCLA Entertainment Law Review* 347–360; Jeffrey H. Brown, '"They Don't Make Music the Way They Used To": The Legal Implications of "Sampling" in Contemporary Music' (1992) *Wisconsin Law Review* 1941–1992; Carlos Ruiz de la Torre, 'Digital Music Sampling and Copyright Law: Can The Interests of Copyright Owners and Sampling Artists Be Reconciled?' (2005) 7 *Vanderbilt Journal of Entertainment Law & Practice* 401–419; Bryan Bergman, 'Into the Grey: The Unclear Laws of Digital Sampling' (2005) 27 *Hastings Communications and Entertainment Law Journal (Comm/Ent)* 619–652; Nicholas B. Lewis, 'Shades of Grey: Can the Copyright Fair Use Defense Adapt to New Re-Contextualized Forms of Music and Art?' (2005) 55 *American University Law Review* 267–306; Melissa Hahn, 'Digital Music Sampling and Copyright Policy – A Bittersweet Symphony? Assessing the Continued Legality of Music Sampling in the United Kingdom, the Netherlands, and the United States' (2006) 34 *Georgia Journal of International and Comparative Law* 713–742; M. Leah Somoano, '*Bridgeport Music, Inc. v. Dimension Films*: Has Unlicensed Digital Sampling of Copyrighted Sound Recordings Come to an End?' (2006) 21 *Berkeley Technology Law Journal* 289–310.

What do I see
Is she walking back to me?
Yeah, she's walking back to me!
Oh, Pretty Woman.

Campbell's song concluded:

Two timin' woman girl you know you am not right
Two timin' woman you's out with my boy last night
Two timin' woman that takes a load off my mind
Two timin' woman now I know the baby ain't mine
Oh, two timin' woman
Oh pretty woman.

Whereas the lyrics of the original song were adoring of the 'pretty woman', Campbell's lyrics were sarcastic. Whereas the original was pleading and resigned in its tone, Campbell's was belittling and cynical. However, the link between the two songs was clear: Campbell's song was derived from the original.

Acuff-Rose brought an action for copyright infringement against 2 Live Crew. The copyright proprietor claimed that it held the exclusive right under copyright law in the United States to reproduce the intellectual property object in copies and sound recordings, and to create derivative works based upon the documented form of the ideational object.[38] 'Pretty Woman', it said, counted as a derivative work of 'Oh, Pretty Woman' for these purposes.[39] In essence, Acuff-Rose Music was claiming that the scope of the intellectual property object established by and related to the

[38] *Copyright Act* 1976, 17 U.S.C. §106: 'Exclusive rights in copyrighted works:.... the owner of copyright ... has the exclusive rights to do and to authorize any of the following: (1) to reproduce the copyrighted work in copies or phonorecords; (2) to prepare derivative works based upon the copyrighted work.'

[39] Ibid., §101: 'Definitions: ... A "derivative work" is a work based upon one or more preexisting works, such as a translation, musical arrangement, dramatization, fictionalization, motion picture version, sound recording, art reproduction, abridgment, condensation, or any other form in which a work may be recast, transformed, or adapted. A work consisting of editorial revisions, annotations, elaborations, or other modifications which, as a whole, represent an original work of authorship, is a "derivative work"'.

documented form of 'Oh, Pretty Woman' was broad enough to encompass 'Pretty Woman'.

Despite differences between the two works, Campbell did not dispute this element of Acuff-Rose Music's claim. The Supreme Court's decision recorded, 'It is uncontested here that 2 Live Crew's song would be an infringement of Acuff-Rose's rights in "Oh, Pretty Woman," ... but for a finding of fair use through parody.'[40] In other words, it was agreed by all parties that the intellectual property object associated with 'Oh, Pretty Woman' was indeed expansive enough to encompass the different lyrics of 'Pretty Woman' under US copyright law. The case therefore provides a vivid illustration of the broad scope over which the intellectual property object can extend, and a clear example of the distinction between the ideational object, the documented form, and the intellectual property object.

As an interesting aside, the case also provides a demonstration of how legal defences operate to counteract what might otherwise be harsh or unwanted effects that might stem from enforcing private rights over sweeping and perhaps ill-defined intellectual property objects.

Campbell argued that his use of Acuff-Rose Music's intellectual property object was legally permissible in the circumstances. His defence was that 'Pretty Woman' was intended 'through comical lyrics, to satirize the original work....'[41] Campbell thus relied on the defence of parody under the 'fair use' provisions of the relevant copyright legislation, which establishes that certain reproductions of copyright material are permissible – and therefore do not infringe the proprietor's monopoly rights to use the intellectual property object – when the copying occurs for purposes such as criticism, comment, news reporting, teaching, scholarship, or research.[42] Campbell's argument was successful, effectively making

[40] *Campbell v Acuff-Rose Music*, above n. 35, per Souter J.

[41] Ibid., ¶3.

[42] *Copyright Act* 1976, above n. 38, §107: 'Limitations on exclusive rights: Fair use – Notwithstanding the provisions of sections 106 and 106A, the fair use of a copyrighted work, including such use by reproduction in copies or phonorecords or by any other

'Oh, Pretty Woman' a *permissible* or *non-infringing* use of Acuff-Rose Music's intellectual property object. In other words, whilst it was agreed by all that Campbell's song – although different from the documented form – did encroach on Acuff-Rose Music's intellectual property object, the court accepted that this was permissible in the circumstances because 2 Live Crew's version constituted a permissible parody under another copyright provision. The case thus became a watershed in the development of the fair use doctrine in the United States, greatly extending the scope of the fair use defence against claims of copyright infringement in parody cases.[43]

Acuff-Rose Music v Campbell is an example from US copyright law. However, the same distinctions between the ideational object, its documented form, and the scope of the intellectual property object can be witnessed in other intellectual property doctrines such as the patent and trademark laws of the United States and other jurisdictions.

3.4.2. A Trademark Example

The UK trademark registration case of *Criminal Clothing Ltd v Aytan's Manufacturing (UK) Ltd* (2005)[44] provides another illustration, as depicted in Figure 3C. Criminal Clothing Ltd applied to register as a trademark a 'device' (ie, a logo) bearing the word 'Criminal' written in a cursive script, reminiscent of a style common among graffiti artists. It proposed to use the trademark on clothing, headwear, and footwear.

means specified by that section, for purposes such as criticism, comment, news reporting, teaching (including multiple copies for classroom use), scholarship, or research, is not an infringement of copyright.'

[43] For discussions of this aspect of the case, see, eg, Lisa M. Babiskin, 'Oh, Pretty Parody: *Music, Inc*' (1994) 8 *Harvard Journal of Law & Technology* 193–230; Nels Jacobson, 'Faith, Hope & Parody: *Campbell v Acuff-Rose*, "Oh, Pretty Woman," and Parodists' Rights' (1994) 31 *Houston Law Review* 955–1026; and Andrew Buckland, 'Rap, Parody, and Fair Use: *Luther R Campbell aka Luke Skywalker, et al v Acuff-Rose Music, Inc*' (1995) 17 *Sydney Law Review* 599–610.

[44] *Criminal Clothing Ltd v Aytan's Manufacturing (UK) Ltd* [2005] EWHC 1303.

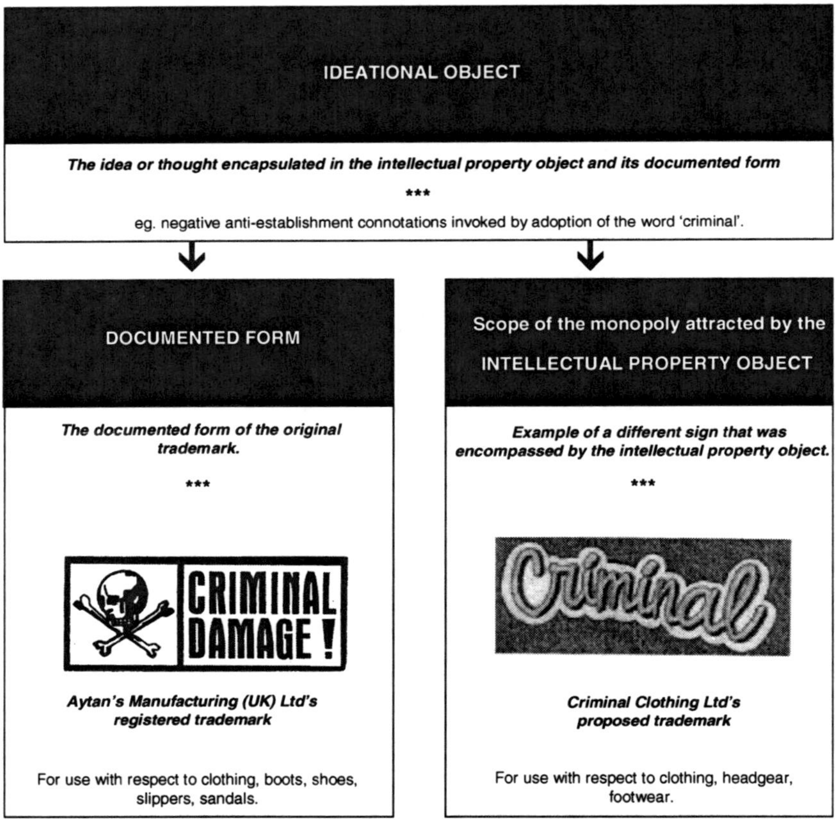

Figure 3C. ***Criminal Clothing Ltd V. Aytan's Manufacturing (UK) Ltd*** **(2005):** Illustrating the distinction and relationship between an ideational object, its documented form, and the scope of the monopoly it attracts (ie. the intellectual property object) under trademark law

'Criminal Damage' trademark kindly provided by Aytan's Manufacturing (UK) Ltd

Criminal Clothing's application was opposed by Aytan's Manufacturing (UK) Ltd, which was the proprietor of earlier device trademarks depicting the words 'Criminal Damage!' beside a picture of a skull and crossbones. The symbol was reminiscent of a sign warning of dangerous chemicals. Aytan's Manufacturing's earlier marks were registered in the United Kingdom and throughout the European Community for use with respect to clothing, boots, shoes, slippers, and sandals. Aytan's Manufacturing claimed that Criminal Clothing's proposed trademark was confusingly similar to its own, and that use of Criminal Clothing's proposed mark would amount to passing off of the goodwill associated with Aytan's Manufacturing's commercial reputation.[45]

When assessing Criminal Clothing's application for registration of its mark, the UK trademark registry's hearing officer upheld Aytan's Manufacturing's opposition. He found that both marks were 'inherently distinctive for the goods at issue and both would enjoy a wide penumbra of protection'[46] and that they were visually dissimilar. However, he also found that the marks sounded alike and that they had conceptual similarities ('negative anti-establishment connotations') that would lead consumers to form similar mental pictures of the goods with respect to which the marks were used. Applying the 'global appreciation test' that determines the scope of the monopoly covered by a trademark in the United Kingdom and European Community,[47] the hearing officer concluded:

> [G]iven the wide penumbra of protection the ['Criminal Damage!'] mark enjoys, the degree of aural/oral and conceptual similarity between the respective marks, the identical/closely similar nature of

[45] 'Passing off' protects unregistered trademarks in some jurisdictions. It is based on the premise that 'nobody has any right to represent his goods as the goods of somebody else': *Reddaway v Banham* [1896] AC 199, per Lord Halsbury. Passing off affords a property right – in essence, an intellectual property right – to monopolize indicia of trade (such as brand names and logos) in which the trader has established a commercial reputation with respect to goods and/or services. The foundational principles of passing off in English law are set out in *Warnink v Townend* [1979] AC 731 and *Reckitt & Colman Products v Borden Inc* [1990] All ER 873.

[46] *Criminal Clothing Ltd v Aytan's Manufacturing (UK) Ltd*, above n.44 at ¶8, considering an appeal against a decision by the hearing officer, Mike Knight.

[47] This test was established and expanded upon in several important decisions of the European Court of Justice: *Sabel BV v Puma AG, Rudolf Dassler Sport* [1998] RPC 199; *Canon Kabushiki Kaisha v MGM* [1999] RPC 117; *Lloyd Schuhfabrik Meyer & Co GmbH v Klisjen Handel BV* [2000] FSR 77. It essentially requires that, in examining for overlap, a 'global appreciation' should be determined of the impact of the interdependent similarity between the marks, similarity of the goods and/or services with respect to which the mark was registered for use, and the likelihood that the average consumer would be confused.

> the goods at issue, the traits of the average consumer when purchasing items of clothing, the manner in which the goods are marketed, and allowing for imperfect recollection, I am satisfied that there is a real likelihood of confusion and the opposition under section 5(2)(b) succeeds accordingly.[48]

Criminal Clothing appealed, and the case was heard by the UK High Court (Chancery Division). The judge upheld the hearing officer's decision.

In making this decision, the judge essentially approved the hearing officer's reasoning as to where the boundaries fell around Aytan's Manufacturing's intellectual property object. Although both signs gave expression to an ideational object that could not itself be monopolized under intellectual property law (ie, 'negative anti-establishment' sentiments) in the context in which it was used, the documented form of Aytan's Manufacturing's 'Criminal Damage!' trademark established an intellectual property object whose boundaries encompassed the territory desired by Criminal Clothing Ltd's 'Criminal' logo. Thus, although it looked different from the 'Criminal Damage!' trademark and expressed its negative anti-establishment sentiments in a different manner, it was held that use of Criminal Clothing Ltd's 'Criminal' logo would encroach on an intellectually property object monopolized by Aytan's Manufacturing under UK trademark law.

3.4.3. Conclusion

The possibility that a different but similar piece of writing will infringe copyright in an earlier poem or song, that a different logo with a similar theme will infringe trademark rights in an earlier commercial symbol, or that building a different but similar object will infringe the patent covering the earlier invention, indicates the lack of necessity for a strict coincidence between the documented form and the content covered by the related copyright, trademark, or patent. It demonstrates that an object

[48] *Criminal Clothing Ltd v Aytan's Manufacturing (UK) Ltd*, above n. 44 at ¶12.

of intellectual property can be different from the ideational object from which it is derived or with which it allegedly coincides, and it can be different again from the physical object that it purports to shield against unauthorized replication.

3.5. Constructing Intellectual Property's Institutional Facts

As the preceding two case studies illustrate, the institutions created by intellectual property law thus define into reality intellectual property objects that can be identified and regulated. The entire process operates within the sphere of legal institutions, although it may be triggered by events outside the legal system (eg, lobbying of government in trade negotiations) and, as with most applications of legal doctrine, the effects spread far beyond the legal system into society more generally. The operation of the institutional fact of intellectual property can thus be described as 'autopoietic' in the sense described by Niklas Luhmann[49] and other sociological legal theorists. That is, intellectual property is created by and operates as a self-referential entity within the legal system's department of intellectual property law, although it is influenced by external events and decisions.

An interesting perspective on the production of intellectual property objects can be gained by examining theoretical literature concerning parts of the legal system – such as intellectual property law – that produce their own objects of regulation.

The brute facts of the documented form and the ideational object may or may not coincide precisely with the institutional fact of the intellectual property object. As an institutional fact, the intellectual property object is socially constructed according to the rules and regulations that law-makers (often in response to lobbying by interest groups) have constructed as 'intellectual property law'. Whether the brute and institutional facts coincide will be random, with subjective outcomes dependent on

[49] Niklas Luhmann, *Social Systems* (Stanford, CA: Stanford University Press, 1996).

the effect of objective laws when applied to particular fact situations. Sometimes an intellectual property object will be created with a view to maximizing its scope under intellectual property law. But often the intellectual property object will be created without regard to its legal status, which will be considered only subsequently when its value is recognized. In every case, the particular ideas, information, and knowledge that constitute the brute fact of the ideational object, combined with the type of documented form, will interplay with the institutional facts of the intellectual property law. The result will be a unique – and sometimes unpredictable – outcome: the institutional fact of an intellectual property object.

Intellectual property law is therefore an unusual sort of 'double' social construct because it is both constructed and it constructs its own objects of regulation. In other words, people create intellectual property law, which they in turn use to create and regulate intellectual property objects. Both the laws and the objects they create and regulate are socially constructed 'institutional facts'. The production of intellectual property objects occurs within a self-referential, autopoietic legal system, and this institution is 'self-productive' to the extent that it creates the intellectual property objects that it then regulates. To draw on the two empirical examples given earlier by way of illustration: The US legal system, Congress, and the courts, acting on behalf of the people, constructed the copyright provisions that in turn constructed the intellectual property object whose scope and boundaries were discussed in the 'Pretty Woman' case.[50] Once created, the song lyrics (the ideational object put in a documented form) performed by Roy Orbison and 2 Live Crew were brute facts that existed irrespective of any legal regulations affecting them. The intellectual property objects related to those songs were institutional facts produced by operation of the copyright law, and their use was then regulated by that law. Similarly, the British Parliament and courts, acting on behalf of the people, constituted the trademark law under which Aytan's

[50] *Campbell v Acuff-Rose Music*, above n. 35.

Manufacturing's 'Criminal Damage' device mark was registered.[51] Once created, Aytan's Manufacturing's logo was a brute fact that existed irrespective of the legal system and its effects. Once registered as a trademark, the logo was transformed into an intellectual property object (the 'Criminal Damage' device mark), an institutional fact whose use was regulated by trademark law. As will become clear in the next chapter, this manner in which the self-productive mechanism of doctrines such as copyright and trademark law operates is a key factor that distinguishes 'intellectual property' from many other legal doctrines.

Gunther Teubner describes self-productive systems as those that produce their own components.[52] Intellectual property law is such a system, but this does not mean that all the forces that cause production of the components are within the system[53] or are self-produced. Indeed, the system is influenced by social, economic, and political factors in its environment. The reasons for the generation of intellectual property objects arguably lie outside the legal system, primarily in politics and diplomacy, and lobbying by interested parties. A self-producing system reproduces itself by identifying new elements in what occurs, by extracting and constituting these, and then by creating selective links between them.[54] In the case of intellectual property, this helps to explain how new doctrines can be identified and absorbed into the legal system's department of intellectual property law, even though no clear 'criterion' of intellectual property may have been identified.

In other words, the system produces 'components recursively by the network of components'.[55] It does this by observing developments within itself and defining its own components in response (processes that sociological jurisprudence might describe, respectively, as 'self-observation' and reflexive 'self-reference'). When these new definitions are adopted

[51] *Criminal Clothing Ltd v Aytan's Manufacturing (UK) Ltd*, above n. 44.

[52] Gunther Teubner, *Law as an Autopoietic System* (Oxford: Blackwell, 1993) at 20.

[53] Ibid. at 21.

[54] Ibid.

[55] Ibid. at 32.

and absorbed by the system, becoming part of the way in which it operates, the system can be said to have constituted itself.[56] 'Self-constitution' occurs when the legal system defines behaviour and objects in terms of legal categories that are used to determine how it regulates its objects. These are derived from the core legal–illegal distinction[57] – frequently referred to in sociological jurisprudence as the law's 'binary code' – which determines what falls within the law's ambit and what does not:

> The law is forced to describe its components using its own categories. It begins to establish norms for its own operations, structures, processes, boundaries, and environments – indeed, for its own identity. When it actually uses these self-descriptions, it has begun to constitute its own components.[58]

This pattern of behaviour is apparent in the operation of intellectual property law.

Each of the doctrines that make up the legal system's department of intellectual property contains a body of rules that creates categories. Each doctrine establishes norms that delineate how it operates, what its procedural requirements will be, what will fall within and outside its jurisdiction, and how these rules will interact with those of other legal doctrines and society as a whole. An example would be the rules within intellectual property doctrines that mediate between the awarding of private monopolies over the use of ideas, information and knowledge, and social claims to communicate freely.[59]

As each doctrine applies and refines the norms that it has established, it creates new intellectual property objects and distinguishes these from

[56] Ibid.

[57] Ibid.

[58] Ibid. at 32.

[59] For a discussion about the tension between monopolies over and use of intellectual property objects, see David L. Lange and H. Jefferson Powell, *No Law: Intellectual Property in the Image of an Absolute First Amendment* (Stanford, CA: Stanford Law Books, 2009). For arguments in favour of information and its documented forms being freely available, see the collection of essays in Joshua Gay (ed.), *Free Software, Free Society: Selected Essays of Richard M. Stallman* (Boston: GNU Press, 2002).

ideational objects. And, in creating these intellectual property objects, it further entrenches its norms and reproduces itself. The more it does this, the more intellectual property's doctrines create their own objects of regulation. These objects are part of a reality that exists within the intellectual property department of the legal system, constructed by the operation of intellectual property law.[60] Within the legal system, these objects are operative facts (albeit institutional ones). To lay observers, they may look more like 'legal fictions'.

3.5.1. Intellectual Property as a Legal Fiction?

One method by which it has been suggested that the legal system constructs intellectual property is by using the device of a legal fiction. This can be described as a statement that is made by officers of the legal system and that the speaker knows to be false.[61] It is explained succinctly by John Hill Burton as 'saying something exists which does not exist, and acting as if it existed; or vice versa.'[62]

The legal fiction is a common tool of law-makers, and its location within an institution of the legal system changes its nature so that a statement that its speaker knows to be untrue should not be considered to be a lie because it is not intended to deceive.[63] A good example of such a fiction would be the aforementioned stipulated definition of 'skiing' to include figure skating and snowboarding.[64] The aim of such a stipulation is presumably not to confuse or deceive anyone into believing that figure skating and/or snowboarding are done in the same way as skiing or that

[60] Michael King and Chris Thornhill (eds.), *Luhmann on Law and Politics: Critical Appraisals and Applications* (Oxford: Hart, 2006) at 17.

[61] Lon Fuller, *Legal Fictions* (Stanford, CA: Stanford University Press, 1967) at 1.

[62] Burton was the editor of Jeremy Bentham's *Works*. See C. K. Ogden, *Bentham's Theory of Fictions* (London: Kegan Paul, Trench, Trubner, 1932) at xvii.

[63] Fuller, above n. 61 at 6. Note, however, that Jeremy Bentham strongly criticized the 'legal fiction', describing it as a 'wicked lie': Jeremy Bentham, 'Legal Fictions', in Ogden, above n. 62, App. A at 141.

[64] See discussion in Chapter 2.

they use the same equipment. Rather, the law-makers who use this fiction almost certainly do so for ease of reference and economy of speech while trying to achieve their purpose of regulating adventure sports that involve moving over frozen water.

The legal fiction is alive and well in the field of intellectual property. It may occur when one object or behaviour is described or treated as if it were another, or when something is said to exist that would not exist but for this statement being made in the context of a legal system. For example, Dan Burk notes the 'dual legal fictions' that exist when copyright law treats each author of a collaborative work as the author of the work in its entirety and regards the work as if it were that of a single person.[65] Barton Beebe argues that the trademark referent (ie, the object that the trademark refers to or stands for) is now little more than a legal fiction because the trademark need not refer to any particular commodity.[66] In a 1978 case in the United States, a judge described the requirement to pay a 'reasonable royalty' as compensation for patent infringement as a legal fiction because it posits a mythical licensor and licensee entering negotiations, when in fact no license exists, the payment is compensatory, and the infringer is usually prevented from continuing to exercise rights over the patented product.[67] The argument that an invention can be found to have the requisite degree of novelty for patentability by being given a new use has also been described as a legal fiction.[68] The examples are numerous.

[65] Dan L. Burk, 'Copyright and Feminism in Digital Media' (2006) 14 *American University Journal of Gender, Social Policy & the Law* 519–550 at 538.

[66] Barton Beebe, 'The Semiotic Analysis of Trademark Law' (2004) 51 *UCLA Law Review* 621–704 at 625.

[67] *Panduit Corp v Stahlin Bros Fibre Works Inc*, 575 F.2d 1152 at 1159, 197 USPQ (BNA) 726 at 731–732 (6th Circuit, 1978), per Chief Judge Markey.

[68] Edson Beas Rodrigues, Jr., and Bryan Murphy, 'Brazil's Prior Consent Law: A Dialogue between Brazil and the United States over Where the TRIPS Agreement Currently Sets the Balance Between the Protection of Pharmaceutical Patents and Access to Medicines' (2006) 16 *Albany Law Journal of Science & Technology* 423–456 at 433, citing Philip W. Grubb, *Patents for Chemicals, Pharmaceuticals and Biotechnology: Fundamentals of Global Law, Practice and Strategy* (Oxford: Oxford University Press, 2004) at 240.

The legal fiction is not without its critics. Perhaps its strongest critic has been Jeremy Bentham, who suggested that a legal fiction is employed only for the nefarious purpose of justifying the unjustifiable and 'affords presumptive and conclusive evidence of the mischievousness of the act of power in support of which it is employed.'[69] Bentham accused those who invented and first employed a legal fiction of 'moral turpitude',[70] and argued that the practice had caused 'intellectual weakness, stupidity and servility, in every nation by which the use of it is quietly endured.'[71] The legal fiction is therefore a somewhat controversial feature among political philosophers and legal theorists. In the context of intellectual property, Peter Drahos proposes that the use of fictional entities in judicial decisions suggests that the reasoning behind those judgments is 'pragmatic and based on conventions.'[72] The legal fiction is nonetheless commonplace and widely utilized.

For the purposes of the current discussion, it is arguably not the reasons for the use of legal fictions concerning intellectual property that are the most significant for understanding what intellectual property is, but the way(s) in which they are used.

However, it is not only aspects of the rules that constitute intellectual property's doctrines that have been argued to be legal fictions. Peter Drahos contends that intellectual property is itself a non-existent legal fiction, as it is composed of (allegedly) non-existent abstract objects. He describes these abstract objects of intellectual property as 'convenient legal fictions',[73] which are 'subsistent entities' or 'convenient mental constructs'. Drahos concludes that the law may be using the technique of a legal fiction when it proposes that abstract objects exist, 'a fiction on which, as it happens, much power rests.'[74]

69 Ogden, above n. 62 at cxvi, citing Jeremy Bentham, *Works*, vol. IX at 77–78.

70 Ibid. at cxvii.

71 Ibid.

72 Drahos, above n. 34 at 153.

73 Ibid. at 4. Drahos's use of the term 'abstract object' covers, in this context, both the aforementioned terms 'ideational object' and 'intellectual property object'.

74 Ibid. at 151.

Whether one accepts this argument will depend upon one's understanding of the nature of 'existence'. 'Ontology' – the study of existence and conceptions of reality – is a matter of broad philosophical debate, coverage of which is outside the scope of the current discussion. Suffice to say here that, if one takes the 'nominalist' view that abstract objects have no independent existence and are only names (ie, the only criterion uniting various objects with the same name is their name), and thus that only physical objects can truly exist, then 'intellectual property' does not exist by definition. 'Conceptualists' would argue that abstract objects exist only within minds and have no tangible existence or connection with objects external to the mind. This view would require a conclusion that 'intellectual property' is just a figment of the human imagination. However, the 'realist' approach accepts the existence of abstract objects. On this view, existence is assessed by the object's effects, in which case both mental and physical objects can be said to 'exist'. Viewed from this perspective, intellectual property's existence is surely indisputable. Could intellectual property, in this case, still be a legal fiction?

The very nature of a legal fiction is that it is a mental construct. Like the notions of 'social construction' and 'institutional fact', a 'legal fiction' comes into existence by virtue of its role in the legal system. It is a notion that helps to provide an understanding of what intellectual property *is*, and its relevance becomes clearer when one considers how intellectual property constitutes its own objects of regulation. However, it is arguable that, while legal fictions do operate within intellectual property doctrines, intellectual property law is no more fictitious than any other area of law, and intellectual property objects may have fiction-like characteristics but are not themselves fictions.

The intangible objects of intellectual property law are arguably legal fictions because they are teleological social constructs: they do not describe a reality that is external to human society or the legal system but are instead devised to create a new 'reality' that serves a legal regulatory purpose.[75] This can perhaps be illustrated most simply by comparing intellectual property with a tangible object to which the device of a legal fiction has also been applied.

An Australian criminal statute contains a good example of a legal fiction in its amusingly artificial definition of 'cattle', which includes 'any horse, mare, gelding, colt, foal, filly, ass, mule, bull, cow, ox, steer, heifer, calf, ram, ewe, sheep, lamb, pig, goat, deer, alpaca, llama, vicuna, camel, or dromedary, and every hybrid or cross thereof'.[76] In effect, the term 'cattle' is used as a synonym for 'livestock',[77] and this overly broad legal conception of 'cattle' requires human institutions to sustain its existence. Outside the context of that specific piece of legislation, pigs remain pigs and cattle remain cattle. The two species are brute facts that pre-exist the law, are easily distinguished by onlookers, and are probably not often confused with one another. In practice, the linguistic object (the word 'pig') and the material object (the animal scientifically identified as *Sus scrofa scrofa*; often kept as a farm animal from which meat cuts such as pork, bacon, gammon, and ham are obtained; and similar in appearance to the animal featured in the sketch in Figure 3D) habitually coincide. When the NSW *Crimes Act* 1900 calls pigs 'cattle', it is utilizing a legal fiction in a context in which the brute fact or reality does not need to correspond with the legal definition for the intended regulatory purpose to be served.

But what happens when the object being defined and regulated is intangible? What happens when the object being defined and regulated exists only as a constructed product of the legal definition?

[75] See, eg, L. Ray Patterson, 'Free Speech, Copyright, and Fair Use' (1987) *Vanderbilt Law Review* 1–66, especially at 5–6. Patterson argues that historically the US Congress has treated copyright as regulatory in nature, and that 'copyright functions as a regulatory concept and should be recognized as such.'

[76] *Crimes Act* 1900 (NSW), s.4.

[77] See, eg, ibid., s.19, which sets out rules concerning liability for livestock that trespass upon public land.

Figure 3D. 'Cattle' or a Pig?

Pig illustration used by permission. © Art Parts / Ron and Joe, Inc. / www.fotosearch.com

The difference between sheep, pigs, camels, alpaca, and cattle, on the one hand, and intellectual property, on the other, is that the former are self-evident, brute facts that exist regardless of the existence of human institutions. They are real, tangible creatures that we can see, hear, smell, touch, and taste. Like Shakespeare's rose ('What's in a name? / That which we call a rose / By any other name would smell as sweet'),[78] Juliet's Romeo ('So Romeo would, were he not Romeo called, / Retain that dear perfection which he owes, / Without that title'),[79] and Honoré's umbrella ('"He owns that umbrella", proffered as a translation of "Ce parapluie est à lui" ... mean[s] the same'),[80] physical objects retain their constituent properties even if we change the definitional labels by which they are known.[81] By contrast, intellectual property law and the legal objects it

[78] William Shakespeare, *Romeo and Juliet*, act II, scene II, ll. 43–44, in *The Complete Works of William Shakespeare* (Cambridge: Galley Press/Cambridge University Press, 1987) at 741.

[79] Ibid., ll. 45–47.

[80] Anthony M. Honoré, 'Ownership', in Anthony Gordon Guest (ed.), *Oxford Essays in Jurisprudence* (Oxford: Oxford University Press, 1961), 107–147 at 108.

[81] For a clear explanation of how the philosophy of language's 'referential theory' (the use of words to represent things) operates in a legal context, see Dennis Patterson, *Law and Truth* (Oxford: Oxford University Press, 1996) at160ff.

creates and regulates are constructed entirely by definition. Their effects may well be as intense (or even stronger) and far reaching as those of physical objects, but that is a separate issue.

A large proportion of the things controlled by law are physical objects that exist prior to and separately from the laws that regulate them. Cows, pigs, people named 'Romeo', roses, and umbrellas constitute just a handful of examples. Even if we perceive such an object as ***x*** but call it ***y***, it will ultimately be reducible to and definable by its physical form in some way. Thus, if the law says that 'cattle' includes pigs, and that people should prevent their cattle from straying onto public land, the owner of pigs that stray onto public land will be guilty of an offence under that law. Whether the offence has occurred will depend on whether some physical part of an animal included in the definition of 'cattle' was present on the public land, which is an assessment that someone present at the time of the alleged offence could make by recourse to her or his five human senses. Even if several varieties of pigs or cows are involved and the law is called upon to determine whether one or other of these constitutes the sort of animal being regulated by the statute in question, the task is one of categorizing pre-existing physical objects. The law establishes rules of taxonomy by which it creates the categories into which the pigs or cows are sorted. Cows may be considered cows for these purposes, in which case the legal categorization would simply reflect common usage of the word 'cattle' and commonsense understandings about what the term refers to: a brute fact. Pigs may also be considered to be cows for these purposes, in which case the tool of the legal fiction is being employed, as the categorization does not reflect common usage; the use of the terminology in this manner creates an instrumental institutional fact that operates only in the context of the legal institutions that created it.[82] In such cases, the law is a social

[82] The same arguably holds true for more complicated cases that involve sorting pre-existing characteristics of brute facts into legal categories. For example, when is a human being not a 'legal person'?

(a) Humans who are excluded by law for discriminatory reasons. Under the US Declaration of Independence of 4 July 1776, written by Thomas Jefferson, the thirteen

construct that defines what it is regulating (eg, 'cows'). That definition ('pigs are cows') may not accord with non-legal reality (that pigs are not cows), but the items being regulated are nonetheless physical objects that exist regardless of human interaction and whose nature, characteristics, and boundaries can be determined by scientific experimentation. They are objects that are identified – rather than devised – and classified by people. To use an analogy that would be familiar to patent lawyers, they are discovered, not invented.

states declared, 'We hold these truths to be self-evident, that all men are created equal.' Even allowing for the language of the time, not all humans fell within Jefferson's text. Humans who were not considered equal – and therefore fell outside the definition of 'man' – included those with 'black' skin, people indigenous to North America, slaves, indentured servants, and women.

(b) Infants and humans under a certain age. Andrew Banham and Stephen Cretney, *Children: The Modern Law* (Bristol: Jordan, 1993), chart the history of the child as a 'legal person' in English law at 9–19, pointing out that a person is not entitled to full legal capacity until he or she reaches the age of majority (which is age eighteen or twenty-one in many jurisdictions).

(c) Humans who are deemed mentally incompetent to make decisions. For example, a party to a commercial contract should have sufficient soundness of mind to understand the general nature of what he or she is committing to. If another party realized the first party's lack of understanding, the transaction might not be binding: Brian E. Porter and Mark B. Robinson, *Protected Persons and Their Property in New South Wales* (Sydney: Law Book Company, 1987) at 20–21; Gordon Ashton and Adrian Ward, *Mental Handicap and the Law* (London: Sweet & Maxwell, 1992) at 22ff.

(d) Humans who are convicted of certain offences and/or imprisoned. See, eg, John Haslam, *Medical Jurisprudence as It Relates to Insanity* (New York: Garland, 1979; reprint of 1817 edition) at 2, which notes that it is an old provision of English law that "[i]f [the person accused] be insane he will be acquitted on the proof of his insanity – if he be not of insane mind, he must be treated an ordinary delinquent."

Each of these characteristics distinguishes certain human beings from the category of a 'legal person'. A person may be considered legally incompetent for some purposes (such as entry into a contract) but not for others (such as consent to medical treatment). These persons remain physically the same regardless of the legal labels attached to them and are therefore brute facts. The labels are indicative of institutional facts. At the same time, corporate entities can be regarded as persons for the purposes of law, meaning that a human might not be a 'legal person' at the same time that a non-human is a 'legal person'. R. H. Graveson, *Status in the Common Law* (London: University of London, Athlone Press, 1953) at 74 observes that the distinction between natural and artificial persons can be traced to Edward Coke (1552–1634). See also the discussion of legal 'status' in ibid. at 1–6. An interesting discussion of this topic can be found in A. J.

Intellectual property lacks these physical qualities; as already indicated, it is simply a product of a legal definition. It is invented, not discovered. It describes the extent of an incorporeal object over which monopoly rights can be enforced by the intellectual property proprietor. This domain is intangible; as described earlier, it goes further than the documented form whose materiality projects an image of the intellectual property object, but it is likely to be more limited than the thoughts (ideational objects) that inspired it. Intellectual property law thus creates a legal zone in which the object is real – it 'exists' as an institutional fact and a legal fiction – but it cannot be perceived except by its effects.

Intellectual property thus shares many similarities with legal fictions. Both are institutional facts. Both have their source in the legal system. Given the use of legal fictions in intellectual property law, and the manner in which the law uses fiction-like devices to create institutional facts, it is of value to understand the mechanics of how this comes about. An explanation can be found in theory concerning 'performative utterances'.

3.5.2. The Role of Performative Utterance ('Speech Acts')

Within the legal system, the institutional facts of intellectual property objects are arguably created through the use of 'performative utterances'.[83] These are declarations that, when uttered by the appropriate person in the appropriate context, have the effect of creating the state of affairs they describe. John Searle explains performative utterances as follows:

> Because saying certain things counts as entering into a contract or adjourning a meeting, you can perform those acts by saying you are performing them.... The same words said by the wrong person or in the wrong circumstances will have no such effect. Because the constitutive rule enables the

Ayer, *The Concept of a Person and Other Essays* (London: Macmillan, 1964) at 82–128. See also the discussion of legal 'status' in Graveson, above at 1–6.

[83] For a discussion of performative utterances in law, see Neil MacCormick and Zenon Bankowski, 'Speech Acts, Legal Institutions, and Real Laws', in Neil MacCormick and

> function to be imposed on a speech act, then just performing that speech act in appropriate circumstances can constitute the imposition of that function, and thus will constitute a new institutional fact.[84]

A common example of a performative utterance is the statement 'I now declare you man and wife'. This has the effect of uniting two people in marriage when uttered by a legally recognized marriage celebrant in the context of a wedding ceremony, but it has no such effect when uttered by a six-year-old child playing make-believe weddings in the school playground. Similarly, the consequence of a head of state announcing 'I hereby declare war on [name of neighbouring country]' could be catastrophic because it is a performative utterance that creates an institutional fact that changes the way people behave within society. It is highly likely to be followed by military action, violence, and bloodshed. However, the same statement uttered by an actor in a scene in an action movie with a fictional storyline would not create an institutional fact or have the same consequences.

In the context of intellectual property law, if a judicial officer who is called upon to adjudicate in a case concerning the boundaries of an intellectual property object declares that those boundaries fall at a particular place, that declaration will have the effect that the boundaries will indeed fall at that point. The same statement made by someone who merely claims rights with respect to that intellectual property object would not have the same effect, nor would the same comment if made as an off-the-cuff observation by an off-duty judicial officer while attending a barbeque with friends. It is the institution of law, the rules of the department of intellectual property law within the legal system, and the conditions that those laws create, that imbue such statements with the force to convert ideational objects into intellectual property objects when made by certain people under certain conditions. The institutional identity of these people is therefore important.

Peter Birks (eds.), *The Legal Mind: Essays for Tony Honoré* (Oxford: Oxford University Press, 1986),121–133.

[84] Searle, above n. 18 at 54.

3.5.3. Who Determines the Boundaries of Intellectual Property Objects?

Many contracts and other documents make claims about what constitutes intellectual property objects, usually in the context of a 'copyright warning' or a notice of a 'registered trademark' or 'patent pending'. These notices act like surveyor's pegs, marking the scope of the intellectual property objects over which rights are claimed according to intellectual property law. They can look most authoritative, but they are not definitive. Indeed, they are often very unreliable, and it is quite common for such notices to be overly broad and lay claim to intellectual property objects quite incorrectly. The 'Regents Guide to Understanding Copyright and Educational Fair Use' states that such overreaching notices are extra-legal and inefficacious, and can be disregarded.[85] However, this does not prevent the chilling effect caused when potential users are nonetheless warned off using material by such a copyright notice.[86]

The scope of an intellectual property object is not certain until ruled upon by a court or tribunal[87] in a given situation and, even then, one can never be sure quite where all the other boundaries of that intellectual property object lie. Objects of intellectual property are multi-faceted and context dependent. An intellectual property object's boundaries are multi-dimensional, and they are usually impossible to determine except when measured against the scope of other (actual or potential)

[85] See, eg, L. Ray Patterson et al., 'Regents Guide to Understanding Copyright and Educational Fair Use' (1997) 5 *Journal of Intellectual Property Law* 243–305 at 284. See also 258 (noting that the US copyright statue does not allow the overriding of fair use provisions by the use of overbroad copyright claims) and 283–284: 'Copyright notices are often inflated to read as if the copyright holder's right to copy is absolute, saying, for example, that no one may copy any portion of the book in any manner without the written permission of the publisher. Literal compliance with such inflated notices would do away with the right of fair use, a clear signal that such notices are incorrect' (notes omitted).

[86] The chilling effect is described in Chapter 1, §1.2.3.

[87] Including, eg, a hearing officer in a trademark, patent, or design registry, or the 'Appointed Person' of UK trademark law.

intellectual property objects. Even after a judicial ruling – a performative utterance – has been made to determine the boundaries of a particular piece of intellectual property in one context (eg, vis-à-vis another object of intellectual property), there remains the potential for a new assessment of the same piece of intellectual property vis-à-vis a seemingly infinite array of other intellectual property objects.

Whereas the full extent or placement of the ideational object's boundaries can arguably never be known, the boundaries of an intellectual property object are fuzzy. Whereas clear lines can be drawn to indicate where the physical aspects of a documented form begin and end, the boundaries of the intellectual property object it signifies are usually delineated only when they are assessed against those of other objects in order to determine infringement issues and contests about boundaries. These other objects may pre-exist the intellectual property object in question, or they could be created subsequently.

Creators and users of ideational objects must be cautious so as not to encroach unlawfully on rights held by proprietors of existing intellectual property objects. Those proprietors are advised to be vigilant in the protection of their rights. For creators, users and proprietors alike (and note that often the same person or organization will fall into each of these categories with respect to different intellectual property objects),[88] a task occasioned by the establishment of intellectual property law is the comparison of any intellectual property object in which they have an interest or which they might like to use with other material over which they perceive an intellectual property monopoly might apply. The scope of

[88] An intellectual property proprietor may well have used another person's copyright or other proprietary material in creating a new intellectual property object. Sometimes the difficulty of identifying the owner of copyright material that a creator would like to use, or the cost of obtaining a license to use that material, or the refusal of the copyright proprietor to allow that material to be used, will affect the form of a new work. Sometimes it may even prevent the new work from being produced at all. This effect has been described as the 'tragedy of the anticommons': Michael A. Heller, 'The Tragedy of the Anticommons: The Transition from Marx to Markets' (1998) 111 *Harvard Law Review* 621–688.

the monopoly depends in part on the location of the boundaries of the intellectual property objects claimed by others.[89]

Where the boundaries of each person's intellectual property lie will depend on the legal definitions to be applied in the context, with the arbiters of this being officers of the law.

For intellectual property objects that require registration before they are defined into existence – such as those created by patent, trademark, and some design laws – the relevant legal officers are initially the staff of intellectual property registry offices, such as the UK Intellectual Property Office,[90] the United States Patent and Trademark Office, and IP Australia. These people, generally guided by arguments from legal practitioners (eg, attorneys, solicitors, barristers, patent and trademark attorneys, and in-house legal advisors within corporations) determine the registrability of intellectual property objects with respect to which legal authority to enforce monopoly rights has been requested. Appellate bodies may adjudicate in difficult cases. The hearing officer's determination in the aforementioned case of *Criminal Clothing Ltd v Aytan's Manufacturing (UK) Ltd*[91] is an empirical example of a registry office determination that

[89] For example, a patent will be awarded only over inventions that are novel (ie, those that cannot be found in the 'prior art'). To the extent that parts of an invention are already known – regardless of whether they are or have been the subject of a patent – no valid patent will be awarded, even if the inventor subjectively thought that his or her invention was completely new. Likewise, copyright will subsist only in work that is original (ie, work that is not copied). To the extent that a work is copied – even from the copyright-protected material of others or from material found in 'the commons' – copyright law will not afford the author ownership of the material. Note, however, that the law in relation to this second example is not well developed in all jurisdictions. For example, authority can be found in Australian and UK law stating that copyright may be found to subsist in a work that itself infringes an earlier copyright work. See, eg, *Wood v Boosey* (1868) LR 3 QB 223 at 229; *Redwood Music v Chappell* [1982] RPC 109 at 120; *ZYX Music GmbH v King* [1995] All ER 1 at 9–11. However, in *Ashmore v Douglas Horne* [1987] FSR 533, the court refused copyright protection for a part of a play that infringed an earlier copyright play.

[90] 'UK Intellectual Property Office' became an operating name of The Patent Office (established in 1852) from 2 April 2007.

[91] *Criminal Clothing Ltd v Aytan's Manufacturing (UK) Ltd*, above n. 44.

was then sent to an appellate tribunal (in this case, the UK High Court) for review.

Some intellectual property objects (such as those created by copyright and passing off laws) are deemed to arise automatically when certain criteria are met, including the expression in a documented form of part of an ideational object. The formal assessment of whether such an intellectual property object has been created happens after the event. This ex post facto type of evaluation tends to occur when the boundaries of intellectual property objects that users and alleged proprietors have (often unwittingly) claimed and/or negotiated become contested during a dispute and arrive before a court for determination. The aforementioned *Campbell v Acuff-Rose Music* case provides an empirical example of this,[92] and such determinations are also requested in litigation involving the alleged infringement of registered forms of intellectual property.

Courts and tribunals are the official forums in which authoritative pronouncements about the boundaries of intellectual property objects are traditionally made in Western intellectual property systems, and in which disputes are therefore resolved (in principle, if not always in practice). However, 'alternative' methods of dispute resolution such as mediation and arbitration are becoming increasingly popular in intellectual property cases.[93] The use of such dispute resolution methods can effectively bypass the determination of the boundaries of intellectual property objects by formal legal mechanisms in favour of pragmatic, conciliated settlements (which will usually also be legally recognized, and which will be enforceable by recourse to contract law, contempt proceedings, or another agreed-upon penalty). Such outcomes effectively sidestep

[92] *Campbell v Acuff-Rose Music*, above n. 35.

[93] See, eg, E. Casey Lide, 'ADR and Cyberspace: The Role of Alternative Dispute Resolution in Online Commerce, Intellectual Property and Defamation' (1996) *Ohio State Journal on Dispute Resolution* 192–222. It is notable that, in 1994, the WIPO Arbitration and Mediation Center was established as an independent and impartial body to offer alternative dispute resolution services in commercial disputes, particularly those involving intellectual property issues.

the need to judicially determine the boundaries of intellectual property objects in favour of a compromise that is perceived to have practical utility. This can obviously affect outcomes on a case-by-case basis. In common law systems governed by the 'doctrine of precedent' (also known as the 'doctrine of *stare decisis*', by which a legal principle made by a higher court is considered binding in cases in lower courts) or civil law systems in which the concept of *jurisprudence constante* operates (according to which the application of a legal principle in earlier decisions by higher courts is persuasive in later cases), it can also slow refinement of the legal rules that determine where the boundaries of intellectual property objects will fall. Hilary Astor and Christine Chinkin note that, in resolving disputes, courts also govern and regulate people publicly in a form of social ordering. They observe:

> The task of courts is not simply one of maximising the ends of the parties, or even of keeping the peace, but of explaining and giving force to rules that are themselves public and subject to challenge. In contrast, '[p]ositive law norm enforcement is subordinated in the ADR process; compromise predominates.'[94]

In the context of intellectual property law, the 'positive norm subordination' side effect of alternative dispute resolution processes is perhaps most likely to be significant when existing principles are being applied in new areas and to innovative 'types' of intellectual property object, such as those deriving from new technologies.[95] Ultimately it is only through the development of a body of case law indicating how intellectual property

[94] Hilary Astor and Christine M. Chinkin, *Dispute Resolution in Australia* (Sydney: Butterworths, 1992) at 55 (references omitted), quoting E. Brunet, 'Questioning the Quality of Alternative Dispute Resolution' (1987–88) 62 *Tulane Law Review* 1–56 at 14. 'ADR' refers to 'alternative dispute resolution'.

[95] For a general discussion of the benefits and limitations of alternative dispute resolution methods when compared with traditional court adjudication of cases, see Lon L. Fuller 'The Forms and Limits of Adjudication' (1978) 92 *Harvard Law Review* 353–409, and critiques of Fuller's work, as well as more general discussions of alternative dispute resolution, in Michael Freeman (ed.), *Alternative Dispute Resolution* (Aldershot: Dartmouth, 1995).

laws are applied in practice that predictability – not certainty – about the application of the law evolves.

3.5.4. The Predictability Created by Intellectual Property Law

The role of an external adjudicator in determining the scope of an intellectual property object reflects the difficulty and uncertainty entailed in the application of abstract legal concepts in a practically useful manner within the department of intellectual property law. A key role of the legal system is said to be its creation of stability, as it affords people sufficient expectation that others will comply with legal rules to allow them to make plans with reasonable predictability as to outcomes.[96] This principle is encapsulated in the notion of the 'rule of law' (the principle that society should be governed by legal rules that are clear, fair, well publicized and understood, and regulate and protect humans equally),[97] which

[96] This is a foundational principle of the English legal tradition. See, eg, Catherine Elliott and Frances Quinn, *English Legal System* (Harlow: Pearson Education, 2002) at 22: 'Certainty: Judicial precedent means litigants can assume that like cases will be treated alike, rather than judges making their own random decisions, which nobody could predict. This helps people plan their affairs'; John Wheeler, *The English Legal System* (Harlow: Pearson Education, 2002) at 122: 'Legal certainty requires that the law should, as far as possible, be available to whom it applies so that they can order their affairs and make necessary plans. In the context of this overarching principle there are three related principles: legitimate expectations, non-retroactivity and vested rights.' See also Joseph Raz, *The Authority of Law: Essays on Law and Morality* (Oxford: Clarendon Press, 1979) at 169–171, discussing the functions of law.

[97] The 'rule of law' was a term used by Oxford law professor Albert Venn Dicey, who explained: '[I]t means, in the first place, the absolute supremacy or predominance of regular law as opposed to the influence of arbitrary power, and excludes the existence of arbitrariness, of prerogative, or even of wide discretionary authority on the part of the government. Englishmen are ruled by the law, and by the law alone; a man may with us be punished for a breach of the law, but he can be punished for nothing else.' See A. V. Dicey, *A Introduction to the Study of the Law of the Constitution* (London: Macmillan, 1959, 10th ed.) at 202. Dicey's approach has significant influence in British constitutional law and that of jurisdictions that inherited or adopted the British legal system. See, eg, the discussion in Ian Loveland, *Constitutional Law: A Critical Introduction* (London: Butterworths, 1996) at 29ff; and Ian Harden and Norman Lewis, *The Noble Lie: The British Constitution and the Rule of Law* (London: Hutchinson, 1986), chap. 1.

acts as a self-regulating mechanism of social control in jurisdictions that embrace it. However, its function is obviously weaker in situations in which the law does not generate a high level of predictability or when a law is commonly disregarded.

When it is unclear where the boundaries of intellectual property objects fall until they have been adjudicated upon, uncertainty is created. Such uncertainty can have far-reaching effects. For example, investors may show less interest in merchandizing an invention unless they believe that they will be able to register and enforce patent and trademark rights that relate to it. The aforementioned chilling effect occurs when artists and musicians are less likely to engage in the creation of 'derivative works' (ie, pieces that reinterpret or are influenced by earlier works in obvious ways) if they want to avoid legal problems and it is unclear whether their proposed use will infringe copyright in the earlier works.[98] And widespread flouting of the law occurs when the rules are not clearly understood or are popularly considered to be immoral,[99]

[98] In UK law, a derivative work is considered 'original' for copyright purposes if it incorporates 'some quality or character which the raw material did not possess, and which differentiates the product from the raw material': *MacMillan v Cooper* (1924) 40 TLR 186 at 188. One commentary notes: 'It is very difficult to define what the something special is that distinguishes original and non-original derivative works. In part this is because it is difficult to describe in positive terms exactly what it is that the originality requirement invokes': Lionel Bently and Brad Sherman, *Intellectual Property Law* (Oxford: Oxford University Press, 2001) at 86.

[99] Studies of legal compliance have found that people are more likely to disobey laws if they believe them to be immoral. See Tom R. Tyler, *Why People Obey the Law* (Princeton, NJ: Princeton University Press, 2006) at 36–37: 'In studies of [legitimacy and the effects of personal morality], people are asked to what extent a law or rule accords with their own judgments of right and wrong, and these judgments are correlated to whether they obey the law. Five studies of this kind found that personal assessments of the morality of the law typically have a strong influence on whether citizens say that they break the law.... [A]bout 20 percent of variance in obedience to the law can be explained by differences in judgments about the morality of law.' These findings were reflected also in studies of compliance with intellectual property laws: Tom R. Tyler, 'Compliance with Intellectual Property Laws: A Psychological Perspective' (1996–1997) 29 *New York University Journal of International Law and Politics* 219–235 at 226–229.

illegitimate,[100] outmoded and open to change,[101] unworkable, or unenforceable.[102] These patterns permeate the various doctrines that subsist within the legal system's department of intellectual property law. When intellectual property laws produce chilling effects or are ignored – because they are unclear, are not well publicized or understood, or are impractical – they are even less effective as generators of predictable outcomes.

The creation of predictability requires consistency in the determination of the scope of intellectual property objects. Indeed, this has been a justification for the standardization of intellectual property laws worldwide through the *TRIPS Agreement* and bilateral accords. Whether the ultimate delineations of individual intellectual property objects' boundaries come about as a result of decisions by registry officers, judicial officers in tribunals or courts, agreement, or alternative dispute resolution mechanisms, the boundaries drawn in intellectual property cases set de facto or de jure precedents. When these build upon each other in a systematic manner, they create an 'order of things' known as 'intellectual property'.[103] Within this order, existing boundaries come to represent

[100] See, eg., Jon M. Garon, 'Normative Copyright: A Conceptual Framework for Copyright Philosophy and Ethics' (2003) 88 *Cornell Law Review* 1278–1360 at 1283: 'Central to the question of copyright ethics, morality, and normative modelling, is the very legitimacy of copyright itself. Unless there is a valid conceptual basis for copyright laws, there can be no fundamental immorality in refusing to be bound by them. The ethics of the law must be grounded in fundamental notions of justice and fairness, for without this, the rules devolve into conveniences which will be obeyed only when punishment is close at hand. If the only reason to respect copyright is to avoid being caught, it has outlived its purpose.'

[101] Tyler, *Why People Obey the Law*, above n. 99, reports that people are more likely to flout the law when they have a sense that their behaviour will effect beneficial change (at 33).

[102] Tom Tyler reports that 'certainty [of punishment] plays a clear but minor role in determining law-related behaviour'. Tyler, 'Complying with Intellectual Property Laws', above n. 99 at 221. Tyler concludes that 'reliance upon threats of punishment to enforce intellectual property laws is a strategy that is likely to be ineffective.... Instead, legal authorities need to focus on creating the values that underlie voluntary compliance with the law' (at 234).

[103] The notion of an 'order of things' is that of Michel Foucault, *The Order of Things: An Archaeology of the Human Sciences* (London: Routledge Classics, 1989), first published

norms[104] within the institutional framework of intellectual property's doctrines and in the minds of professionals who work within that framework. These boundaries become institutionalized through the 'reciprocal typification of habitualized actions by types of actors'.[105] In other words, when it becomes typical to place a boundary in a certain way, and particularly when officers of the legal system affirm and thus reinforce the placement of such boundaries, such typification becomes institutionalized.[106] The resulting institution becomes known as 'intellectual property law', and it constitutes and reproduces itself through the ongoing production of norms.

Once people defer to intellectual property norms by complying with the rules established by intellectual property law that regulate behaviour with respect to intellectual property objects, the socially constructed institutional facts created by these rules take on a 'material' nature. They become metaphysically 'real' because they have actual – and often powerful – effects in that they prompt people to act in ways in which they would not otherwise act, often leading to materially identifiable results.

in French as *Les mots et les choses* (Paris: Éditions Gallimard, 1966). Foucault states at xxiii of the English edition: 'I am concerned to show … in the mainstream of a culture such as ours: in what way, as one traces – against the current, as it were – language as it has been spoken, natural creatures as they have been perceived and grouped together, and exchanges as they have been practised; in what way, then, our culture has made manifest the existence of order, and how, to the modalities of that order, the exchanges owed their laws, the living beings their constants, the words their sequence and their representative value; what modalities of order have been recognized, posited, linked with space and time, in order to create the positive basis of knowledge as we find it employed in grammar and philology, in natural history and biology, in the study of wealth and political economy.'

[104] This conclusion follows that of Hans Kelsen, *Introduction to the Problems of Legal Theory* (Oxford: Clarendon Press, 1992) at 68. Kelsen views adjudication as a means of norm production. See also Hamish Ross, *Law as a Social Institution* (Oxford: Hart, 2001) at 158–159.

[105] Peter L. Berger and Thomas Luckmann, *The Social Construction of Reality: A Treatise in the Sociology of Knowledge* (London: Penguin, 1991) at 72 (notes omitted); see also 83–84.

[106] Ibid.

Once constructed and institutionalized, and once they start to become powerful within society, institutional facts such as intellectual property laws and the objects they create become part of the social status quo. As Peter L. Berger and Thomas Luckmann have observed:

> Habitualized actions, of course, retain their meaningful character for the individual although the meanings involved become embedded as routines in his general stock of knowledge, taken for granted by him and at hand for his projects into the future.[107]

Thus, members of society – including those very people who were responsible for their construction – tend to take institutional facts such as intellectual property law and intellectual property objects for granted, and the intentional method by which they came about can even be forgotten. In this way, society internalizes intellectual property law and its objects of regulation, and the rules of intellectual property law become norms by which it becomes usual for society to regulate the use of ideas, information, and knowledge.

3.6. Conclusion

Intellectual property can thus be understood as an institutional fact that is subject to regulation within a socially contingent department of law. The analysis in this chapter has indicated how the various components of that department fit together to create and regulate objects that are recognized as 'intellectual property'. The unusual conclusions drawn about the distinction between the ideational object and the intellectual property object point to a central criterion that characterizes intellectual property abstractly, and the following chapter will further explore how this feature helps to give intellectual property law a recognizable character.

From a broad metaphysical perspective, declarations about the objects created by intellectual property laws are similar to statements about legal

[107] Ibid. at 71 (notes omitted).

fictions. These objects are institutional facts that are dependent on law for their existence, but they have a tendency to masquerade as statements of brute fact.[108] In other words, ideational objects and documented forms are brute facts, the intellectual property laws that regulate their use are institutional facts, and each intellectual property object created by these laws is an institutional fact.

However, identifying something as a social construction or a brute or institutional fact suffers from a definitional defect in that it still does not explain clearly what intellectual property *is*. This is because identifying something as a social construct or a brute or institutional fact involves drawing conclusions about how it came about and how it operates rather than about what it consists of. It helps to generate an understanding of the general nature of intellectual property law and its objects of regulation, and this could have valuable effects if used to improve the drafting and operation of intellectual property laws. However, like the definitional methodologies outlined in the preceding chapter, a metaphysical analysis of the type offered here is unsatisfactory if one is seeking an explanation of what (if anything) the term 'intellectual property' intrinsically refers to. As do the definitional approaches surveyed in Chapter 2, the metaphysical explanation offered in this chapter invites the conclusion that 'intellectual property' may be capable of being stretched to cover almost endless types of objects and behaviours with which both ideational objects (such as a concept, idea, or mental image) and a documented form could be associated. The reason for this would appear to lie in the lack of a clear conceptual or tangible constraint that limits what may be 'intellectual propertized'.

Chapter 4 addresses this feature by focusing on how intellectual property's abstract objects and rules operate to create 'intellectual property'

[108] See J. L. Austin, *How to Do Things with Words: The William James Lectures Delivered at Harvard University in 1955* (Oxford: Oxford University Press, 1975) at 4, n. 2. Austin comments: 'Of all people, jurists should be best aware of the true state of affairs.... Yet they will succumb to their own timorous fiction, that a statement of "the law" is a statement of fact.'

and effect 'intellectual propertization'. When anchored below the definitional and constitutive analyses offered so far in Chapters 2 and 3, this helps to uncover the distinctive nature of 'intellectual property' and assists in explaining why some ideational objects have been defined as falling within this legal department while others remain outside it.

4 Intellectual Property's Core Criteria

THE SELF-CONSTRUCTED NATURE OF INTELLECTUAL property's objects and rights is a distinctive characteristic of intellectual property doctrines that immediately sets them apart from many other departments of law and other objects of legal regulation. Narrowing the focus of analysis and concentrating on these two elements – the substance of the intellectual property object, and the 'rights' that intellectual property law creates to regulate human behaviour towards such objects – this chapter examines several additional features that characterize intellectual property doctrines. It argues that intellectual property is typified by bodies of rules that generate abstract intellectual property objects from communicated thoughts, and by 'rights' that regulate behaviour with respect to those objects.

This chapter focuses on identifying the nature of the intellectual property object and rights that are, and are created by, intellectual property law. That is, it examines the substance ('intellectual property objects') being created and regulated through the application of several 'core conceptual criteria' and the 'rights' by which the regulation is effected. The key to understanding the nature of intellectual property arguably lies in these building blocks: its conceptually based objects and rights.

The way in which the intellectual property system produces its own objects of regulation is a key feature of intellectual property doctrines, and the resulting characteristics are a combination of the structure typical of its doctrines and the unique nature of the objects that these doctrines regulate. This chapter suggests that the substance of the self-generated intellectual property object depends on the application of the conceptual notions of an ideational object, documented form, creatorship, and originality (concepts that may not accord with ordinary social understandings of the terms). These are the core concepts on which the 'subsistence' of intellectual property objects is based but, as the chapter indicates with case study examples, they do not necessarily correlate well with the social contexts in which they are applied. Intellectual property law then puts rights in place to regulate human behaviour with respect to these objects.

4.1. Intellectual Property's Conceptual Building Blocks

Intellectual property's various conceptions are composed of a series of unstable doctrines that in turn consist of 'objects' and 'regulations'. Key among these regulations are the 'rights' that allow proprietors to govern various uses of their intellectual property objects. Each of intellectual property's doctrines is an institutional fact, as are their objects and regulations, and changing either their definitions or the relationships between them alters the scope, meaning, and effects of 'intellectual property' per se. Each variation affects the span and strength of intellectual property overall, thereby producing successive new conceptions of what 'intellectual property' means. Yet, despite its flexibility, intellectual property seems to remain recognizable as a discrete department of law, albeit one with ill-defined boundaries and that is subject to some academic disagreement about what is to be 'intellectual property'.

The legal department of intellectual property has been expanding as new rights and objects are built layer upon layer on existing principles, and these changes are often attributed to the need for new laws in response to new technologies and commercial conditions. Examples that have occurred in many jurisdictions include the extension of trademark law to services (previously trademarks could be registered only with respect to their application to goods), the extension of patent law to cover business methods and life forms (in most jurisdictions, these were previously implicitly or explicitly excluded from patentability), and the extension of the copyright term (which was originally 28 [14 + 14] years in eighteenth-century England,[1] then extended to 'the life of the author plus 25 years',[2] then to 'the life of the author plus 50 years',[3] and then to 'the life of the author plus 70 years' in the United States[4] and

[1] *Statute of Anne*, 8 Anne, ch.19 (1710).

[2] See, eg, the *Universal Copyright Convention* (as revised at Paris on 24 July 1971), which requires this duration for many types of copyright works. Article IV(2)(a) states: 'The term of protection for works protected under this Convention shall not be less than the life of the author and twenty-five years after his death. However, any Contracting State which, on the effective date of this Convention in that State, has limited this term for certain classes of works to a period computed from the first publication of the work, shall be entitled to maintain these exceptions and to extend them to other classes of works. For all these classes the term of protection shall not be less than twenty-five years from the date of first publication.'

[3] This is the standard requirement for copyright works found in the *Berne Convention for the Protection of Literary and Artistic Works* (1886; Paris text, 1971). Article 7(1) states: '(1) The term of protection granted by this Convention shall be the life of the author and fifty years after his death.' Subsequent provisions elucidate the rules in relation to specific types of works.

[4] This amendment was brought about by the *Sonny Bono Copyright Term Extension Act* 1990; S 505, Pub. L. 105–298, 11 Stat. 2827 (1998) (amending 17 U.S.C. §§301–304). This law was passed by both the House of Representatives and the Senate on 7 October 1998, and signed by President Clinton on 21 October 1998. For discussions of copyright term extension in the United States, see Philip Alberstat, 'Copyright Extension in the United States: The Mouse That Roared' (1999) 10:3 *Entertainment Law Review* 61–63; Hank Brown and David Miller, 'Copyright Term Extension: Sapping American Creativity' (1996) 44:2 *Journal of the Copyright Society of the USA* 94–102.

Europe,[5] and in Australia[6] in the first decade of the twenty-first century).[7] Meanwhile, publicity rights, moral rights, geographical indications, plant

[5] Harmonized copyright term standards within the European Union were amended by the *Council Directive 93/98/EEC of 29 October 1993 Harmonizing the Term of Protection of Copyright and Certain Related Rights*, Official Journal L 290, 24/11/1993 P. 0009–0013. For a discussion of these changes see, eg, Robert L. Bard, *Copyright Duration: Duration, Term Extension, the European Union and the Making of Copyright Policy* (San Francisco: Austin & Winfield, 1999); Peter Coles, 'Copyright Duration: The European Community Adopts "Three Score Years and Ten"' (1996) 18:7 *European Intellectual Property Review* 379–383; Tim Morely, 'Copyright Term Extension in the EC: Harmonization or Headache?' (1992) 24 *Copyright World* 10–17; Peter Weinand, 'Copyright Term Harmonisation in the European Union' (1994) 40 *Copyright World* 24–28.

The directive's requirements were then implemented by the individual laws of various Member States. For example, the UK's *Copyright, Designs and Patents Act* (1988) was amended by the *Duration of Copyright and Rights in Performances Regulations* (1995) (Statutory Instrument 1995, No. 3297). For a discussion of these amendments see, eg, John Norman Adams and Michael Edenborough, 'The Duration of Copyright in the United Kingdom after the 1995 Regulations' (1996) 18:11 *European Intellectual Property Review* 590–596.

Subsequently, the UK government's *Gowers Review of Intellectual Property* recommended that further amendments to extend the copyright term for sound recordings and performers' rights from fifty to seventy years should not be introduced by the European Commission: Andrew Gower, *Gowers Review of Intellectual Property* (London: HM Treasury, 2006) at 56 following ¶4.40. See, eg, the discussion in Andreas Rahmatian, 'The Gowers Review on Copyright Term Extension' (2007) 29:9 *European Intellectual Property Review* 353–356.

A European Parliament committee announced in 2009 that the copyright term for music recordings would be extended in the European Union to ninety-five years. See, eg, Patrick Foster, 'Musicians Celebrate Victory as Go-ahead Given for Copyright to be Extended to 95 Years' (13 February 2009) *Times*, http://entertainment.timesonline.co.uk/tol/arts_and_entertainment/music/article5720510.ece [accessed 16 January 2010]. For a discussion of the issues, see Natali Helberger, 'Never Forever: Why Extending the Term of Protection for Sound Recordings Is a Bad Idea' (2008) 30:5 *European Intellectual Property Review* 174–181.

[6] This amendment was implemented by the *US Free Trade Agreement Implementation Act* 2004 (Cth), Part 6 ss.120–128 in order to fulfil Australia's obligations under Chapter 17, 'Intellectual Property Rights', of the *Australia–United States Free Trade Agreement* (1994). For discussions of this change, see Christopher Arup, 'The United States–Australia Free Trade Agreement: The Intellectual Property Chapter' (2004) 15:4 *Australian Intellectual Property Journal* 205–226; Christopher Moore, 'Creative Choices: Changes to Australian Copyright Law and the Future of the Public Domain' (2005) 114 *Media International Australia* 710–782; and Matthew Rimmer, 'Robbery Under Arms: Copyright Law and the Australia–United States Free Trade Agreement' (2006) 11(3) *First Monday*, http://firstmonday.org/htbin/cgiwrap/bin/ojs/index.php/fm/article/view/1316/1236 [online journal, accessed 15 January 2010]; also available at SSRN: http://ssrn.com/abstract=855805 [accessed 15 January 2010].

[7] For general discussions about the perpetuation of copyright terms, see Kamal Puri, 'The Term of Copyright Protection: Is It Too Long in the Wake of New Technologies?'

variety types, traditional knowledge, and other sui generis doctrines have been absorbed into the intellectual property systems of various jurisdictions and international intellectual property treaties. Despite this, and despite fluidity around the edges of its doctrines, intellectual property has apparently retained sufficient unity to remain identifiable as a distinct department of law. That this has happened even despite so many changes suggests that there might be one or more core criteria that, alone or in combination, characterize 'intellectual property'. This chapter identifies and discusses characteristics that may perform this function.

4.1.1. Core Criteria?

Having earlier concluded that the difficulty of defining 'intellectual property' stems from its lack of a clear or simple criterion whose presence distinguishes 'intellectual property' doctrines from other areas of law,[8] one risks accusations of inconsistency or contrariness by immediately seeking to identify core characteristics that typify intellectual property law. This is a conundrum that is possibly inherent in defining concepts:[9] they do have characteristics that allow them to be grouped together (even if only by application of something as vague as the 'elephant test'[10] or the notion of 'family resemblance'[11]), but there is no easy definition.

The current chapter proposes that intellectual property doctrines share a number of core characteristics – here dubbed 'criteria' – that can be found in almost all cases of 'intellectual property'.

The core criteria are functional in nature. They may take different forms, have different justifications, and be of variable significance in different doctrines, but they serve the same function in each situation. In the

(1990) 12 *European Intellectual Property Review* 12–20; Peter Schonning, 'Survey of the Term of Protection of Authors' Rights' (2000) 11:4 *Entertainment Law Review* 59–72.

[8] See Chapter 3.

[9] See Alexandra George, 'The Difficulty of Defining "Property"' (2005) 25:4 *Oxford Journal of Legal Studies* 793–813.

[10] See Chapter 2.

[11] This term is Ludwig Wittgenstein's. See reference and explanation in Chapter 5, §§5.1 and 5.6.

early laws that established modern principles of copyright, trademark, patent, and design laws, these criteria seem to have been necessary, but not necessarily sufficient, for a finding of intellectual property. Moreover, probably not every law to which the core criteria apply will be an instance of 'intellectual property' law.

There are also more recent expansions of the subject matter covered by intellectual property doctrines in which one of the core criteria seems to be missing from a modern intellectual property doctrine. This could reinforce a suspicion that the presence of these criteria is common, but perhaps not compulsory, thanks to the use of practices – discussed in the preceding chapter – such as 'definition by intuition' or 'definition by stipulation'. Where one or more of the core criteria is absent and a doctrine is nonetheless treated as intellectual property (eg, in a treaty), it is likely that the doctrine is clustered with existing 'intellectual property' doctrines by stipulation only. In such situations, the doctrine is arguably 'faux intellectual property', having that status by virtue of a legally binding performative utterance[12] rather than as a result of its intrinsic status (if there is such a thing) or philosophical characteristics. Alternatively, a doctrine may be classified as 'intellectual property' because it is related or similar to other intellectual property doctrines and has therefore been grouped with its relatives for pragmatic or administrative reasons, even though its resemblance may be somewhat superficial. An example of this may be 'trading standards' or 'trade practices' law[13] that prohibits false and misleading commercial conduct and resembles trademark law, but whose heritage lies in the areas of consumer protection rather than intellectual property laws.[14] This chapter suggests that a key feature that sets

[12] See Chapter 3, §3.5.2.

[13] Such as the *Australian Consumer Law* 2010, s.18 (replacing the *Trade Practices Act* 1974 (Cth), s.52, from 1 January 2011), which states: 'A person shall not, in trade or commerce, engage in conduct that is misleading or deceptive or is likely to mislead or deceive.'

[14] See, eg, the Australian case of *Taco Co (Aust) v Taco Bell* (1982) 42 AR 177 at 199, in which Deane and Fitzgerald JJ noted: 'The backgrounds of s.52 and of the law of

'intellectual property' law apart from 'quasi–intellectual property' law (such as breach of confidence law)[15] is a series of core criteria.

The presence of the core criteria is thus a useful guideline as to the likelihood that a legal doctrine should be classified as intellectual property, and the examination of the presence or lack of these criteria in intellectual property–like doctrines in the following chapter may help to refine, confirm, and reinforce such a conclusion. However, it must be emphasized that the presence of such characteristics is not determinative. There is arguably no central arbiter that decides definitively whether something is or is not 'intellectual property' and, even if there were, the use of some of the definitional techniques described in Chapter 2 (eg, stipulation, enumeration, or intuition) could distort the categories. Despite this caveat, the use of the core criteria as an analytic tool arguably remains a useful method of better understanding the nature of 'intellectual property' than is offered by the definitions surveyed in Chapter 2.

What, then, are the core criteria that characterize intellectual property? They arguably fall into two categories, which can be summarized, respectively, as 'conceptual criteria' (an ideational object, a documented form, creatorship, and originality) and 'rights' (these vary according to the intellectual property doctrine in question, but they include rights 'to copy' copyright-protected material, 'to use' a trademark, 'to exploit' a

passing-off are quite different. Their respective purposes and the interests which they primarily protect are contrasting. Their areas of operation do not coincide. The indiscriminate importation into s.52 cases of principles and concepts involved in passing-off and the associated area of trade mark law is likely to be productive of error and to give rise to arguments founded on false assumptions.'

[15] The common law doctrine of 'Breach of Confidence' is an example of quasi-intellectual property. Although it is routinely covered in intellectual property textbooks, there are reasons to argue that it should not be considered a doctrine falling under the intellectual property law umbrella. See, eg, *Federal Commissioner of Taxation v United Aircraft Corp* (1943) 68 CLR 525 at 534; cf. *Smith Kline & French Laboratories (Australia) Ltd v Secretary, Department of Community Services and Health* (1990) 17 IPR 545 at 592–594, per Gummow J. See also the discussions in Sam Ricketson, 'Confidential Information: A New Proprietary Interest?' (1977) 11 *Melbourne University Law Review* 223–245; Mark Thomas, 'Information as Property: Humanism or Economic Rationalism in the Millenium?' (1998) 14 *Queensland University of Technology Law Journal* 203–213.

patented invention, and to authorize others to do these things). To provide a preview of the territory to be charted in the remainder of this chapter, these two categories – 'conceptual criteria' and 'rights' – will be outlined briefly, before being surveyed in greater depth in the pages that follow.

4.1.1.a Conceptual Criteria

The first category consists of conceptual criteria that are common across the classic forms of intellectual property doctrines and whose role is to define and delineate – and thereby create as objects of regulation – the subject matter with respect to which intellectual property laws are applied. These criteria are fundamental to the existence and function of intellectual property law; once given a legally enforceable role, they effectively create intellectual property objects. More specifically, a survey of existing intellectual property doctrines suggests that they are created and invoked in situations in which an *ideational object* is identified that bears a degree of *originality* and that can be represented in a *created* and *documented form*. This becomes the 'intellectual property object'. For instance:

- Copyright law creates an intellectual property object out of a thought that is fixed in an 'original' manner in a tangible form (eg, written down or recorded) by a creator known as an 'author'.
- Trademark law creates an intellectual property object out of an authored sign (such as a word, logo, sound, or colour) that can be depicted graphically (eg, written down in specifications or drawn) and that is original to the extent that it is not identical or similar to an existing trademark that is used on identical or similar goods or services, and that is not identical or similar to a 'well-known' trademark. Thus, it takes an ideational object (a sign) that displays the required degree of originality (not identical or similar to an existing trademark), has an identifiable creator (the first user of the trademark), and is presented in a documented form (graphical representation).

- Patent law creates an intellectual property object out of an invention that is described in claims (ie, written down according to prescribed rules) and that is original to the extent that it involves an 'inventive step' and is 'novel' (in jurisdictions such as the United Kingdom and Australia) or is 'non-obvious' (in the United States). In doing so, it converts an ideational object (invention) that is original to the extent that it has not been published or used publicly by an identifiable creator (the inventor) by putting it into a documented form (the patent specifications).

Distinct similarities between the doctrines can therefore be identified in the form of similar core conceptual criteria. These conceptual criteria operate together in a similar manner in each of the intellectual property doctrines, with the law defining an intellectual property object into existence by isolating abstract elements of an ideational object and reconstituting them as an object of legal regulation. To do this, the ideational object must be documented in a sufficiently original manner and in a way that complies with the relevant intellectual property doctrine's requirements. These conditions vary from doctrine to doctrine and are expressed in different ways for different types of intellectual property object, but the requirements being described seem to share strikingly similar features that are found across the range of doctrines and objects that are typically considered to fall within the legal department of 'intellectual property'. These core features or conceptual criteria are arguably common to various intellectual property doctrines, even though contention over whether certain doctrines are correctly classified as 'intellectual property' remains a constant reminder of the contested nature of intellectual property and its component doctrines.

4.1.1.b Rights

The second category of core criteria contains the rights by which the legally constructed intellectual property object is regulated. Intellectual property's rights are probably less conceptually complicated than intellectual property's core conceptual criteria.

Just as the core conceptual criteria share distinct similarities from doctrine to doctrine, so too are there clear similarities between many of the rights associated with various intellectual property doctrines. Just as proprietors of real property and personal property have legally recognized rights to exercise with respect to their property, intellectual property law sets out the exclusive rights of proprietors. These rights define the ways in which an intellectual property object may be monopolized by its owner. They may also be accompanied by duties or responsibilities (such as the duty to use a registered trademark), and they may be tempered by limits. Exceptions, such as fair use/fair dealing in copyright law, descriptive use of a trademark,[16] or use of a trademark in comparative advertising,[17] describe ways in which intellectual property rights may legally be used by someone without the owner's authorization.

Intellectual property *rights* are similar in many ways to other kinds of property rights. While the objects whose use is regulated by real property rights and other types of personal property rights are usually quite different in substance and delineation from those whose use is regulated by intellectual property rights, the rights themselves bear many resemblances. They stem from a right to use the object, authorize use of the object, or exclude others from using the property. Corollaries are rights to earn income from exploiting the intellectual property, as well as rights to license or assign interests in the intellectual property.

[16] See, eg, s.122(1)(a) and (b), *Trade Marks Act* 1995 (Aust.): 'When is a trade mark not infringed? (1) In spite of section 120, a person does not infringe a registered trade mark when: (a) the person uses in good faith: (i) the person's name or the name of the person's place of business; or (ii) the name of a predecessor in business of the person or the name of the predecessor's place of business; or (b) the person uses a sign in good faith to indicate: (i) the kind, quality, quantity, intended purpose, value, geographical origin, or some other characteristic, of goods or services; or (ii) the time of production of goods or of the rendering of services.'

[17] See, eg, s.122(1)(d) *Trade Marks Act* 1995 (Aust.): 'When is a trade mark not infringed? (1) In spite of section 120, a person does not infringe a registered trade mark when: (d) the person uses the trade mark for the purposes of comparative advertising.'

4.1.1.c Conclusion

The core conceptual criteria and rights make up the structural framework of intellectual property doctrines. As a general rule, an intellectual property doctrine arguably does not exist or function if either is missing: the conceptual criteria create the object of regulation, and then rights determine how that regulation occurs. It is arguably particular sorts of criteria and rights that are indicative of the presence of intellectual property. These elements deserve deeper analysis.

4.2. Constructing the 'Intellectual Property Object'

The core conceptual criteria can be thought of as a series of requirements that underpin each of intellectual property's doctrines. They operate together to construct the 'intellectual property object' with which rights are associated and with respect to which human behaviour is then regulated.

In particular, four key conceptual criteria seem to be common to the traditional forms of intellectual property's constituent doctrines, and determinative in creating intellectual property law's objects of regulation:

- *an ideational object* (a specified type of thought) is propertized into an intellectual property object;[18] and
- aspects of the ideational object are *documented* in a manner that allows them to be physically recorded so that they can be accessed in the future;
- they are documented by a *creator*; and
- the documented form of the ideational object displays the required degree of *originality*.

The terminology adopted here to describe these criteria has been chosen for its clarity. It more closely resembles copyright terminology

[18] See the discussion of this point in Chapter 3, §3.3.3.

than that of other intellectual property doctrines but, as explained later, it arguably applies across the doctrines.

A table summarizing the application of these four core concepts is set out in Figure 4A. The top row lists the fundamental conceptual properties that characterize the objects created by various intellectual property doctrines. It simplifies descriptions of the manner in which the conceptual criteria are applied to each of the doctrines, translating the doctrinally specific tests and terminology into generic descriptions that can be applied to most jurisdictions and are compatible with the concepts used in the major international treaties dealing with intellectual property. The first column lists examples of intellectual property doctrines, and the body of the table indicates key essential requirements – expressed using the relevant legal terms of art typical of each doctrine – that are prerequisites for acquiring intellectual property rights under copyright, trademark, design, and patent law.

While intellectual property's various doctrines use different jargon to explain these requirements, their diverse terminology only lightly masks the functional commonalities between the concepts that express equivalent requirements and serve similar purposes in their respective fields. It is the resemblance among these underlying features that is significant in the current context. Like that found in many other departments of law, the jargon of intellectual property often imbues words with meanings that are more specific than or different from those found in everyday usage of the same terms. 'Terms of art' are a common feature of law, which uses a variety of techniques to delineate and define the objects it regulates. Intellectual property law is no exception.

Recognizing and understanding the definitional techniques used in a particular situation can throw light on the nature of a legal regulation, and it is arguably in core concepts that are common to its various doctrines that intellectual property's inherent or distinguishing features can be identified. These concepts may be known by different names and may display distinct variations across the doctrines. Nonetheless, common underlying conceptual criteria that help to loosely bind together

Intellectual Property Doctrine	Ideational Object (thought)	Intellectual Property Object	Documented Form of Intellectual Property Object	Creator	Originality
Copyright	A story, sentiment, fact, knowledge, theory, picture, diagram, music, choreography, etc.	'Literary, Dramatic, Artistic or Musical Work', or derivative thereof.	'Material Form' (UK/Australia); 'Fixation in a tangible medium of expression'(US).	'Author' (or author's employer) – often without requiring registration	'Original' (that is, not copied).
Design	Appearance of a product.	'Shape, configuration, pattern, ornament'.	'Graphical Representation'	'Designer' (or designer's employer or commissioner) – may require registration.	'Novelty'
Patent	Technique for making or doing something, or the resulting product.	'Invention'	'Claims' (within the patent 'specifications')	Inventor (unless by agreement with inventor) – requires registration before rights are awarded.	'Novel' and involves an 'inventive step' or is 'non-obvious'.
Trademark	Symbolic association between a trader and its goods/services.	'Sign'	'Graphical Representation'	First commercial user – usually requires registration.	'Distinctive': not identical or similar to an existing trademark.

Figure 4A. Conceptual Requirements for Converting Ideational Objects into Intellectual Property Objects

intellectual property's components can arguably be identified in the terminology that describes each of the doctrines' central tenets. If intellectual property is a legal construct, an understanding of how the law's jargon is used in its construction can help to clarify how intellectual propertization of an object occurs, thus providing insight into the nature of 'intellectual property' more generally.

The role of these concepts is to act as the abstract building blocks that are employed when the law is used to transform raw ideational objects into intellectual property objects. It is only once these concepts have been applied to the thoughts that arise and circulate in human societies that intellectual property objects are created, and it is only once intellectual property objects have been defined into existence by the operation of intellectual property law that legal rights can be claimed and enforced with respect to them. The point at which 'intellectual propertization' occurs is that at which there is a change in legal status from an ideational object to a privately owned intellectual property object. That is, there is a change in status from a pre-legal object, at least in the sense that it is not regulated by any intellectual property doctrine,[19] to one regulated by intellectual property laws.

In the interests of clarity, it should be noted that an object may not be recognized as 'intellectual property' at the point at which it is created, even though it would then be eligible for such recognition. For example, in jurisdictions applying *Berne Convention* principles, a copyright work (ie, an intellectual property object) automatically comes into existence at the time the work is created or published, provided that it fulfils certain conditions. Despite the work being covered by copyright law, the notional proprietor may for some reason not recognize or exercise its rights over the work. Such rights may be recognized and applied retrospectively, so

[19] However, the same object may be the object of legal regulation by some other department of law. For example, a statement that is not regulated by intellectual property law may be regulated by defamation and anti-hate laws. It would therefore be recognized by the law, though not as an intellectual property object.

the point at which intellectual propertization occurs would arguably be that at which copyright in the work subsisted rather than that at which it was recognized. Therefore, it subsists at the point at which the proprietor could enjoy the benefits of its status as intellectual property, regardless of whether the proprietor in fact decides to do so. By contrast, a trademark (ie, an intellectual property object) comes into being at the time at which a trademark is registered, even though legally its rights may be backdated to the 'priority date' on which the application for its registration was lodged.[20]

Thus, an intellectual property object comes into being when the foundational conceptual criteria of creatorship, originality, and adequate documentation are applied to ideational objects in the manner required by a specific intellectual property doctrine. The following discussion offers some explanation and illustration of how this occurs.

4.2.1. Propertization of an Ideational Object Using the Core Conceptual Criteria

Elements of intellectual property that can be dubbed 'ideational objects' and 'documented forms' were introduced in the preceding chapter, where they were described as brute facts that underpin intellectual propertization. It is timely to now build on that earlier discussion to indicate from a more practical perspective how these characterizations are interpreted in various intellectual property doctrines.

In addition to the requirements of an 'ideational object' and 'documented form', a degree of 'originality' seems to be a uniform condition across a range of classic intellectual property doctrines. This goes hand in hand with 'creatorship', a concept that attributes credit – and from which stems proprietorship (commonly referred to as 'ownership') – for the originality of an intellectual property object. Originality and creatorship

[20] This is the case, for example, with respect to Australian and UK trademarks, as well as the 'Community Trade Mark' (CTM) of the European Union.

are arguably legal constructs that intellectual property law uses as conceptual tools to create the institutional facts of intellectual property objects by distinguishing them from brute fact ideational objects. The manner in which these concepts are engaged by the intellectual propertization process is perhaps indicative of the criterion or criteria that characterize(s) intellectual property laws, and this section discusses the nature of these factors in their various doctrinal contexts to help demonstrate how intellectual property law operates structurally. It builds on concepts that were introduced in the earlier discussion of intellectual property's foundational building blocks[21] by considering how various intellectual property doctrines apply essentially similar foundational concepts to different kinds of thoughts.

4.2.2. Ideational Object

Intellectual property statutes, cases, and texts tend to make little or no overt reference to the ideational object, yet its presence is always implicit. Without the existence of an underlying ideational object, there is no possibility of the creation of an intellectual property object or its documented form. In other words, an idea must be thought before it can be expressed, documented, and converted by law into 'intellectual property'. While this may be a statement of the obvious, it is a far from redundant observation when the existence and nature of the ideational object (the thought) are so commonly overlooked in intellectual property law and theory.

Each of intellectual property's various doctrines provides for the propertization of thoughts about different types of things. The sorts of thoughts that fall within the scope of an intellectual property doctrine are the 'ideational objects' that were described earlier. The exponential expansion of intellectual property law since the 1990s has had the effect of intellectual propertizing ever increasing categories of thoughts, resulting

[21] See Chapter 3.

in a greater number of ideational objects being converted into intellectual property objects. For example, from an intellectual property perspective, computer programs and moral rights used to be mere ideational objects in Australia. Computer programs certainly existed, as did the books, paintings, and other works that were elsewhere recognized as the subject matter of not only copyright but also moral rights laws.[22] However they were the types of thoughts that circulated within Australian society without the use of their contents being regulated by intellectual property laws that now extend to them. In 1984[23] and 2000,[24] respectively, these types of thoughts underwent intellectual propertization in Australia as new laws converted them into new intellectual property objects.

[22] For example, perpetual and inalienable 'moral rights' (*droits moraux*) – as distinct from 'copyright' or economic rights (*droits patrimoniaux*) – have long been recognized under Art.121 of France's *Code de la propriété intellectuelle*. These include rights to first publication, attribution, integrity, withdrawal, and the protection of the honour and reputation of the author. Similarly, Art. 6 *bis*(1), which was introduced by the 1971 Paris Amendments to the *Berne Convention for the Protection of Literary and Artistic Works* (1886) states: 'Independently of the author's economic rights, and even after the transfer of the said rights, the author shall have the right to claim authorship of the work and to object to any distortion, mutilation or other modification of, or other derogatory action in relation to, the said work, which would be prejudicial to his honor or reputation.'

[23] A 1984 amendment to the *Copyright Act* 1968 recognized computer programs as 'literary works' under Australian copyright law. In *Apple Computer Inc v Computer Edge Pty Ltd* (1983) 50 ALR 581, the High Court of Australia had held that the object code in computer programs was not a 'literary work' within the meaning of the *Copyright Act* 1968 (Cth) and was therefore not covered by copyright law. This law was changed by the *Copyright Amendment Act* 1984 (Cth), after which computer programs were regarded as literary works in which copyright could subsist.

[24] Moral rights were explicitly introduced into Australian copyright law by the *Copyright Amendment (Moral Rights) Act* 2000 (Cth). Before 2000 it was argued by some that the prohibition by the *Copyright Act* 1968 on falsely attributing work to an author (Part IX) was similar or equivalent to moral rights protection, and ss.35(5) and 55(2) were likewise argued to grant an author a right equivalent to the moral right of integrity. The Copyright Law Review Committee advised against the introduction of explicit moral rights in Australia (a recommendation initially adopted by the Commonwealth Attorney General) in its *Report on Moral Rights* (Canberra: Australian Government Publishing Service, 1988). These developments are outlined in Maree Sainsbury, *Moral Rights and Their Application in Australia* (Sydney: Federation Press, 2003) at 32–33.

The range of thoughts covered by intellectual property doctrines is expansive. Copyright doctrine, for example, draws its subject matter from a broadly defined range of literary, artistic, musical, and dramatic ideas. Trademark law propertizes certain types of signs used in commercial settings. Patent law propertizes thoughts about new ways of making or doing things. Design rights propertize the appearance of a product. Publicity rights propertize indicia of reputation associated with famous people. Geographical indications propertize thoughts linking goods or services with places. And so on. Any thought falling within these categories is an ideational object that can potentially form the raw material on which an intellectual property object will be based in jurisdictions with relevant laws. Whether or not this in fact occurs depends on the way in which the rules of a discrete intellectual property doctrine operate in a particular jurisdiction, and these rules are usually concerned with determining how and by whom the thought (and/or its documented form) is developed, expressed, and/or used.

It is interesting to note that many of the thoughts recorded in people's memories are actually the property – the intellectual property – of other people. While merely thinking thoughts whose documented form is owned by others is not (yet) a legally infringing act,[25] it is enlightening to reflect on the large proportion of one's daily thoughts that do involve the use of others' intellectual property objects.

It is similarly enlightening to consider the kinds of thoughts that have not yet been intellectual propertized.[26] Examples of the sorts of

[25] Apart from policy objections that the implementation of such a rule would invite, 'infringement by thought' would be virtually impossible to police or prove in the absence of a confession. In the current state of knowledge, such a law would therefore be impractical. It would also suffer from the 'don't think of an elephant problem' discussed by philosopher George Lakoff, whereby an audience is instructed not to think of an elephant, thus prompting everyone to immediately think of an elephant and rendering counterproductive the instruction not to think of an elephant. See George Lakoff, *Don't Think of an Elephant: Know Your Values and Frame the Debate* (White River Junction, VT: Chelsea Green, 2004).

[26] See also Chapter 5 for examples of intellectual property–like doctrines that have not undergone intellectual propertization.

ideational objects that are not yet, or not usually, covered by intellectual property laws include emotions (such as happiness, sadness, worry, satisfaction, euphoria, jealousy, misery and hurt), identification with social groups (such as national identity and patriotism, familial identity, gender identity, identity associated with one's sexual orientation, and loyalty to a school, employer, or other organization), beliefs or schools of thought (such as the doctrines of Christianity, Islam, and Judaism),[27] and most ephemeral communications that are not recorded in a documented form.[28] Most intellectual property doctrines also exclude from their catchments the types of thoughts whose free circulation in society the law has considered to be in the public interest.[29] Legal systems

[27] Although note that the holy texts of some religions, or certain editions or translations of these texts, may themselves be the subject of copyright law. See, eg, *A Brief Guide to Liturgical Copyright: Liturgical Texts for Local Use: Copyright Information* (London: Church House, 1994).

Copyright in the King James Version (also known as the 'Authorized Version') of the Holy Bible is covered by Crown Copyright until 2039 in the United Kingdom under transitional arrangements of the *Copyright, Designs and Patents Act* 1988, Schedule 1, s.13(1): '*Perpetual copyright under the Copyright Act 1775*. The rights conferred on universities and colleges by the [1775 c. 53.] Copyright Act 1775 shall continue to subsist until the end of the period of 50 years from the end of the calendar year in which the new copyright provisions come into force and shall then expire', replacing the *Copyright Act* of 1775.

A distinction should be made here between protection of a religion itself as the intellectual property object (as in the case of protection of a holy book) and a religion that constitutes intellectual property law. See also Chapter 5, §5.2, where this point is described in the context of indigenous cultures.

[28] Confidential information laws, if classified as an intellectual property doctrine, may provide an exception to this example.

[29] For example, copyright law is typified by 'fairness' exceptions (eg, 'fair use' in the United States and 'fair dealing' in jurisdictions including the United Kingdom and Australia) that allow for the continued free circulation in society of uses of thoughts that it would not be in the public interest to propertize and limit. Similarly, under *Council Regulation (EC) No 207/2009 of 26 February 2009 on the Community Trade Mark*, the European Office for Harmonization in the Internal Market (OHIM) will not register as Community Trade Marks, inter alia, signs devoid of distinctive character (Art.7(1)(b)), signs that consist exclusively of indications of geographical origin (Art.7(1)(d)), or signs that are contrary to public policy or accepted standards of morality (Art.7(1)(f)). Meanwhile, the UK Court of Appeal has held that copyright law may not be enforced over material that is contrary to public policy: *Hyde Park Residence v Yelland* [2000] Ch 143. For a discussion of the use of 'public policy' defences to copyright infringement,

tend to leave such ideas outside the realm of private property, and thus outside intellectual property law, although thoughts about such material may nonetheless be 'captured' if they can be demonstrated to meet the conditions for propertization under an intellectual property doctrine. For example, it may not be possible to monopolize a descriptive symbol under trademark law, but it may be possible to monopolize that symbol using copyright law.

Why are some types of thoughts intellectual propertized while others are not? The answer can usually be found in the diverse public policy rationales that are applied to the intellectual propertization, or not, of different types of thoughts. Examples of the sorts of documented forms of thoughts that have been explicitly excluded from the coverage of intellectual property laws as a matter of public policy include offensive signs that cannot be registered as trademarks, 'public interest' material over which the courts will not enforce copyright law, and the scientific and medical theories and processes over which patents will not be granted. Most intellectual property doctrines also carry public interest–based exceptions or defences to infringements, such as the non-commercial use of trademarks, and independent authorship or fair use/dealing of a work covered by copyright law. In addition, the unrecorded ideas and thoughts that flit through human minds, such as likes and dislikes, memories of times gone by, fantasies, and plans for the future or things to be done have not been intellectual propertized thus far.[30]

However, it would be misleading to suggest that such unpropertized thoughts are not ideational objects – in an intellectual property sense – because they do not have the potential to underpin intellectual property

see Rachel A. Yurkowski, 'Is *Hyde Park* Hiding the Truth? An Analysis of the Public Interest Defence to Copyright Infringement' (2001) 32:4 *Victoria University of Wellington Law Review* 1053–1086.

[30] For a discussion of ways in which intellectual property law may come to transcend existing material constraints in response to future scientific and technological advances, see Alexandra George, 'Propertizing the Immaterial: The Commodification of Valuable Intangibles', in Rachel Moffat and Eugene de Klerk (eds.), *Material Worlds* (Cambridge: Cambridge Scholars Press, 2007), 134–147.

objects. Intellectual property rights may not have been awarded over memories or emotions per se but, as already discussed, this does not mean that particular instances of documented records of these memories, emotions, or other non-intellectual-propertized thoughts cannot support an intellectual property object. For example, an emotive poem or a tear-jerker movie may be covered by copyright law, effectively limiting the ability of others to legally describe their emotions in the same or very similar terms for the duration of the copyright.[31] Thus, such thoughts may not themselves have been targeted by law-makers as categories of ideational objects underpinning an intellectual property doctrine in its own right, but they may nonetheless be intellectual propertized if they can be shown to have been expressed and documented in a manner that falls within one of the established intellectual property doctrines. These doctrines are largely subject matter neutral, so they may – if they are expressed in a manner that falls within the scope of an intellectual property doctrine – happen to capture subject matter that society would tend to assume would be better left unpropertized (such as certain expressions of emotions or sexual preferences). Such thoughts may similarly be intellectual propertized if legal standards change. For example, methods of non-cosmetic medical treatment of the human body traditionally lay outside the reach of Australian intellectual property law, but the decision in a 1992 court case concerning this issue brought such developments within the scope of patent law.[32] Similarly, the well-known US Supreme Court case of *Diamond v Chakrabarty* (1980) brought a 'human-made micro-organism' within the scope of patent protection for the first time in that jurisdiction.[33]

[31] In many jurisdictions, this rule is subject to the Doctrine of Independent Creation. This would allow for independently created renditions so long as they are not copied from one another.

[32] *Rescare Ltd v Anaesthetic Supplies Pty Ltd* (1992) 25 IPR 119 (a majority of the Full Bench of the Federal Court of Australia held that claims detailing processes for methods of treating the human body were patentable subject matter).

[33] *Diamond v. Chakrabarty*, 447 U.S. 303 (1980).

The ideational underpinning of intellectual property objects is therefore one of their core features. The manner in which it is distinguished from their documented form is another.

4.2.3. Documented Form

Intellectual property objects can be distinguished from ideational objects by their documented form. A characteristic that seems common to the traditional forms of intellectual property's classic doctrines is the requirement that aspects of the ideational object be set in a material or tangible – that is, a 'documented' – form. This essentially demands that an expression of the thought be embodied in or attached to a physical object from which it can be copied or reproduced without recourse to the human brain or mind that originated the thought. Peter Drahos calls this the 'corporealization' of an abstract object.[34]

The sort of documented form required for intellectual propertization to occur varies among intellectual property doctrines. Copyright law is explicit in its demand for a 'material form' in which the ideational object is expressed[35] (although note that – in what may be an example of copyright subject matter being extended by use of the definitional techniques of intuition and/or stipulation – broadcasts attract copyright protection in many jurisdictions regardless of whether or not they are recorded in a documented form). Patents, trademarks, and the law of registered designs tacitly oblige the provision of a documented form by requiring that the intellectual property object be recorded in an official register. Either way, intellectual propertization occurs when a thought to which some claim of originality (including first use) is made by a creator is embodied in communication that is documented in a prescribed manner.

[34] Peter Drahos, *A Philosophy of Intellectual Property* (Aldershot: Ashgate, 1996) at 153.

[35] Article 2(2) of the *Berne Convention for the Protection of Literary and Artistic Works* (9 September 1886) states, 'It shall, however, be a matter for legislation in the countries of the Union to prescribe that works in general or any specified categories of works shall not be protected unless they have been fixed in some material form.'

Patent law, for example, requires the lodging of 'claims' with a registry office before a patent will be granted. In order to obtain a patent, an inventor documents the invention in claims that comprise a written description and often also a diagrammatic depiction of the subject matter over which a monopoly is requested. The claims form part of a 'specification', which provides greater detail about the problems the invention solves, how it achieves this, and how its effect might be reproduced. The documented description of the invention given in the patent application must be sufficient to enable a person who has ordinary levels of skill in the relevant field to make and use the invention. In essence, patent law thus regards as 'an inventor'[36] someone who had, and registered a documented form of, a previously unpublished thought about how to make or do something. The requirement of a documented form is an essential element in the functioning of the intellectual property doctrine of patent law.

Trademark law grants registration only after a graphical representation or depiction has been submitted for assessment by registry officers. The graphical representation documents the 'sign' that is intended to serve as the trademark. This sign traditionally had to be capable of reproduction in the old-fashioned pages of a booklike register that could be inspected by the public,[37] so the sign tended to take the written form of a word, a name, or a drawing of a logo known as a 'device'. The register has evolved into an electronic database in many jurisdictions. European Union law, for example, has developed a requirement that the sign be depicted either visually or by the graphical use of images, lines, or characters in a manner that is clear, precise, self-contained, easily accessible, intelligible, durable, and objective.[38] EU trademark law has been interpreted to mean that

[36] See discussion at §4.2.4.

[37] The reasoning is that members of the public could inspect the register to determine which trademark indicates the goods/services of which trader, and other traders could discover which signs are already trademarks and therefore should not be used except in accordance with the rights of the registered proprietor.

[38] *Ralf Sieckmann v Deutsches Patent- und Markenamt* [2003] ETMR 466.

'anything which can convey information' can constitute a sign that may function as a trademark so long as it meets certain requirements.[39] One of these requirements is the prerequisite of the sort of documented form that is known in English trademark law as a 'graphical representation'. US trademark law takes an alternative but arguably parallel approach by requiring 'use' of the trademark, which has led to the de facto requirement of a documented form to evidence use. This is illustrated by the demand for 'affixation' of the trademark to the goods or their container under US common law, and the *Lanham Act* states that a mark is used in the manner required for trademark registration when

> it is placed in any manner on the goods or their containers or the displays associated therewith or on the tags or labels affixed thereto, or if the nature of the goods makes such placement impracticable, then on documents associated with the goods or their sale.[40]

The range of signs attracting legal recognition as trademarks has expanded to encompass the depiction of words, names, slogans, phrases, colours, shapes, sounds, personas, gestures and movements, holograms, and potentially smells and tastes. Each type of sign has different requirements as to how it can be adequately documented, but so long as these are met and the documented form is neither identical nor similar to an existing trademark for identical or similar goods or services,[41] and so long as the proposed mark does not fall foul of specific prohibitions on the sorts of signs that are permitted to function as trademarks (such as requirements that the mark not be offensive, too descriptive, or the emblem of certain non-governmental organizations),[42] it can be expected to proceed to registration.

[39] *Philips v Remington* (1998) RPC 283, per Jacob J. This finding was made at first instance and not overturned on appeal.

[40] *Lanham (Trademark) Act* 15 USCA §1127 (2000).

[41] This is known as a 'relative grounds' assessment within the trademark law of the European Union.

[42] These are known as 'absolute grounds' for refusal to register a trademark under European Union law.

Other intellectual property doctrines also require the objects they propertize to be recorded in a documented form. In the United Kingdom, for example, registered design law requires the submission of a graphical representation or specimen,[43] copyright's moral right of attribution requires the written assertion of authorship of a work over which rights are claimed,[44] and passing off law requires that goodwill be expressed via indicia of reputation such as a name or logo[45] (which, in practice, are evidenced in documented forms). Indeed, the demand for an intellectual property object to be expressed in a documented form seems to be a de jure or de facto characteristic common to the classic doctrines that make up the department of intellectual property law.

4.2.4. Creatorship

The person who puts elements of the ideational object into the documented form can be thought of as the 'creator' of the intellectual property object. Like that of a 'documented form', the notion of 'creatorship' flows across intellectual property's classic doctrinal divides in diverse forms that vary according to the type of intellectual property object being created. It is sometimes referred to as 'authorship', but the term 'creatorship' has been adopted here as 'authorship' is so closely associated with copyright law. 'Creatorship' is a more generic term that avoids the risk of doctrinal confusion when used with respect to intellectual property doctrines other than copyright. Whether it takes the form of copyright's 'author', the first user of a trademark, patent law's 'inventor', or the 'designer' of an industrial design, each doctrinal conception of creatorship refers to the person to whom a particular documented form of an ideational object can be attributed. This creator is the person who gives rise to – and is

[43] See, eg, *Registered Designs Rules*1995 (SI 1995/2912 and SI 2001/3950), r. 17: 'There shall be furnished in connection with an application two identical representations of the design, in a form satisfactory to the registrar, or two specimens.'

[44] *Copyright, Designs and Patents Act* 1988, s.78(1), (2).

[45] *Powell v Birmingham Vinegar* [1897] 14 RPC 720; *BBC v Talksport* [2001] FSR 53.

therefore usually entitled to claim – proprietorship of the resulting intellectual property object.

The distinction between the creator and proprietor varies from doctrine to doctrine and jurisdiction to jurisdiction. 'Proprietor' is often used as a general term to describe the creator (including the author, inventor, designer, and so on) of intellectual property rights, but the creator does not necessarily become the proprietor. For example, an invention produced in the course of employment is likely to belong to an employer, as is copyright in a report written in the course of employment.[46] In such situations, moral rights can temper the effect of 'alienation' from one's creation that can occur when copyright proprietorship can be claimed by someone other than the author or authors whose creative input generated its production. The relationship between creatorship and proprietorship in any given situation is likely to depend on terms in a specific jurisdiction's intellectual property statutes, and also on any relevant contracts (such as an employment contract or publishing contract). For the purposes of the current discussion, the focus is on the concept of creatorship rather than the proprietorship that may arise from this.

In most jurisdictions and intellectual property doctrines, the legally recognized creator may be an individual human or a corporate entity. It may be a group of people, but usually only if the members of that group can be individually identified. The bottom line is that the creator is the person whose labour led directly to the formation of the documented form of the object.

[46] Exceptions to these norms occur where employment contracts indicate otherwise. This was traditionally common, for example, with respect to copyright in academic contracts. See, eg, Corynne McSherry, *Who Owns Academic Work? Battling for Control of Intellectual Property* (Cambridge, MA: Harvard University Press, 2001). Statutes may also specify exceptions, such as the Australian *Copyright Act* 1968, which provides exceptions for employed journalists (s.35(4)), and provides for variations to the standard rules regarding ownership of works produced by photographers contracted for private or domestic purposes (as opposed to employed photographers), such as those who are commissioned to photograph a wedding (s.35(5)).

The role of the creator is foundational to intellectual property discourse. The author of copyright law is not just the stereotypical person who pens a letter or writes a book. Copyright's author includes those who write poetry, prose, and plays, draw diagrams, paint pictures, design buildings, or compose music. Even those who compile lists of telephone numbers, draft betting forms, and write computer software have qualified for the label 'author' under copyright law. Patent law's version of the creator is the inventor who devises a new product or method of doing something, while design law's creator is the designer who devises the industrially applied shape or appearance of an object. Thus, the conceptual creator of modern intellectual property doctrines may equally be, inter alia, a scientist, an engineer, an architect or draftsperson, a fashion designer or graphical design artist, a computer programmer, a corporation that engages such professionals, or a lone writer penning a novel in an attic.

While creatorship is critical to the practical operation of intellectual property law, it is also important to note that creatorship is a highly artificial concept, and the notion of a solitary, identifiable creator – often resembling copyright's author – creating an original work has been widely discussed and criticized in literary studies scholarship.[47] The differences between intellectual property law's doctrines' use of the creatorship concept and ordinary social conceptions of creatorship can be quite distinct.

[47] The concept of 'authorship' has been the subject of much extra-legal discussion and criticism, particularly in the field of literary studies. See, eg, Roland Barthes, 'The Death of the Author', in Stephen Heath (ed. and trans.), *Image-Music-Text* (New York: Hill & Wang, 1977); Kenneth Dauber, *The Idea of Authorship in America: Democratic Poetics from Franklin to Melville* (Madison: University of Wisconsin Press, 1990); Stanley Fish, *Is There a Text in This Class? The Authority of Interpretive Communities* (Cambridge, MA: Harvard University Press, 1980); Michel Foucault, 'What Is an Author?' in *The Foucault Reader*, ed. Paul Rabinow (New York: Pantheon, 1984); Karl Miller, *Authors* (Oxford: Clarendon Press, 1989); Mark Rose, 'The Author as Proprietor: *Donaldson v Becket* and the Genealogy of Modern Authorship' (1988) 23 *Representations* 51; Brad Sherman and Alain Strowel (eds.), *Of Authors and Origins* (Oxford: Clarendon Press, 1994); Martha Woodmansee, *The Author, Art, and the Market: Rereading the History of Aesthetics* (New York: Columbia University Press, 1994); Martha Woodmansee and Peter Jaszi (eds.), *The Construction of Authorship: Textual Appropriation in Law and Literature* (Durham, NC: Duke University Press, 1994).

This sheds light on the constructed notion of 'intellectual property' and the artificiality of that construction in a social and cultural context. Both the theory and practice of these conceptions are therefore deserving of deeper attention.

4.2.4.a The Romantic Author

The concept of the creator – in the form of the 'author' – is central to copyright law. Copyright subsistence revolves around the putative author's 'qualification' in terms of jurisdiction, duration, and contribution to the making of the work. Claims of others – licensees, assignees, and other third parties (such as employers) – depend on their ability to trace an appropriate connection to the author of the copyright work. In trademark law, too, the right to register a sign as a trademark in some jurisdictions depends on the ability to demonstrate that the applicant is the author of the mark.[48] Likewise, patents are awarded only to inventors and those who derive rights through the inventor, and the term 'inventor' is essentially patent law's synonym for what copyright refers to as 'the author'. The designer of design law plays the same role. In each of these intellectual property doctrines, the role of the creator is central. Without the creator, the intellectual property object does not come into being and rights do not attach to that object. However, the notion of the creator is far from uncontroversial.

The creators recognized by intellectual property laws arguably reflect a particular 'Romantic' conception of creativity that developed

[48] For example, the Australian *Trade Marks Act* 1995, s.27(1) states: '(1)A person may apply for the registration of a trade mark in respect of goods and/or services if: (a)the person claims to be the owner of the trade mark.' Australian passing off law establishes that the owner of an unregistered mark that has been used is the person who, or group that, has built goodwill with respect to goods and/or services. With respect to an application to register an unused mark, the owner of the mark is the 'author' of the mark who has applied for registration with the intent of using the mark on or in connection with the goods or services, and the 'author' in this context is the person who first adopted the mark for use with respect to the relevant goods and/or services: *Shell Co of Australia Ltd v Rohm & Haas Co* (1949) 78 CLR 601 at 625.

alongside the Romantic conception of authorship identified in literary scholarship.[49] Intellectual property historian Lionel Bently offers insight into these parallel depictions of 'the author' in literature and intellectual property law, observing:

> The claim that the concept of authorship in literature is intimately related to that which operates in law is principally an historical claim that copyright law, romantic authorship and the overpowering significance of the author were 'born together.' That is, the link established in law between an author and a work, and the romantic conceptualisation of the work as the organic emanation from an individual author, emerged simultaneously at the end of the eighteenth century.

The Romantic period in art, literature, and music lasted from the early/middle nineteenth century[50] until the early twentieth century, and was characterized by artistic trends that emphasized creativity, expressiveness, and freedom from the strict artistic rules that had characterized the earlier Classical period. As the person responsible for implementing these principles to create new works, the author became a focus of attention and was elevated to a new status.

The Romantic period was a time of aesthetic genius. Artistic feeling and emotional expression gained respect and popularity, with compositions increasingly interpreted in light of the identity and imagination of the artists who created them. For example, European composers Wolfgang Amadeus Mozart, Ludwig van Beethoven, Franz Liszt, Felix Mendelssohn, and Frédéric Chopin were all of the Romantic period, as were the British poets William Wordsworth, Samuel Taylor Coleridge,

[49] Lionel Bently, 'Copyright and the Death of the Author in Literature and Law' (1994) 57:6 *Modern Law Review* 973–986 at 974 (notes omitted).

[50] In music, the Romantic period is generally considered to have spanned the years 1815–1910. In art, it lasted from around 1800 to 1900: Graham Hopwood, *Handbook of Art* (Melbourne: Graham Hopwood, 1971) at 106–107 and 154. In literature, it lasted for about three decades after the outbreak of the French Revolution in 1789 (there is some scholarly disagreement about its exact dates): Aidan Day, *Romanticism* (New York: Routledge, 1996) at 2–4.

William Blake, Lord Byron, and John Keats. Painters such as J. M. W. Turner and John Constable were also of this era.

The opening words of Michel Foucault's well-known essay 'What Is an Author?' speak of the birth of the 'author' concept during this period as 'the privileged moment of individualization in the history of ideas, knowledge, literature, philosophy, and the sciences.'[51] Taking this notion of the individualistic author beyond the creative context discussed by Foucault, and situating it in a broader social context, Andrew Bennett has argued that this new Romantic idea of authorship "with its stress on individuality, on uniqueness and originality, on the conscious intention of the autonomous object, has also been seen as part of a more general development of the idea of the self.'[52] This notion of the self and individuality blossomed in the philosophy and political ideologies that were developing and gaining popularity during this period.

Placed in the historical context of its development, it is arguably easier to understand the legal conception of creatorship that is now so central to intellectual property doctrines. At a time when society was starting to place a greater emphasis on imagination, individuality, and creativity – all encapsulated in the notion of the 'genius' – it seems natural that laws would emerge that reflected these priorities and rewarded individual creative endeavour. Hence, it is perhaps not surprising that copyright law's emphasis on individualistic creatorship and originality was first identified as such during this era.[53] The same emphasis in design law can also be traced to this period, and patent law similarly reflected the emphasis on creativity in its abstractions of 'inventiveness'

[51] Foucault, above n. 47 at 101.

[52] Andrew Bennett, *The Author* (London: Routledge, 2005) at 56–57.
Bently, above n. 49 at 978 states: 'According to Foucault himself, prior to the eighteenth century, attribution of authorship had been orthodox in relation to scientific texts but not literary discourse, and the period merely saw a reversal of that orthodoxy.'

[53] Note, however, that recognition of the author's role in copyright did exist in England before the Romantic period. See, eg, John Feather, 'From Rights in Copies to Copyright: The Recognition of Authors' Rights in English Law and Practice in the Sixteenth and Seventeenth Centuries', in Woodmansee and Jaszi (eds.), above n. 47 at 191–209.

and 'novelty' that could be traced to an inventor with similar Romantic characteristics.

4.2.4.b Literary Critiques of the Authorship Concept

While the history of 'the Romantic author' has been well documented and discussed in both literary and legal contexts, it is not without strong critics. In summary, the critics argue that creatorship is a fiction that fails to take into account the reality of the ways in which human creativity occurs. They suggest that creators are typically not Romantic-style geniuses, that creators are typically not individuals who independently generate their artistic works or scientific inventions from their imaginations, that many works are created collaboratively, and that creators typically do not spontaneously produce 'originality'.[54] Writers use language – vocabulary and grammatical structures – that necessarily pre-exist their writing, and they tend to fit within literary styles that are referenced and/or evolve as each new work is added to them. Likewise, musicians use notes, chords, and musical structures that pre-exist their compositions and performances, and their work tends to fall into genres such as Baroque, Classical, Pop, or Hip-Hop. Most artists also use materials, styles, and artistic techniques that pre-exist their efforts. In other words, the Romantically influenced conception of creatorship is flawed to the extent that it fails to correspond to or accord with the ways in which works are in fact created in society.[55] The Romantic creator is a somewhat artificial abstraction that may not fit well with the realities of collaboratively derived or piecemeal creative output. Yet it is primarily this type of Romantic-style creator that is rewarded by intellectual property laws.

Arguably the most powerful attack on Romantic conceptions of creatorship stems from the essay 'The Death of the Author', written by

[54] See also the critique of 'originality' conceptions at §4.2.5.

[55] Bently, above n. 49 at 985, citing Peter Jaszi, 'On the Author Effect: Contemporary Copyright and Collective Creativity', in Martha Woodmansee and Peter Jaszi (eds.), *The Construction of Authorship: Textual Appropriation in Law and Literature* (Durham, NC: Duke University Press, 1994), 29–56 at 50.

French literary critic Roland Barthes in the 1960s.[56] Barthes argues that a work results from many social influences and is thus layered with multiple meanings. As it is influenced by a diverse range of sources, it can be understood only by reference to those influences. These include fragments of other texts, the pre-existing meanings of the language that is used, and other 'innumerable centres of culture',[57] which Barthes describes collectively as the 'tissue of quotations'[58] that constitute the text.

Barthes condemns the Romantic conception of creatorship (referred to as 'authorship'), suggesting that the identity of the individual who created a text becomes irrelevant once that person has released the text into society. Once the work is released into society by its creator, inter-textuality – the interpretation of the work in its literary and social context[59] – becomes the most important interpretative tool. So, rather than trying to interpret the text by identifying its creator and searching for the creator's intent in order to establish a work's meaning, the interpretative focus should be on the text in its social and cultural context, as well as readers' responses to it. Creators are themselves part of the structure of a creative work.[60] In this sense, creatorship is merely a product of writing, and the Romantic notion of 'the author' is declared to be dead.

Avant-garde movements seek to break free of artistic norms and chart new territory, challenging aesthetic frontiers. Jazz musicians improvise, as do abstract artists. Yet even these texts are created in a cultural context. The creator brings the text into being, but its ultimate meanings are as much created by the responses of those who interpret it as by anything imbued by the creator. All of this happens in a social context that gives a text a life of its own once the creator has released it into society. As Michel Foucault argues, the text 'indicates itself, constructs itself, only

[56] Barthes, above n. 47 at 142–148.

[57] Ibid. at 146.

[58] Ibid.

[59] Daniel Chandler, *Semiotics: The Basics* (London: Routledge, 2002) at 201 defines 'intertextuality' as 'allusions to other texts'.

[60] Foucault, above n. 47.

on the basis of a complex field of discourse.'[61] The recognition of this was an important watershed in literary discourse, but it has not been reflected in intellectual property's conceptions of creatorship.

While the identity of the creator may be irrelevant to the interpretation of a text,[62] and the author may be dead for the purposes of literary analysis, the creator of intellectual property law plays a different role. The role of the literary author that Barthes criticizes is one of interpretation of meaning. In other words, Barthes objects to the suggestion that the creator should not only play the role of putting ideas into a documented form, but should also perform a second task: that of imbuing that documented form with meaning. It is the second of these that is important to literary discourse and that Barthes challenges (with the first role being relevant chiefly as a condition of the second; the work must come into being before it can be interpreted). However, in intellectual property law it is the first of these roles – that of the physical creator – that is important. The second function – that of the giver of meaning – is relevant only to the extent that it affects the creation and sustainability of the intellectual property object.

Thus, the author in literary discourse and the creator in intellectual property law serve different purposes. Even if the literary author has died, as Barthes claims, the creator of an intellectual property object arguably lives on. Perhaps a more important legal consideration is to contemplate the identity of the creator. Perhaps the more important question for intellectual property law is not whether it recognizes a creator, but who it identifies as that creator. Is the creator whose role coincides with the notion of the 'Romantic author' really deserving of all the glory and rewards that intellectual property rights can confer?

[61] Michel Foucault, *The Archaeology of Knowledge*, trans. A. M. Sheridan Smith. (London: Routledge, 2002) at 26.

[62] As argued by Michel Foucault, *The Order of Things: An Archaeology of the Human Sciences*(London: Routledge Classics, 2002). Foucault suggests that literary writing is not about the author's expressiveness or communication, but about the circulation of language. He queries the relevance of the author in a literary context, suggesting that it is irrelevant who created a text.

4.2.4.c Critiques of Intellectual Property Law Creatorship

The notion of the Romantic author is reflected in the US Constitution, which gives primacy to 'the author' by empowering Congress to legislate '[t]o promote the progress of science and useful arts, by securing for limited times *to authors and inventors* the exclusive right to their respective writings and discoveries.'[63] James Boyle describes the Romantic author of contemporary copyright law as someone who adds novelty to the raw materials found in nature or already circulating in culture,[64] suggesting that it is this role that justifies the property rights that she or he then obtains over the intellectual property objects that arise.[65] This plays on the classic stereotype of a solitary poet or novelist toiling in a garret over the creation of 'his' masterpiece.[66] It is generally accepted by historians of intellectual property that copyright law picks up on the theme of the Romantic author quite directly, although Oren Bracha convincingly challenges some common assumptions about the significance of this influence in a study of US copyright history.[67] The relationships between the

[63] *Constitution of the United States of America*, Art. 1, Sec. 8, Clause 8. This provision is colloquially referred to as 'the copyright clause', the 'copyright and patent clause', or the 'progressive clause' (emphasis added).

[64] James Boyle, *Shamans, Software and Spleens: Law and the Construction of the Information Society* (Cambridge, MA: Harvard University Press, 1997) at 54.

[65] Note that this accords with 'Lockean' reasoning described in the appendix to this volume.

[66] 'Romantic authors' of this ilk were traditionally men. Indeed, female authors of the Victorian Era often took male names in order for their work to be taken seriously and published. Examples include Charlotte Brontë (who wrote under the pseudonym Currer Bell), Emily Brontë (writing as Ellis Bell), and Mary Ann Cross (née Evans, writing as George Eliot). Australian writers Ethel Florence Lindesay Richardson (writing as Henry Handel Richardson) and Stella Maria Sarah Miles Franklin (Miles Franklin) are other well-known examples of authors who disguised their gender by using male pen names.

[67] Oren Bracha, 'The Ideology of Authorship Revisited: Authors, Markets and Liberal Values in Early American Copyright' (2008) 118 *Yale Law Journal* 186–271. Bracha argues: 'Is the construct of authorship the key for understanding modern American copyright law and its history? Yes and no! the myth of the author is indeed a central element in modern copyright law, but as a matter of legal doctrine, copyright does not directly rest on and, more importantly, never has directly rested on this myth' (at 189).

creatorship concept and Romantic notions of individualistic creativity are arguably also apparent – albeit less obviously – in the other classic intellectual property doctrines of patent, design, and trademark law.

In intellectual property scholarship, criticism of copyright's notion of 'the author' is similar to that of the literary author, but Lionel Bently suggests that the effective critiques of literary authorship have not destabilized copyright's authorship concept. He notes that '[t]he post-structuralist critique of authorship appears so far to have had no significant influence on copyright law which has continued to employ romantic images of authorship, at least in some contexts.'[68] This is arguably because the author of literary studies and the creators found in intellectual property doctrines serve different functions even though they share the same identity.[69]

As already suggested, identification and analysis of the literary author is an interpretative tool whose role is to provide a context for the creative work and assist in understanding its content and meaning. By contrast, the creator of intellectual property law serves the purpose of fixing a point of creation to which 'attribution' attaches, and from which legally enforceable proprietary rights can be traced. As Lionel Bently points out in the context of copyright authorship, the creatorship concept can also act as a limitation on the subject matter protected by intellectual property law,[70] a limitation on the threshold of protection (used to determine whether the 'originality' threshold is met),[71] a limitation on the breadth

[68] Bently, above n. 49 at 977. Indeed, Bently agrees with Jaszi, *above* n. 55 at 35, that the Romantic concept of authorship instead thrives in copyright law: 'The instance of moral rights is but one example of how Romantic conception of authorship is displaying a literally unprecedented measure of ideological autonomy in legal context. Recent copyright decisions show that even as scholars of literary studies elaborate a far-reaching critique of the received Romantic concept of authorship, American lawyers are reaching out to embrace the dull range of its implications.'

[69] David Saunders, *Authorship and Copyright* (London: Routledge, 1992) at 223.

[70] Lionel Bently, 'R. v the Author: From Death Penalty to Community Service' (2008) 32:1 *Columbia Journal of Law and the Arts* 1–109 at 92–94 (Bently describes this as a 'limitation on the field of copyright').

[71] Ibid. at 95–98.

of rights (by choosing to adopt a narrow view of creatorship rather than a broader one),[72] and a limitation on the length of protection (particularly where, as in copyright law, the term of protection is related to the date of the author's death).[73]

The meaning, content, and context of an intellectual property creator's work are irrelevant to the operation of the law (except when the work fails to receive protection as an intellectual property object on content-related grounds). Indeed, the creation of intellectual property objects is content neutral,[74] and their meaning is largely irrelevant to both the subsistence of intellectual property in the first place, and the application of rights in relation to the intellectual property object that has been created.[75] The creator in intellectual property jurisprudence is cast more in terms of the worker being rewarded for an investment of time and labour.[76] Indeed, Leon Seltzer argues that the Founding Fathers of the United States chose the 'author' and 'inventor' as instruments by which economics could be used to benefit society through the implementation of selected intellectual property laws.[77]

Recognition of the instrumental role of the intellectual property creator is important for understanding the concept. It also provides a simple

[72] Ibid. at 98–99.

[73] Ibid. at 99–101.

[74] 'Content neutrality', also known as 'subject matter neutrality', is a concept borrowed from First Amendment literature in US scholarship. See, eg, the discussion in Wojciech Sadurski, *Freedom of Speech and Its Limits* (Dordrecht: Kluwer Academic, 1999), chap. 4.

[75] Bently, 'Copyright and the Death of the Author', above n. 49 at 982: 'In so far as Barthes' claim is an extension of Saussurean linguistics – that the meaning of texts derives from a system of "signifiers" and "signifieds" rather than from the author – it is difficult to see exactly what this would mean for copyright law. This is because the relationship between copyright law and "meaning" is extremely troublesome. In some ways copyright is not about meaning at all, so that the radical critique would fail to bite.'

[76] See the appendix to this book.

[77] Leon E. Seltzer, *Exemptions and Fair Use in Copyright: The Exclusive Rights Tensions in the 1976 Copyright Act* (Cambridge, MA: Harvard University Press, 1978) at 8: '1. The *purpose* of copyright is to benefit society. 2. The *mechanism* by which this purpose is achieved is to be economic. 3. Society's *instrument* in achieving this purpose is the author.'

answer to critics of intellectual property's creatorship conceptions who argue that creatorship does not reflect the way in which works are actually produced in society. The starting point for the defence is provided by Lionel Bently, who writes:

> In law, authorship is a point of origination of a property right which, thereafter, like other property rights, will circulate in the market, ending up in the control of the person who can exploit it most profitably. Since copyright serves paradoxically to vest authors with property only to enable them to divest that property, the author is a notion which needs only to be sustainable for an instant. This means that copyright law is able to imply and invent authors where there is no corresponding (cultural or other) 'reality'.[78]

Having recognized this instrumental role of intellectual property's creators, it is helpful to examine criticisms of creatorship in light of this. The definition of the *author* in terms of the original creator – 'the originator and therefore the owner of a special kind of commodity, the work'[79] – does seem to derive from an historical notion of the creator as the originator and beneficiary of copyright works. However, it is perhaps wrong to assume that the intellectual property creator fits the Romantic image.

A key criticism of intellectual property's creatorship conceptions rests on their general failure to acknowledge the collective, collaborative manner in which many works are produced. For example, Peter Jaszi notes that copyright law frequently fails to engage with the 'realities of contemporary polyvocal writing practice – which increasingly is collective, corporate and collaborative.'[80] It also fails to recognize new ways of creating works, such as the spontaneous viral or memetic ways in which many modern intellectual property objects are actually produced. In light of the technical role of creatorship in intellectual property doctrines, this criticism merits more detailed analysis.

[78] Bently, 'Copyright and the Death of the Author', above n. 49 at 980–981.

[79] Rose, above n. 47 at 1.

[80] Jaszi, above n. 55 at 38.

4.2.4.d Collaborative and Collective Creatorship

Collaborative and collective creatorship (which are often two features of a single work) provide a good example of a situation in which intellectual property law's creatorship conceptions do not necessarily accept or reflect the realities of the ways in which art, literature, computer programs, inventions, designs, commercially valuable symbols, and others, are created. Yet these conceptions are nonetheless very important in determining – and thus possibly distorting understanding about – who the creator is. While intellectual property doctrines have come to recognize the commercial practice of collective creatorship in the area of trade symbols such as 'geographical indications' and 'collective marks',[81] this is arguably the exception rather than the rule. Doctrines such as copyright and patent laws have been subject to convincing criticisms regarding their insistence on recognizing only identifiable creators who have made identifiable contributions.

Intellectual property laws – and particularly copyright law – have traditionally had some difficulty accepting collective creatorship. They sometimes allow for joint ownership of copyright works and invented material;[82] however, such provisions tend to require positive

[81] In the United Kingdom and Australia, for example, the common law doctrine of passing off has come to recognize 'collective goodwill', where a group of traders has collectively contributed to the building of mental associations in the minds of consumers between the product and a trade symbol. Examples include the word 'champagne', which describes the sparkling wines produced by wine-makers of the Champagne region of France, and the word 'Palma' to describe the smoked ham produced in the Palma region of Italy. Collective marks are discussed further in Chapter 5, §5.6.1.a.

[82] Patent and design law also allow more than one person to be considered the inventor or designer – and therefore entitled to proprietary rights over their creation – where more than one person's contributions culminated in the creation. In each of these examples, those who have proprietary claims can be individually identified on the basis of their individual contributions to, or use of, the intellectual property object in question.

Australian and UK copyright law, by contrast, allows for the recognition of 'joint authorship' (whereby all recognized authors hold ownership as tenants-in-common) when the work is a cumulative effort that would not have come about but for the individual contributions of each of the authors. See, eg, the Australian case of *Prior v Lansdowne Press Pty Ltd* (1975) 12 ALR 685, where the Supreme Court of Victoria

identification of individual creators and their contributions to the creative process, which are deemed to be equally important, so shared equally. That is not always realistic. The result is that works, or their creators, that do not fall into the individualistic Romantic conception of creatorship reflected by copyright and other classic intellectual property laws are less likely to qualify for protection. In an environment in which the scope of intellectual property laws has been expanding quite rapidly, this restriction on the identification of creatorship is an interesting paradox that hints at internal conceptual confines that restrict intellectual property law's boundaries. It points to a structural boundary that is associated with the creatorship concept that is a core tenet of intellectual property. That is, intellectual property laws are based on conceptions of creatorship, but those conceptions are bounded by abstract limits found in the emphasis on Romantic-style creatorship within this department of law.

Intellectual property doctrines generally prefer individual creators, or at least a limited number of specified creators (as opposed to a communal creative group of people). This leads to a limited, and possibly more manageable, list of owners unless rights are subsequently divided. This preference may be tied to intellectual property doctrines' historical roots. It seems that the Romantic conception of individual creatorship that underpins or influences intellectual property doctrines has, thus far, withstood challenges from the collaborative styles of creatorship that have been increasingly common in a world of digital and multimedia technologies.[83] Yet, while it has been suggested that intellectual property's doctrines have preferred the model of the individual Romantic creator in the

held that co-authors held copyright as tenants-in-common (not joint tenants), and thus in equal shares.

[83] See, eg, John Blossom, *Content Nation: Surviving and Thriving as Social Media Changes Our Work, Our Lives, and Our Future* (Indianapolis: Wiley, 2009). The book describes a multitude of ways in which the Internet and new methods of communicating and publishing (such as the use of social networking websites) are allowing individuals to shift from their traditional passive roles as media consumers to more active roles as writers, directors, and actors.

interests of simplicity,[84] this does not explain why intellectual property – which has been so flexible and receptive to expansionary change in other ways – has been so resistant to admitting a more expansive conception of creatorship.

Economist Yoram Barzel has argued that multiple ownership may in fact be preferable to sole ownership in certain circumstances, such as complex transacted commodities with many attributes, because various individuals gain comparative advantages from such an arrangement.[85] Perhaps a fear is that recognizing too many creators will lead to a 'tragedy of the anticommons'[86] situation, where the need to obtain licenses or assignments from each of several owners before using an intellectual property object will make it too expensive or complicated to use that object, thus producing a chilling effect that leaves it underutilized.

Intellectual property's doctrines recognize certain types of creatorship – those falling within the conception of Romantic authorship, whether they be by writers, musicians, playwrights, painters, sculptors, inventors, designers, draftspeople, or others – leaving creators who do not fit within these conceptions unrewarded and their works possibly unpropertized. As such, intellectual property doctrines can deal quite easily with situations in which there is a single identifiable creator whose contribution is specific and quantifiable. They are less successful at dealing with situations in which a group of people has collaborated and their individual contributions cannot easily be determined or are not the sorts of contributions that intellectual property law recognizes (eg, intellectual property's

[84] Bently, 'Copyright and the Death of the Author', above n. 49 at 981: 'Because a single property owner means that assignments and licences of copyright are easier and cheaper to effect, copyright law prefers to minimise the number of authorial contributions it is prepared to acknowledge rather than reflect the "realities" of collaborative authorship.'

[85] Yoram Barzel, *Economic Analysis of Property Rights* (Cambridge: Cambridge University Press, 1997) at 55.

[86] For a discussion of this idea, see Michael A. Heller, 'The Tragedy of the Anticommons: The Transition from Marx to Markets' (1998) 111 *Harvard Law Review* 621–688, and Michael Heller, *The Gridlock Economy: How Too Much Ownership Wrecks Markets, Stops Innovation, and Costs Lives* (New York: Perseus, 2010).

copyright doctrine easily recognizes the Romantic-style authorship of a playwright who pens a dramatic work, but not the more ephemeral contribution of a director who suggests to actors how they should interpret and perform their roles in the play).[87] A consequence is that people who contribute to the creation of works can miss out on recognition and reward under intellectual property doctrines such as copyright and patent law. This is perhaps a more potent criticism of intellectual property doctrines' creatorship conceptions than is the literary critique, for it unmasks intellectual property's creatorship concept as a legal construct that does not always coincide with how creatorship occurs empirically.

Intellectual property doctrines acknowledge creatorship in order to award property rights to those responsible for having put an idea, or a piece of information or knowledge, or a sign, into a documented form. They reward these creators for having given materiality to an idea, but those who were responsible for generating the pre-documented idea in the first place, and those who later give that documented form meaning, may go unacknowledged and unrewarded. Intellectual property laws seem to have particular difficulty accommodating within their conceptual and jurisprudential frameworks situations in which creatorship has occurred incrementally, over an extended period of time, and with input from various (often unidentified) members of a community. This implicit internal limitation on the recognition of collective, collaborative creatorship seems to be a classic trait of intellectual property doctrines.

It is easy to find examples of intellectual property objects whose value is largely dependent on meanings created by the collaborative contributions of collective, often anonymous creators whose inputs are not recognized as creatorship by intellectual property laws, and understanding this issue is central to appreciating the way in which the legal system constructs intellectual property objects. Three case studies of collaborative

[87] For a discussion of this issue see, eg, Brent Salter, *Copyright, Collaboration and the Future of Dramatic Authorship* (Strawberry Hills, Sydney: Currency House, 2009) at 2–3.

creatorship are therefore offered to illustrate this point in the context of intellectual property's most dominant doctrines:

- collective creatorship of brands (trademark);
- collective creatorship of indigenous works (copyright); and
- collective creatorship in scientific publishing (copyright and patent).

They will be explored in turn.

The first of these examples illustrates how registered trademarks can acquire valuable connotations that were not envisaged by their proprietors but that were constructed by consumers. In this sense, trademark law's attribution of creatorship is somewhat contrived.

4.2.4.e Brands: A Case Study

Consumers who use a trademark in a symbolic manner and thereby contribute to creating its meaning are neither acknowledged nor rewarded as creators of the mark under trademark law, even where they are identifiable individually or as part of a group.[88]

Steven Wilf argues that trademark law's conception of creatorship should reflect the public's role in creating meaning, suggesting, 'It is the collective personality of culture that participates in the authorship of trademarks and that act of collective labor establishes a stake to trademark symbolism contemporaneous with any private claims.'[89] However, creating an association with a trademark is not legally considered to be creatorship of a trademark unless it is done by the registered proprietor, regardless of how valuable that association proves to be. The reason is that trademark law protects the association between a trademark and the goods and/or services with respect to which it is used.[90] The trademark

[88] For a discussion of a similar issue from the perspective of copyright law see, eg, Rebecca Tushnet, 'Payment in Credit: Copyright Law and Subcultural Creativity', (2007) 70 *Law & Contemporary Problems* 135–174, especially 161ff.

[89] Steven Wilf, 'Who Authors Trademarks?' (1999) 17 *Cardozo Arts and Entertainment Law Journal* 1–46 at 4–5.

[90] See, eg, the statement by the European Court of Justice in *Sieckmann v Deutsches Patent-und Markenamt* [2003] RPC 38 at 691: 'The essential function of a trade mark

proprietor gains the right to monopolize commercial uses of this association. Other brand associations – such as use on banners indicating support or fandom – are extrinsic to this protected association, even if they make the trademark more valuable.[91] This can lead to situations in which creatorship of meanings of a trademark that have been constructed by non-commercial uses by consumers – such as use as badges of 'support, loyalty or affiliation'[92] – is automatically (and thus artificially) attributed to the trademark proprietor, thus bolstering the traditional trademark conception of creatorship. The Harley Davidson brand provides a vivid example of how this can occur.

Harley Davidson makes motorbikes. Its brand – and its related intellectual property in its trademarks – provide an excellent illustration of the creatorship conception within trademark law and the awkward way in which that creatorship conception operates with respect to consumer-driven brand reputation.

Motorbike gang members who adopted Harley Davidson bikes and branded merchandise as part of their unofficial uniform and, in doing so, drove the Harley Davidson brand's popularity as a symbol of rebellion,

is to guarantee the identity of the origin of the marked product or service to the consumer or end-user by enabling him, without any possibility of confusion, to distinguish that product or service from others which have another origin and that, for the trade mark to be able to fulfill its essential role in the system of undistorted competition which the EC Treaty seeks to establish, it must offer a guarantee that all the goods or services bearing it have been manufactured or supplied under the control of a single undertaking which is responsible for their quality.'

[91] For example, in relation to the added popularity that a strong fan base can give to a celebrity, Michael Madow notes that '[a] Madonna T-shirt may be worth *more*, not less, to consumers precisely because millions of her fans are already wearing them.... Similarly, the marketing of Madonna T-shirts may actually increase the demand for other sorts of Madonna paraphernalia: posters, buttons, and so on. In the merchandising context, where faddism and emulation are important forces, sometimes it is "the more the merrier".' See Michael Madow, 'Private Ownership of Public Image: Popular Culture and Publicity Rights', (1993) 81 *California Law Review* 127–240 at 222.

[92] See, eg, the UK case of *Arsenal Football Club Plc v Reed* [2001] RPC 46 at 939–940, where Justice Laddie discussed the possibility that a trademark could be used for non-commercial purposes such as 'a badge of support, loyalty or affiliation to those to whom they are directed.'

are not considered by law to be the creators of the trademark's meaning. This is despite the fact that rebel connotations were not originally envisaged or intended by the trademark proprietors and were officially adopted only once the popularity and commercial potential of these alternative meanings were recognized.[93] Indeed, legend has it that Harley Davidson's trademark proprietors initially resisted the rebel connotations, even manufacturing golf carts to present a more conventional and acceptable corporate image.[94] In time, however, the Harley Davidson company acknowledged the marketing potential of rebel connotations and adjusted its brand image and marketing campaigns accordingly.[95]

The trademarked name 'Harley Davidson', and the trademarked logos associated with that name, subsequently became iconic symbols of rebellion, freedom, and individuality. Movies such as *The Wild One* (1953) and *Easy Rider* (1969) immortalized the image of the bad boy rebel riding a motorcycle.[96] Loose association with the Hells Angels Motorcycle Club, which is outlawed in some jurisdictions,[97] accentuated the bad boy rebel image. The sight of Hells Angels members riding Harley Davidson bikes

[93] One brand commentator notes that the Harley Davidson company took 'existing beliefs within the community that might have already formed around [its] brand or cult and simply articulate[d] them': Douglas Aitkin, *The Culting of Brands: When Customers Become True Believers* (New York: Portfolio, Penguin Books, 2004) at 104.

[94] Shaun Barrington, *Harley-Davidson, an Illustrated History* (Castle Hill, Sydney: Lifetime Distributors, 1994) at 122.

[95] As the *Two Wheeled Warriors: The Story of Harley-Davidson in Australia* exhibition at Sydney's Powerhouse Museum states, 'Harley-Davidson is the world's most widely recognised and imitated motorcycle brand. It has achieved icon status through clever marketing of Harley-Davidson as a way of life, not just a method of transport.' See http://www.powerhousemuseum.com/previous/harley_legend.asp [accessed 18 January 2010].

[96] Although the prominent motorcycle brand shown in the film *The Wild One* was Triumph (the lead character, played by actor Marlon Brando, rode a Triumph Thunderbird 6T), the film's 'bad boy biker' image arguably created cultural associations that Harley Davidson would draw on in the future.

Other movies that prominently featured the Harley Davidson brand were *Harley Davidson and the Marlboro Man* (1991) and *Wild Hogs* (2007).

[97] For example, in 2005 a Canadian court in Ontario declared the Hells Angels to be a 'criminal organization' under anti-gang legislation. See 'Hells Angels Criminal Organization, Judge Rules' (1 July 2005) *CBC News*, http://www.cbc.ca/canada/story/2005/07/01/

and wearing its merchandise reinforced that image.[98] In essence, consumers adopted the Harley Davidson trademark as a way of telling a story about an attitude and lifestyle.[99] In this context (which is not 'use as a trademark' from a legal perspective, and so is not likely to amount to infringing dilution),[100] the context meant that the tellers of that story did not become legally recognized creators of the trademark. From a cultural perspective, the consumers were constructing meaning for the trademark, not acting as a passive audience or consumers of a mark divorced from its context. However, from a legal perspective, the input of those consumers is not considered to be creatorship.

Harley Davidson's relationship with the Hells Angels (which has its own portfolio of registered trademarks)[101] seems symbiotic. Branding

bikers-ruling.html [accessed 23 January 2010]. However, in 2008 a Canadian court in British Columbia ruled that Hells Angel members were not part of a 'criminal organization'. See 'Hells Angel Member Not in Criminal Organization' (27 March 2008) *CTV News*, http://www.ctv.ca/servlet/ArticleNews/story/CTVNews/20080327/hellsangels_guilty_080327/20080327?hub=CTVNewsAt11 [accessed 23 January 2010].

[98] Aitkin, above n. 93 at 22–23, refers to the Hells Angels as the accidental 'High Priests' of the Harley Davidson cult: '[T]hey have never been officially endorsed by the company, but you can be sure the brand manager covertly prays to the god of benevolent serendipity for such outstanding "product placement".'

[99] The notion of 'telling a story' in this sense is adapted from David Tan, 'Beyond Trademark Law: What the Right of Publicity Can Learn From Cultural Studies' (2008) 25 *Cardozo Arts and Entertainment Law Journal* 914–994 at 988 n. 324, citing Leo Braudy, *The Frenzy of Renown: Fame and Its History* (New York: Oxford University Press, 1986) at 591–592: 'Fame is metamorphic.... The famous person is thus not so much a person as a story about a person.'

[100] In *Mattel, Inc v MCA Records*, 28 F.Supp. 2d 1120 (C D California, 1998), *affirmed* 296 F.3d 894 (9th Cir., 2002), the US Supreme Court stated that trademarks offer a 'a limited property right in a particular word, phrase or symbol, but cannot be used to allow trademark owners to eviscerate all discussion of their marks they might find annoying or offensive' (at 1141).For a discussion of the possibility that fan fiction could constitute diluting use of a trademark (whether through 'blurring', which reduces the capacity of the mark to distinguish goods/services, or 'tarnishment', which taints the connotations of the trademark), see Meredith McCardle, 'Fan Fiction, Fandom, and Fanfare: What's All the Fuss?' (2003) 9 *Boston University Journal of Science and Technology Law* 443–468, Part IIIE.

[101] See, eg, the following US Trademarks: Registration No. 3666915 (registered 11 August 2009); Registration No. 3338837 (registered 20 November 2007); Registration No. 1943341

commentator Douglas Aitkin notes that Harley Davidson loyal consumers – including Hells Angels members – have been responsible for creating much of the brand's meaning:

> Harley has a wealth of unofficial iconography created by the membership itself. Much of it is specifically designed to distance the cult from society. It repels outsiders by fetishizing society's taboos. Most of it is borrowed from that inner circle of members, the High Priesthood of the cult: the Hells Angels.[102]

Distinct similarities can be found between some of Harley Davidson's and Hells Angels' iconography. For example, both have sought to register trademarks[103] depicting skulls (possibly wearing caps or motorcycle helmets) encircled by a 'halo' effect and featuring their names in capital letters and similar (though not identical) fonts. For Harley Davidson, the halo is formed with the wing-like flames and ribbon-like banners trailing from its name. For the Hells Angels, the halo is created by angel-like wings.

It is possible that the similarities between Harley Davidson's and the Hells Angels' brand symbols are accidental. Perhaps they are a result of no more than both having been created within, and to catch the attention of, a particular social subculture (motorcycle riders), thus appealing to common themes within that subculture.[104] However, it is arguable that the

(registered 26 December 1995). The trademarks can be found in the 'Trademark Electronic Search System' (TESS) of the United States Patent and Trademark Office, http://tess2.uspto.gov/bin/gate.exe?f=tess&state=4004:n340lu.1.1 [accessed 12 May 2010].

[102] Aitkin, above n. 93 at 29.

[103] See, eg, the Harley Davidson application for USPTO trademark serial number 78708686. The application was filed on 8 September 2005, and withdrawn on 19 October 2006. It can be found online at http://tess2.uspto.gov/bin/jumpto?f=doc&state=4006:r45008.2.2 4 [accessed 23 January 2010].

[104] From a trademark registration/infringement perspective, 'motorcycles' (goods in *Nice Convention* Class 12) and 'entertainment services being services associated with the staging of events, competitions, meetings and concerts' (services in *Nice Convention* Class 41), which would include motorbike rallies, are likely to be regarded as 'closely related goods and services'.

similarities are not entirely coincidental and that Harley Davidson has intentionally adopted brand connotations 'authored' by its consumers.

Harley Davidson has become what branding commentator Alex Wipperfürth calls a 'cult brand'.[105] That is, it has been the target of a 'brand hijack' in which consumers have commandeered the brand. They have wrestled it from the clutches of marketing professionals and have driven its development.[106] In more recent times, Harley Davidson's brand has become what Wipperfürth describes as a 'co-created hijack', in which the company's brand managers effectively invited sub-cultures to 'co-create a brand's ideology, use, and persona, and pave the road for adoption by the mainstream'[107]. Co-created hijacked brands signify ways of life,[108] and the work of loyal brand followers (sometimes known in marketing literature as the 'cult' or 'brand tribe')[109] has helped to entrench Harley Davidson as a mainstream symbol of freedom, independence, and rebellion. Tales of accountants who wear a Harley Davison trademark tattoo under their suits and 'weekend warriors' who break free from social conventions by donning the unofficial Harley uniform of 'tattoos, leather, bandannas, beards, and ripped and dirty jeans' on their days off[110] are somewhat clichéd.[111] Yet a survey of Melbourne tattoo parlours by

[105] Alex Wipperfürth, *Brand Hijack: Marketing without Marketing* (New York: Portfolio, Penguin Books, 2005) at 139.

[106] Ibid. at 12.

[107] Ibid. at 61.

[108] Ibid. at 82–83.

[109] Ibid. at 131. This notion of a sub-culture as a tribe draws on symbolic anthropology, which investigates the social expression of meaning through cultural symbols, such as brands. See, eg, Mary Douglas, *The World of Goods: Towards an Anthropology of Consumption* (New York: Routledge, 1996). It is used by brand and marketing consultants and scholars to describe customers loyal to a brand. See, eg, Giles Lury, *Brandwatching: Lifting the Lid on Branding* (Dublin: Blackhall, 2001) at 23: 'We like the "Just do it!" attitude of Nike. We like to feel that everyone else is wearing Nike trainers too. We want to be part of that "brand tribe" – we want to belong to that club.' Lury also uses the term 'brand clans' to describe the same notion (at 109).

[110] Aitkin, above n. 93 at 28.

[111] This stereotype inspired the storyline of the comedy movie *Wild Hogs* (2007), in which a group of four middle-aged suburban men (a dentist, a computer analyst, a plumber/

Australian trademark attorney firm Nicholas Weston in 2009 indicated that the Harley Davidson trademark is the most frequently requested tattoo in that city,[112] and this is reportedly also the case in the United States.[113]

Branding specialists suggest that affiliation with the Harley Davidson brand is commonly displayed by people who are not bikers or whose jobs may require them to conform to conservative social norms. Al and Laura Ries note that many people who buy Harley Davidson motorcycle jackets do not ride motorcycles,[114] while Laurence Vincent suggests that 'many white-collar riders enjoy the association with the outlaw imagery.'[115] Shaun Smith asks: 'When you think of Harley-Davidson, do you think of grizzly, tattooed middle-aged Hells Angels? Think again.... The reality is that a Harley-Davidson is more likely to be ridden by a professional female than by a middle-aged tearaway.'[116]

For those who do associate themselves with the established brand image, Harley Davidson may be a socially acceptable way of expressing their own core values that happen to coincide with values defined by the Harley Davidson company.[117] These original values were adopted

writer, and a businessmen) from Cincinnati (US) break free of their mundane lives on a road trip on their Harley Davidson motorcycles.

[112] Caroline Marcus, 'Stop Me If My Tag Is Showing' (17 May 2009) *Sydney Morning Herald*, http://www.smh.com.au/lifestyle/lifematters/stop-me-if-my-tag-is-showing-20090516-b6pk.html [accessed 31 January 2010].

[113] David A. Aaker, *Building Strong Brands* (London: Simon & Schuster UK, 2002), claims that 'the most popular tattoo in the United States is the Harley-Davidson symbol' (at 138).

For a discussion of intellectual property rights in tattoos generally, see Thomas F. Cotter and Angela M. Mirabole, 'Written on the Body: Intellectual Property Rights in Tattoos, Makeup, and Other Body Art' (2002–2003) 10 *UCLA Entertainment Law Review* 97–138.

[114] Al Ries and Laura Ries, *The Origin of Brands: How Product Evolution Creates Endless Possibilities for New Brands* (New York: HarperCollins, 2004) at 253.

[115] Laurence Vincent, *Legendary Brands: Unleashing the Power of Storytelling to Create a Winning Market Strategy* (Chicago: Dearborn, 2002) at 192.

[116] Shaun Smith, 'Brand Experience', in Rita Clifton and John Simmons (eds.), *Brands and Branding* (Princeton, NJ: Bloomberg Press, 2004) at 107.

[117] As brand consultant Giles Lury states, 'A brand's image and personality, which is based on such factors as its name, how it is packaged, the way it is promoted and advertised,

and adapted (ie, authored or created in a socio-cultural sense) by followers who constituted a Harley Davidson sub-culture,[118] and ultimately the brand redefined itself in terms of the new 'pseudo-rebel' in a cycle that continually strengthens and reinforces the brand's meaning.[119] The brand tribe thus plays an important role in creating the Harley Davidson persona, which gives its trademarks their commercial value. It does so in a manner that is now partly orchestrated by the company (through membership, eg, in H.O.G. – the 'Harley Owners Group®' – which advertises itself as 'one million people around the world united by a common passion: making the Harley-Davidson® dream a way of life.'),[120] and that builds on and reflects the brand values adopted by the Harley Davidson company partly in response to its followers.

Analysis of the Harley Davidson brand would thus suggest that the popular association between the brand and its meaning, which resides in the minds of consumers,[121] has been created – perhaps to quite a great extent – by the brand tribe. At the very least, the brand tribe has implicitly collaborated with the Harley Davidson company to create the meanings and connotations popularly associated with the Harley Davidson

the values it projects, all encourage you to believe it also says something about you to others.' Lury, above n. 109 at 24.

[118] Wipperfürth, above n. 105 at 168 notes: 'Hijacked brands take on a human quality. One Duet user confessed to Silverman's research team, "It's part of my family." The brands' actions are driven by an organic instinct rather than a marketing campaign's series of calculated pretences. This natural, uninhibited, and spontaneous relationship between manufacturer and market is read by consumers as authenticity, that precious attribute missing from the heart of modern politics, media, corporations, and, above all, marketing. Hijacked brands are differentiated primarily by intrinsic values.... The brand's authenticity allows the market to intuitively grasps what these values are without having to be told, or without the companies even having to express the values precisely.'

[119] Smith, above n. 116 at 107.

[120] This is a statement taken from the home page of the Harley Owners Group website in the United States. See http://www.harley-davidson.com/wcm/Content/Pages/HOG/HOG.jsp?locale=en_US [accessed 23 January 2010].

[121] Lury, above n. 109 at 105: 'What both successful brands and stars can command is instant recognition. They own a space in our minds. Their appearances, and key images of them, have become cultural icons.'

brand. Yet that collaborative creatorship is not recognized by the relevant intellectual property doctrine, trademark law.

Trademarks are the legal apparatus that underpin brands,[122] and trademarks thus provide the legal vehicle that allows Harley Davidson to prevent unauthorized uses that do not accord with its chosen values and to profit from its brand image. Trademark law protects a brand owner's formal ability to monopolize brand image and profit from its legal monopolization of a brand's popularity, and it allows the trademark proprietor to sue for certain uses of the trademark that would dilute or tarnish its image.

Branding is about more than just creating a trademark and using it on a product. Successful branding instils and cultivates brand meaning that captures the public imagination and comes to reside in the minds of consumers. As branding expert Wally Olins has argued, branding has increasingly developed into a process by which consumers are co-opted to participate in the authoring of brand meaning:

> Branding these days is largely about involvement and association; the outward and visible demonstration of private and personal affiliation. Branding enables us to define ourselves in terms of a shorthand that is immediately comprehensible to the world around us. Diesel, Adidas and W hotels is one lifestyle; Hermès, Ralph Lauren and the Ritz is another. You can mix 'n' match to customize, enhance and underline your own particular self-perception.... Brands were created by marketing people inside large companies to seduce consumers – to sell products by creating and projecting colourful but simple ideas clearly, again and again.[123]

Thus, while Harley Davidson's lawyers have worked to protect the company's trademarks – including an attempt to register the distinctive 'roar' sound of a Harley Davidson bike's engine as a trademark in the United

[122] For a discussion of this phenomenon, see Alexandra George, 'Brand Rules: When Branding Lore Meets Trade Mark Law' (2006) 13:3 *Journal of Brand Management* 215–232.

[123] Wally Olins, *On B®and* (London: Thames & Hudson, 2004) at 14.

States[124] – its marketing people have encouraged its growth as an experiential brand[125] that helps to build a sense of group membership and belonging among its customers.[126] They have encouraged brand hijack by Harley Davidson's customers, even though this has involved relinquishing some control of the meanings associated with the trademark. In other words, Harley Davidson has allowed its market to help devise and shape the popular meanings of its trademarks by allowing the brand tribe to help create and shape the Harley Davidson brand image. These meanings are the 'secondary reputation' or 'secondary meaning' that is protected as goodwill by intellectual property law's passing off doctrine in some common law jurisdictions,[127] and protected as 'acquired distinctiveness' by trademark doctrines.[128] They are linked to iconology – such as a logo, or a

[124] On 1 February 2004, Harley Davidson applied to register the roar sound of its motorbikes' exhausts as a trademark with the United States Patent and Trademark Office (USPTO). The trademark description read, 'The mark consists of the exhaust sound of applicant's motorcycles, produced by V-Twin, common crankpin motorcycle engines when the goods are in use.' See USPTO trademark serial number 74485223. The USPTO record can be found on its online TESS database at http://tess2.uspto.gov/bin/jumpto?f=doc&state=4006:r45008.2.253 [accessed 23 January 2010].

Following oppositions filed by competitor bike companies, Harley Davidson withdrew its trademark application on 22 September 2000. See David Bollier, *Brand Name Bullies: The Quest to Own and Control Culture* (Hoboken, NJ: Wiley, 2005) at 219. For a discussion of the legal merits of the application see, eg, Michael P. Sapherstein, 'The Trademark Registrability of the Harley-Davidson Roar: A Multimedia Analysis' (1998) *Boston CollegeIntellectual Property and Technology Forum*, http://www.bc.edu/bc_org/avp/law/st_org/iptf/articles/content/1998101101.html] [online journal, accessed 23 January 2010].

[125] 'Experiential marketing' encourages consumers to interact with brands. See, eg, Shaz Smilansky, *Experiential Marketing: A Practical Guide to Interactive Brand Experiences* (London: Kogan Page, 2009); Max Lenderman, *Experience the Message: How Experiential Marketing Is Changing the Brand World* (Toronto: McClelland & Stewart, 2007); Bernd Schmitt, *Experiential Marketing: How to Get Customers to Sense, Feel, Think, Act, and Relate to your Company and Brands* (New York: Free Press, 1999).

[126] Wipperfürth, above n. 105 at 83.

[127] See *Reddaway v Banham* [1896] AC 199.

[128] A trademark has acquired distinctiveness when its primary significance is to indicate the source of the goods or services (as opposed, for example, to an indication of quality). See the explanation in Lionel Bently and Brad Sherman, *Intellectual Property Law* (Oxford: Oxford University Press, 2001) at 834–841.

distinctive roar of a particular brand of motorcycle engine – that signals to consumers the source of the product. And they are, in a practical sense, authored in collaboration between the company and its consumer base.

This signalling effect is the essential role of a trademark and, in return for building (or committing to build) 'brand recognition' between a sign and the minds of consumers, the creator of a trademark is rewarded with registration and ownership. However, the Harley Davidson case study indicates that not all of those who have contributed to a brand's meaning (and thus its value as intellectual property) are acknowledged as its creators by intellectual property law. The reason is arguably that the law protects the documented form of the mark, rather than its meaning. It ostensibly rewards those who created the documented form, rather than those who created the meaning. This is somewhat paradoxical when the notion of 'acquired distinctiveness' is considered; in passing off cases, and in the recognition and registration of trademarks that are not inherently adapted to distinguish a trader's goods or services, only signs that have acquired a *secondary meaning* (the type that brand hijack helps to build) are protected as trademarks in some jurisdictions. Moreover, infringement proceedings for 'dilution' allow trademark proprietors to seek compensation ('damages') if another trader damages their brand's meaning. Thus, a trademark's meaning is protected by trademark law, allowing the trademark proprietor to benefit from its monopolization of that meaning. The proprietor can likewise benefit from additions to that meaning that it chooses to adopt, even where the additional meaning has been created by the brand tribe whose members are not acknowledged as creators and are not rewarded.[129] The brand owner thus benefits both ways (to adopt a colloquialism), in that it can also sue for certain additions to the meaning or dilutions of the meaning that the brand owner considers to be damaging.[130]

[129] See, eg, *Arsenal Football Club Plc v Reed*, above n. 92.

[130] An example is the infamous UK 'McLibel Case', which ran from 1990 until 2005. 'McLibel: Longest Case in English History', *BBC News*(15 February 2005), http://news.bbc.co.uk/2/hi/uk_news/4266741.stm [accessed 6 June 2010]. McDonald's sued activists from a London Greenpeace group for distributing a leaflet headlined 'What's Wrong

In effect, therefore, the trademark owner can choose to recognize and use the brand meanings it has created alone, or it can adopt those created by its brand tribe, and either way it will be recognized as the creator entitled to the benefits of legal rights.

It is well recognized by branding and marketing consultants that a trademark's meaning resides in the minds of consumers.[131] In the sense of 'authorship' proposed by Barthes,[132] it is this interpretation by consumers that matters in interpreting a trademark's meaning (and that thus gives it its value as a trademark), not the legally recognized creator who first put the sign into a documented form and used it as a trademark. Nonetheless, as it is the documented form (the registered sign) of the ideational object (the meaning) that is considered to be the intellectual property object (the trademark) to which the property rights attach, the recognized creator of the trademark is considered to be the person who put the mark into a documented form by registering it and/or using it, and it is through that person that proprietorship of the mark is traced. The result is that, regardless of how extensive the contribution of the Hell's Angels and other 'hijackers' to Harley Davidson's brand meaning and consequential trademark value, it is not recognized as creatorship by trademark law.

The Harley Davidson example illustrates that, despite the important role that consumers sometimes have in creating a trademark's meaning, this is not a form of creatorship that is recognized by trademark law or intellectual property law more generally. Even where it is the meaning that gives the intellectual property object its economic value, it is not

with McDonald's – Everything They Don't Want You to Know'. See discussion about the case and use of McDonald's trademarks – and 'Mc' trademarks generally – in Fiona J. L. Donson, *Legal Intimidation* (London: Free Association, 2000), chaps. 5 and 6; Marlene Arnold Nicholson, 'MCLIBEL: A Case Study in English Defamation Law' (2000) 18 *Wisconsin International Law Journal* 1–144.

131 See, eg, Lury, above n. 109 at 4: '[I]t is clear that brands are much more than names. They are more than physical entities: much of what we see and value in them exists in our minds and not in the products themselves. It is our perceptions – our beliefs and our feelings – about a brand that are most important. The true meaning and power of branding exists in the minds of you and me and not in the products themselves.'

132 Barthes, above n. 47.

meaning that is protected by intellectual property law. Intellectual property law is notionally content neutral.[133]

◆◆◆

Each intellectual property doctrine has jurisdiction over certain types of communication, and the scope of each seems to be determined by the role or function played by that communication. For example, if the communication serves as music, art, drama, or a literary work (or a technological reproduction of one of these), it falls within the catchment of copyright law. If the communication functions as an indicator of commercial reputation, it falls within the catchment of trademark and/or passing off law (or geographical indications law, in some contexts). If it describes how to make a product or how to do something, it falls within the catchment of patent law, and if it serves the purpose of decorating a product, it falls within the catchment of design law. It is not what the art depicts or what the literary work says that is important for intellectual property law, nor is the type of invention or the sorts of goods/services on which a trademark is used relevant to the applicability of intellectual property law.[134] Rather, it is an ideational object placed into a documented form by a creator engaging in original creativity that intellectual property law protects. In this sense, intellectual property law is content neutral. It protects the vessel into which meaning is poured, but not the meaning itself. It nominates as 'creator' the person who fashioned the vessel, not those who contributed to filling the vessel with meaning.

Trademark law is not the only intellectual property doctrine that has a view of creatorship that arguably fails to fully reflect or recognize the diversity of ways in which intellectual property objects are collaboratively produced by members of society. Copyright law is another doctrine

[133] This is a concept borrowed from First Amendment jurisprudence in the United States. See, eg, Sadurski, above n. 74.

[134] Certain subject matter may be excluded from subsisting as copyright or passing off's goodwill on the basis of public policy considerations, or may be excluded from registration as a trademark, patent, or design on similar grounds. However, these analyses are applied separately and are not dependent on the 'authorship' concept.

at which this objection has been levelled, as the following case study illustrates.

4.2.4.f Indigenous 'Intellectual Property': A Case Study

Even where traditional lore and conventions regulating the ideas, information, knowledge, and signs of indigenous people have created a form of collectively held customary copyright that continues to operate in those communities alongside Western legal systems, modern intellectual property conceptions may reject the idea of communal ownership of regulated ideational objects that indigenous lore often encompasses.[135] Numerous examples have been recorded of situations in which indigenous peoples' traditional rules regarding intellectual property–like objects have not been protected by Western laws.[136] The case study examined here is chosen because not only is it quite representative, but it vividly demonstrates the 'culture clash' and potential for hurt to a community that can occur when social systems of creatorship (as supported throughout that community's history by indigenous customary law) are not recognized by the legal system's intellectual property doctrines.

A 2003 *New York Times* article described Australian Aboriginal art as 'a hot commodity with a 30,000-year lineage',[137] but it is these

[135] Broader differences between mainstream intellectual property laws and indigenous methods of regulating ideas, information, and knowledge are discussed in more detail in Chapter 5, §5.2.

[136] See, eg, Angel R. Riley, 'Recovering Collectivity: Group Rights to Intellectual Property in Indigenous Communities', (2000) 18 *Cardozo Arts and Entertainment Law Journal* 175–225; Martha Woodmansee, 'On the Author Effect: Recovering Collectivity' (2000) *10 Cardozo Arts and Entertainment Law Journal* 279–292; Terence Dougherty, 'Group Rights to Cultural Survival: Intellectual Property Rights in Native American Cultural Symbols' (1998) 29 *Columbia Human Rights Law Review* 355–399; Richard Hertz, 'Legal Protection for Indigenous Cultures: Sacred Sites and Communal Rights' (1993) 79:3 *Virginia Law Review* 691–716; Robert Clinton, 'The Rights of Indigenous Peoples as Collective Group Rights' (1990) 32 *Arizona Law Review* 739–747; John Moustakas, 'Group Rights in Cultural Property: Justifying Strict Inalienability' (1990) 74 *Cornell Law Review* 1179–1227.

[137] Tony Clifton, 'A Hot Commodity with a 30,000-Year Lineage' (24 April 2003) *New York Times*, http://www.nytimes.com/2003/04/24/arts/a-hot-commodity-with-a-30000-year-lineage.html [last accessed 15 May 2010].

ancient roots that often cause difficulties for those who seek recognition under intellectual property law as the creators – 'authors' in copyright terminology – of indigenous works. As indigenous Australian lawyer Terri Janke explains:

> Indigenous knowledge systems form part of a living heritage. Indigenous knowledge systems contain a wealth of information including traditional knowledge of arts, craft, dance and cultural expressions, belief systems, customary laws, environmental knowledge of plants and animals and kinship systems. [They] have been handed down through the generations, mostly in oral form.... [U]nder Indigenous laws, knowledge may be held by one person, a family or community, and the right to share or disseminate that knowledge is subject to a complex system of consents. There is also a cultural obligation to pass on knowledge, and to guard its cultural integrity.[138]

Although it may cover many of the same types of objects as Western intellectual property law, the conception of creatorship found in customary 'lore' of this ilk often bears little resemblance to the intellectual property 'laws' operated by contemporary societies that have adopted the intellectual property standards required by treaties such as the *Agreement on Trade Related Aspects of Intellectual Property*. A case in point is copyright law.

Much indigenous creative work engages culturally and religiously significant symbols, motifs, and iconology, but the works are deemed 'unoriginal'[139] by copyright law because they comprise artistic 'vocabulary' that has previously been used in the same way by other authors and/or because their first use was so long ago that copyright would by now have expired, had it ever actually applied.

[138] Terri Janke, *Writing Up Indigenous Research: Authorship, Copyright and Indigenous Knowledge Systems* (Sydney: Terri Janke, 2009) at 8.

[139] See discussion of originality at §4.2.5. The work may also fail to satisfy copyright's 'originality' requirement because it is too similar to works in the artistic heritage to which it contributes. See discussion in Terri Janke, *Our Culture: Our Future: Report on Australian Indigenous Cultural and Intellectual Property* (Sydney: Michael Frankel, 1998) at 52, §5.2.2.

Moreover, copyright laws require the identification of an author, or joint authors, of a work. Many artistic, musical, dramatic, and literary works created by indigenous peoples cannot be traced to identifiable, individual authors that would be recognized by copyright law. Not only are many indigenous works created collectively, but the incremental and collaborative nature of those contributions by various creators may be made over numerous generations, resulting in a chronological period of creation and pattern of authorship that is not recognized by copyright law.

Copyright law recognizes works that an identifiable author has (or joint authors have) imbued with a recognized degree of labour, skill, and judgement,[140] and that have not been copied.[141] Many indigenous works – artistic, musical, literary, and dramatic alike – are created communally, gradually evolving as they are reproduced (retold, reperformed, or repainted) by younger generations who have inherited the cultural traditions of their elders and who in turn preserve those traditions for their descendants, sometimes building on them as they do. Such works may also fail to meet the copyright requirement for reproduction in a documented form, as indigenous literary works are often recorded as oral history and indigenous musical and dramatic works have often been passed from generation to generation through practice and performance, so there is no identifiable point at which the ideational object has been translated into a documented form by an author to become an intellectual property object. Without documentation in a material form, indigenous oral traditions and indigenous performance and musical traditions may fall outside the scope of modern copyright law.[142]

[140] See, eg, *of London Press Ltd v University Tutorial Press Ltd* [1916] 2 Ch. 601 at 608–609 (applicable in the United Kingdom and Australia).

[141] *Victoria Park Racing and Recreation Grounds Company Limited v Taylor* (1937) 58 CLR 479 at 511, per Dixon J (Aust.).

[142] Paradoxically, where these works *are* documented in a material form as required by copyright law, the 'author' recognized by copyright law may be a non-indigenous researcher who has recorded the music, drama, or stories by investing the labour, skill,

A graphic example of copyright's traditional discomfort with styles of creatorship that are typical of indigenous traditions is seen in the 1998 Australian case of *John Bulun Bulun & Anor v R & T Textiles Pty Ltd*,[143] in which copyright law was held to require a type of authorship that did not accord with the traditions of an indigenous Aboriginal community affected by alleged copyright infringement.

The case involved the importation into Australia from Indonesia of a fabric print depicting John Bulun Bulun's painting *Magpie Geese and Waterlilies at the Waterhole*. Aboriginal artist Bulun Bulun had not authorized this use of the artwork, and he argued that he held copyright in the painting only as a type of guardian, and that the unauthorized use of the painting appropriated indigenous law and custom of the Ganalbingu clan from North-Central Arnhem Land in Australia. Further, Bulun Bulun claimed that he was merely the custodian or curator of rights in the artwork that were held by the whole clan, a conception of creatorship quite removed from the Romantic, individualized 'author' of Western copyright law.

The court seemed sympathetic, but found otherwise:

> Whilst it is superficially attractive to postulate that the common law should recognise communal title, it would be contrary to established legal principle for the common law to do so. There seems no reason to doubt that customary Aboriginal laws relating to the ownership of artistic works survived the introduction of the common law of England in 1788. The Aboriginal peoples did not cease to observe their *sui generis* system of rights and obligations upon the acquisition of sovereignty of Australia by the Crown. The question however is whether those Aboriginal laws can create binding obligations on

and judgement to write them down or otherwise record them. For a discussion of the issues involved in such situations, see Janke, *Our Culture*, above n. 139.

[143] *John Bulun Bulun & Anor v R & T Textiles Pty Ltd* (1998) 157 ALR 193. For a discussion of this case, see Martin Hardie, 'The Bulun Bulun Case: John Bulun Bulun & Anor v R & T Textiles Pty Ltd' (1998) *Indigenous Law Bulletin* 87; (1998) 4:16 *Indigenous Law Bulletin* 24, http://www.austlii.edu.au/au/journals/ILB/1998/87.html (last accessed 12 May 2010).

> persons outside the relevant Aboriginal community, either through recognition of those laws by the common law, or by their capacity to found equitable rights *in rem*.... Copyright is now entirely a creature of statute. Section 35(2) of the Copyright Act 1968 (Cth) provides that the author of an artistic work is the owner of the copyright which subsists by virtue of the Act. That provision effectively precludes any notion of group ownership in an artistic work, unless the artistic work is a 'work of joint ownership' within the meaning of s10(1) of the Act. In this case no evidence was led to suggest that anyone other than Mr Bulun Bulun was the creative author of the artistic work.[144]

In this case, the Federal Court of Australia's Justice von Doussa noted that equity's principles concerning fiduciary duties may apply in some situations to protect the interests of those who have contributed to a collectively produced work.[145] In so finding, Justice von Doussa creatively discovered a de facto intellectual property right, albeit one not generally recognized as such by contemporary intellectual property law. One reason that this de facto intellectual property right would not be recognized as 'intellectual property' de jure is that it did not conform to the standard copyright definitions of individual or joint authorship. Another reason was that the incremental development over time of some of the artworks in question in cases such as *Bulun Bulun* would not meet the originality standards required by contemporary intellectual property laws.[146]

[144] *John Bulun Bulun & Anor v R & T Textiles Pty Ltd* (1998).

[145] Ibid: 'Whilst the nature of the relationship between Mr Bulun Bulun and the Ganalbingu people is such that Mr Bulun Bulun falls under fiduciary obligations to protect the ritual knowledge which he has been permitted to use, the existence of those obligations does not, without more, vest an equitable interest in the ownership of the copyright in the Ganalbingu people. Their primary right, in the event of a breach of obligation by the fiduciary is a right in personam to bring action against the fiduciary to enforce the obligation' (at 264).

[146] The concept of 'originality' is discussed at §4.2.5. See also reference to this case in Chapter 5, §5.2.2.a The issue of originality in the Bulun Bulun case is discussed in Colin Golvan, 'The Protection of *At the Waterhole* by John Bulun Bulun: Aboriginal Art and the Recognition of Private and Communal Rights', in Andrew T. Kenyon, Megan Richardson, and Sam Ricketson (eds.), *Landmarks in Australian Intellectual Property Law* (Melbourne: Cambridge University Press, 2009), 191–208 at 196–200; collective protection is discussed at 203–207.

Thus, copyright laws can fail to recognize types of quite common collective, collaborative creatorship, such as that typical of indigenous Aboriginal communities in Australia. This does not make those forms of creativity any less valuable to the society in which they exist or to the wider community. Nor does it make them any less respected by art critics. Perhaps it reflects policy decisions to devalue such forms of creatorship at law, although this may be by oversight rather than intentional choice, and it may also reflect the difficulties faced by individual legal systems that might otherwise recognize such forms of ownership but for rigid international treaty obligations. Whatever their effect or the reasons for their existence, the narrow definition of authorship in copyright law provides another illustration of a disjuncture between contemporary intellectual property laws and the ways in which works may in fact be created in society.

◆◆◆

A third case study, this time concerning patent law, gives yet another example of how intellectual property law's construction of creatorship may deviate from conceptions found in other parts of society. Like the trademark and copyright examples, patent law's rendering of creatorship – 'inventorship' – is subject to the criticism that it postulates an individualistic, Romantic view of creatorship and creativity that is divorced not only from the social and scientific context in which it operates, but also from the notion of 'authorship' found in copyright laws that operate alongside it. The issue of 'scientific authorship' further illustrates the limitations of intellectual property doctrines' adoption of the Romantic model of creatorship. In this case, the intellectual property doctrines in question are copyright and patent law.

4.2.4.g Scientific Authorship: A Case Study

Scientific journals are notorious for publishing articles listing numerous contributors as authors.[147] Indeed, sometimes the list of authors on

[147] See the discussion of this phenomenon in Mott Greene, 'The Demise of the Lone Author' (2007) 450 *Nature* 1165.

a scientific article runs to tens, hundreds, or even thousands of names.[148] Despite such lists, copyright law would not necessarily recognize all of the named authors as copyright 'authors' for the purposes of establishing rights to the intellectual property object created when the research (the ideational object) was put into an original 'documented form' by being written up for publication in the journal. The notion of authorship applied in such situations is often quite remote from that of copyright law.

Notions of scientific authorship vary within scientific communities,[149] but they tend to encompass the sorts of contributions set out in guidelines compiled by the US National Institutes of Health, which states that 'those persons designated as authors should make a significant contribution to the conceptualization, design, execution, and/or interpretation of the study, and [be] willing to accept responsibility for the study.'[150] Such notions of creatorship concentrate on a person's contribution to creating the content of the text that is embodied in the intellectual property object, and they thus diverge significantly from legal notions of creatorship under copyright law that protect only the expression of the article, not also the creation or use of the information that it expresses.[151] They

[148] For example, the following article used the name of the research group in the citation, listing 972 authors in an appendix: Investigators, The Gusto, 'An International Randomized Trial Comparing Four Thrombolytic Strategies for Acute Myocardial Infarction' (1993) 329:10 *New England Journal of Medicine* 673–682.

Another article lists 2,926 individual authors as part of a collaborative research group: Collaboration, The Atlas; G. Aad, E. Abat, J. Abdallah, et al., 'The ATLAS Experiment at the CERN Large Hadron Collider' (2008) *Journal of Instrumentation* 3, http://www.iop.org/EJ/abstract/1748–0221/3/08/S08003 [online journal, last accessed 24 January 2010].

[149] For a survey of different scientific conceptions of 'authorship' see, eg, Dale J. Benos, Jorge Fabres, John Farmer, Jessica P. Gutierrez, Kristin Hennessy, David Kosek, Joo Hyoung Lee, Dragos Olteanu, Tara Russell, Faheem Shaikh, and Kai Wang, 'Ethics and Scientific Publication' (2005) 29 *Advances in Physiology Education* 59–74.

[150] National Institutes of Health, Office of the Director, *Guidelines for the Conduct of Research in the Intramural Research Programs at NIH* (Committee on Scientific Conduct and Ethics, National Institutes of Health, Office of the Director, May 2007), http://www1.od.nih.gov/oir/sourcebook/ethic-conduct/Conduct%20Research%20 6–11–07.pdf [accessed 24 January 2010].

[151] Whether a collection of facts into a documented form (such as a database) qualifies for copyright protection is a vexing question. See, eg, *Feist Publications, Inc. v Rural*

also diverge from the legal conceptions of creatorship under patent law, which protects only novel inventions and innovations made by 'an inventor'. Understanding the social context in which they operate helps to clarify the reasons for the scientific conceptions, and they are therefore discussed in turn.

Scientific authorship principles reflect a variety of competing concerns, which could be summarized as primarily attributional and political. Scientific authorship principles have traditionally reflected legal concerns to a far lesser extent. Thus, scientific authorship and legal conceptions of creatorship do not necessarily coincide.

Scientific authorship's *attributional* impetus for listing someone as a creator accords with copyright law's moral right to attribution.[152] It reflects a person's individual contribution to the project discussed in the article, and that person's right to be acknowledged for having made this contribution.

The *political* impetuses for listing someone as a scientific author are more complicated. These are typically connected with the politics of academia and research funding. As Mott Greene comments:

> [I]n a world of clearly shared credit and hazily specified responsibility, [citation counts] as the principal means of establishing scientific prominence and reputation. No matter how many co-authors you have, the more times your name appears on a scientific publication, the more productive you are assumed to be, and the more worthy of support.[153]

The political impetus for including someone's byline in an article's list of authors – and his or her place in that list – can cause problematic

Telephone Service Co. (1991) 499 U.S. 340 (US) and *Nine Network Australia Pty Ltd v IceTV Pty Ltd* [2007] FCA 1172 (Aust.).

152 Art. 6*bis*, *Berne Convention for the Protection of Literary and Artistic Works* (as amended, 28 September 1979).

153 Greene, above n. 147. See also the discussion in Teja Tscharntke, Michael E. Hochberg, Tatyana A. Rand, Vincent H. Resh, and Jochen Krauss, 'Author Sequence and Credit for Contributions in Multiauthored Publications' (2007) 5:1 *Public Library of Science Biology* (*PLoS Biology*) 13–14.

outcomes, including litigation.[154] This has led to significant discussion in scientific communities. One key issue is that of 'first authorship'. Another is that of contribution.

The term 'first author' refers to the person whose byline appears first in the list of authors,[155] and it has traditionally implied status within the research group responsible for the outcome described in the article. It has been common practice for scientific journal articles to list the head of a research group (such as the professor who runs the laboratory in which the research occurred, or who obtained the funding that paid for the research) as 'first author' even though one or more students or post-doctoral fellowship holders may in fact have conducted the research and/or written the paper.[156] With appointments, promotion prospects, and opportunities to obtain future research grants often linked to the quantity and quality of publications 'authored' by a researcher, and sometimes determined by the frequency of citations, the implications of being cited as author of a scientific journal article – and thus being recognized as a person responsible for producing the research findings – can be important for the development of academic careers. The effect of distorting authorship lists with politically motivated 'first authorship' placements could thus be to disadvantage less prominent researchers and reinforce established hierarchies within the research field. It could also be misleading for copyright purposes.

The importance of byline position in listings of authors of scientific journal articles acquires even greater significance in the context of governmental research assessments[157] that count only 'first authorship'

[154] See, eg, Alison Abbott, 'Dispute over First Authorship Lands Researchers in Dock' (2002) 419 *Nature* 4.

[155] Don Riesenberg and George D. Lundberg, 'The Order of Authorship: Who's on First?' (1990) 264:14 *Journal of the American Medical Association* 1857.

[156] For reference to this tendency, see, eg, 'Authorship without Authorization' (editorial) (2004) 3:11 *Nature Materials* 743.

[157] For a discussion of this topic in the context of the 2007 'Research Assessment Exercise' in the United Kingdom (commonly referred to as the RAE), see Aziz Sheikh, 'Publication Ethics and the Research Assessment Exercise: Reflections on the Troubled Question of Authorship' (2000) 26 *Journal of Medical Ethics* 422–426.

listings,[158] effectively disregarding others who may have actually conducted the substantive scientific research or penned the journal article reporting it, and flying in the face of intellectual property principles. This issue has been recognized by scientific communities and has led to the publication of guidelines on the attribution of authorship.[159] For example, guidelines established by the Council of Science Editors rein in the definition of authorship, noting the difference between 'authorship' and 'contributorship', and limiting listings of authors to those who have been substantially involved in producing the article as either an author or contributor.[160] This method of attributing contributions to a publication has been likened to the system of listing credits at the end of a film.[161] It also moves closer to copyright's notions of 'joint ownership' that effectively depend on a 'but for' contribution.[162]

These guidelines extend beyond order of attribution to whether or not someone should be attributed as a scientific author or contributor at all. The Council of Science Editors has identified several forms of 'authorship' that are common to scientific publishing, which it seeks to shift outside the 'authorship' definition. In this sense, the scientific

[158] Agricultural economist Bruce McCarl notes that such quantitative assessments are sometimes conducted by reference only to the 'first author', thus discriminating against those whose names do not appear first on authorship lists. He offers the example of the Social Sciences Citation Index, a commercial service that provides statistical citation data. See Bruce A. McCarl, 'Citations and Individuals: First Authorship Across the Alphabet' (1993) 15:2 *Review of Agricultural Economics* 307–312 at 307.

[159] See, eg, American Medical Association, *American Medical Association Manual of Style: A Guide for Authors and Editors* (Oxford: Oxford University Press, 2007) at 128–140.

[160] See, eg, the Council of Science Editors Editorial Policy Committee, *White Paper on Promoting Integrity in Scientific Journal Publications, 2009 Update* (2009), http://www.councilscienceeditors.org/editorial_policies/whitepaper/entire_whitepaper.pdf [accessed 23 January 2010].

[161] 'A third, radical, response is to scrap the concept of authorship. Instead, we would have a descriptive system something like film credits and talk about contributors rather than authors.' See Richard Smith, 'Authorship: Time for a Paradigm Shift?' (editorial) (1997) 314 *British Medical Journal* 992.

[162] That is, 'but for' the contribution of [name author] this particular work would not have been created.

definition of authorship would become more aligned with the Romantic-style authorship that is recognized by the creatorship conceptions of copyright and patent law.[163]

The practices that the Council of Science Editors wishes to exclude from the authorship definition include the following:

- *Guest authorship*: This occurs when the named 'guest' author has made no discernible contributions to the content of the article, but her or his byline is included to improve the publishability or status of the article.[164] A study by Susan Eastwood et al. in the mid-1990s found that a third of respondents would be 'willing to cite an undeserving author if it would help publication of their work or enhance their career.'[165] The pervasiveness of guest (and 'ghost'; see the following definition) authorship in scientific scholarship became evident during litigation concerning the possible liability of the pharmaceutical company Merck, which had employees ghost-write articles before engaging academic researchers who were bylined and thus posed as the authors.[166] Guest authorship has been a long-standing practice in scientific circles but bears no resemblance to copyright notions of 'authorship' or patent law's 'inventorship'. Indeed, the practice of guest

[163] Frank Davidoff, 'Who's the Author? Problems with Biomedical Authorship and Some Possible Solutions', *Report to the Council of Biology Editors (Now Council of Science Editors) from the Task Force on Authorship* (February 2000), available at the website of the Council of Science Editors, http://www.councilofscienceeditors.org/publications/v23n4p111-119.pdf [accessed 24 January 2010].

[164] Ibid.

[165] S. Eastwood, P. Derish, E. Leash, and S. Ordway, 'Ethical Issues in Biomedical Research: Perceptions and Practices of Postdoctoral Research Fellows Responding to a Survey' (1996) 2 *Science and Engineering Ethics* 89–114, cited in an editorial by Richard Horton and Richard Smith, 'Time to Redefine Authorship' (1996) 312 *British Medical Journal* 723.

[166] See, eg, Joseph S. Ross, Kevin P. Hill, David S. Egilman, and Harlan M. Krumholz, 'Guest Authorship and Ghostwriting in Publications Related to Rofecoxib: A Case Study of Industry Documents from Rofecoxib Litigation' (2008) 299:15 *Journal of the American Medical Association* 1800–1812.

authorship conflicts with copyright law's moral rights prohibition on false attribution of copyright-protected works.[167]

- *Ghost authorship*: This occurs when people who have made substantive contributions to conducting or writing up the research are not named as authors. This may involve, for example, junior staff members who write for their employers, or employees of pharmaceutical companies.[168] The Merck guest authorship example in the preceding paragraph also illustrates how ghost authorship can operate. Not only is ghost authorship unethical, it is also a breach of copyright's subdoctrine of moral rights to attribution as the author of a copyright-protected work.
- *Honorary or gift authorship*: This occurs when the named 'honorary' author has only a 'tenuous affiliation' with the research written up in the article, such as a professor who is the head of the department at the university where the research was conducted but who had no personal role in undertaking the research.[169] In the Eastwood study previously referred to, around half of the researchers surveyed said they would attribute an 'authorship' citation to the laboratory head, and 44 percent said they would grant authorship to those who obtained funding.[170] Yet, as with guest authorship, representing that someone is an author on the basis only of their role in an institution conflicts with copyright's moral right against false attribution. It also sits uncomfortably with patent law's requirement that a named 'inventor' be someone who actually devises the invention[171] by having a material effect on the invention's final concept.[172]

[167] See, eg, Australian *Copyright Act* 1968 (Cth), s.195AC(1): 'The author of a work has a right not to have authorship of the work falsely attributed.'

[168] Davidoff, above n. 163.

[169] Ibid. at 4.

[170] Eastwood, Derish, Leash, and Ordway, above n. 165.

[171] See, eg, UK *Patents Act* 1977, s.7(3).

[172] See *Row Weeder Pty Ltd v Nielsen* (1998) IPR 400 at 405.

Each of these conventions of scientific authorship involves a misattribution that results in the list of authors on an associated publication conflicting with copyright's definition of authorship and moral rights, as well as patent law's definition of inventorship, not to mention notions of scholarly integrity.[173] While the scientific conventions may also conflict with the individualistic notions of creatorship found in intellectual property law, their disjunction with copyright and patent law arguably stems from a different source. The collaborative notion of creatorship reflected in such conventions is based at least partly on the practical and political realities of modern scientific enterprise. It reflects the complex ways in which scientific endeavour is carried out, as well as the numerous people who are involved in various ways and without whom the research findings would not eventuate. It reflects a desire or need – whether heartfelt or politically motivated – to acknowledge these contributions, and it thus serves a purpose that differs from intellectual property law's conceptions of creatorship. As a result, the collaborative conceptions of authorship attribution in scientific publishing do not always sit comfortably with the Romantic-style conception of 'authorship' found in copyright, or with the 'inventorship' of patent law. This causes a disjuncture between scientific publishing and intellectual property law.

In an attempt to stamp out unacceptable forms of 'authorship' attributions from scientific publications, the esteemed scientific journal *Proceedings of the National Academy of Sciences of the United States of America* now follows an editorial policy that states, '*Authorship* should

[173] For further discussions of gift and ghost authorship, see, eg, Annette Flanagin, Lisa A. Carey, Phil B. Fontanarosa, et al., 'Prevalence of Articles with Honorary Authors and Ghost Authors in Peer-Reviewed Medical Journals' (1998) 280:3 *Journal of the American Medical Association* 222–224; Drummond Rennie and Annette Flanagin, 'Authorship! Authorship! Guests, Ghosts, Grafters, and the Two-Sided Coin' (1994) 271:6 *Journal of the American Medical Association* 469–471; Elizabeth Wager, 'Bye Bye By-line, Hello Contributors' (2006) 99 *Journal of the Royal Society of Medicine* 542–543.

be limited to those who have contributed substantially to the work.'[174] Indeed, many reputable scientific journals have started requiring that all named authors specify their respective contributions to the work. For example, the leading medical journal *The Lancet* asks 'all authors, and all contributors (including medical writers and editors), to specify their individual contributions at the end of the text',[175] as does the *Journal of the American Medical Association*.[176] This is the approach also taken by the International Committee of Medical Journal Editors (known as the 'Vancouver Group'), which defines an author as 'someone who has made substantive intellectual contributions to a published study'.[177] Meanwhile, the *British Medical Journal* has adopted a policy called 'Authorship and Contributorship' that states:

> We now list contributors in two ways. Firstly, we publish a list of authors' names at the beginning of the paper and, secondly, we list contributors (some of whom may not be included as authors) at the

[174] This policy can be found on the publication's website at http://www.pnas.org/site/misc/iforc.shtml#ii [accessed 23 January 2010]. Emphasis in original.

[175] 'Information for Authors', *The Lancet* (January 2010). These guidelines are available on the journal's website at http://download.thelancet.com/flatcontentassets/authors/lancet-information-for-authors.pdf[accessed 24 January 2010].

[176] See Drummond Rennie, Annette Flanagin, and Veronica Yank, 'The Contributions of Authors' (2000) 284 *Journal of the American Medical Association* 89–91: 'To provide information on the work done by authors and to resolve the inconsistency between the information provided for those named in the byline vs those listed in the Acknowledgment, *JAMA* will begin requiring authors to indicate specific contributions for all those involved in the manuscript. Consequently, authors will be required to describe their specific contributions as well as the contributions of those acknowledged but not listed in the byline' (at 89).

[177] International Committee of Medical Journal Editors, *Uniform Requirements for Manuscripts Submitted to Biomedical Journals: Writing and Editing for Biomedical Publication* (October 2008) at 2. The policy continues: 'Some journals now request and publish information about the contributions of each person named as having participated in a submitted study, at least for original research. Editors are strongly encouraged to develop and implement a contributorship policy, as well as a policy on identifying who is responsible for the integrity of the work as a whole.' This policy is available from *The Lancet* website at http://www.download.thelancet.com/flatcontentassets/authors/icmje.pdf [accessed 24 January 2010].

end of the paper, giving details of who did what in planning, conducting, and reporting the work.[178]

The classic forms of scientific authorship misattribution previously outlined (ie, guest, ghost, or honorary/gift authorship) conflicted with principles of scientific integrity and transparency, and each of these approaches attempts to minimize the misleading aspects of those forms of misattribution by shifting the focus to the actual author(s) and/or contributor(s). As Michel Foucault noted, scientific scholarship is accepted as reliable ('authoritative') only when it is associated with the name of an author.[179] To associate research with the name of someone who is not actually an author is confusing and undermines its authority.

In attempting to remove the classic forms of misattribution, the reforms also help to shift the notions of 'scientific authorship' closer to the creatorship conceptions found within copyright and patent law. This is a sensible move by publishers wishing to protect themselves legally, as the forms of misattribution that had become so common in scientific publishing were also likely to infringe aspects of copyright law (affecting the subsistence of copyright in the work, as well as increasing the likelihood that the legal author's moral rights may be breached as a result of inaccurate authorship citations), and were likely to be inconsistent with nominations of the 'inventor(s)' on related patents. As correct nomination of the inventor(s) is typically required for registration of a valid

[178] This policy is based on principles set out in an editorial by Richard Smith, 'Authorship Is Dying; Long Live Contributorship' (1997) 315 *British Medical Journal* 696. The policy is available on the *British Medical Journal* website: http://resources.bmj.com/bmj/authors/article-submission/authorship-contributorship [accessed 24 January 2010]. Letters to the editor in response to this statement shed light on the various perceptions of authorship, and the political issues related to authorship, among readers of the *British Medical Journal*. See 'Authorship' (letter to the editor) (1997) 315 *British Medical Journal* 744. See also Raj Bhopal, Judith Rankin, Elaine McColl, Lois Thomas, Eileen Kaner, Rosie Stacy, Pauline Pearson, Brian Vernon, and Helen Rodgers, 'The Vexed Question of Authorship: Views of Researchers in a British Medical Faculty' (1997) 314 *British Medical Journal* 1009.

[179] Foucault, 'What Is an Author?' above n. 47 at 109.

patent, inconsistencies between scientific authorship and legal conceptions of creatorship could conceivably contribute to the rejection of a patent application, and thus the failure to convert an ideational object into an intellectual property object. This leads to the third, and perhaps – in reality – the least influential, category of impetuses for deciding who should be cited as an author: the *legal* impetus.

Even scrupulously accurate authorship lists that indicate the relative contribution of each named author to a research project or the writing up of a scientific article[180] may not coincide with the legal conceptions of authorship that are applied under copyright law to the article in which the research is written up. They may also fail to coincide with the equivalent legal conception applied under patent law to any inventions arising from the research (although at least they are not likely to undermine the ability of those recognized by intellectual property law as authors to claim those rights). This is because the legal conceptions found in intellectual property law reflect policy decisions that privilege the Romantic idea of individual creatorship, or maybe co-creatorship. As noted earlier, intellectual property does not cope well with the demands of what is, in effect, collective creatorship. For example, in order to be regarded as a joint author of a copyright work under Australian law, it is necessary to have produced the work in collaboration between two or more people, where 'the contribution of each author is not separate from the contribution of the other author or the contributions of the other authors.'[181] Having conducted the research that is then written up by someone else would not usually qualify someone as a copyright author under this law.[182]

[180] For example, the Council of Science Editors has published 'group authorship' guidelines regarding appropriate attribution of various contributors to a research project. This document is entitled *CSE Recommendations for Group-Author Articles in Scientific Journals and Bibliometric Databases* and is available at its website: http://www.councilofscienceeditors.org/publications/group_authorship.pdf [accessed 24 January 2010].

[181] *Copyright Act* 1968 (Aust.), s.10; 'Work of Joint Authorship'.

[182] See, eg, *Donoghue v Allied Newspapers* (1938) Ch. 106 (UK), where a journalist attracted copyright in the version of a story that he wrote up, even though the story had been told to him by an interviewee.

Writing up the research in the form of drafting the specifications and claims necessary for patent registration would probably give a person copyright over that material but would not qualify the author (often a patent attorney) to be regarded as an 'inventor' – patent law's version of the creator – for patent registration purposes. Rather, the inventor would be the person(s) who conducted the research. The difference between this intellectual property conception of creatorship and the traditional scientific conventions is also quite distinct.

Clearly the conventions of scientific publishing have grown in a particular context and have been evolving to meet the needs of the readership they serve. Likewise, intellectual property conceptions of creatorship evolved in specific legal contexts, and they serve the purpose of establishing ownership rights, which are typically obtained by only one creator or a very small group of identifiable creators who made certain types of collaborations. There is arguably no particular need for the scientific and legal conceptions of creatorship to coincide (although it would almost certainly reduce confusion, particularly among scientists who may not have been educated in intellectual property law's requirements), just as there was arguably no particular need for branding or literary studies' conceptions of creatorship to coincide with the legal conceptions. To the extent that the legal norms do not coincide with common practices that have evolved in various other disciplines and social systems, the differing conceptions of creatorship displayed in these case studies simply indicate disparities between intellectual property law's conceptions of creatorship and those that operate elsewhere in society.

4.2.4.h Conclusion

In summary, intellectual property creatorship generally depends on intentional communication in a documented form by a creator. The conceptions of creatorship found in social systems[183] other than law are often

[183] The notion of social systems is discussed by Niklas Luhmann, *Social Systems* (Stanford, CA: Stanford University Press, 1996).

broader and more collaborative than this. Like the literary critique of authorship, they leave intellectual property's conceptions of the creator open to challenge and strong criticism by those who perceive the reader or consumer of communication to be also a creator because it is that recipient who interprets and chooses the meaning of the communication. They also leave intellectual property's creatorship conceptions open to challenge by those who would see 'contributorship' as a more relevant basis than Romantic-style 'authorship' for divvying up reputational, financial, and other rewards.

Mark Lemley has suggested (in a copyright context) that analysing 'Romantic authorship' conceptions yields relatively little information about the nature of copyright or why it has evolved into its current forms, and efforts would perhaps be more fruitful if diverted to an analysis of economic explanations of intellectual property.[184] However, even if creatorship does not provide normative explanations of the contemporary forms of copyright, designs, patent, or trademark law, its presence in each of these classic intellectual property doctrines arguably provides useful insight into the ontology of intellectual property as a department of law. Examining the common role that creatorship plays in these doctrines helps to shed light on the nature of intellectual property more generally.

Within the various doctrines of intellectual property law, the ultimate and common role of the creator seems to be to determine who obtains proprietary rights, and there would appear to be little room for collective, collaborative, or incremental creatorship in an intellectual property system premised on notions of individualistic creation. On this view, social contributions to the meaning of an intellectual property object are marginalized by intellectual property laws, as are broader and less direct contributions to the development of an invention or copyright work.

There seems to be no practical need to restrict intellectual property creatorship in this way. If ownership of intellectual property rights can be

[184] Mark A. Lemley, 'Romantic Authorship and the Rhetoric of Property' (1997) 75 *Texas Law Review* 873–906.

shared or apportioned among proprietors contractually, there seems little reason – other than in the interests of simplicity, a goal overlooked by law (including intellectual property law) in many other contexts – to arbitrarily limit who can be intellectual property's creators. Yet intellectual property's creatorship conceptions have remained remarkably resistant to change. Until such change occurs, the conclusion can reasonably be drawn that the Romantic notion of creatorship – however flawed and out of sync with the social practices by which works are created in practice – still lies very much at the heart of intellectual property doctrines.

Thus, the intellectual property system produces its own objects of regulation, in part by creating its own conceptions of creatorship. It defines which creative people it will recognize as creators and in which situations. These definitions may not accord with the notions of creatorship and creativity that operate in non-legal social contexts, but that is largely irrelevant for the purposes of intellectual property. Intellectual property law determines the classifications that will be used to regulate intellectual property objects, including the identification of creators to whom property rights will usually be allocated. Distinctions that attribute some creators and exclude others are constructed within the intellectual property system for regulatory purposes. These may be artificial and arbitrary when viewed in their social and cultural contexts, but they are legitimated by the pragmatic legal function they serve. As such, the various conceptions of creatorship found within intellectual property doctrines (such as copyright's 'author', patent law's 'inventor', and design law's 'designer') help to construct and reinforce the nature of intellectual property law. As non–intellectual property creatorship traditions are marginalized because creators who do not coincide with one of intellectual property law's creatorship conceptions risk missing out on rewards, creative work is increasingly conducted with a view to meeting the requirements of relevant intellectual property laws. Intellectual property law thus constructs and reinforces the creatorship concepts – such as 'authorship' and 'inventorship' – that comprise it and that are used to define its objects of regulation. This is a key feature of intellectual property doctrines, which are arguably constructed around, and themselves construct, the core conceptual criteria of an ideational object, documented form, creatorship, and originality.

4.2.5. Originality

Like the word 'authorship', the word 'originality' is closely associated with copyright concepts, even though different versions of 'originality' that are known by different names are found across the intellectual property spectrum. This may well reflect the historical development of the various doctrines. For example, copyright and design law share a close history, having separated into independent doctrines in the late eighteenth century. This entwined history could help to account for similarities between the conceptions of originality found in copyright and design law. Meanwhile, design and patent law also share very similar conceptions of originality, which may in turn be due partly to their historical categorization as 'industrial property law' and their presence together in the *Paris Convention for the Protection of Industrial Property* (1883). Even though the conceptions of originality found in modern copyright, design, and patent law are prima facie different, they serve common functions and share many similarities.

In many intellectual property contexts, the terms 'originality' and 'novelty' are used to indicate that a creation is new – in the sense that something identical or very similar has not previously existed in this form in society – having been produced by the creator (whichever conception of creatorship applies, depending on the doctrine in question). Thus, much analysis of originality is closely linked to the notion of creatorship, and there is no need to repeat that analysis here.[185] However, rather than 'originality' being left as the other side of the creatorship coin, as is often the case, three additional issues are worthy of recognition:

[185] See §4.2.4.

- the similarity of doctrinal treatments of originality within intellectual property law;
- the relationship between originality and the public domain; and
- the extent to which anything can ever truly be said to be original.

These points help to demonstrate that intellectual property's conceptions of 'originality' are often divorced from the social understandings of the way in which intellectual property objects and their documented forms are constructed.

4.2.5.a Similar Doctrinal Approaches to Originality

Various intellectual property doctrines incorporate 'originality' standards, and these arguably have a common theme. Copyright law demonstrates well the concept and its ambiguity.

Although English copyright law's statute was traditionally silent on the meaning of 'originality', the term was defined by case law. The 1916 UK copyright case of *University of London Press Ltd v University Tutorial Press Ltd* defined 'originality' to mean that a work should 'originate from the author'.[186] However, this does little to elucidate the nature of either creatorship ('authorship' in copyright law) or originality, as it does not identify how different from pre-existing works a creation must be to qualify as 'original'. As already noted, in practice a work is original for copyright purposes if the author has invested the appropriate type and amount of 'labour, skill and judgment' to create the work, and if it has not been copied. Such practical lists are perhaps more helpful, although they inevitably result in questions about the degree to which an author can be influenced by another work before his or her creation is deemed to have been copied and is regarded as unoriginal.

Copyright legislation in the United States protects 'original works of authorship fixed in a tangible medium of expression' but it leaves the

[186] *University of London Press Ltd v University Tutorial Press Ltd* [1916] 2 Ch. 601 at 608.

phrase 'original works of authorship' undefined.[187] A 1976 House Report stated, 'The phrase "original works of authorship", which is purposely left undefined, is intended to incorporate without change the standard of originality established by the courts under the present copyright statute.'[188] In practice, this has been defined by the US Supreme Court to mean 'that the work was independently created by the author (as opposed to copied from other works),[189] and that it possesses at least some minimal degree of creativity.'[190] 'Some minimal degree of creativity' means that the work need only 'possess some creative spark, "no matter how crude, humble, or obvious it might be".'[191] It excludes a 'mere mechanical reproduction' of an earlier work[192] or a purported work that consists of only a word or short phrase,[193] but it otherwise sets a low threshold for originality. The possible exception to this low threshold is found with respect to a 'derivative work' (one that incorporates an existing work or works), which may require a higher degree of creativity that is more than trivial,[194] and which has sufficient originality in itself once the originality of the work(s) on which it is built is disregarded. In the words of Justice Posner, for a derivative work to be original, there must be 'a sufficiently gross difference between the underlying and the derivative work to avoid entangling subsequent artists depicting the underlying work in copyright problems.'[195]

[187] United States: 17 USCA §102(a). See commentary in M. B. Nimmer, P. Marcus, D. A. Myers, and D. Nimmer, *Cases and Materials on Copyright and Other Aspects of Entertainment Litigation Including Unfair Competition, Defamation, Privacy* (St. Paul, Minn.: West, 1991) at 2.

[188] *United States of America: H R Report*, No. 94–1476, 94th Congress, 2d Session (1976).

[189] For a discussion of the treatment of the 'originality' conception in the various contexts under US copyright law, see Jeffrey Malkan, 'What Is a Copy?' (2005) 23 *Cardozo Arts and Entertainment Law Journal* 419–463.

[190] *Feist Publications, Inc. v Rural Telephone Service Co.* (1991) 499 U.S. 340 at 355.

[191] Ibid. at 349.

[192] *Burrow-Giles Lithographic Co. v Sarony*, 111 U.S. 53 (1884); *Bridgeman Art Library v Corel Corp.*, 36 F. Supp. 2d 191 (S.D.N.Y. 1999).

[193] See also *Exxon Corporation v Exxon insurance Consultants International* [1982] 1 Ch. 119 (UK).

[194] *Durham Industries, Inc. v Tomy Corp.*, 630 F.2d 905 (2d Cir. 1980) at 909.

[195] *Gracen v Bradford Exchange*, 698 F.2d 300 (7th Cir. 1983) at 305, per Posner J. See discussion of this case in Steven S. Boyd, 'Deriving Originality in Derivative Works:

Despite these guidelines, the nature of 'originality' in copyright law tends to remain vague. What is an original work? (And, therefore, who is an author?)

The same problem can be found throughout intellectual property's classic doctrines. 'Originality' functions to distinguish newly created intellectual property objects from existing intellectual property objects, and originality conceptions operate in a similar manner in the various intellectual property doctrines.

To take Australian intellectual property law as an example, similar conceptions of originality can be found in copyright, patent, design, and trademark law. In Australian copyright law, *original* creations are protected by copyright,[196] while other works – such as copies – fall into the public domain,[197] where they can usually be used by anyone, anytime, and for any purpose. In Australian patent law, *novel* inventions are those that meet a required standard of originality when compared with the existing body of knowledge (known as the 'prior art'). Similarly, the *novel* designs that may be protected by registered design rights in Australia are, in effect, those displaying sufficient originality when compared with pre-existing designs. And the *distinctive* signs that may be registered as Australian trademarks because they are neither identical nor similar to an existing trademark (and usually are not applied to similar goods and/or services as an existing similar trademark) are, in effect, signs that are sufficiently original in the way in which they are used. In each case, whether or not a documented ideational object is sufficiently original is determined by the rules of the doctrine in question.

Considering the Quantum of Originality Needed to Attain Copyright Protection in a Derivative Work' (1999–2000) 40 *Santa Clara Law Review* 325–378 at 362–365.

[196] The legal standard of originality in Australian copyright law is discussed in Patricia Loughlan, 'Qualitative Standards for the Protection of Literary and Artistic Works', in Alice Ehr-Soon Tay and Conita S. Leung (eds.), *Australian Law and Legal Thinkers in the 1990s: A Collection of 32 Australian Reports to the XIVth International Congress of Comparative Law* (Athens, 31 July–6 August 1994) at 263. For a more general discussion of 'originality' see F. Meltzer, *Hot Property: The Stakes and Claims of Literary Originality* (Chicago: University of Chicago Press, 1994).

[197] See the discussion at §4.2.5.b.

Intellectual property objects are thus created from ideational objects with respect to which a sufficient degree of originality can be demonstrated when they are put into a documented form. Unoriginal texts, inventions, designs, commercial symbols, and potential subject matter of other intellectual property doctrines remain in the public domain. The definition and required standard of originality may vary according to jurisdiction, doctrine, and historical context, but the concept of originality – and the difficulty of delineating exactly when something is or is not original – remains a common, prominent, and enduring feature of intellectual property doctrines.

4.2.5.b Originality and the Public Domain

The notion of originality arguably arose as a conceptual boundary to divide new intellectual property objects from existing ones, and to differentiate privately owned works from those in the public domain.[198]

Sometimes referred to as 'the commons', the 'public domain' has been described as an 'elastic and inexact' term,[199] with a variety of meanings.[200] It is often used as a concept that encompasses ideational objects and their documented forms that are not covered by monopoly rights granted by intellectual property laws.[201] It is thus the non–intellectual property side[202] of the proverbial 'copyright balance',[203] and the non–intellectual

198 See S. Ricketson, 'The Concept of Originality in Anglo-Australian Copyright Law' (1991) 9 *Journal of the Copyright Society of Australia* 265–288; Jessica Litman, 'The Public Domain' (1990) 39 *Emory Law Journal* 965–1024 at 974–975.

199 David Lange, 'Reimagining the Public Domain' (2003) 66 *Law and Contemporary Problems* 463–483 at 463. See also David Lange, 'Recognizing the Public Domain' (1981) 44 *Law and Contemporary Problems* 147–178; and see the discussion in James Boyle, 'The Second Enclosure Movement and the Construction of the Public Domain', (2003) 66 *Law and Contemporary Problems* 33 at 59.

200 Lange, "Reimagining', above n. 199 at 483.

201 See, eg, the discussion in ibid. at 464; and Ronan Deazley, *Rethinking Copyright: History, Theory, Language* (Cheltenham: Edward Elgar, 2006) at 103.

202 James Boyle, 'Forward: The Opposite of Property' (2003) 66 *Law and Contemporary Problems* 1–32.

203 The 'copyright balance' is described by Gillian Davies, *Copyright and the Public Interest* (London: Sweet & Maxwell, 2002) at 7: 'The copyright system as it has developed

property side of equivalent balances in other areas of intellectual property law, that supposedly reach equilibrium by balancing the public interest in having access to ideas, information, and knowledge against the private interest in monopolizing the opportunity to profit from the ideas, information, and knowledge that one gives to society.

The attractiveness of private monopoly rights is supposed to function as an incentive for creators to make and release their work into society. The public domain is a little like a special intellectual property doctrine – additional to copyright, patents, trademarks, and so on – that draws together those results of creative output that are not collected by any of the other intellectual property doctrines and places them outside private ownership. It is like a safety net under the intellectual property rubric that catches all the material that is not gathered up by any other doctrine (eg, material that did not meet minimum creatorship or originality standards and was therefore not converted into a regular intellectual property object). In other words, material that is not intellectual propertized by one of the classic or sui generis doctrines falls by default into the public domain.

In his seminal article describing the public domain, David Lange defined it as 'a place of sanctuary for individual creative expression, a sanctuary conferring affirmative protection against the forces of private appropriation that threatened such expression'.[204] The public domain is therefore a concept describing material that may have some, but not all, of the attributes of intellectual property objects – an ideational object, a documented form, creatorship, and originality – and

over the past nearly 300 years, has created, in the public interest, a balance between the rights of the authors, on the one hand, and the interest of the public in access to protected works, on the other.... This balance has been described in Article 27 of the Universal Declaration of Human Rights which provides: (i) everyone has the right freely to participate in the cultural life of the Community, to enjoy the arts and to share in scientific advancement and its benefits; (ii) everyone has the right to the protection of the moral and material interests resulting from any scientific, literary or artistic production of which he is an author.'

[204] Lange, 'Reimagining', above n. 199 at 466.

that therefore does not qualify as an object of regulation by intellectual property law.[205]

With respect specifically to the core intellectual property concept of 'originality', the role of the public domain is clear. Rather than being regarded as private intellectual property, material that is not original falls by default into the 'public domain'. In the United States, the United Kingdom, and Australia alike, this includes material that was never eligible for intellectual property, such as commercial symbols that were too descriptive to be used as trademarks or that were unregistrable due to their obscene nature, inventions that were too similar to other inventions that could be found in the prior art, and literary or musical works that were too similar to earlier works. It also includes material whose term of intellectual property protection has expired, such as inventions that were patented more than twenty years ago, trademarks whose registration has not been renewed or that have become generic and have thus been removed from the register, and artistic works produced by creators who died more than seventy years ago and whose copyright period has therefore lapsed. Jessica Litman argues that the public domain thus fortifies copyright law and its core concept of originality:

> The public domain … permits us to continue to exalt originality without acknowledging that our claims to take originality seriously are mostly pretense. It furnishes a crucial device to an otherwise unworkable system by reserving the raw material of authorship to the commons, thus leaving that raw material available for other authors to use. The public domain thus permits the law of copyright to avoid a confrontation with the poverty of some of the assumptions on which it is based.[206]

Unoriginal material resides in the public domain, where it is available to anyone to use freely. It is 'the commons' of ideas, information, knowledge,

[205] See Chapter 5 for examples of such material. However, note that even when not covered by 'intellectual property' law, material that is nonetheless covered by other departments of law may not be left in the public domain.

[206] Litman, above n. 198 at 1023.

and symbols. By taking from the commons and adding something new that is not owned by anyone, a creator can produce something that would itself qualify for intellectual property protection. The constant – and perhaps greatest – difficulty for intellectual property doctrines is determining the point at which a creation passes the originality threshold and qualifies for intellectual property protection, thus transforming in status from an article in the public domain to an item of private property. The conceptual fence around the public domain depends on the threshold points at which sufficient originality is added to material that already exists in society, to qualify for protection under one or more intellectual property doctrines.

4.2.5.c Is Anything Original?

Originality is not an unproblematic concept. The well-known phrase that there is 'nothing new under the sun'[207] captures the spirit of strong objections to originality, which are also tied clearly to the difficulties raised by intellectual property's conceptions of creatorship. Post-structural critiques of the Romantic author, and criticisms of intellectual property's failure to adequately recognize collaborative creatorship, are also associated with flaws in the concept of pure originality.

The requirement that original thought or expression be attributed to a creator strains the meaning of 'original' when most thought and expression is highly dependent on the socio-cultural influences to which the thinker's mind/brain has been exposed. As Story J commented with respect to the implausibility of a pure authorship conception in the US copyright case of *Emerson v Davies* (1845):

> In truth, in literature, in science and in art, there are, and can be, few, if any, things, which in an abstract sense, are strictly new and original throughout. Every book in literature, science, and art, borrows, and

[207] Rosalind Fergusson, *The Penguin Dictionary of Proverbs* (Harmondsworth: Penguin Books, 1983), ¶17.40 (at 23).

> must necessarily borrow, and use much which was well known and used before.[208]

By affording protection to the documented form rather than the ideational object, it is less the originality of the thought or idea than the originality of the documented form into which it is translated that intellectual property doctrines reward. This is reflected across the spectrum of intellectual property doctrines by the operation of such concepts as 'originality' in copyright law, 'novelty' in design and patent law, 'inventiveness' in patent law, and 'distinctiveness' in trademark law. Each rewards an original way of putting a thought into a documented form, rather than originality per se. Originality thus seems to be a common concept unifying various doctrines under the intellectual property umbrella. It is a common familial trait[209] that functions as a core conceptual feature of intellectual property doctrines.

However, intellectual property law's notions of an *original* work (copyright), *novel* invention or design (patent/design), and *dissimilar* sign (trademark) are arguably disingenuous to the extent that each fails to acknowledge the social context in which thought and expression build on prior expressive influences. Each awards proprietorship only over material that represents an advance over what existed before it came into being. It is this gap between what existed previously and what is covered by the new work that is regarded as 'original' and rewarded by intellectual property laws. However, as noted earlier, deciding where to place the boundary between the old and the new is not a simple matter.

This issue is perhaps most problematic when a new work has been created by presenting an old work in a new way or by mixing several old works in a new way that leaves recognizable parts of the old works in the new one. Such situations are common. Examples include the discovery of a new use for an old invention,[210] the application of an iconic cultural symbol as

[208] *Emerson v Davies*, 8 F.Cas 615 at 619 (CCD Mass, 1845), per Story J.

[209] See references to Ludwig Wittgenstein on 'family resemblance' in Chapter 5, §5.1.

[210] A controversial example of this is patent 'evergreening', where a patent is awarded over a new use for an old or known drug. This can effectively extend the patent period of a pharmaceutical. For a discussion of patent evergreening in an Australian context,

a brand for a business or product,[211] and the mixing of old, familiar pieces of music to create a new piece of music.[212] Appropriation art and music sampling are obvious examples of situations in which originality conundrums arise. The difficulty in each such case is to decide the point at which the old becomes new, and thus at which originality begins. From a policy perspective, the difficulty is to define how much and what sort of originality is required before intellectual property law rewards it with monopoly rights over its use. The difficulty is to determine the boundary between the old and the new. Policy determinants are not always clear.

Perhaps 'originality' is a concept that only masquerades as an objective standard used to distinguish ideational objects from intellectual property objects in order to satisfy politically motivated goals that are not necessarily explicit, and that may express rationales that diverge from those offered for the relevant legal principle itself. With respect to copyright law, Diane Zimmerman suggests:

> What looms behind the door marked 'originality' is a question that is rarely acknowledged by the courts and never definitively answered: what exactly is the purpose of copyright? What values are we protecting and why? Until that question is finally answered as a legal matter, it will remain impossible ... to identify and defend the level of required 'creativity'.[213]

see Robert Chalmers, 'Evergreen or Deciduous: Australian Trends in Relation to the Evergreening of Patents' (2006) 30 *Melbourne University Law Review* 29–61.

211 Such as the use of 'Nike' (the name of the ancient winged Greek goddess of victory) to sell sporting goods. The goddess had appeared on medals won by Olympic athletes since 1928, portrayed holding a palm and waving a victor's laurel wreath crown above her head. In 1978 sporting goods company Blue Ribbons Sports changed its name to Nike, Inc., after early success marketing a model of shoe that bore the goddess of victory's name. For a discussion of this topic, see David Jary, 'The McDonaldization of Sport and Leisure', in Barry Smart (ed.), *Resisting McDonaldization* (London: Sage, 1999), 116–134 at 125; Robert Goldman and Stephen Papson, *Nike Culture: The Sign of the Swoosh* (London: Sage, 1998).

212 See, eg, Olufunmilayo B. Arewa, 'From J. C. Bach to Hip Hop: Musical Borrowing, Copyright and Cultural Context' (2005–2006) 84 *North Carolina Law Review* 547–645.

213 Diane Zimmerman, 'It's an Original!(?): In Pursuit of Copyright's Elusive Essence' (2005) 28 *Columbia Journal of Law and the Arts* 187–212 at 189.

Such objections may undermine the integrity of intellectual property doctrines that rely on originality as a core definitional concept in the identification of their objects.

Nonetheless, 'originality' (like authorship) has displayed dogged longevity, having survived around two hundred years in copyright law[214] and well over five hundred years in patent law.[215] There may be at least two reasons for this.

First, contemporary intellectual property doctrines arguably acknowledge – though perhaps only by implication and not fully – the social context of an 'original' intellectual property object and the subjectivity of originality standards. The very dichotomy between the unoriginal and original acknowledges that the material that comes before is the material against which any alleged originality is to be assessed. Moreover, intellectual property doctrines implicitly recognize that common social referents may inspire similar or identical work, and some doctrines (notably copyright and trademark law) allow for this phenomenon. For example, copyright law's principle of 'independent creation' allows for the coincidental independent creation of identical or very similar works by authors who have not directly or indirectly copied from one another (the fact that both may have been inspired by a common factor is not fatal to either's claim of independent creation). Meanwhile, trademark and passing off law allow for the 'honest concurrent use' of identical or deceptively similar indicia of trading reputation with respect to similar goods or services when both traders have adopted the signs without nefarious intent.

[214] See, eg, Oren Bracha, above n. 67 at 201: 'Originality doctrine [in the United States] was shaped by the dialectical interaction between commercial interests and ideology. It appeared as a doctrinal concept starting in the late 1920s in various copyright disputes in which defendants argued lack of originality in order to deprive copyrighted works of protection and escape infringement charges.'

[215] The *Venetian Patent Law* of 19 March 1474 stated: '[E]ach person who will make in this city any *new ingenious* contrivance, *not made heretofore* in our dominion, as soon as it is reduced to perfection....' Quoted in Dominique Guellec and Bruno van Pottelsberghe de la Potterie, *The Economics of the European Patent System: IP Policy for Innovation and Competition*, trans. Luigi Sordelli (Oxford: Oxford University Press, 2007) at 16 (emphasis added).

In each situation, the law recognizes that creators may independently develop similar works, and in doing so it perhaps acknowledges the social and cultural influences on which creators build to create their 'original' works. Even if such buffers against doctrinal rigidity do not reflect the full reality of the way intellectual property laws' 'originality' conceptions operate in society, they perhaps give them sufficient credibility to make the legal standards of 'originality' workable at a practical level.

A second (related) reason is arguably found in the traditional utility of originality conceptions. Although the notion that originality and creatorship are objectively measurable standards may be somewhat artificial, conventions have developed that organize the ways in which these legal concepts are used in practice. As a result, notions such as creatorship and originality have become entrenched as practically useful tools by which the legal system employs intellectual property doctrines to regulate uses of ideas, information, and knowledge. They are institutional facts whose rules are created by – and in turn create – the intellectual property doctrines that they are part of. Within intellectual property law they perform the function they were designed to perform. As such, they are sustainable within intellectual property doctrines, even if they seem problematic when viewed from a broader social or cultural perspective. Thus, criticisms of the artificiality of the creatorship and originality concepts in intellectual property law are arguably both valid and misplaced, depending on the perspective from which they are viewed. Such a paradox is a common feature throughout intellectual property law.

Similarly, the answer to the question 'is anything original?' is probably 'yes and no'. Good illustrations of this paradox in practice can be found in the history of Western music and art. The following case study focuses on cultural notions of 'originality' and creative influences in the work of Spanish artist Pablo Picasso. Was Picasso's work original? Arguably, 'yes, wildly so!' Arguably, 'no, not in some respects.' The case study concludes by contrasting Picasso's use of references from other works with the application of intellectual property law by Picasso's estate to control uses of the artist's name and work.

4.2.5.d Originality and Influences in the Art of Pablo Picasso: A Case Study

In thirteenth- and fourteenth-century Europe, painters were craftspeople whose role was to paint church altars depicting biblical tales in a manner that could be understood by a largely illiterate community.[216] They followed strict traditions in which standard iconology was reproduced in recognizable ways. For example, depictions of important characters were larger than those of marginal ones (a technique known as the 'perspective of meaning'),[217] and the divine nature of biblical figures was represented by the golden halos that encircled their heads. As apprentices, young craftspeople were trained by master artists, who passed to them the techniques and professional secrets of generations of painters.[218] Part of this inherited knowledge was the body of artistic traditions that would influence the way in which future artists developed their skills. Painters learned by replicating the works of those who preceded them, so copying the work of others was an essential aspect of an artist's education.[219]

From the mid–sixteenth century, the Dutch Reformed Church virtually stopped commissioning works of art, and painters in the Netherlands lost their role as church artists and turned to more secular work as a livelihood.[220] The traditional training of the young artist as a craftsperson remained, with apprentices learning by copying drawings, models, and works of the masters. However, with the secularization of Dutch art,

[216] Anna C. Krausse, *The Story of Painting: From the Renaissance to the Present* (Cologne: Könemann, 1995) at 6–7.

[217] Ibid. at 7.

[218] Ibid. at 9.

[219] It should be noted that this tradition of learning by copying the masters was not confined to Europe or Western schools of art. Such practices were also common in, for example, Asian artistic traditions. See, eg, Brenda G. Jordan and Victoria Louise Weston, *Copying the Master and Stealing His Secrets: Talent and Training in Japanese Painting* (Honolulu: University of Hawaii Press, 2003); and William P. Alford, *To Steal a Book Is an Elegant Offense: Intellectual Property Law in Chinese Civilization* (Stanford, CA: Stanford University Press, 1997).

[220] See Jonathan Janson, 'A Brief Overview of the Dutch Art Market in the 17th c', http://www.essentialvermeer.com/dutch-painters/dutch_art/ecnmcs_dtchart.html [accessed 15 May 2010].

artists accepted commissions for non-religious work and would sell copies of these as well as copies of works of the great masters that their apprentices had painted.[221] In time, these practices spread throughout Europe.

At the Museu Picasso de Barcelona[222] in Barcelona, Spain, visitors can trace the evolution and maturing of the artistic skill of Pablo Ruiz Picasso (1881–1973) as he followed in this tradition, from his youthful drawings, to the copies of masters he made while training as an artist, to his more adventurous work that led to Cubism and the 'Variations'.

During Picasso's childhood, his art teacher father educated him in a classic tradition that involved copying the works of such masters as Italian Renaissance artist Raphael (1483–1520) and Spanish Baroque painter Diego Velázquez (1599–1660). Picasso continued this practice throughout his training, spending many hours as a late teen in Madrid's Museu Prado copying the works of masters such as Velázquez.[223] For example, Velázquez's *Portrait of Felipe IV* and the copy Picasso painted of it[224] are depicted in Figures 4B and 4C, respectively.[225]

221 Ibid.

222 Museu Picasso de Barcelona, Carrer Montcada 15–23, 08003 Barcelona, Spain. Website: http://www.museupicasso.bcn.es/en/ [accessed 15 May 2010].

223 The website of the Museu Picasso de Barcelonastates: 'Picasso spends the academic year, 1897–1898, in Madrid. Encouraged by his family, he enriched his artistic training at the San Fernando Royal Academy of Fine Arts in Madrid.... Apart [f]rom academic exercises during this stay in Madrid, the artistic activity of the young Picasso was focused on scenes of everyday life and copying great masters of painting in the Prado Museum': http://www.museupicasso.bcn.es/eng/collection/cont_collec.htm#p1 [accessed 15 May 2010].

224 It is questionable whether copyright would subsist in this painting due to its lack of originality (ie, because it is a copy). If copyright does subsist, it would now be owned by Picasso's estate. Picasso died in 1973 and, in most jurisdictions, copyright will extend for another seventy years beyond the year in which the author died. Therefore, if copyright subsists in this painting, it would not expire until 2043 in many parts of the world.

225 An analysis of Picasso's copy of Velázquez's portrait of Philip IV can be found in Elizabeth Cowling, 'Competition and Collaboration: Picasso and the Old Masters', in Johanna Stephenson (ed.), *Picasso: Challenging the Past* (London: National Gallery, 2009), 11–25 at 16–17. This volume is a catalogue published to accompany the 'Picasso: Challenging the Past' exhibition at the National Gallery, London, 25 February to 7 June 2009, and colour plates of the paintings in Figures 4B and 4C can be compared side by side at 16–17.

Figure 4B. Diego Velázquez, *Portrait of Felipe IV* (1652–1653)

Diego Velázquez, Philip IV of Spain © The National Gallery, London.

Inspired by French Modernist artist Paul Cézanne's geometric patterns,[226] a more mature Picasso became the co-founder (with Georges Braque) of the Analytic Cubist school of art.[227] Later in life, Picasso arguably blended elements of Cubism with the tradition of copying works of past masters, adopting a new style that art critics refer to as the 'Variations on Past Masters'. As suggested by their name, Picasso's

[226] Paul Cézanne (1839–1906) has been described as the 'Father of Classical Modernism'. Anna C. Krausse explains: 'By reducing nature to individual geometrical elements and basing his pictorial arrangements on the intrinsic value of colour, he became the most important predecessor of the art of the 20th century.' Krausse, above n. 216 at 124. Cézanne's own work was in turn heavily influenced by the Impressionist artists, who were themselves influenced by earlier artistic schools.

[227] 'Analytic Cubism' was the style Picasso developed between 1909 and 1912. The style is characterized by the deconstruction of objects into their elemental shapes, painted with monochrome browns and neutral colours.

Figure 4C. Pablo Picasso, copy of Diego Velázquez's *Portrait of Felipe IV* (1897)

Variations reinterpreted in new styles works that had been painted by earlier master artists.

In 2008 the *Picasso and the Masters* exhibition in Paris exhibited side by side Picasso's Variations and the works that he had referenced in them. Speaking in this context, exhibition co-curator and director of Paris's Picasso Museum, Anne Baldassari, described Picasso as a 'cannibal'. '[H]e ate up works and let them digest. Then he would produce something entirely his own,' she told an interviewer.[228] They were not original, and yet they were highly original. The great originality of Picasso's interpretations is rarely questioned, yet the Variations were in some respects

[228] Associated Press and France 24, 'Picasso et les maîtres' (8 October 2008), http://royalandco.wordpress.com/2008/10/08/picasso-et-les-maitres/ [accessed 15 May 2010].

Figure 4D. Diego Velásquez, *Las Meninas* (c1656)

Image courtesy of Dover Publications.

'copies' that were heavily inspired by the creative work of others, and influenced by the social context of Picasso's era.

Perhaps the best known of Picasso's Variations are his fifty-eight interpretations of Velázquez's *Las Meninas* (The Maids of Honour,

Figure 4E. Pablo Picasso, *Las Meninas after Velázquez* (1957).

Las Meninas, No.1, 1957 (oil on canvas) by Picasso, Pablo (1881–1973) Museo Picasso, Barcelona, Spain/ Giraudon/ The Bridgeman Art Library.

1656).[229] Figures 4D and 4E[230] use one of the most famous works in the *Las Meninas* series of variations to indicate the similarities and differences between Velázquez's and Picasso's interpretations of the theme, and to demonstrate how Picasso was influenced by – and reinterpreted – the earlier master's work.[231]

An analysis by Elizabeth Cowling in the catalogue accompanying the 2009 *Picasso: Challenging the Past* exhibition at the National Gallery,

[229] Incidentally, Margaret Theresa – depicted in *Las Meninas* – was the daughter of King Philip IV of Spain; Velásquez's painting of Philip IV (see Figure 4B) was copied in 1897 by Picasso, aged sixteen (see Figure 4C).

[230] Colour plates of the paintings in Figures 4D and 4E can be compared side by side in Stephenson, above n. 225 at 128–129.

[231] For a clear analysis of the artistic technique involved in Picasso's variations on *Las Meninas*, see Susan Grace Galassi, 'Picasso's "Old Master" Period', in Stephenson, above n. 225 at 114–115.

London, notes a 'sense of companionship [between Picasso and] his great predecessor' that is evident in this Variation.[232] She argues that Picasso's interpretations of *Las Meninas* recast Velázquez's seventeenth-century original in terms of Picasso's twentieth-century era, using a style that was different from that of Velázquez, depicting the scene from different perspectives than did Velázquez, and emphasizing different objects in it.[233] Picasso thus paid homage to his antecedent while at the same time critiquing *Las Meninas*, offering a 'shrewd but sympathetic commentary on Velázquez and his masterpiece.'[234]

Cowling argues that '[c]ensorious critics at the time [who] accused him of completely running out of ideas of his own and living parasitically on the old masters out of sheer desperation'[235] misunderstood Picasso's work. Rather, she suggests, this copying – the dialogue between the past and present, and his collaboration with past masters – was a hallmark of Picasso's creativity throughout his career.[236] Her interpretation accords with the seminal discussion of Picasso's variation on Velázquez's *Las Meninas* by philosopher Michel Foucault.[237]

Foucault used the new perspectives on the old masterpiece that were offered by Picasso's depiction to illustrate the argument that 'truth' is ordered by a code of signs that is constructed by a society and varies according to historical periods. Just as appreciation of the scene in Velázquez's *Las Meninas* can change when seen from the viewpoint offered by Picasso, so too can understandings of the world – and the things in it – change according to the time, place, and perspective from which it is viewed.[238] Just as Foucault's analysis drew on Picasso's work

[232] Cowling, above n. 225 at 14.

[233] Ibid. at 15.

[234] Ibid. at 16. Cowling notes that this painting was created at a point in his life when Picasso was increasingly anxious about his own place in art history.

[235] Ibid. at 16.

[236] Ibid. at 16 and 23.

[237] Michel Foucault, *The Order of Things: An Archeology of the Human Sciences* (London: Routledge Classics, 2002), chap. 1, 'Las Meninas', 3–18. This book was first published in French as *Les mots et les choses* (Paris: Éditions Galliard, 1966).

[238] This theory has obvious relevance to the subject matter of this book. As Velázquez's *Las Meninas* could be viewed as a metaphor for the analytical technique of looking

to make an original and important contribution to the development of contemporary social theory, Picasso 'copied' Velázquez's *Las Meninas* to make an original and important contribution to the development of Western art. The originality lies not only in the painter's brush strokes, but also in the meanings those markings convey.

Commenting from an aesthetic perspective on the transformation of the image in Picasso's variation of Velázquez's work, Justin R. Erenkrantz writes:

> By making small and not-so-small variations to a well-known physical image, Picasso proceeded to create a brand new spiritual image. An interesting duality then arises – Picasso copied a masterpiece, yet it was clearly not a copy because he distorted the physical aspects of the painting. Hence, Picasso created an entirely different image than the original Velázquez work. By varying some details of a masterpiece, Picasso took the risk of destroying what made the original so great. Or, as Picasso himself predicted, the copy could become an original in its own right.[239]

Picasso was clearly mindful of the issues surrounding artistic copying: he is famous for having stated, 'To copy others is necessary, but to copy oneself is pathetic'[240] and 'Don't expect me to repeat myself. My past doesn't interest me any more, I would rather copy others than repeat myself. At least I would inject something new into them.'[241] With the latter quote, he summarized the artistic principle that all art is produced in a social context.

behind the prima facie appearance of something to explore its structure, meaning, and context, it seemed an appropriate choice for cover art of a volume that looks behind the standard definitions of 'intellectual property' to explore the content, meaning, and structure of this area of law.

239 Justin R. Erenkrantz, 'The Mask and the Mirror', http://www.erenkrantz.com/Words/TheMaskAndTheMirror.shtml [accessed 15 May 2010].

240 Carol Strickland, *The Annotated Mona Lisa: A Crash Course in Art History from Prehistoric to Post-Modern* (Kansas City: Andrews McMeel, 1992) at 137. The same quote is offered in the context of more detailed discussion in Dore Ashton, *Picasso on Art: A Selection of Views* (London: Thames & Hudson, 1972) at 53: 'Why should one stick desperately to everything that has fulfilled its promise? Would you have a man only able to repeat himself? Repetition is contrary to the laws of the spirit, to its flight forward. Copying others is necessary, but what a pity to copy oneself!'

241 Ashton, above n. 240 at 52.

From an intellectual property perspective, copyright law would probably consider a Picasso 'variation' to be a 'derivative work', which would be considered 'original' only to the extent that it did not copy from existing works. An artist making too close a reproduction of another artist's work would be expected to obtain permission in the form of a license before creating such a 'variation', and to refrain from copying if permission was withheld.[242] Many of the works that Picasso copied were not covered by copyright law, having been created before copyright laws came into force or having fallen into the public domain following the expiration of their copyright periods. Picasso's works also displayed a degree of creativity that would arguably have led to their being deemed by a court to be 'original' for copyright purposes. However, it would be interesting to see how a contemporary court would apply copyright law to the Variations, were they to be created today with respect to works still covered by copyright. Surely society would have been poorer had the enforcement of intellectual property law prevented Pablo Picasso from offering the world his artistic variations on culturally significant works such as Diego Velázquez's *Las Meninas*.

Interestingly, Picasso was bound by copyright law. His homeland, Spain, became a signatory to the *Berne Convention for the Protection of Literary and Artistic Works* (1886) on 5 December 1887, as did France, where Picasso spent much of his working life. Both jurisdictions also became signatories of the *Universal Copyright Convention* (1952) in the mid-1950s, and both had comprehensive copyright laws during Picasso's lifetime. Picasso's level of personal knowledge of, and/or attitude towards, intellectual property laws does not seem to have been recorded.[243]

[242] This becomes a problem for artists who would like to draw on – by copying, modifying, and/or reinterpreting – the work of someone who will not grant permission to do so. It is an impediment to the creation of 'appropriation art' (including techniques such as audio mash ups, and culture jamming), which is premised on recycling culturally interesting sources in new ways. For a discussion of this issue, see Kembrew McLeod and Rudolf Kuenzli (eds), *Cutting Across Media: Appropriation Art, Interventionist Collage, and Copyright Law* (Durham, NC: Duke University Press, 2011).

[243] Searches have been made in the English-language literature. However, it is possible that such information has been recorded in other languages, such as Spanish or French.

Perhaps paradoxically, Pablo Picasso's heirs have been active in seeking to enforce the artist's intellectual property rights since his death. For example, in a French case involving copyright in a catalogue of Picasso's artwork that was alleged to have been copied by another catalogue publisher, the Paris Court of Appeals avoided deciding the painter's heir's claim to hold copyright in the original paintings.[244] In another example, the maker of *Surviving Picasso*,[245] a 1996 biographical film about the artist, was prevented on copyright grounds from reproducing Picasso's paintings in the film following legal action by the artist's son Claude Ruiz Picasso. Claude reportedly took the action because he was unhappy with the film's portrayal of his father.[246]

The estate of Pablo Picasso reportedly takes legal action around twenty times per year to fight alleged misappropriation of the Picasso name (rights to which were determined by a French court in 1989).[247] The estate licenses the Picasso name for certain purposes – it has chosen to associate the name with 'high-quality' products, such as Citroen cars, Cognac Hennessy Picasso, and an ST Dupont Picasso cigarette lighter – and lawyers for the estate claim that more than two hundred attempts

[244] Translation obtained from Anne Pigeon-Bormans and Pierre Lautier, 'Photographies of Picasso's Work Protected by Copyright' (6 September 2004), http://www.avocats-publishing.com/Photographies-of-PICASSO-S-WORK, the website of Paris intellectual property law firm Avocats en propriété intellectuelle [accessed 15 May 2010].

[245] *Surviving Picasso* (2006). The film was made by Merchant Ivory Films, distributed by Warner Bros, directed by James Ivory, and produced by Ismail Merchant, David L. Wolper, and Humbert Balsan (co-producer), and stars Anthony Hopkins as Pablo Picasso. It is based on Arianna Stassinopoulos Huffington, *Picasso: Creator and Destroyer* (New York: Avon, 1989).

The film avoids showing Picasso's artwork in a manner that would infringe copyright. For further discussion, see 'Portraits of Picasso' (18 October 1996), *The Atlantic Online*, http://www.theatlantic.com/past/docs/unbound/flashbks/picasso/picasso.htm [accessed 10 May 2010].

[246] Richard Hurowitz, 'Surviving Copyright Infringement: Fair Use of Protected Works in "Biopics"' (1998) 22 *Columbia Journal of Law & the Arts* 247–268 at 247 n. 2. This article discusses the case in some detail.

[247] Alan Riding, 'A Family Feud over a Picasso (on Wheels): A New Car's Logo Divides the Heirs of a Lucrative Name' (19 April 1999) *New York Times*, http://www.nytimes.com/1999/04/19/arts/family-feud-over-picasso-wheels-new-car-s-logo-divides-heirs-lucrative-name.html?pagewanted=all [accessed 15 May 2010].

per year are made to use the Picasso name for commercial purposes.[248] The estate authorizes numerous requests to reproduce the artist's work in books and catalogues but fights unauthorized uses of his name and artistic reputation.

In 1998 the Australian Trade Marks Office was asked by Picasso's son Claude to prevent a pizza restaurant in the Sydney suburbs of Newtown and Randwick from registering a trademark containing the words PIZZA PICASSO PIZZAS OF ART and a palette device with respect to '[p]roviding food – restaurant, takeaway & delivery' in Class 42. The device was depicted as shown in Figure 4F.

Claude Picasso held trademarks in the words PABLO PICASSO, PICASSO and the Picasso signature, for use with respect to textiles, chinaware, ceramics, and glassware, and copyright in the Picasso signature. He argued that allowing the PIZZA PICASSO PIZZAS OF ART registration would cause confusion among consumers, who would infer a connection between the artist Pablo Picasso and the Sydney pizza restaurants. Although similar arguments had been accepted in decisions in the United States, the Australian Registrar's delegate rejected this argument. He stated that '[w]hile the mere mention of [Picasso's] name might immediately evoke images of his art and artistic genius, it does not likewise summon up visions of pizza.'[249] Registration of the pizza trademark was

[248] 'Every year there are at least 200 attempts by people to claim the Picasso trademark without authorization,' Picasso estate lawyer, Ms. Andrieu, explained. 'Add to that, there are 42 different classes of trademarks for names and logos. There's a Spanish company that has filed both the name and the logo in 30 classes, so that's 60 separate disputes. I'd say that at present, around 800 of the 1,043 registered trademarks using the Picasso name are unauthorized.' See ibid.

[249] *Re: Opposition by Claude Ruiz Picasso to registration of trade mark application 754587(42) – PIZZA PICASSO PIZZAS OF ART and device – filed in the name of Robyn Thomas* (7 September 2001), available at the IP Australia website: http://www.ipaustralia.gov.au/pdfs/trademarks/hearings/754587.pdf [accessed 10 May 2010] The Registrar's delegate, Jock McDonagh, stated: 'There is no evidence before me to indicate that any person in Australia would assume that the trade mark would connote a connection, sponsorship, approval or endorsement of the applicant's restaurants and

Figure 4F. 'PIZZA PICASSO PIZZAS OF ART and Palate Device' trademark (Aust.)

Image kindly provided by Robyn Thomas (all rights reserved).

therefore permitted, and the attempt by the artist's heirs to use intellectual property law to, in effect, monopolize associations with Picasso's legacy not authorized by his estate was therefore frustrated in this instance.

It is understandable that Picasso's heirs would wish to profit from his reputation and would employ intellectual property laws in aid of this goal. Nonetheless, there is a certain irony that the estate of an artist whose work is so associated with variations on the work of his artistic predecessors would seek to prevent others from borrowing references from the cultural associations and art of Pablo Picasso. It is ironic that intellectual property laws are apparently used by his heirs to prevent

pizzas by Picasso or his estate. I am not aware of any connection that Pablo Picasso might have had with restaurants or pizzas in his lifetime. While the mere mention of his name might immediately evoke images of his art and artistic genius, it does not likewise summon up visions of pizza. In my opinion, there is nothing in the mark itself to give the imprimatur of endorsement. There is no evidence, in either anecdotal or survey form, before me to find otherwise.' (This quote can be found at p. 8 of the published decision.)

'variations' on the work of someone so noted for his 'variations' on the work of others.

From a broader jurisprudential perspective, the Picasso case study illustrates the differing conceptions of 'originality' applied by copyright law and the art world. It illustrates that permissive artistic notions of originality do not necessarily accord with copyright's narrower conception of originality. It is another example of how the legal system can produce internally defined objects of intellectual property regulation that operate alongside, and influence, the social production of ideational objects and their documented forms, and that are in turn regulated by intellectual property laws. This internal creation and reinforcement of the core concepts that define both the law and its objects of regulation is a key characteristic of intellectual property doctrines.

4.2.6. The Artificiality and Factuality of Intellectual Property Concepts in Practice

Viewed outside the context of the intellectual property doctrines in which they operate, damaging objections can thus be cast at the concepts of 'creatorship' and 'originality'. However, these concepts form an integral part of the institutional apparatus that allows intellectual property law to operate, and abandoning or greatly altering them would fracture the doctrines they sustain. Without the endurance of doctrinal variants of the concepts of 'creatorship', 'originality', and a 'documented form' of an ideational object, recognizable forms of the intellectual property doctrines that encompass them would undoubtedly collapse. The concepts are therefore central to the perpetuation of intellectual property doctrines as currently understood. Furthermore, identification of such concepts within an area of law points to the likelihood that that area of law falls within the department of intellectual property.

It may be that some of these concepts are legal fictions. In society, thoughts build on earlier thoughts, and copyright-protected work often builds on earlier works, patented inventions often incorporate parts of earlier inventions, and trademarks frequently contain elements found in earlier marks and/or symbols from language and culture generally.[250] Recognition of this is imported into the calculus that is used to determine the threshold levels of creatorship and originality that draw lines between existing and new intellectual property objects and between ideational objects and intellectual property objects. The placement of these lines delineates the boundaries of intellectual property objects; the lines operate like abstract fences. As noted earlier, determining their location is a routine challenge faced by practitioners in the application of intellectual property laws.[251]

Unoriginal components of intellectual property objects are not themselves protected; nor are elements whose intellectual property rights have expired. However, even these may attract a degree of de facto intellectual property protection if they come to play new roles as part of larger or derivative objects that are deemed to be original and that do otherwise fall within the catchment of an intellectual property doctrine.[252]

Yet, despite the law's implicit recognition that 'creatorship' and 'originality' are relative measures by which the documented form of ideas can be compared with their predecessors, they are often treated as absolutes. Like much legal jargon, these words operate as terms of art within intellectual property doctrines, where their significance is different from that of the ordinary English meanings of the terms. It can be difficult to explain the related concepts of creatorship and originality to those

[250] See Garrett Hardin, 'The Tragedy of the Commons' (1968) 162 *Science* 1243–1248. For a discussion of the costs that patterns of multiple layers of intellectual property rights can trigger, see Heller, 'The Tragedy of the Anticommons', above n. 86; and Heller, *The Gridlock Economy*, above n. 86.

[251] See Lange, 'Recognizing the Public Domain', above n. 199.

[252] An obvious example of this is the evergreening of patents.

who are not intellectual property specialists, and harder still to expect the general public to comply with laws built on concepts that are so difficult to understand and apply in practice. Perhaps the stronger critique of the intellectual property concepts of creatorship and originality is not, therefore, that they are legal fictions or that they fail to reflect the operation of common practices in the societies in which they apply (although, as discussed earlier, such criticisms may be valid). Perhaps the great flaw of creatorship and originality is instead that they are so difficult to understand and to apply consistently.

4.2.6.a Conclusion

Creatorship, originality, and the documented form all operate as mechanisms that help to define the intellectual property object. In summary, they work together as a conceptual apparatus that can allow for the propertization of almost any idea that can be linked to a tangible object. Where an idea is reproduced as a tangible representation, the possibility exists for intellectual propertization to occur. The physical representations are the documented form of the idea, and these are recognizable as an intellectual property object. Whether such an object will be brought into existence depends on the application of the further criteria of creatorship and originality. These establish a temporal barrier that allows intellectual property objects to be identified only if they have been created by an identifiable person within a delineated timeframe. The documented form of these creations must also meet the required minimum standards of originality in comparison with other intellectual property and/or ideational objects that apply to the intellectual property doctrine in question.

Where each of these conditions is met, an intellectual property object can potentially be identified. Thus, intellectual property law is fundamentally an institution that provides for the conversion of ideational objects into private property through the application of a series of conceptual requirements. These conceptual requirements – creatorship, originality, and a documented form – each take effect through different conceptions in different intellectual property doctrines. Each is also capable of being endlessly adjusted to meet the changing interpretations of those responsible for the implementation and operation of intellectual property doctrines, and in response to shifting conditions in the society in which the law operates.

Once intellectual property objects have been defined into existence, their use is regulated by additional rules set down within the relevant intellectual property doctrine. Many of these are 'rights' that delineate the nature and scope of the monopoly awarded by the doctrine to the intellectual property proprietor. Like the conceptual components that give intellectual property objects their identity, intellectual property's rights are also susceptible to endless amendment and adjustment.

Within the realms of intellectual property law, all of this makes sense. Outside, it may not. Delete intellectual property laws, and intellectual property objects would cease to exist as such; they would fade into mere ideational objects. Their documented forms may continue to exist, but they would not be affected by the 'intellectual property' rules restricting the ways they could be used. Ideational objects are pre-legal (where they exist before law regulates them) or post-legal (where intellectual property law has been exhausted,[253] or dismantled, or the term of its operation has expired), or they may be the ideas, information, facts, signs, and so on underlying an intellectual property object. By contrast, intellectual property objects are legal in nature: they are entirely dependent on the law for their existence and form.

[253] Used in the context of intellectual property law, the term 'exhaustion' refers to a proprietor's right to use the intellectual property object before anybody else does, with the proviso that some or all rights in the object will be 'exhausted' (ie, expired and lost) after that first use by the proprietor. This principle is sometimes known as the 'first sale' doctrine, and it is particularly relevant in parallel importation cases (where authentic/licensed goods from outside the jurisdiction are brought into the jurisdiction by someone other than the local trademark, patent, or copyright proprietor). In such a case, a proprietor may be unable to enforce its rights in one jurisdiction if those rights have been exhausted in another jurisdiction.

4.3. Intellectual Property Rights

Compared with the subsistence issues examined in earlier sections (ie, the core criteria of an ideational object, documented form, creatorship, and originality), intellectual property *rights* seem very straightforward. They fall into relatively neat lists of benefits that an intellectual property holder may claim and enforce at law and, in many ways, they resemble the rights that attach to real property and other types of personal property.

4.3.1. *Typical Intellectual Property Rights*

Legal recognition that a good is property generally implies that its proprietor has rights to exploit it (such as rights to consume, sell, rent, mortgage, transfer, or destroy the property) and rights to authorize or exclude others from engaging in these activities.[254] Rights over intellectual property objects tend to include monopoly privileges to obtain, use, make, provide to others, and authorize others to do these things with respect to the intellectual property object. Like other property rights, the rights of an intellectual property proprietor might be limited by general laws or intellectual property laws. For example, a person may not be permitted to publish, sell, or otherwise distribute photographs that depict child pornography regardless of whether the person holds copyright in those photographs. Or the proprietor of a patent may not be permitted to exploit its invention to the extent that doing so would infringe the rights of another patent holder.[255]

[254] This list of 'standard incidents of ownership' is generally attributed to Anthony M. Honoré, 'Ownership', in Anthony Gordon Guest (ed.), *Oxford Essays in Jurisprudence* (Oxford: Oxford University Press, 1961), 107–147 at 112ff.

[255] For this reason, patents are often described as rights to exclude, not rights to use. See, eg, the US case *Herman v. Youngstown Car Manufacturing Co.*, 191 F. 579 at 584–85, 112 CCA 185 (6th Cir. 1911): A 'patent is not the grant of a right to make or use or sell. It does not, directly or indirectly, imply any such right. It grants only the right to exclude others. The supposition that a right to make is created by the patent grant is obviously inconsistent with the established distinctions between generic and specific patents, and

Rights in intellectual property laws arguably differ from other property rights only so much as to reflect the different – abstract – nature of the objects being regulated. Rights to 'use' take different forms depending on the type of intellectual property object in question.[256] For example, in copyright law the right to use amounts to a right to copy, whereas in design law it amounts to a right to use a product embodying, the design. These rights can also be abridged by conflicting rights.[257] Intellectual property law thus respects and reflects the functional roles of the core conceptual concepts that create objects in each of its various doctrines by adjusting the rights to suit the ways in which the documented form of those doctrinal objects can be used.

The rights attached to the classic intellectual property doctrines can be summarized as variations on the following: a right to obtain (including make or import), a right to use (including use, exploit, copy), a right to provide to others, and a right to authorize others to do any of the other rights.

The intangible nature of an intellectual property object means that its rights are cast in terms of use of the documented form of the intellectual property object, such as the book in which a copyright-protected literary work appears or a product to which a trademark has been applied.

It is noticeable that almost all the rights just catalogued are 'economic rights'. That is, they are rights to exploit the economic opportunities that arise from the limited monopolies granted by intellectual property laws. They accord well with the economic rights that are associated with objects of property law generally.

A clear exception to the economic nature of intellectual property rights is found in copyright's group of 'moral rights'. Article 6 *bis* of the *Berne Convention* requires member states to implement laws giving

with the well-known fact that a very considerable portion of the patents granted are in a field covered by a former relatively generic or basic patent, are tributary to such earlier patent, and cannot be practiced unless by license thereunder.'

[256] As noted in ibid., not all intellectual property doctrines include a right to use.

[257] Ibid.

authors rights to claim authorship and to object to certain modifications and other derogatory actions with respect to their work that is recognized to subsist under copyright law.[258] In jurisdictions where this requirement has been followed and moral rights have been enacted, they tend to take the form of:

- a right to attribution;
- a right against false attribution; and
- a right to the integrity of, or against derogatory treatment of, one's work.

These rights protect non-economic interests that an author may have in a work, and they are often attributed to Hegelian theory that argues that a person should not be alienated from the products of her or his creative labour.[259] Moral rights thus allow an author to maintain some formal connections with a copyright-protected work, even after the economic rights of that work have been sold or otherwise assigned by the author. Although moral rights provide an exception to the general rule that intellectual property rights are economic rights, they are arguably only a minor exception because these non-economic rights arise only when copyright objects have already been identified (ie, through the application of the core criteria, which were devised in the context of economic rights and were used to delineate copyright objects prior to the introduction of moral rights requirements in many jurisdictions). The rights

[258] Article 6*bis* reads: '(1) Independently of the author's economic rights, and even after the transfer of the said rights, the author shall have the right to claim authorship of the work and to object to any distortion, mutilation or other modification of, or other derogatory action in relation to, the said work, which would be prejudicial to his honor or reputation. (2) The rights granted to the author in accordance with the preceding paragraph shall, after his death, be maintained, at least until the expiry of the economic rights, and shall be exercisable by the persons or institutions authorized by the legislation of the country where protection is claimed.' Available from the World Intellectual Property Organization's Treaties website: http://www.wipo.int/treaties/en/ip/berne/trtdocs_wo001.html#P123_20726 [accessed 15 May 2010].

[259] For a summary of this justification for intellectual propertization, see the appendix to this volume.

contained in intellectual property laws are thus very similar to property rights more generally.

4.3.2. Property Theory and Intellectual Property Rights

Discussions of 'rights' are typically given much less attention in intellectual property theory than are discussions about subsistence (for intellectual property doctrines whose objects come into being by automatic operation of the law) and registrability (for intellectual property doctrines whose objects come into being when they are registered by a governmental organization). In this respect, they perhaps differ from general discussions about property, which typically discuss the rights associated with objects of property in greater depth.

Two characteristic dichotomizations of property rights are between, first, 'choses in action' and 'choses in possession' and, second, rights '*in rem*' and rights '*in personam*'.

Choses in action relate to the objects of property that depend on a proprietor's ability to take an action in a court rather than take physical possession of the object.[260] The intangible nature of intellectual property objects would seem to put them clearly in this category.[261] However, J. E. Penner argues that, while they are similar to choses in action 'because they are abstract legal rights, with no direct connection to any thing, tangible or intangible',[262] intellectual property rights differ from typical choses in action because they do not involve claims to part of the property of others.[263]

[260] Tim Murphy, Simon Roberts, and Tatiana Flessas, *Understanding Property Law* (London: Sweet & Maxwell, 2004) at 57.

[261] As Murphy, Roberts, and Flessas observe: 'You can reclaim a book or a cow that belongs to you by regaining physical control of it. But if someone interferes with intangible personal property, you can only bring a legal action to stop the interference and obtain financial compensation; you cannot take it back because it has no physical form.' Ibid.

[262] J. E. Penner, *The Idea of Property in Law* (Oxford: Oxford University Press, 1997) at 119.

[263] Ibid.

The intangibility of intellectual property objects also affects application of the second dichotomy. Rights *in rem* are rights that a proprietor can enforce against all members of society with respect to the object of property, such as rights to exclude strangers from growing flowers on your land and rights to exclude people from entering your house. By contrast, rights *in personam* are personal rights that bind only certain individuals, such as rights enforceable under the terms of a contract or the result of a judicial order.[264]

Intellectual property rights tend to be classified as rights *in rem*.[265] However, a feature of rights *in rem* would normally be that of excludability. That is, the proprietor obtains rights to exclude others from doing certain things with respect to the property, and other people have an obligation or duty to abstain from interfering with the property.[266] Sukhninder Panesar notes that this principle is founded in pragmatism:

> The aspect of 'excludability' is taken by the courts as a central requirement before a resource can be admitted into the category of private property. If it is not feasible for a person to exercise regulatory control over the access of strangers to various benefits inherent in the resource, the resource cannot be an object of private property [and will] be confined to common property.[267]

This principle may relate to property law generally, but it presents special challenges when applied to ideational objects. How does an owner exclude people from its intellectual property?

[264] For a deeper discussion of these distinctions, see Sukhninder Panesar, *General Principles of Property Law* (Harlow: Pearson Education, 2001) at 11ff.

[265] See, eg, Penner, above n. 263 at 119: '[Intellectual property rights] are rights directly to a practice of exclusion, as directly as are property rights in chattels or land, correlating to duties *in rem* by which all subjects of the legal system have a negative duty not to do something.'

[266] Tony Honoré, 'Rights of Exclusion and Immunities against Divesting' (1960) 34 *Tulane Law Review* 453–468 at 458–459. See also Penner, above n. 263, chap. 4, 'The Right to Property: The Exclusion Thesis'.

[267] Panesar, above n. 265 at 12.

Whatever the reasons, it can be very difficult for a member of society to avoid trespassing on others' intellectual property when the boundaries are invisible and experts do not always agree where those boundaries lie. Two or more different intellectual property lawyers or judges may view exactly the same 'intellectual property object' and apply exactly the same intellectual property laws, but reach different views about where intellectual property law's conceptual fences should properly be placed in order to correctly delineate the objects of intellectual property regulation. This is presumably a result of differing worldviews and experiences coming to bear on the assessment and is relatively common, as evidenced by differing conclusions on the facts drawn by panels of appellate court judges who have viewed precisely the same evidence as a trial judge whose opinion they disagree with (yet whose findings of fact the appellate court is typically bound to accept).[268]

In order to exclude, boundaries have to be established. As discussed earlier, there are certain difficulties associated with erecting conceptual fences around abstract objects of property rights. Even if these boundaries are established, society must be alerted to the status of the intellectual property–protected objects. Otherwise, people may accidentally wander onto private property – albeit intellectual property – thinking they are in the commons, or they may use another's intellectual property thinking mistakenly that it is their own (eg, when they make a derivative work). Or it may not occur to them to contemplate issues of intellectual property ownership at all. Signs such as the ©, ®, and ™ symbols indicate claims to rights, as does appearing in trademark, patent, and design registers. Even despite such 'evidence', individuals may find it difficult to determine the

[268] See, eg, the Australian case of *Universal City Studios v Zeccola* (1982) 67 FLR 225, in which an appellate court commented on the findings of fact of the trial judge in a copyright case. The trial judge had compared the movie *Jaws*, about a shark terrorizing a seaside community, with another movie with a similar plot, *Great White*. The majority judgement of the appellate court noted a differing impression of the similarity between the two films upon the same application of the copyright law: 'Whilst our own viewing of the films did not instil in us the same degree of conviction that his Honour felt, we are not persuaded that his Honour was wrong' (at 230).

conceptual boundaries of individual intellectual property objects. It is a problematic issue: How can you exclude people if you cannot agree on the boundaries of the property they are being excluded from? Complicating matters further are difficulties associated with excluding people from property that can be endlessly consumed without anyone having any less of it (that is thus 'non-rival').

Non-excludability and non-rivalrousness are characteristics typical of intellectual property objects and the application of intellectual property rights to those objects, but they are not necessarily typical of other types of property. They influence the sorts of rights that are awarded to enable intellectual property proprietors to enjoy their property rights, and thus additional characteristics of intellectual propertization.

The current chapter concludes by applying the core concepts discussed earlier to a case study that illustrates how they apply in practice. In doing so, it demonstrates that intellectual propertization occurs when law-makers apply the core criteria – the concepts of creatorship, originality, and a documented form – together to allow parts of ideational objects to be isolated and converted into intellectual property objects. Rights can then be added to the law to determine who may use the intellectual property object and how. The case study illustrates how this works in the empirical context of copyright law in practice; it indicates how intellectual propertization occurs and how 'rights' are then applied to the objects created by intellectual property laws.

4.4. The Operation of Intellectual Property's 'Objects' and 'Rights'

Whether consciously or not, law-makers who create intellectual property must go through a two-stage process. They must identify what will be regulated by the law: these are the doctrine's *objects*, which are defined by applying a combination of the aforementioned core concepts of creatorship, originality, and documented form to a raw 'ideational object'. They must also determine what regulations will apply with respect to those objects. They do this by creating rules that allow a proprietor to enforce *rights* with respect to its intellectual property and that sometimes also require observance of responsibilities by that proprietor. Together, the objects, the rights, and the legal regulations that create them, shape the framework of intellectual property's doctrines. The way in which these work together within the legal department of intellectual property to create and regulate intellectual property objects is the process of intellectual propertization.

The following example is drawn from UK copyright law and demonstrates how these principles are applied. It also illustrates how the process of intellectual propertization involves not only the identification of an intellectual property object and its associated rights, but subsequent changes – often extensions – to the scope of those objects. UK copyright law was chosen as the case study because, not only is it quite representative of copyright laws worldwide and of various intellectual property doctrines more generally, but it is the parent of many copyright regimes found in many other jurisdictions today. Not only is it found in the United Kingdom, but it remains influential in jurisdictions that were formerly British colonies,[269] perhaps most notably the United States.[270] It also reflects early *Berne Convention* principles,[271] as updated by later *Berne Convention* amendments, and can therefore be viewed as a model of 'standardized copyright'. This copyright example provides a simple illustration of how the theory described in this volume thus far translates into the construction and operation of intellectual property law in practice.

[269] For a discussion of copyright issues (and international concerns) in British colonies, see Simon Nowell-Smith, *International Copyright Law and the Publisher in the Reign of Queen Victoria* (Oxford: Clarendon Press, 1968), 85–105, chap. 5.

[270] For an historical treatment of the influence of English copyright principles in the post-colonial United States, see Catherine Seville, 'From Pirates to Eagles: America's Changing View of Copyright' (2007) 29:10 *European Intellectual Property Review* 406–410.

[271] Ibid. at 90: 'The late eighties were a time of copyright ferment not only in the new world but in Europe and throughout the British empire. 1885 saw the first draft of the Berne international convention. Several of its provisions conflicted with existing British law. A new international copyright act (49 & 50 Vict. C.33) was accordingly passed in order to iron out the discrepancies and the opportunity was taken to remove outstanding colonial grievances. Copyright registered in a colony was given validity throughout the empire.'

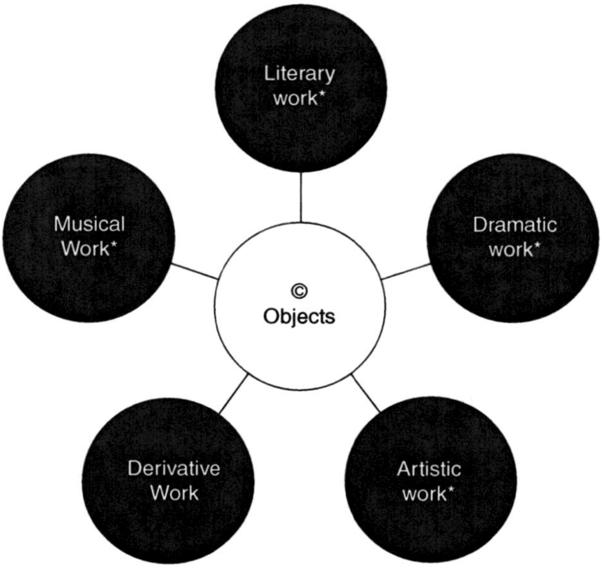

Figure 4G. Copyright's Objects:
Intellectual Property Objects Protected by Copyright Law (UK)
(* denotes it must also be original, substantial, and in a material form)

4.4.1. The Intellectual Propertization Process: A Copyright Example

UK copyright law – with its 'subject matter' requirement and its rules about how that subject matter can be used – provides a clear example for the purposes of illustrating an intellectual property doctrine whose structure consists of objects and rights. The subject matter constitutes copyright's 'intellectual property object', while the rules about who may access and copy that subject matter and the conditions under which they may do so constitute its 'rights'. These are depicted in diagrammatic form in Figures 4G and 4H, respectively.

4.4.1.a Subsistence (Creating Copyright's Intellectual Property Objects)

In the United Kingdom, copyright attaches to 'works' (or 'subject matter'), and these must 'subsist' before copyright law will apply. In

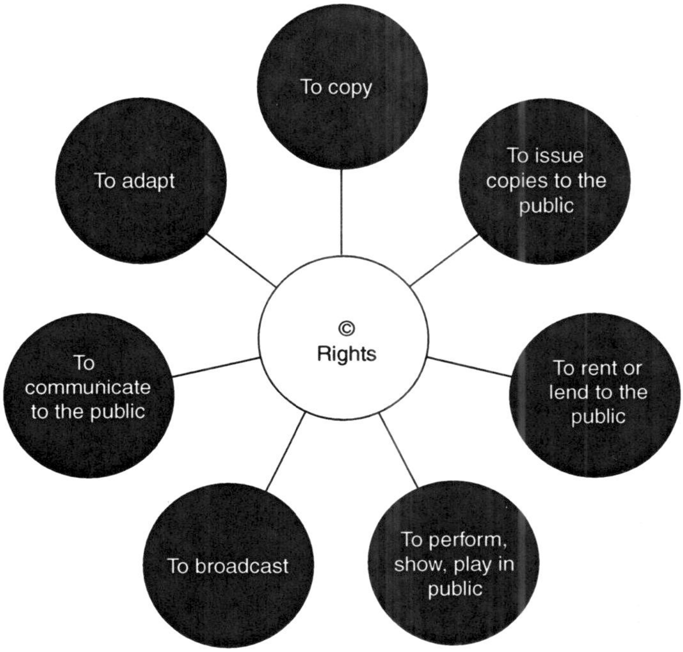

**Figure 4H. Copyright's Rights:
The Proprietor's Legally Awarded Exclusive Rights to Control Intellectual Property Objects (UK)**

other words, they must meet the requirements necessary for part of an ideational object to be regarded as an intellectual property object that is created and regulated by the doctrine of copyright law. To do this and thus fall within the scope of copyright law, the work must be, inter alia,[272]

- an authored,
- literary, dramatic, musical, or artistic work[273] (or an adaptation of one of the first three of these categories);[274]

[272] This analysis does not extend to secondary works, such as cinematograph films.

[273] *Copyright, Designs and Patents Act* 1988, s.1(1)(a), and defined in s.3(1).

[274] Ibid., s.16(e). An adaptation may, for example, take the form of a translation of a literary work, an arrangement, altered version, or translation of a computer program, or an arrangement or transcription of a musical work; see s.21(3).

- recorded in a material form;[275]
- original;[276] and
- substantial enough to merit the attention of copyright law.[277]

As none of these criteria – 'literary work', 'dramatic work', 'musical work', 'artistic work' (which are the objects of copyright), and 'authored'; 'material form', 'original', 'substantial' (rule-based, comparative, qualitative, and quantitative features of the intellectual property object, which are reliant on the application of the core concepts) – has a self-evident meaning, each requires further legal definition. Some of these definitions are provided by the legislation, but all are ultimately subject to interpretation by the courts and are elastic in meaning.

4.4.1.b Rights

For the proprietor, UK copyright law provides legally enforceable rights to copy, issue copies to the public, perform, show or play in public, broadcast, communicate to the public, rent or lend to the public, or adapt a more than insubstantial portion of the material covered by copyright law (the 'subject matter'). It is these rights that enable the copyright proprietor to collect royalty payments in return for giving others permission ('licenses') to do any of these things.

[275] Ibid., s.3(2): 'Copyright does not subsist in a literary, dramatic or musical work unless and until it is recorded, in writing or otherwise.' This is UK copyright law's version of a documented form requirement. While the statute does not specify that an artistic work must be recorded in a documented form, arguably this requirement is implicit in the types of artistic works enumerated in s.4: graphic work (defined as 'any painting, drawing, diagram, map, chart or plan, and any engraving, etching, lithograph, woodcut or similar work'), photograph (defined as 'a recording of light or other radiation on any medium on which an image is produced or from which an image may by any means be produced, and which is not part of a film'), sculpture (including a cast or model made for purposes of sculpture), or collage, a work of architecture being a building (including any fixed structure and a part of a building or fixed structure) or a model for a building, or a work of artistic craftsmanship. Arguably the very nature of each of these types of artistic work leads them to take a material form.

[276] Ibid., s.1(1): 'Copyright is a property right which subsists ... in the following descriptions of work – (a) *Original* literary, dramatic, musical or artistic works' (emphasis added).

[277] See, eg, *Francis Day and Hunter v 20th Century Fox* [1940] AC 112.

For the layperson and the user of copyright-protected materials, copyright is the legal doctrine that prohibits, for example, the unauthorized photocopying of a whole book, the unauthorized use on a website of a photograph taken by someone else, the unauthorized downloading of certain music and videos from the Internet, and the unauthorized installation of a piece of 'proprietary' (as opposed to 'open source')[278] computer software on numerous machines. However, the rights of the proprietor are tempered by exceptions, and unauthorized uses of a copyright-protected work may be permitted when they constitute 'fair dealing' or would otherwise be in the public interest.

'Fair dealing' – a narrower concept than its counterpart, 'fair use', in the United States[279] – allows copyright-protected works to be used without explicit prior permission for purposes such as non-commercial research,[280] or making a criticism or review that is also made available to

[278] When used in this context, the term 'proprietary' indicates that the software is protected under copyright laws, and that the proprietor – as identified by that law – has the legal right to either authorize use or refuse to do so. 'Open source' suggests the author or owner has voluntarily forfeited some of these rights.

[279] The US 'fair use' doctrine allows unauthorized use of another's copyright material when it falls into the category set out in the *Copyright Act* 1976, 17 USC §107, and further elucidated in case law: 'Notwithstanding the provisions of sections 17 USC §106 and 17 USC §106A, the fair use of a copyrighted work, including such use by reproduction in copies or phonorecords or by any other means specified by that section, for purposes such as criticism, comment, news reporting, teaching (including multiple copies for classroom use), scholarship, or research, is not an infringement of copyright. In determining whether the use made of a work in any particular case is a fair use the factors to be considered shall include:

- the purpose and character of the use, including whether such use is of a commercial nature or is for nonprofit educational purposes;
- the nature of the copyrighted work;
- the amount and substantiality of the portion used in relation to the copyrighted work as a whole; and
- the effect of the use upon the potential market for or value of the copyrighted work.

The fact that a work is unpublished shall not itself bar a finding of fair use if such finding is made upon consideration of all the above factors.'

[280] *Copyright, Designs and Patents Act* 1988, s.29(1).

the public,[281] so long as it is accompanied by sufficient acknowledgement. Under the United Kingdom's fair dealing provisions, copyright works (excluding photographs) may also be used for the purposes of reporting current events,[282] and copyright in a work may be unenforceable in cases where this would serve the public interest.[283]

4.4.1.c The Elasticity of Intellectual Property Doctrines

One way of altering the scope of intellectual property is to expand or contract the definition of the objects that fall within its doctrines. For example, UK copyright's notion of a 'literary work' expanded when it was deemed to encompass databases and computer programs. This stretched the scope of copyrightable works and extended the reach of copyright (and it therefore stretched the definition of intellectual property more generally).

Tinkering with the boundaries of existing definitions is not the only way of adjusting the number and type of objects of intellectual property laws. Another method is to add new categories of protectable material or to remove old ones. For example, copyright traditionally protected the types of subject matter outlined earlier. Legislative action added the

[281] Ibid., s.30(1).

[282] Ibid., s.30(2). The law contains a proviso that sufficient acknowledgement of the original work must be included.

[283] The *Copyright, Designs and Patents Act* 1988 does not explicitly provide a public interest defence, although s.171(3) does provide that '[n]othing in this Part ["copyright"] affects any rule of law preventing or restricting the enforcement of copyright, on grounds of public interest or otherwise.' The common law contains examples of cases where a public interest defence to copyright infringement has been accepted in the United Kingdom, eg, *Lion Laboratories v Evans* [1985] QM 526 (where the public interest in knowing that a make of breathalyser was allegedly faulty overrode the plaintiff's copyright in a confidential internal memorandum). However, in *Hyde Park Residence v Yelland* [2000] EMLR 363, the majority of the Court of Appeal found no public interest defence to an action for copyright infringement. This approach was then rejected in *Ashdown v Telegraph Group Ltd* (2001) 3 WLR 1368 by a differently constituted Court of Appeal, which referred to s.171(3) and with approval to *Lion Laboratories v Evans*, and said a public interest defence to copyright infringement may apply in very rare circumstances.

notion of 'secondary works' – also referred to as 'entrepreneurial subject matter',[284] which covers sound recordings, films, broadcasts, and cable programmes – to the scope of intellectual property objects created and regulated by copyright law.[285] In doing so, the law increased the varieties of material that copyright law could be used to protect and thus also expanded the reach of intellectual property law.

The scope of an intellectual property object, such as copyright work, can thus be enlarged or reduced by

1. adjusting the meanings of definitional terms (eg, modifying what is encompassed by the legal definition of a 'literary work') and/or
2. adding or removing definitional terms (eg, adding or removing 'dramatic work' as one of the types of copyright 'works').

It can also be changed by adjusting the properties of copyright works. 'Works' is a doctrinal term synonymous with 'intellectual property object' within copyright law, and works are themselves defined by reference to the above-mentioned properties of 'material form', 'originality', 'substantiality', 'creatorship', and so on.

A 'property', in this sense, refers to a characteristic, quality or trait of a thing. In the context of the current discussion, these operate together to make up the property protected by 'intellectual property' law (the latter use of the term 'property' implying ownership or possession). An example of properties being adjusted and this altering the scope of intellectual property would be the lowering of the threshold of originality that a work must meet in order to qualify for copyright protection.

Another common route to varying intellectual property's reach and nature is to adjust the rights that attach to the objects of its doctrines. Although the acronym 'IPRs' (for 'intellectual property rights') is often used as a shorthand, catchall phrase in relation to intellectual property

[284] In Australian law, these are called 'subject matter other than works'.

[285] While these types of works do not themselves require originality, they are usually representations of works that do attract copyright protection (eg, recordings of underlying musical works or films of underlying dramatic works) or that have done so in the past.

law, its use can be misleading unless employed in a context in which the necessity of a prior intellectual property object is recognized.[286] It is important to distinguish between an intellectual property object and the rights that can be enforced in relation to it. To reiterate, intellectual property objects are original ideas, information, knowledge, or symbols put into a documented form by a creator, with respect to which control is conferred by intellectual property rights. In the case of copyright, the works are the objects of copyright protection, while the rights are effectively the rules about who can do what with the objects.

Modifying the rights also modifies intellectual property's reach. For example, copyright's scope can be changed by adjusting the rights that attach to the works or the categories of person (natural and legal) who can exercise these rights. A copyright law that gives a proprietor an exclusive right only to copy a work is much more limited than one that also gives the proprietor exclusive rights to broadcast, or even access, a work. Similarly, a copyright law that gives the power to exercise rights only to an author who is a natural person and only during that person's lifetime is much narrower than a copyright law that allows the rights to be exercised also by the author's employer, the heirs and successors of the author, or also by a legal person (entity) such as a publishing company. The variable breadth of rights embodied in empirical intellectual property laws is indicative of the flexibility of the definitions contained in these laws. The definitions can be altered by law-makers at any time,[287] and doing so can

[286] This may seem obvious, but it is relatively common for claims to rights to be made by those seeking legislative 'intellectual propertization', even though the object they are asking for rights over has yet to be recognized legally as their intellectual property object. See, eg, discussion in Chapter 2, §2.1.1.

[287] In practice, however, this prerogative is somewhat limited by membership of international organizations and treaties that establish minimum intellectual property requirements for members. The effect has been that, unless their domestic provisions already exceed the international requirements established by TRIPs, members cannot amend definitions to make them more favourable to intellectual property proprietors unless the 'standard' definitions are altered centrally. This phenomenon is observed in relation to the *TRIPs Agreement*. When jurisdictions adopt intellectual property standards that

have a domino effect with respect to both the nature of the doctrine in question and the very concept of 'intellectual property'.

Each of the three mechanisms just described has been used (either alone or in conjunction with another) to change the scope of copyright and other intellectual property doctrines as a reaction to lobbying by interested parties and in response to new technologies and changing commercial environments.[288] Amending the objects of any one of intellectual property's doctrines in any of these ways changes the ambit of that doctrine as a whole, and this in turn has implications for the nature and scope of the legal system's department of intellectual property more generally. If intellectual property's definition is flexible and can be added to or subtracted from so easily in response to environmental conditions, 'intellectual property' is a rather chameleonic concept. It implies meaning and is used to communicate in a meaningful way, but there is no particular object that it represents.

With its objects and rights both so susceptible to continuous redefinition by law-makers, copyright – like other intellectual property doctrines – is an extremely flexible area of law. As Mark Lemley notes with regard to the evolution of this area of law in the United States:

> Copyright law has gone through numerous statutory iterations over the past 210 years, almost always changing in the direction of expanded protection for copyright owners – increasing the number of things that are copyrightable, increasing the duration of copyright protection, making it easier to qualify for copyright protection, and increasing the rights copyright owners have to control uses of their works.[289]

are in excess of those required under TRIPs – typically as an outcome of entering into a bilateral agreement with another nation – the resulting intellectual property laws are referred to as 'TRIPs-plus'. See, eg, Susan K. Sell, *Private Power, Public Law: The Globalization of Intellectual Property Rights* (Cambridge: Cambridge University Press, 2003), chap. 6, at 121–162.

[288] See, eg, the discussion in the introduction of Alexandra George (ed.), *Globalization and Intellectual Property* (Aldershot: Ashgate, 2006), xi–xl.

[289] Lemley, 'Romantic Authorship', above n. 184 at 886–887 (notes omitted).

The numerous changes have stretched copyright law so much that some parts of it barely resemble the earlier laws on which they were built. Despite this, copyright has retained an identifiable identity as a discrete intellectual property doctrine. The features that give it this character are arguably its doubly constructed objects (ie, its self-generated objects of regulation that are constructed first by being defined into existence by copyright law and, second, by being regulated by the operation of copyright law) and the particular conceptual building blocks that comprise those objects (ie, ideational object, documented form, creatorship, originality, and rights). The conceptual building blocks are common features of intellectual property, which also help to set intellectual property doctrines apart from other areas of law. However, as will be seen in the following chapter, they are not completely determinative in themselves.

The copyright example just discussed provides an indicative model of the manner in which intellectual property's doctrines are constructed, and it shows how the core criteria identified in this book operate in practice. An analysis of patent, trademark, or design law would have resulted in a similar depiction, as would have studies of many of the less mainstream sui generis intellectual property doctrines. Each doctrine consists of a body of 'rights' that attach to intellectual property 'objects' that have been defined into existence by the doctrine's own rules. These intellectual property objects are institutional facts that have arisen when the rules of an intellectual property doctrine were applied to ideational objects and condensed into a documented form. Thus, intellectual property objects are arguably self-generated objects of legal regulation, and the particular manner in which intellectual property doctrines create their own objects of regulation is a defining characteristic of intellectual property law. This gives rise to the description in this chapter of intellectual property's conceptual tools of self-creation – ideational object, creatorship, originality, and the documented form, and the rights that are then applied to the resulting object – as 'core criteria' of intellectual property law.

The following chapter tests this theory against intellectual property–like doctrines that, despite obvious similarities to intellectual property, are not themselves classified as such.

5 'Family Resemblance' and Intellectual Property

METHODS OF REGULATING THE USE OF IDEATIONAL objects such as ideas, information, knowledge, and signs have been evolving since time immemorial, but only some of these methods have developed into intellectual property laws. This chapter examines doctrines that are similar to those of intellectual property law, in that they too delineate and regulate the use of ideational objects and/or their documented forms, but whose objects of regulation are not treated by the law as 'intellectual property'.

Examining some of these intellectual property–like doctrines, this chapter tests the theory proposed in Chapters 3 and 4. It concludes that such doctrines may not be included in contemporary intellectual property doctrines because they may not bear all of the core criteria that were earlier suggested to be common to or characteristic of intellectual property doctrines.[1] They may not, for example, require a documented form or originality before regulating an ideational object. Or they may not have an identifiable creator or associated rights. Such cases would support a conclusion that the core criteria offer a reliable definition of 'intellectual property'.

[1] That is, an ideational object, represented in a documented form, that has an identifiable creator and is original, and that is governed by law that has created its object of regulation in this form.

However, some other intellectual property–like doctrines do display versions of the core criteria, despite not being generally recognized as doctrines of 'intellectual property' law. Some are customs, traditions, commercial practices, lore, and laws that regulated the use of ideational objects before the development of intellectual property laws per se. Others operate alongside contemporary intellectual property laws and can be credited as intellectual property's extended family. This begs the question, why are these regulations not treated as 'intellectual property'? Is it because the core criteria are also typical of non–intellectual property doctrines? Or does it suggest that something beyond the internal structural characteristics identified earlier may help to identify a law as 'intellectual property'?

Adopting a Hartian approach to defining by context, this chapter asks under what types of conditions intellectual propertization occurs. It concludes that the presence of political will, particularly when supported by normative justifications, creates conditions in which a regulatory doctrine is likely to be transformed into a doctrine within intellectual property law.

5.1. Intellectual Property's Extended Family

This book has focused thus far on the structure found within doctrines that are clearly recognized within society as 'intellectual property'. It has drawn conclusions from that analysis that can then be applied in a broader setting. At this point, the focus shifts from intra-departmental analysis (ie, within acknowledged intellectual property doctrines) to inter-departmental analysis (ie, comparing intellectual property with other legal and regulatory systems). The shift is from an analysis of the specific features of intellectual property doctrines to those of doctrines found outside the department of intellectual property.

Ludwig Wittgenstein described common features among related objects as a 'family resemblance':

> I can think of no better expression to characterize these similarities than "family resemblances"; for the various resemblances between members of a family: build, features, colour of eyes, gait, temperament, etc., etc. overlap and criss-cross in the same way.[2]

The department of intellectual property is like a family whose members (doctrines) have various resemblances: abstract objects of regulation defined in terms of creatorship and originality, documented forms, associated rights, and so on, as examined in the preceding chapter.

Drawing on this notion, the current chapter examines intellectual property–like laws and regulations – those with a family resemblance to intellectual property in that, like intellectual property laws, they also regulate human behaviour with respect to ideas, information, knowledge, or signs (and they share similarities with intellectual property's rights) but are not generally considered to be part of the intellectual property family. It investigates whether they display the core criteria of intellectual property identified in Chapters 3 and 4.

If these intellectual property–like regulations do not display them, the core criteria would appear to offer a self-sufficient method of identifying 'intellectual property'. In that case, the intellectual property–like doctrines may be considered to be ancestors (ie, precursors to) or relatives (ie, laws and conventions that perform functions similar to those performed by intellectual property but operate in a different manner) of intellectual property, but not be considered intellectual property themselves.

However, if intellectual property–like doctrines do share the core criteria but are nonetheless not treated as 'intellectual property', this begs the question why? Obtaining this outcome to an examination of intellectual property–like doctrines could give rise to the suggestion that the core criteria are not typical only of intellectual property doctrines, in which case the conclusion could be reached that something more than

[2] Ludwig Wittgenstein, *Philosophical Investigations*, trans. G. E. M. Anscombe (Oxford: Blackwell, 2003) at 27[e]–28[e], §67.

the core criteria is needed before certain laws and regulations attain their status as 'intellectual property'.[3]

In this way, the chapter tests the theoretical structure of intellectual property proposed earlier in this book. Whereas previous chapters have reached conclusions about the core criteria based on an examination of doctrines that *are* generally recognized as 'intellectual property', this chapter takes an external perspective, examining marks that generally are *not* considered to be 'intellectual property'. The benefit of this shift in perspective is the depth that it adds to the study. That is, 'intellectual property' is explored not only in its own terms, but also in a broader context.

5.1.1. Testing the Core Criteria: Subjects of Analysis

In testing the core criteria, intellectual property–like doctrines (rather than those from within quite separate legal departments, such as family law or constitutional law) have been chosen for examination precisely because of the similarities between their rules and the rights of intellectual property doctrines.

It would be relatively easy to reach the conclusion that the core criteria are not characteristic of the numerous non–intellectual property doctrines that bear little or no resemblance to intellectual property, either in form or in function. For example, it is not difficult to find a

[3] With respect to the idea of intellectual property as 'status': David Lange, 'Reimagining the Public Domain' (2003) 66 *Law and Contemporary Problems* 463–483, uses at 474 the term 'status' when distinguishing the 'public domain' (ie, the conceptual area covering goods that are not subject to regulation by intellectual property laws) from 'intellectual property'. He writes: 'Imagine the public domain as a status that arises from the exercise of the creative imagination, thus to confer entitlements, privileges and immunities in the service of that exercise; a status independently and affirmatively recognized in law, sometimes collective in nature and sometimes individual, but omnipresent, portable and defining; and a status meanwhile paramount to whatever inconsistent status may be conferred upon a work of authorship (or its author) from time to time, whether that work is protected as intellectual property, or is included within a so-called liability regime, or is otherwise provided for.' This notion of 'status' could be extended as suggested by the use of the term in the text.

range of differences between intellectual property law and family law or employment law. Neither relies on the core concepts of 'creatorship' or 'originality' to construct its own objects of regulation, as intellectual property doctrines do, and they are also very different in what they regulate (compared with the intellectual property object) and how they do so (compared with intellectual property's rights).

Differences are harder to discern when the comparison is made between intellectual property doctrines and doctrines that regulate similar things (ie, human behaviour towards abstract objects such as information and signs) in similar ways (ie, with rules or rights about access to and/or use of those objects). The focus in this chapter is thus on examining bodies of rules that are similar to intellectual property laws in structure or effect, but that are not treated as 'intellectual property' by the legal system. The results are likely to be interesting and informative. The similarities between those doctrines and intellectual property doctrines also mean that the results are unpredictable, in that it would not be surprising if the results either coincided with or diverged from the core criteria discussed in earlier chapters.

A finding that the intellectual property–like doctrines do not share utilization of the core criteria in creating their own objects of regulation would support a conclusion that the core criteria are particular characteristics of 'intellectual property' doctrines. It would suggest not only that the core criteria are characteristic of intellectual property doctrines, but also that they are probably not characteristic of doctrines that are not generally considered to be 'intellectual property'.

By contrast, a finding that some or all of the intellectual property–like doctrines do use the core criteria may either undermine the value of these criteria in identifying and defining 'intellectual property', or point to a need for refinements of the original theory. It would beg the question as to whether there is something about their structure – including what they regulate and how they do so – that sets them apart. Is there an additional factor or factors that validate some doctrines as 'intellectual property', while marginalizing others in this respect?

5.1.2. Methodology

This chapter examines examples of conventions and legal regulations of signs and other intangible objects that bear some resemblance to intellectual property laws but that are not generally recognized as 'intellectual property'. It tests the theoretical structure of 'intellectual property' proposed in Chapters 3 and 4 against these intellectual property–like doctrines that are not considered to be intellectual property. It does this by examining each doctrine and asking: Do the core conceptual criteria create an object of regulation from an 'ideational object' that is represented in a 'documented form' to which rights attach?

Selecting appropriate examples for analysis posed a dilemma. The extended family of intellectual property is well illustrated by examples of intellectual property–like regulatory systems such as customary indigenous laws governing arts, crafts, and traditional medicines; Roman law that did not expressly refer to intellectual property but did recognize and regulate certain incorporeal things; heraldic systems that governed the use of certain crests and symbols; rules about the branding of animals; law and custom concerning the use of hallmarks on items made of precious metals; and patronage systems that have given rise to some of the great masterpieces of art and music; as well as scientific breakthroughs; film, television programming, and coverage of news and current affairs. They are too numerous for each to be surveyed, so which should be chosen?

Most of the intellectual property–like doctrines surveyed in this chapter contain elements that might be described as examples of intellectual property's 'pre-history'.[4] In some cases, they can be traced back more than five hundred years and pre-date the earliest laws that are commonly

[4] The term 'pre-history' has been used elsewhere in relation to intellectual property, but in slightly different contexts. See, eg, Ronald V. Bettig, *Copyrighting Culture: The Political Economy of Intellectual Property* (Boulder, CO: Westview Press, 1996) at 11–15. It is also used in the introduction to Alison Firth (ed.), *The Prehistory and Development of Intellectual Property Systems* (London: Sweet & Maxwell, 1997) at v–vi, but is not defined.

regarded as intellectual property laws. In some cases, their influence on modern intellectual property laws is evident, yet they are not generally included in intellectual property treaties or administered by governmental intellectual property bureaucracies. This is particularly interesting when these regulatory forms have continued to operate alongside modern intellectual property laws. Contrasting intellectual property doctrines with similar forms of regulation that are not generally categorized as intellectual property provides insight into what distinguishes intellectual property doctrines from non–intellectual property.

An exhaustive survey of intellectual property's ancestors or its relatives is outside the scope of this book; the need here is only to test the theory proposed earlier (ie, that intellectual property doctrines are characterized by use of the core criteria to create documented objects of regulation that are separate from their underlying ideational objects), not to provide a comprehensive study of intellectual property–like bodies of regulation. Ultimately, the doctrines selected to be surveyed in this chapter are the following:

- indigenous customary law/lore;
- heraldry;
- the branding of animals; and
- workers' marks (guild marks, hallmarks, and standards).

It is suggested that, while each of these doctrines pre-dates modern intellectual property law in some ways, some of them may be thought of as intellectual property's ancestors. Others more closely resemble relatives who live in the neighbourhood of intellectual property.

Other examples that could equally have been included are doctrines regulating communicative systems as diverse as the use of Scottish tartan (traditional and modern),[5] certain uniforms, patronage systems,

[5] See, eg, Ross D. Petty, 'Of Tartans and Trademarks' (2004) 94 *Trademark Reporter* 859–880; Matthew A. C. Newsome, 'Restricted Tartans and Copyright' (April 2007) *Scottish Banner*, http://www.albanach.org/restricted.htm [accessed 14 June 2010].

Roman law traditions of regulating abstract objects, colour identification systems such as Pantone, cataloguing methods such as Dewey Decimal Classification or the Library of Congress Classification System, and methods of communicating via 'artificial' languages such as sign language and Morse Code.[6] The examples that have been included for examination in this chapter have been selected because of their prima facie similarities to intellectual property doctrines and because they are quite representative of the issues involved. The typical nature of the examples chosen means that the chapter's findings could be expected to apply to other examples not included in the survey.

In testing the theory proposed earlier in this volume, this study commences by searching for the core criteria in indigenous customary intellectual property–like laws that have not been drawn within the legal department of intellectual property.

5.2. Indigenous Customary Lore

Modern intellectual property laws are a relatively recent phenomenon. Most intellectual property laws took their modern forms during the Industrial Revolution and afterwards.[7] However, rules regulating ideational objects and their documented forms have existed since time immemorial. An examination of the laws of indigenous societies indicates a rich diversity of traditions in these areas.

The customary intellectual property–like rules and regulations observed by indigenous peoples will hereafter be referred to as 'lore' to

[6] Examples include signs and codes that have been systematically and intentionally created by humans, such as sign language for the deaf, which was invented by Juan Pablo de Bonet in 1620, and Morse Code, which was invented by Samuel Morse in the 1830s–1840s.

[7] See, eg, Brad Sherman and Lionel Bently, *The Making of Modern Intellectual Property Law: The British Experience, 1760–1911* (Cambridge: Cambridge University Press, 1999); Lyman Ray Patterson, *Copyright in Historical Perspective* (Nashville: Vanderbilt University Press, 1968); and Ronan Deazley, *Rethinking Copyright: History, Theory, Language* (Cheltenham: Edward Elgar, 2008).

distinguish them from the laws of the 'Western' societies that colonized many indigenous nations,[8] that spread around much of the world under the influence of the *Berne* and *Paris Conventions*, and that now comprise the minimum standards of 'intellectual property' law required to be implemented by World Trade Organization members under the *Agreement on Trade Related Aspects of Intellectual Property* 1994. The term 'lore' also reflects that such traditions and rules may not have the status of legally binding law (ie, they may not be enforceable by recourse to a state's legal apparatus) within the jurisdictions in which such lore survives.

For the purposes of this discussion, the 'intellectual property–like' lore of Australian Aboriginal cultures will be examined.[9] This example has been selected because it provides a clear demonstration of customary lore regulating ideational objects and their documented forms.

Despite the representative nature of these examples of indigenous Australian lore, it should be emphasized that important differences can be found between the lore of different indigenous communities, even those in close geographical proximity. This would be very evident were further examples from the South Pacific or other regions such as North America or Africa to be compared with the Australian Aboriginal lore discussed here.[10] Nonetheless, certain themes do seem to be quite common to the

[8] Note that such Western 'laws' could include 'customary law' in the sense of 'sources of law'. For a discussion of the use of customary principles in de jure intellectual property law, see Jennifer E. Rothman, 'The Questionable Use of Custom in Intellectual Property' (2007) 93 *Virginia Law Review* 1899–1982.

[9] Indigenous Australian conceptions of 'authorship' were discussed in some detail in Chapter 4, §4.2.4.f. The current survey of Aboriginal 'intellectual property' lore is directed at the system of regulation found in indigenous Australian communities, as well as their similarities to and differences from the traditions found in the Western intellectual property laws enacted by the Australian government.

[10] For discussions of customary intellectual property–like laws in other jurisdictions and the effects of globalization on those systems, see Paul Kuruk, 'Role of Customary Law under Sui Generis Frameworks of Intellectual Property Rights in Traditional and Indigenous Knowledge', (2007) 17 *Indiana International and Comparative Law Review* 67–118; Danielle M. Conway, 'Indigenizing Intellectual Property Law: Customary Law, Legal Pluralism, and the Protection of Indigenous Peoples' Rights, Identity, and Resources' (2008–2009) 15 *Texas Wesleyan Law Review* 207–256; Erica-Irene Daes, 'Intellectual

types of regulations that traditionally governed – and, in some cases, continue to govern – the use of ideational objects and their documented forms in many indigenous societies. These general themes are outlined in the following section, before being examined in context in the case study offered later.

5.2.1. Common Themes in Indigenous 'Intellectual Property' Lore

The heritage of many indigenous cultures has traditionally been governed by rules that regulate the use and transmission of history, kinship, and beliefs (such as spiritual traditions and religious convictions), knowledge (such as language, medicines, agricultural methods, use of land, and information about aspects of nature such as plants, animals, and weather patterns), and arts and rituals (such as ceremonies, songs, stories, dances, and paintings).[11] Social status, responsibilities, obligations, and privileges could also form part of the system regulated by such lore, and thus customary intellectual property–like lore often regulated a wider scope of subject matter than modern 'Western' intellectual property laws may do. For example, instead of dividing knowledge into 'artistic' and 'musical' works as copyright does, or into 'inventions', 'designs', and 'trademarks' as the international industrial property convention does,[12] indigenous lore

Property and Indigenous Peoples' (2001) 95 *American Society of International Law Proceedings* 143–150; Susan Scafidi, 'Intellectual Property and Cultural Products' *(2001)* 81 *Boston University Law Review* 793–842; Peter W. Jones, 'Indigenous Peoples and Intellectual Property Rights' (1996) 4 *Waikato Law Review* 117–140; Peter K. Yu, 'Cultural Relics, Intellectual Property, and Intangible Heritage' (2008) 81 *Temple Law Review* 433–506; Irma De Obaldia, 'Western Intellectual Property and Indigenous Cultures: The Case of the Panamanian Indigenous Intellectual Property Law' (2005) 23 *Boston University International Law Journal* 337–394.

[11] Terri Janke, *Our Culture: Our Future: Report on Australian Indigenous Cultural and Intellectual Property Rights* (Sydney: Michael Frankel, 1998) at 2.

[12] The *Paris Convention for the Protection of Industrial Property* (as amended, 28 September 1979) covers, inter alia, patent, design, and trademark law, as opposed to 'artistic property'.

may regulate ideational objects alongside tangible objects. Erica-Irene Daes describes the role and nature of such regulation in the following terms:

> Heritage includes all expressions of the relationship between the people, their land and the other living beings and spirits which share the land, and is the basis for maintaining social, economic and diplomatic relationships – through sharing – with other peoples. All of the aspects of heritage are interrelated and cannot be separated from the traditional territory of the people concerned. What tangible and intangible items constitute the heritage of a particular indigenous people must be decided by the people themselves.[13]

Some of the characteristics of such indigenous lore are that it forms a living tradition that evolves through its ongoing transmission and helps to form a society's continuing identity and culture.[14] Lore often has a holistic nature,[15] which makes attempts to separate it into legal departments or categories familiar to Western legal systems, such as tort or contract, or 'real property', 'personal property', and 'intellectual property', artificial.

Communal ownership or custodianship of both tangible and intangible objects is common in indigenous lore. Often a particular individual or group within a community is the nominated caretaker of a specified aspect of cultural heritage, and consent to use or communicate that aspect of cultural heritage for various purposes is a matter of decision-making by the society rather than by an individual.[16] Furthermore, systems of indigenous intellectual property–like lore are often concerned more with the preservation of resources and heritage than with economic issues.[17]

[13] Erica-Irene Daes, *Study on the Protection of the Cultural and Intellectual Property of Indigenous Peoples*, E/CN.4/Sub.2/1993/28 (28 July 1993), cited in Janke, above n. 11 at 2–3.

[14] Janke, above n. 11 at 7.

[15] Ibid. at 8.

[16] Ibid. at 8–9.

[17] Ibid. at 10.

Examples taken from Australian indigenous customary lore – hereafter referred to also as 'Aboriginal' lore – illustrate these characteristics and provide a distinct contrast with the classic intellectual property doctrines[18] whose standards are increasingly globalized.[19]

5.2.2. Australian Aboriginal 'Intellectual Property' Lore: A Case Study

Before 1788, the land that is today known as the 'Commonwealth of Australia' was home to an estimated 250 distinct language groups,[20] each representing different cultural traditions. Around 200 of these languages survive,[21] although many are no longer passed down to younger generations. The loss of indigenous languages is indicative of the loss of culture and traditions in many Australian indigenous communities.

Traditionally, much of the collective knowledge within Aboriginal communities was passed down through oral traditions, as was the interpretation of heritage that was recorded in documented forms such as rock art and tools.

Following British settlement in Australia in 1788, the customary patterns by which heritage was passed on within Aboriginal societies were upset by the destruction of communities through introduced diseases to which Aboriginal people lacked resistance, through the removal of people from their traditional lands, families, and communities,[22] and through the dilution of Aboriginal traditions by influences from other cultures.[23]

[18] For reference to the 'classic intellectual property doctrines', see Chapter 1, §1.5.2.

[19] For references to the globalization of intellectual property, see Chapter 2, §2.1.1.c.

[20] Michael Walsh, 'Overview of Indigenous Languages of Australia', in Suzane Romaine (ed.), *Language in Australia* (Cambridge: Cambridge University Press, 1991), 27–48 at 27.

[21] David Nathan (ed.), 'Aboriginal and Torres Strait Islander Languages', *The World Wide Web Virtual Library*, http://www.dnathan.com/VL/austLang.htm [accessed 30 May 2010].

[22] Janke, above n. 11 at 9.

[23] Heather McRae, Garth Nettheim, Laura Beacroft, Luke McNamara, and Shelley Wright, *Indigenous Legal Issues: Commentary and Materials* (Sydney: Law Book Company,

Although diverse in many ways, Aboriginal societies across the Australian continent were traditionally united by shared notions of 'the Dreaming'.[24] The Dreaming incorporates the culture and heritage of indigenous Australian communities as inherited from ancestors and passed from generation to generation through song, dance, storytelling, visual art, sacred sites, and oral history. It includes creation stories, customary lore, social structures, values and rules for behaviour, relationships with other people as well as with nature and the land, history, spirituality, and identity.[25] The Dreaming traditionally provided the 'legal' institutions of an Aboriginal community, including the regulation of people's behaviour towards other people with respect to intangible objects and their documented forms. As such, the Dreaming arguably operated as the traditional 'intellectual property' lore of Aboriginal communities.

5.2.2.a The Dreaming as Intellectual Property Lore

The concept of 'law' in Aboriginal communities prior to colonization was distinct from, and far broader than, the concept of 'law' introduced by British settlers. Traditional Aboriginal conceptions of 'law' encompass traditional culture or heritage, and they are therefore much more pervasive and wider in scope than Western concepts of a 'legal system' or 'system of justice'.[26]

2003), vividly summarize this effect at 75: 'For the most dispossessed peoples, much of their law was irretrievably lost. Others were left to reconstruct their laws as best they could, out of new affiliations forged with land and kin in a variety of environments: missions, reserves, cattle stations, rural towns and cities. Those fortunate enough to remain on their own land had to cope with introduced threats to their laws: the influence of missionaries, the introduction of alcohol, the removal of their children, the destruction of sacred sites, and the interventions of Australian law.'

[24] For a list of ways in which Aboriginal peoples' 'intellectual property rights' under indigenous lore differ from Western 'intellectual property', see Heather McRae, Garth Nettheim, Thalia Anthony, Laura Beacroft, Sean Brennan, Megan Davis, and Terri Janke, *Indigenous Legal Issues: Commentary and Materials* (Sydney: Law Book Company, 2009; 4th ed.) at 398, §8.120.

[25] For a more detailed introduction to the Dreaming, see Howard Murphy, *Aboriginal Art* (London: Phaidon Press, 1998) at 4–7.

[26] Kathryn Trees, *Contemporary Issues Facing Customary Law and the General Legal System: Roebourne – A Case Study*, Background Paper No. 6 (Perth: Law Reform

Describing Aboriginal customary lore, Kenneth Maddock draws on research by anthropologists working in various indigenous communities:

> In the Gibson Desert of Western Australia, for example, the Mardudjara have the word *julubidi*, glossed as 'law' by those who speak English. To say that an action is *julubidingga*, 'according to the Law', is to commend it. In the opinion of the anthropologist Robert Tonkinson the Mardudjara term 'connotes a body of jural rules and moral evaluations of customary and socially sanctioned behaviour patterns'; it is practically a synonym for 'traditional culture'. The rules and practices comprised in this culture are said by the Aborigines to have originated in the Dreamtime, that mythical era in which creative beings shaped the land and imposed life's order.[27]

Referring to another Aboriginal community, the Walbiri from the land north and northwest of Alice Springs, Maddock explains:

> *[D]jugaruru* [means] 'an established and morally-right order of behaviour (whether of planets or of people), from which there should be no divergence'; it can be translated as 'the law', 'the line' or 'the straight or true way'. Actions as diverse as the making of fire (human technique), the mating of bandicoots (animal behaviour) and the avoiding of mothers-in-law (social convention) are subsumed under *djugaruru*. This breadth of meaning makes sense in the light of the Walbiri world-view. Like the Mardudjara they suppose

Commission of Western Australia, 2004) at 218: 'To understand customary law it is necessary to appreciate the relationship between the inadequate concepts of "dreamtime" and "law". These terms are both impositions on Aboriginal cultures. Both the use of English and needing to speak to people outside their language groups has required Aboriginal people to use such terms (or variations of them). "Law" and "customary law" are inadequate because they cannot be free of the western concepts and power ascribed to the word "law" and the status of law as somehow above or separate from other aspects of our daily lives. "Dreamtime" is a derisory and simplistic term for an ancient belief system. It is necessary to have the information in both of these concepts, and a sense of spirituality, to understand customary law, because they are indistinguishable' (notes omitted).

[27] Kenneth Maddock, 'Aboriginal Customary Law', in Peter Hanks and Bryan Keon-Cohen (eds.), *Aborigines and the Law* (Sydney: George Allen & Unwin, 1984), 212–237 at 212 (notes omitted).

> nature and culture to have been formed in the same period by acts of the same beings.[28]

In such conceptions, 'law' means something encompassing both 'laws of nature' (eg, gravity and biological structures) and 'laws of human conduct' (including human behaviour towards other humans and with respect to things, tangible and intangible), both of which were inherited by humans from the ancestral forms who walked the land during the time of the Dreaming. 'The Dreaming' thus comes to stand for the law.[29]

Within this social system, human behaviour with respect to intangible objects and the documented forms of intangible objects are part of the Dreaming. Thus, Aboriginal methods of regulating intellectual property–like objects through the Dreaming amount to an indigenous system of customary intellectual property lore. These systems entail rights/privileges and duties, which may be one and the same. For example, in the case of *John Bulun Bulun & Anor v R & T Textiles Pty Ltd* (1998),[30] Aboriginal artist John Bulun Bulun gave evidence about a painting he had made, and his cultural obligation to do so, as passed from father to son through generations:

> My father ... painted the dreaming stories of our tribe, the Gunilbingu, including waterhole scenes.... His teaching was of importance in

[28] Ibid. at 212–213 (notes omitted).

[29] An analogy could arguably be drawn here between the regulatory function of the Dreaming and the regulatory function of orthodox or fundamentalist religious groups (who typically believe that their religion dictates a code of behaviour by which all people should live). For a discussion of Islam as intellectual property law – in a similar sense to which the Dreaming is being described here as intellectual property lore – see Ali Khan, 'Islam as Intellectual Property' (2000–2001) 31 *Cumberland Law Review* 631–684. See also Steven D. Jamar, 'The Protection of Intellectual Property Under Islamic Law' (1992) 21 *Capital University Law Review* 1079–1106.

[30] *John Bulun Bulun & Anor v R & T Textiles Pty Ltd* (1998) 41 IPR 513. See discussion in Chapter 4, §4.2.4.f, where the case is discussed in the context of the requirement of 'originality' for copyright to subsist under Australian copyright law. The case involved the reproduction of a painting, *At the Waterhole*, by John Bulun Bulun on T-shirts. Bulun Bulun joined other artists whose work had also been infringed to sue for copyright infringement and breach of the *Trade Practices Act* 1974 (Cth).

> imparting to me the traditional techniques of bark painting, and the dreaming traditions and images of our tribe. I am training my own son in the same manner.[31]

Explaining his duties or responsibilities, and the role of his artwork in preserving his cultural heritage, Bulun Bulun gave evidence:

> Barnda not only created the place we call Djulibinuyamurr but it populated the country as well. Barnda gave the place its name, created the people who follow him and named those people. Barnda gave us our language and law. Barnda gave to my ancestors the country and the ceremony and paintings associated with the country. My ancestors had a responsibility given to them by Barnda to perform the ceremony and to do the paintings which were granted to them. This is a part of the continuing responsibility of the traditional Aboriginal owners handed down from generation to generation.... In the same way my creator ancestor formed the natural landscape and granted it to my human ancestors who in turn handed it to me. My creator ancestor passed on to me the elements for the artworks I produce for sale and ceremony. Barnda not only creates the people and landscape, but our designs and artworks originate from the creative acts of Barnda. They honour and celebrate the deeds of Barnda. This way the spirit and rule of Barnda is kept alive in the land.[32]

[31] Colin Golvan, 'The Protection of *At the Waterhole* by John Bulun Bulun: Aboriginal Art and the Recognition of Private and Communal Rights', in Andrew T. Kenyon, Megan Richardson, and Sam Ricketson (eds.), *Landmarks in Australian Intellectual Property Law* (Melbourne: Cambridge University Press, 2009), 191–208 at 195.

[32] *John Bulun Bulun & Anor v R & T Textiles Pty Ltd* (1998) 41 IPR 513 at 518. See also discussion of this case in Aron Ping D'Souza, *Special Protections: The Ethics of Copyright and Aboriginal Iconography* (Carlton, Vic.: Elias Clark Group, 2008) at 125ff. See also Golvan, above n. 31. Bulun Bulun also gave evidence: '[M]y work is very closely associated with an affinity for the land. This affinity is the essence of my religious beliefs. The unauthorized reproduction of artworks is a very sensitive issue in all Aboriginal communities. The impetus for the creation of works remains their importance in ceremony, and the creation of artworks is an important step in the preservation of important traditional customs. It is activity which ... represents an important part of the cultural continuity of the tribe.'

In addition: 'This reproduction has caused me great embarrassment and shame, and I strongly feel that I have been the victim of the theft of an important birthright'. He said he had stopped painting as a result of the infringement.

The connection between the Dreaming and the lore regulating indigenous 'intellectual property' thus meant that the two could not be separated within this Aboriginal tradition.

Not only did such traditions award duties to paint and regulate the use of paintings, they also provided for penalties for infringers of the lore. For example, Maddock recounts a case in the nineteenth century in which several Aboriginal men were seized by their community and killed after they broke an object during a ceremony.[33] Whether it was the abstract significance (the ideational object) of this item (the documented form), or the symbolism of this item's documented form itself, that prompted the punishment, an analogy can be drawn with misuse of a copyright object or a breach of the moral right to integrity, both of which are found in Australian copyright law.

In another example, a Pitjantjatjara man was killed by his tribe after being secretly accused of disclosing tribal secrets to women.[34] Parallels can be drawn with the Australian law of breach of confidence, which punishes the unauthorized discloser of certain secrets.

In yet another example, a woman took a shortcut to a spring, walking within sight of a store of ritual objects. When her footprints were discovered, she was speared to death by her community.[35] Again, a comparison can be drawn with Western intellectual property laws that punish offences such as the disclosure of secrets and unauthorized access to and/or use of intellectual property objects.

While the precise behaviour being regulated, the objects with respect to which that behaviour was regulated, the rights and/or responsibilities that accompany custodianship or proprietorship, and the penalties for misuse of the object, may diverge, both the customary lore of the Dreaming and Australian intellectual property law regulate human behaviour with respect to ideational objects and/or their documented

[33] Maddock, above n. 27 at 224: 'Their necks were twisted around till the vertebrae had been dislocated, and they were probably choked to death as well.'

[34] Ibid.

[35] Ibid.

forms. The Dreaming can therefore be said to constitute 'intellectual property' lore within traditional Aboriginal societies.

5.2.2.b 'Infringement' of the Dreaming

Although the Dreaming's customary laws still operate to regulate uses of traditional heritage in some Aboriginal communities, they do not have the force of law in Australia,[36] and its rules have no enforceability against people external to those communities. They do not bind non-indigenous Australians, and they do not bind people who are not residents or citizens of Australia.

Concerns have been raised by some indigenous Australians about the use of Aboriginal heritage by unauthorized people with respect to the appropriation of indigenous art and methods of cultural expression.[37] Examples include the unauthorized use of symbols typical of Aboriginal art and the creation of non-authentic artworks adopting characteristically Aboriginal styles (such as those incorporating the use of dots, cross-hatching, and 'x-ray' imagery), the retelling of stories from the Dreaming, the unauthorized use of material that is secret and/or sacred within Aboriginal communities, the appropriation of spirituality from indigenous communities (such as non-Aboriginal authors writing and selling books and/or making films that record and discuss indigenous rituals, dance, and music, and thereby commercializing those materials), and the appropriation of indigenous art, music, and cultural objects (such as the acquisition of certain Aboriginal paintings by museums or private collectors). Such complaints have been made about Australians and foreigners outside Australia, as well as about Aboriginal people who have been alienated from their traditional heritage and have used culturally

[36] For a discussion of the application of Aboriginal lore under Australian law, see Alison Humphry, 'An Opportunity Lost for Aboriginal Self-Determination: Australia's Compliance with ILO 169' (1995) 2:1 *Murdoch University Electronic Journal of Law*, http://www.murdoch.edu.au/elaw/issues/v2n1/humphry21.html [accessed 7 June 2010].

[37] The concerns catalogued in this paragraph are discussed in more detail by Janke, above n. 11 at 19–41.

significant artistic motifs even though they would traditionally not have had the authority to do so. In addition, Aboriginal people have objected to bio-prospecting, and to the collection of indigenous remains and artefacts by museums in Australia and abroad.[38]

5.2.2.c The Dreaming and Intellectual Property Law

The destruction of Aboriginal cultures and the influences of non-Aboriginal society have left indigenous Australians often unable to protect their heritage using traditional lore. Yet they may be equally unable to avail themselves of Australian law appropriate to the situations that they object to. Aboriginal 'intellectual property' lore is different from Australian intellectual property law.

Trademarks, designs, and patents have to be registered in Australia before the respective signs, designs, and inventions can be protected. Trademarks are registrable only for commercial uses, so they are inappropriate and inapplicable to non-economic signs. They are therefore of little use in protecting the designs traditionally used by Aboriginal artists, although they may be useful for protecting modern artists' reputations.[39]

It was hoped that the introduction of a special authenticity label protected by trademark law would enable people to easily identify works of art created by Aboriginal and Torres Strait Islander Australians, thus

[38] See, eg, Tim Elliott, 'Spirits Cannot Rest So Far from Home' (13 March 2010), *Sydney Morning Herald*, http://www.smh.com.au/national/spirits-cannot-rest-so-far-from-home-20100312-q45t.html [accessed 30 May 2010]; Paul Turnbull, 'Theft in the Name of Science' (2008) 21 *Griffith Review*, http://www.griffithreview.com/images/stories/edition_articles/ed21_pdfs/turnbull_ed1.pdf [accessed 30 May 2010]. For a general discussion of the appropriation of cultural heritage such as art and ethnographical objects, see Jeanette Greenfield, *The Return of Cultural Treasures* (Cambridge: Cambridge University Press, 1995).

[39] For a more extensive discussion of the use of trademarks in this sense, see Terri Janke, 'Use of Trade Marks to Protect Traditional Cultural Expressions', Case Study 2 in *Minding Culture: Case-Studies on Intellectual Property and Traditional Cultural Expressions* (Geneva: World Intellectual Property Organization, 2003), available at http://www.wipo.int/export/sites/www/tk/en/studies/cultural/minding-culture/studies/trademarks.pdf [accessed 14 June 2010].

reducing the incidence of non-authentic 'Aboriginal' art being sold as Australian indigenous works.[40] Hence, the National Indigenous Arts Advocacy Agency (NIAAA) introduced the 'Label of Authenticity', which represents a boomerang or tick.[41]

It was registered as an Australian trademark in 1988[42] for use with respect to '[r]etail services in connection with indigenous arts and crafts' (Class 35) and '[t]he authentication of works of art or craft including indigenous arts and crafts; implementing, managing, and enforcing a certification program for authentic works of indigenous arts and crafts' (Class 42). Two identical marks[43] were registered as 'Certification Marks' covering many areas of business.[44] However, the initiative was found to

[40] Marianna Annas, 'The Label of Authenticity: A Certification Trade Mark for Goods and Services of Indigenous Origin' (1997) 3:90 *Aboriginal Law Bulletin* 4; Leanne Wiseman, 'The Protection of Indigenous Art and Culture in Australia: The Labels of Authenticity'(2001) 23 *European Intellectual Property Review* 14–25.

[41] For a discussion of the introduction and operation of the Label of Authenticity, see Matthew Rimmer, 'Australian Icons: Authenticity Marks and Identity Politics' (2004) 3 *Indigenous Law Journal* 139–179.

[42] Australian registered trademarks 772563 and 772564. Details may be found at the IP Australian ATMOSS trademarks database. See, eg, for trademark 772563, http://pericles.ipaustralia.gov.au/atmoss/Falcon_Details.Show_TM_Details?p_tm_number=772563&p_detail=DETAILED&p_search_no=5&p_ExtDisp=D#ENDORSEMENT772563 [accessed 14 June 2010].

[43] Australian registered trademarks 772564 and 772565.

[44] For example, registered trademark 772565 was registered for use with respect to '*Class 2* Dyes for clothing, paints and paint boxes; *Class 4* Candles; *Class 8* Hand tools and implements including artists tools such as chisels; *Class 9* Recordings (whether on compact disk, video tape, software or any other medium) which feature aboriginal art or craft works; *Class 14* Jewellery, precious stones and objects made of precious stones, watches and clocks, other works of art made of or with precious metals in this class; ornaments in this class; *Class 15* Musical instruments, including indigenous instruments; *Class 16* Paper, cardboard and goods made from these materials, printed matter, photographs, stationery, artists materials, paint brushes, instructional and teaching material, works of art or craft made of or on paper, lithographic works of art; *Class 18* Leather goods, art or craft works made on or with animal skins or hides; walking sticks, whips, harnesses and saddlery; *Class 20* Furniture, mirrors, picture frames; works of art or craft made of or with wood including bark paintings, spears, shields, woomeras and indigenous weapons; works of art or craft made of or on reed, bone, shell, mother-of-pearl and substitutes for these materials, wax, plaster or plastic; *Class 21* Household or kitchen utensils and containers, combs and brushes (except paint brushes); brassware,

be largely ineffective in practice,[45] and lawyer Terri Janke notes a lack of support amongst indigenous artists:

> There were relatively small numbers of artist[s] applying for the label in regional and local bodies. Many regional bodies are already using their own trade marks and logos to sell and distribute their art via Aboriginal arts center networks. Many centers feel they do not need to apply for the NIAAA mark to show that their products are 'authentic'. Moreover, the costs of the mark may preclude use by Indigenous artists, who have to pay for the cost of applying the label to their works.

The NIAAA closed in 2002 (after its funding ceased), and the authenticity marks were removed from the trademark register in 2009 after the expiry and non-renewal of the registered marks.[46]

Meanwhile, other Australian intellectual property laws are similarly ineffective at protecting traditional Aboriginal heritage. Australian design and patent laws require a description of a 'novel' design or invention. As Aboriginal designs and knowledge are often ancient, having been passed from generation to generation, the aspects of their heritage that

porcelain and earthenware including works of art or craft made of or on porcelain, terra-cotta or glass; *Class 22* Works of art or craft made of or with ropes, string and other fibrous textile materials; fishing nets and baskets within this class; *Class 24* Textiles and textile goods; works of art or craft made on or with textiles; *Class 25* Clothing, footwear, headgear; *Class 27* Carpets, rugs, mats and matting, wall hangings; *Class 41* Educational and training services relating to indigenous arts and crafts; entertainment, cultural activities or events relating to indigenous arts or crafts.'

[45] Terri Janke, 'Indigenous Arts Certification Mark', Case Study 8 in *Minding Culture: Case-Studies on Intellectual Property and Traditional Cultural Expressions* (Geneva: World Intellectual Property Organization, 2003) at 14, http://www.wipo.int/tk/en/studies/cultural/minding-culture/studies/indigenousarts.pdf [accessed 14 June 2010]. Janke also writes: '[T]he Label of Authenticity has failed to gain wide support at the primary production level, particularly among Aboriginal Arts and Craft Centres that are the major producers of Aboriginal art in the regions' (at 1).

[46] Details of the trademarks' history can be obtained from IP Australia's ATMOSS trademark database. Details of trademark 772563 (by way of example) are available at http://pericles.ipaustralia.gov.au/atmoss/Falcon_History.Summary_Page?p_tm_number=772563&p_search_no=5&p_detail=DETAILED&p_Extdisp=D [accessed 14 June 2010].

indigenous people would like to protect from appropriation by outsiders often cannot be registered under these intellectual property doctrines because they do not display the requisite kinds of creatorship, originality, and/or documented form. Even if expressions of the Dreaming could be registered by design and patent law, the duration of protection would be relatively short (five years, renewable for another five years, in the case of designs; a maximum of twenty years for patents). After rights under these laws expired, the ideational objects would again be left unprotected by intellectual property law.

Copyright law is likewise inapplicable to many of the things that Aboriginal people would like to protect from activities that would be considered misappropriation or misuse under traditional lore. Copyright law requires a work to be documented in a 'material form' before an intellectual property object will be identified in which rights can subsist. By its very nature, heritage that has been passed through generations of oral history is unlikely to have a documented form. Even when it is put in a documented form, the creator of the resulting 'work' will be considered by copyright law to be the person who converted it from an ideational object into that documented form. This may not be the same person who is the indigenous owner or caretaker of the heritage. Indeed, non-indigenous researchers have become the copyright proprietors of the documented forms of Dreamtime stories and histories of Aboriginal families and clans that they have recorded, causing upset and anxiety in some communities.[47] Although such problems can be alleviated by contract, the ability to transfer ownership of a work from the legally recognized creator to the traditional owner depends on the participation of that creator. This is clearly problematic in various situations, such as where one or more of the participants are unaware of the operation of the law, where a traditional owner is unaware that a work has been created, or where the traditional owner is being exploited.

[47] Terri Janke, *Writing Up Indigenous Research: Authorship, Copyright and Indigenous Knowledge Systems* (Sydney: Terri Janke, 2009).

Under indigenous Aboriginal lore, the creator of a work may be a communal group whose authorship is not recognized by Australian copyright law,[48] or the author may have died so long ago that the work is no longer covered by copyright law. The work may also have been made following a particular community tradition, and it is perhaps identical or very similar to earlier works within that community, meaning it would fall short of 'originality' requirements under Australian law. In any of these circumstances, the work is unlikely to be covered by copyright law but will instead lie in the public domain, where it may be freely copied by anyone, even if doing so would offend Aboriginal traditions.

Even if copyright law does apply and indigenous people are considered to be the creators to whom rights are awarded, fair dealing exceptions will allow unauthorized uses of the works in certain circumstances, such as for the purposes of research and study, reporting the news, or parody. Thus, copyright law does not necessarily provide the type of protection that an indigenous community seeks over its works;[49] people unconnected with the Aboriginal community have legally protected freedom to use the work for fair dealing purposes, even if the customary lore of a particular community would not allow use of it for those purposes or would discriminate in determining who was permitted to use the work. Australian copyright law is therefore unlikely to be an appropriate legal doctrine for indigenous communities to rely upon to protect their cultural heritage in accordance with the lore of the Dreaming.

5.2.3. Conclusion

Thus, indigenous, customary systems of lore can fulfil a role in indigenous communities akin to – although different from and sometimes broader in

[48] See, eg, the discussion of this issue in Chapter 4, §4.2.4.f.

[49] For a discussion of the unsuitability of copyright law to act as a proxy for indigenous lore in this respect, see Anne Barron, 'No Other Law? Author-ity, Property and Aboriginal Art', in Lionel Bently and Spyros Maniatis (eds.), *Intellectual Property and Ethics* (London: Sweet & Maxwell, 1998), 39–87.

scope than – 'intellectual property' law. They may overlap with Western intellectual property laws but are not typically regarded as 'intellectual property' themselves. Some would say the reason for this lies in a form of cultural or legal 'imperialism'.[50] Intentionally or not, this may indeed be the case. However, whether or not imperialism does help to explain the exclusion of indigenous lore from intellectual property law, theoretical explanations may also be offered.

The non-recognition of Aboriginal traditions with respect to intellectual property–like objects can likewise be explained in terms of legal imperialism; that is, Western laws trump Aboriginal lore. Yet Aboriginal lore has been incorporated into, or respected by, Australian law in other contexts where the legal device of 'incorporation' has allowed discretionary recognition of elements of Aboriginal customary law by lawmakers.[51] This sometimes occurs when courts incorporate aspects of Aboriginal customary law into their common law decisions.[52] For example, in *R v Jagamara* (1984), the Northern Territory Supreme Court took into account the customary punishment already meted out to an offender accused of killing a man with whom his wife was allegedly unfaithful.[53] Other examples occur when statutes provide for governmental decision-makers to take Aboriginal customary law into account as a legitimate part of their decision-making processes.[54]

In this context, it is more surprising that elements of Aboriginal lore regulating the use of ideational objects and their documented forms have not been recognized by Australian intellectual property law. Perhaps the

[50] See, eg, Keith Aoki, "Neocolonialism, Anticommons Property, and Biopiracy in the (Not-So-Brave) New World Order of International Intellectual Property Protection" (1998) 6 *Indiana Journal of Global Legal Studies* 11–58; Samuel A. Oddi, 'TRIPS: Natural Rights and a "Polite Form of Economic Imperialism"' (1996) 29 *Vanderbilt Journal of Transnational Law* 415–470.

[51] Greg McIntyre, *Aboriginal Customary Law: Can It be Recognised?* Background paper (Perth: Law Reform Commission of Western Australia, 2005) at 344.

[52] Ibid.

[53] *R v Jagamara* (Unreported, Northern Territory Supreme Court, 28 May 1984).

[54] McIntyre, above n. 51 at 344–346.

explanation lies – at least in part – in structural incompatibilities between the two bodies of law.

Adopting the structural perspective set out in Chapters 3 and 4, one might explain the reasons for excluding customary lore from the intellectual property rubric in terms of the core criteria. That is, much of the Aboriginal customary lore that traditionally regulated the use of ideational objects and/or their documented forms in indigenous communities does not exhibit creatorship or originality in the sense required by Australian intellectual property laws. Some of the traditional lore did not require a documented form, particularly where heritage was passed from generation to generation through the medium of oral history and performance traditions (especially in pre-literate societies). Some therefore regulated intangible knowledge and the ideational object, distinguishing them further from the model of 'intellectual property' identified earlier in this book that regulates use of the documented form. In these ways, indigenous customary systems of regulating 'intellectual property' differ metaphysically from Western intellectual property doctrines, and this could explain their exclusion from intellectual property's immediate family in Australia.

5.2.4. The International Intellectual Propertization of Customary Lore

Against this backdrop, it is interesting to note that 'traditional knowledge' (often referred to as 'TK') has become an area of much discussion and debate in intellectual property circles worldwide. Notwithstanding its divergence from intellectual property doctrines, an intellectual-propertized method of protecting indigenous heritage known as 'traditional knowledge' may be being assimilated within the Western intellectual property family.

The World Intellectual Property Organization offers the following definitions:

> Traditional knowledge (TK), genetic resources (GRs) and traditional cultural expressions (TCEs, or 'expressions of folklore') are economic and cultural assets of indigenous and local communities and their countries. WIPO's work addresses the role that intellectual property (IP) principles and systems can play in protecting TK and TCEs from misappropriation, and in generating and equitably sharing benefits from their commercialization and the role of IP in access to and benefit-sharing in genetic resources.[55]

This would suggest that WIPO's ambition is to create traditional knowledge as a doctrine of intellectual property law in its own right, incorporating and protecting common values found in indigenous culture. The Dreaming is an example of the sort of heritage that might be protected. However, from statements made by WIPO, it seems likely that such protection might be achieved by employing the core criteria rather than by adopting principles typical to indigenous systems of lore.

In the year 2000, WIPO established the WIPO Intergovernmental Committee on Intellectual Property and Genetic Resources, Traditional Knowledge and Folklore, a group tasked with drafting an international agreement to protect the genetic resources, traditional knowledge, and folklore of indigenous peoples (and others). The sorts of issues the committee is considering in drafting the agreement include: definitions of the material that should be protected; who should hold rights over the material; who should benefit from the protections/rights; whether economic or moral objectives should be the focus of the agreement; what exceptions or limitations will attach to the protection/rights; the duration of the protection/rights; interaction with existing intellectual property laws that may cover the same material; sanctions and penalties for infringing the new laws; and the extent to which the rules should be mandated internationally or left to national governments to determine.[56] As such,

[55] WIPO Traditional Knowledge, Genetic Resources and Traditional Cultural Expressions/ Folklore website: http://www.wipo.int/tk/en [accessed 8 June 2010].

[56] WIPO Traditional Knowledge, Genetic Resources and Traditional Cultural Expressions/ Folklore, Intergovernmental Committee 'Lists of Issues' website: http://www.wipo.int/ tk/en/igc/issues.html [accessed 8 June 2010].

the committee seems to be importing conceptions of the core criteria of intellectual propertization, and in doing so it may indeed end up creating a new doctrine of 'intellectual property law' with respect to traditional knowledge.[57] Only time will tell whether such a doctrine would replicate or replace the traditional intellectual property lore of various indigenous peoples around the world.

◆◆◆

At this point, our attention shifts from the macro-perspective of identifying intellectual property doctrines in systems of law to a more focused analysis of intellectual property–like regulatory doctrines that exist in jurisdictions such as the United Kingdom, the United States, and Australia, but that are not recognized by the law as intellectual property doctrines in their own right. The regulatory systems of heraldry, animal brands, and workers' marks (such as guild marks, hallmarks and standards) will be analysed in turn.

5.3. Heraldry

Heraldry grew out of ancient systems of military identification such as the pictures of animals found on the shields and armaments of Greek and Roman warriors, and the symbols on Norman and Saxon shields and banners that can be seen on the renowned Bayeux Tapestry.[58] Heraldry shares similarities with trademark laws, yet it has not developed into a modern 'intellectual property' doctrine that is recognized by intellectual property treaties or national intellectual property bureaucracies.

From around the tenth to the twelfth century, modern heraldic systems began to evolve in several European countries. Military tournaments

[57] For a discussion of how donor jurisdictions can themselves be affected and changed by global intellectual propertization processes see, eg, Kenneth D. Crews, 'Harmonization and the Goals of Copyright: Property Rights or Cultural Progress?' (1998) 6 *Indiana Journal of Global Legal Studies* 117–138.

[58] L. G. Pine, *The Story of Heraldry* (London: Country Life, 1952) at 19–20; J. P. Brooke-Little, *Boutell's Heraldry* (London: Frederick Warne, 1970) at 3.

were popular during this period, with participants identifying themselves with insignia worn on their armour. Coinciding with the Roman Catholic pope's call for Crusaders to fight Muslims in Palestine in the twelfth century, these conditions encouraged consolidation in the practice of marking one's armour, banners, and shields with crests and other insignia to identify the affiliations of their bearers.[59] The result was the development of an organized system of heraldry and the emergence of professional heralds with knowledge of insignia and of the rules and terminology that governed their use.[60] These professional heralds formally administered the system.

Within this system, various heraldic symbols represented the bearer's heritage, principles, and beliefs, as well as factual information such as lineage and gender. Rolls of arms were established, and heraldic regulatory bodies compiled and organized the use of the symbols and language of heraldry. In some respects, this system resembled an early military version of the trademark system that would later develop in the field of commerce.

Initially, armorial bearings could be granted by a herald or they could be adopted by someone who wished to use symbols not already in use.[61] From the early fifteenth century, the right to use armorial bearings could be obtained only through inheritance or by award by a herald. In England, for example, the College of Arms in London was established by a patent from King Richard III in 1483 to supervise the use of arms.[62] Many other European jurisdictions created equivalent heraldic authorities.[63]

[59] Ibid. at 4–6; Pine, above n. 58 at 20–21; Thomas Arundell, *Historical Reminiscences of the City of London and Its Livery Companies* (London: Richard Bentley, 1869) at 389.

[60] Brooke-Little, above n. 58 at 3.

[61] Pine, above n. 58 at 23, quoting Nicholas Upton, *Doctorum sui temporis Maecenas* (published in the early fifteenth century, though the publication details are unclear).

[62] Noel Cox, 'The Intellectual Property Law and the Protection of Armorial Bearings' (2001) 12 *Australian Intellectual Property Journal* 143–152 at 143 n. 2.

[63] Francis J Grant (ed.), *The Manual of Heraldry: A Concise Description of the Several Terms Used, and Containing a Dictionary of Every Designation in the Science* (Edinburgh: John Grant, 1929) at 11.

Heraldic systems still operate with the force of law in some jurisdictions. Armorial bearings are granted by the ancient College of Arms in London and Court of the Lord Lyon in Scotland, while the Office of the Chief Herald grants arms in Ireland. In continental Europe, state heraldic authorities continue to grant arms in Belgium,[64] Denmark,[65] Latvia,[66] Lithuania,[67] Luxembourg,[68] the Netherlands,[69] Portugal,[70] Russia,[71] Slovakia,[72] parts of Spain,[73] and Sweden.[74] Outside Europe, official heraldic authorities grant arms in Kenya, South Africa, Zimbabwe, Azerbaijan, and the Caribbean state of Antigua and Barbuda. The Canadian Heraldic Authority was established in 1988 to grant and register arms in that jurisdiction.

In some jurisdictions where no government authority has been established to grant arms, private organizations have been established to register arms. For example, the United States does not have an official heraldic authority, but several private organizations offer heraldic registration services. Although the assumption and registration of arms with such a service may be evidence of the adoption of arms, it has no other legal basis.[75]

[64] Arms are granted by the Raad van Adel or Conseil de la noblesse, Vlaamse Heraldische Raad and the Conseil d'héraldique et de vexillologie de la Communauté française de Belgique.

[65] Arms are granted by the Statens Heraldisk Konsulent.

[66] Official and municipal arms are granted by the State Heraldry Commission, within the President's Office.

[67] Official and municipal arms are granted by the Heraldry Commission, within the President's Office.

[68] Arms are granted by the Commission héraldique de l'état.

[69] Arms are granted by the Hoge Raad van Adel.

[70] Arms are granted to corporations only by the Gabinete de Heraldica Corporative.

[71] Arms are granted by the State Heraldry Service, within the President's Office.

[72] Arms are granted by the Heraldic Commission.

[73] Arms are granted by the Cronistas de Arms within the provinces of Castile and León only.

[74] Arms are granted by the Statens Heraldiska Namnd.

[75] See, eg, the information provided by the American Heraldry Society, which suggests the registration of arms with such a service: 'Registration establishes a date certain when the arms were in use as a hedge in case a legal protection regime is established in

In modern times, the uses of heraldic symbols extend far beyond military and familial foundations, and the influences of heraldry are found in diverse places. Many flags follow heraldic principles, and although some contemporary trademark laws explicitly regulate the manner in which heraldic imagery may be incorporated into registered trademarks,[76] many contemporary trademarks adopt traditional heraldic symbolism. For example, Porsche cars carry the arms of Stuttgart superimposed on those of Württemberg (Germany), Alfa Romeo cars carry parts of the coats of arms of Milan (Italy), and – as depicted in Figure 5A – the trademark of Saab cars[77] bears part of the arms from Scania (Sweden).[78] The colours of the Milanese football clubs Inter and AC Milan derive from the sixteenth-century tinctures of two of the city's districts.[79] Indeed, many modern trademarks display heraldic influences.

Heraldry and trademark law are alike in several ways. Using English heraldry as an example, it can be observed that armorial bearings and intellectual property objects appear to share the same core criteria. They each display an ideational object, used in a documented form, governed

the future. Customarily, the person who first uses a particular coat of arms in any given jurisdiction is considered to have a superior right to it. If the time comes when it is possible to bring legal action to protect armorial bearings, it will probably be important to be able to document the first use of the arms': http://www.americanheraldry.org/pages/index.php?n=Registration.Domestic [accessed 7 June 2010].

[76] See, eg, the UK *Trade Marks Act* 1994, which prohibits the (unauthorized) registration of a trademark that consists of or contains the royal arms, or any of the principal armorial bearings of the royal arms, or any insignia or device so nearly resembling the royal arms, or any such armorial bearing as to be likely to be mistaken for them or it (s.4(1)(a)); the armorial bearings or any other state emblem of a Convention country that is protected under the *Paris Convention* or the WTO agreement (s. 57(2)); and the armorial bearings of international intergovernmental organizations of which one or more *Paris Convention* countries are members (s.58).

[77] Community Trade Mark 001814284, registered to Saab Automobile AB, Sweden. Details available at CTM-Online (OHIM database): http://oami.europa.eu/CTMOnline/RequestManager/en_DetailCTM_NoReg [accessed 4 June 2010].

[78] Per Mollerup, *Marks of Excellence: The History and Taxonomy of Trademarks* (London: Phaidon, 1998) at 22–23.

[79] Michael Pastoureau, *Heraldry: Its Origins and Meaning*, trans. Francisca Garvie (London: Thames & Hudson, 1997) at 93–94.

Figure 5A. Use of Scania Heraldic Image in Saab Trademark (EU)
Coat of Arms of Scania (*top*) and registered trademark of Saab Automobile (*bottom*)

Top: Image by Lokal_Profil at Wikimedia Commons (Skåne län vapen.svg), under CC-BY-SA-2.5.
Bottom: Image kindly provided by Saab Inc (all rights reserved).

by and dependent on laws (in some jurisdictions, these laws are explicit; in others, they are customary rules of heraldic organizations that may or may not be enforced through the legal system), created, and displaying a degree of originality at the time of grant. The similarities may reflect the influence of heraldry on early trademark regimes, and/or perhaps they reflect English heraldry's heritage in early patent law.[80]

Despite the similarities between heraldry and intellectual property, it appears to be only in Zimbabwe that heraldry has been incorporated within a state intellectual property bureaucracy. In that jurisdiction, arms can be granted by the Registrar of Names, Uniforms, Badges and Heraldic Representations,[81] located within the Zimbabwe Intellectual Property Office. The website of the Ministry for Justice and Legal Affairs states:

> The office deals with all registration of Industrial Designs, Trade and service Marks, renewal of registered Trade Marks and Patents, Name changes, granting of letters of patents assignments, restoration and administration of copyrights and neighbouring rights including Armorial Bearing, Names, Uniforms and Badges registration although these do not constitute Intellectual Property.[82]

Thus, even where heraldry is formally administered with intellectual property law, distinctions can be drawn between heraldry and modern intellectual property. A catalogue of their differences points to reasons for this.

[80] Cox, above n. 62: 'The letters patent issued by Henry V to the sheriffs of three counties in 1418 required that only those men possessed of arms by ancestral right, or by grant from someone possessing the authority to grant arms, could bear arms' (at 143 n. 2).

[81] This is governed by Chapter 10:01 of Zimbabwe Law, the *Armorial Bearings, Names, Uniforms And Badges Act* (Acts 12/1971, 40/1977, 29/1981 (s.59), 7/198, 22/2001 (s.4); S.I. 490/1981 (s.3)).

[82] Website of the Zimbabwe Ministry for Justice and Legal Affairs, Department of Deeds, Companies, Trade Marks, Patents and Industrial Designs: http://www.justice.gov.zw/index.php?option=com_content&view=article&id=51%3Adepartment-of-deeds-companies-trade-marks-patents-and-industrial-designs&catid=35%3Adepartments&Itemid=55 [accessed 7 June 2010].

First, intellectual property doctrines tend to apply to and operate in commercial environments, whereas this is not an inherent feature of heraldry, and commercial use of a heraldic symbol is subordinate to the purpose regulated by the heraldic system. In intellectual property law, passing off requires use as a trader before indicia of reputation will be protected, and trademark law requires commercial use if a registered mark is to be valid. Where armorial bearings are not used in a commercial context, they would be unprotected by passing off law and unregistrable as trademarks.

Second, the documented form of the ideational object represented by an heraldic crest stems from a royal grant. As Noel Cox notes, armorial bearings are therefore 'a form of Crown-licensed monopoly ... akin to a form of royal honour.'[83] Arms are granted by letters patent from the Crown, which delegates its authority to the Kings of Arms at the College of Arms in London. Arms will be granted only if the Earl Marshal issues a warrant to this effect.[84] While anyone may petition the Earl Marshal for armorial bearings, not all petitioners are granted arms. The College of Arms explains:

> [T]here are no fixed criteria of eligibility for a grant of arms, but such things as awards or honours from the Crown, civil or military commissions, university degrees, professional qualifications, public and charitable services, and eminence or good standing in national or local life, are taken into account. When approaching a herald with a view to petitioning for a grant of arms it is desirable to submit a curriculum vitae.[85]

Thus, the rules for grant of armorial bearings are discretionary and uncertain. By contrast, intellectual property law nominates clear standards (albeit ones that may be difficult to interpret and apply precisely when one is delineating the scope of intellectual property objects) about what

[83] Cox, above n. 62 at 149.

[84] College of Arms (UK) website: http://www.college-of-arms.gov.uk/About/08.htm#a [accessed 14 June 2010].

[85] Ibid.

and when intellectual property objects subsist or when ideational objects become intellectual property objects through registration.

Third, the legal enforceability of heraldic law is problematic in some jurisdictions. The English High Court of Chivalry has jurisdiction to intervene where arms are being used without authorization, but it 'has been inactive for some centuries.'[86] Moreover, despite New Zealand and Australia having inherited the English legal system, there appears to be no enforceable legal protection in either country[87] for armorial bearings that have been properly granted by the English College of Arms (which is the appropriate heraldic authority to which citizens of those nations would apply for a grant of arms). However, a dearth of litigation means this issue has not actually been tested in the Australian courts' common law jurisdiction.[88] By contrast, intellectual property ownership and rights are enforceable at law.

Fourth, not all jurisdictions have heraldry systems. For example, it was noted earlier that the United States has no formal system for registering armorial bearings. US citizens may apply to the Earl Marshal in London for honorary arms,[89] or they may simply assume arms and register them with informal registries. The absence of a heraldic system in one of the nations that has been most responsible for driving the global intellectual propertization agenda in recent times may also help to account for its absence from the intellectual property family.

[86] Cox, above n. 62 at 146.

[87] Ibid. at 145.

[88] See, eg, Andrew G. A. George, 'The Law of Arms in Queensland' (2008) 49 *Heraldry News* 3–6 at 4: '[I]n almost 150 years, the Queensland Courts have had the fortune of never hearing a case specifically on the law of arms and thus armorial common law is particularly vague.'

[89] See College of Arms website: http://www.college-of-arms.gov.uk/About/08.htm#a [accessed 16 June 2010]: 'American citizens may be granted honorary arms. They must meet the same criteria for eligibility as subjects of the Crown, and in addition must record in the official registers of the College of Arms a pedigree showing their descent from a subject of the British Crown. This may be someone living in the north American colonies before the recognition of American independence in 1783, or a more recent migrant.'

Figure 5B. Trademarks (*left & middle*) and Logo (*right*) of the University of Sydney (Aust.)

Images kindly provided by The University of Sydney, Australia (all rights reserved).

Fifth, armorial bearings may be registered as trademarks for use in a commercial context. For example, the University of Sydney holds several trademarks depicting heraldic emblems. Those depicted on the left and middle in Figure 5B are registered trademarks, while the image on the right illustrates the manner in which these arms have been incorporated into the University's latest logo.[90]

If they are sufficiently original, coats of arms may also be protected as artistic works under copyright law. Copyright protection would arise automatically in *Berne Convention* jurisdictions, although trademark protection of an heraldic emblem would require registration. Passing off may also protect monopoly rights to use arms in commercial contexts in some jurisdictions. Thus, even in jurisdictions that offer specific systems of

[90] *Left*: Australian registered trademark 187871, granted to the University of Sydney in 1964. *Middle:* Australian registered trademark 793395, granted to the University of Sydney in 1999. The armorial bearings were first granted to the University of Sydney by letters patent on 14 May 1857. A description and explanation of the coat of arms can be found at an online exhibition at the University of Sydney website: http://sydney.edu.au/heraldry/coat_of_arms/index.shtml [accessed 16 June 2010]. *Right*: Logo of the University of Sydney, introduced 11 January 2010. For an explanation of the logo and its relationship with the University of Sydney's Coat of Arms, see http://sydney.edu.au/about/publications/logo.shtml [accessed 7 October 2011].

protection for heraldry, the ease with which intellectual property protection can be afforded over armorial bearings may make it a more practical and attractive manner of protecting heraldic imagery than traditional heraldic systems.

Despite this catalogue of differences, the structural similarities between heraldry and intellectual property law beg the question of whether heraldry is an example of the presence of the core criteria in the absence of an intellectual property doctrine.

The answer is perhaps yes and no. Yes, versions of the core criteria are present in heraldry, yet it is not treated as an intellectual property doctrine. No, heraldry itself may not be considered to be intellectual property, but it operates alongside classic intellectual property doctrines – trademark law, and perhaps also passing off and copyright law – that perform overlapping functions, thus rendering heraldry largely obsolete in legal terms.

Heraldry grew from a customary system of identifying opponents in battle and developed into a royal grant in a period that pre-dated modern intellectual property laws, and it has arguably not grown much beyond that point. This may be because it is largely superfluous in modern society, with few armorial bearings now being granted[91] and the alternative possibility of using mainstream intellectual property doctrines to protect commercial uses of heraldic emblems. It may also be indicative of ideological factors, with heraldry commonly perceived as inegalitarian and somewhat irrelevant, and therefore unlikely to attract the attention of many law-makers or voters. In this sense, heraldry has stagnated as a body of regulatory rules, while other systems of regulating ideational

[91] The College of Arms website records: 'In 2009, 132 grants and transfers of armorial bearings were made by the English Kings of Arms, of which 10 were to corporate bodies (including Glyndwr University, City University, Oriel College Oxford, Green Templeton College Oxford, Stowe School, the Worshipful Company of Glass Sellers, the Town Council of Lavenham, and the Essex Society for Archaeology and History). There were 83 grants of badges, eight grants of supporters, and six grants of arms to grantees in the same patent as their spouse.' See http://www.college-of-arms.gov.uk/About/08.htm#a [accessed 14 June 2010].

objects – particularly those that meet commercial imperatives and accord better with mainstream philosophical ideals such as equality – have been incorporated into the modern family of 'intellectual property'. If this is correct, the conclusion may be drawn that, rather than an exception to the core criteria of intellectual propertization, heraldry represents a pre-cursor to 'intellectual property'. It is one of intellectual property's ancestors, and it also survives in its own right as a sort of living cultural relic. Its modern commercial functions have been largely usurped by intellectual property's trademark doctrine, and what remains is little more than the continuation of an age-old body of tradition.

5.4. Branding of Animals

The marking of animals with brands that indicate their owners or other information about them has been a traditional practice of herders and livestock owners for many centuries. The word 'brand' is derived from *brandr*, the Old Norse verb 'to burn',[92] and it traditionally referred to the marking of animals with symbols burned into their hides.

The branding of animals with hot irons can be traced back at least five thousand years, with Egyptian tombstones from 3000 BC illustrated with branded domestic animals. For example, the Egyptian tomb of Khemuheted at Beni Hassan dates from around 1900 BC and shows a man leading an ox branded with hieroglyphics.[93]

Farmers traditionally branded their animals to indicate ownership in case they strayed, were stolen, or mingled with other farmers' animals. In order to demonstrate that certain sheep or cattle belonged to them, they branded their livestock with unique symbols. Even in pre-literate societies, this made it easy for farmers to discern the animals of one from those of another.

Brands also functioned as marks of quality. Once an animal was sold, brands were an instant indication of where the beast had come from and

[92] J. B. Sykes (ed.), *The Concise Oxford Dictionary of Current English* (Oxford: Clarendon Press, 1976, 6th ed.) at 119.

[93] Mollerup, above n. 78 at 27.

who had reared it: designators of source and quality. These simple brands thus functioned as badges of origin or de facto trademarks.[94]

In addition to brands made on an animal's hide, earmarks (slits in an animal's ear) are also a traditional method of marking livestock. Many jurisdictions have laws concerning the earmarking of branded animals, where use of a registered brand indicates ownership of livestock, and use of a registered earmark aids the identification of animals. For example, the *Brands Act* 1918 in the Australian state of Queensland[95] provides that cattle and pigs over a certain weight must be branded before being sold, and other livestock may be branded and earmarked to assist with identification and avoid disputes if animals stray. Cattle earmarks are constructed from a set 'alphabet' comprising certain signs that may be combined and then allocated and registered with the Queensland Primary Industries and Fisheries Brands Office. Figure 5C depicts some of the signs that can be combined to create earmarks suitable for registration in Queensland.

A national Australian database – the National Livestock Identification System – records all transportation of cattle, sheep, goats, and pigs from birth until export or death (either natural or by slaughter), with the animals identified by their brands and earmarks. Similar systems operate in many other jurisdictions and seem quite intellectual property–like in nature. For example, the California Department of Food and Agriculture will register a brand that does not

> conflict with any other recorded brand in this State ... is capable of producing a like design when applied to the hide of an animal ... is capable of readily symbolizing the intended design to any person who views it [and] lends itself to common verbal description.[96]

[94] Gerald Ruston, 'On the Origin of Trademarks' (1955) 45 *Trade-Mark Reporter* 127–144 at 128.

[95] In conjunction with the *Brands Regulation* 1998 (Qld).

[96] These instructions on the California Department of Food and Agriculture website (http://www.cdfa.ca.gov/ahfss/Livestock_ID/Brand_Registration_Info.html#Cattle [accessed 4 June 2010]) paraphrase the requirements of the *Food and Agricultural Code*, s.20661–20672.

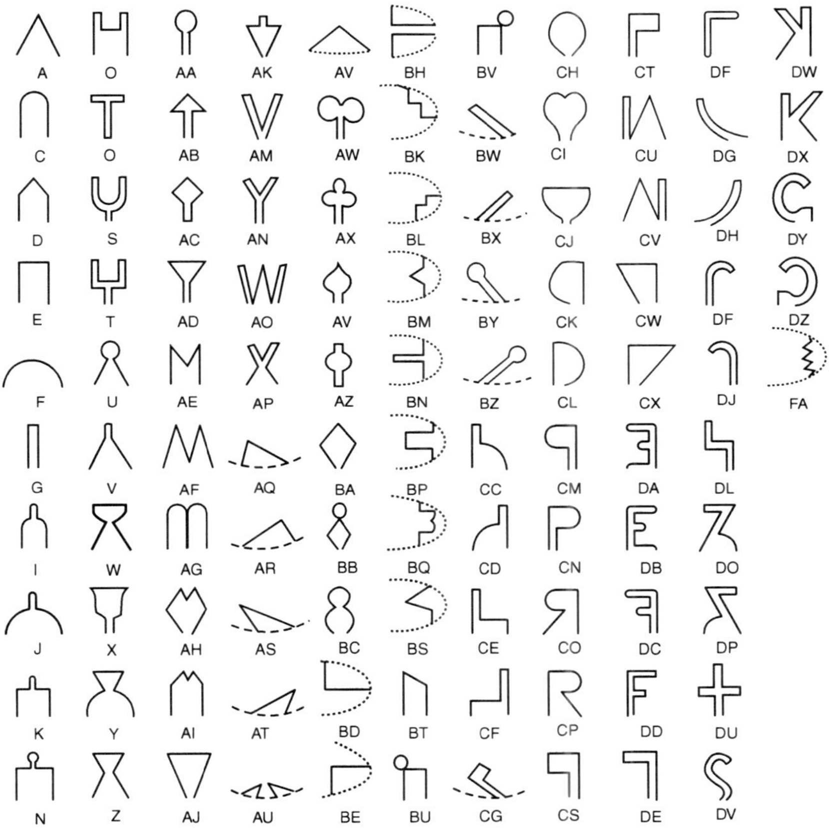

Figure 5C. Cattle Earmark Codes and Shapes (Queensland, Australia)

Diagram provided by courtesy of The State of Queensland, Australia, (Department of Employment, Economic Development and Innovation)

These requirements sound very much like those of trademark law, where a distinctive (ie, original) sign is registered (ie, represented in a documented form) to denote a trader's (ie, author's) goods (in this case, livestock). Yet, despite their similarities to intellectual property, animal branding systems are not covered by international intellectual property treaties or administered by governmental intellectual property administrations such as IP Australia, the Intellectual Property Office (UK), or the United States Patent and Trademark Office.

There seems to be no reason why a livestock brand that otherwise meets requirements could not also be registered as a trademark or protected by the law of passing off. It might also be covered by copyright law. Livestock owners can therefore draw on both a jurisdiction's specific branding rules and mainstream intellectual property law to protect their indicia of livestock ownership and identification. It is not entirely clear why animal branding remains outside intellectual property's nuclear family, but – as with heraldry – it may be because it can be replicated by trademark law. It therefore operates in conjunction with and parallel to intellectual property. Maybe animal branding is yet another of intellectual property's ancestors, some of whose features are replicated in its descendants (such as trademark law), but which also lives on in its own right as part of intellectual property's extended family.

5.5. Workers' Marks

Guild marks, pottery marks, and hallmarks are likewise precursors of intellectual property laws that display some distinct functional similarities to trademarks and the law of passing off. However, the governing structures overseeing the adoption and use of these original industrial marks set them apart from modern intellectual property doctrines.

Workers' marks are perhaps the earliest forms of intellectual property, some dating back thousands of years. Pottery marks have been traced back to the Stone Age, around 50,000 BC, and have been found in the tombs of Egyptian kings dating from the First Dynasty, around 3000 BC.[97] Marks such as thumbprints and symbols (eg, a fish, star, or cross)

[97] Craig Hovey, *The Patent Process: A Guide to Intellectual Property for the Information Age* (New York: Wiley, 2002) at 58.

have been found on clay pots from ancient Etruria, Greece, and Rome,[98] and pottery marks were common on European pottery from the 1700s onwards.[99] Branding expert Tom Blackett notes:

> Some of the earliest manufactured goods in 'mass' production were clay pots, the remains of which can be found in great abundance around the Mediterranean region, particularly in the ancient civilisations of Etruria, Greece and Rome. There is considerable evidence among these remains of the use of brands, which in their earliest form were the potter's mark. A potter would identify his pots by putting his thumbprint into the wet clay on the bottom of the pot or by making his mark: a fish, a star or cross, for example. From this we can safely say that symbols (rather than initials or names) were the earliest visual form of brands.[100]

The purpose of these marks was to identify the potter, and therefore the origin of the object. A reputation for quality could be summarized by the mark, and a culprit could more easily be traced in the case of poor craftsmanship. This was the standard reasoning behind workers' marks.

Workers' marks have taken various forms. The following pages will examine, in turn,

- guild marks;
- hallmarks; and
- standards.

Although each developed separately, each has similarities with intellectual property law. And, like the examples of heraldry and animal brands surveyed earlier, each operates in parallel with intellectual property law.

[98] Tom Blackett, 'What Is a Brand?' in Rita Clifton and John Simmons (eds.), *Brands and Branding* (New York: Profile, 2003), 13–25 at 14.

[99] Geoffrey A. Godden, *Encyclopaedia of English Pottery and Porcelain Marks* (London: Herbert Jenkins, 1964) at 13.

[100] Blackett, above n. 98 at 14.

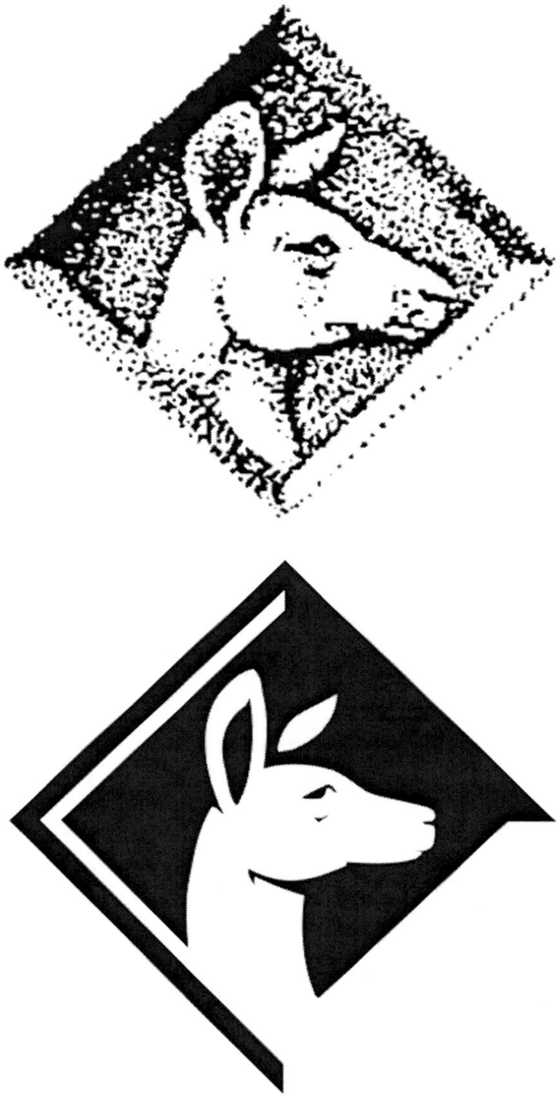

Figure 5D. Guild Mark (*top*) and Registered Trademark (*bottom*) of the Gold and Silversmiths Guild of Australia (Aust.)

Images kindly provided by The Gold and Silversmiths Guild of Australia (all rights reserved).

5.5.1. Guild Marks

The formation of guilds to protect artisans and craftspeople led to formal systems of workers' marks. Guild members were required to brand their work with the marks of both the guild and the individual craftsperson,[101] and early guilds kept registers of the 'devices' used to indicate who had made particular products.[102] This led to systems of de facto 'trademark' registration in many industries,[103] some of which were backed by statute.

For example, pottery marks were formally regulated in Britain from the fourteenth century when potters merged with the guild protecting armourers and braziers to protect their work against counterfeiters.[104] From this period, armourers and sword-makers were also required to place a unique mark on their metalwork to indicate its source.[105]

Similar systems were put in place to regulate the use of furniture marks, stonemasons' marks, printers' marks, and watermarks. Some artisans still use marks to identify their products, although the general purpose is more to keep tradition – and the values served by those traditions – alive than to comply with legal requirements.

[101] Hovey, above n. 97 at 59: 'Guilds usually mandated that anything made by a craftsman show both the symbol of the guild and the mark of the individual who produced the article.'

[102] Edward S. Rogers, "The Social Value of Trade-marks and Brands" (1947) 37 *Trade Mark Bulletin* 249–254 at 252.

[103] See, eg, Hovey, above n. 97 at 59, who notes: 'In English law the first known statute applying to trademarks comes from 1266, when bakers were required to have their own marks for each type of bread they made. In the fifteenth and sixteenth centuries armorers, metal workers, paper workers, weavers, printers, tanners, and smiths used trademarks to identify their goods, and tough laws existed to punish whoever copied somebody else's trademark. Once an innkeeper was hanged for trying to sell a cheap wine as Rudesheimer. In addition to merchants, it became common for well-off families to develop their own form of trademark, the coat of arms, many of which we continue to see today.'

[104] W. Care Hazlitt, *The Livery Companies of the City of London: Their Origin, Character, Development, and Social and Political Importance* (London: Swan Sonnenschein, 1892) at 133. Note, however, that records from this time are limited.

[105] Rogers, above n. 102 at 251.

Even where not required by law, modern guilds have sometimes been established to preserve the traditions of their trades by using guild marks to continue ancient practices of applying guild and markers' marks. A good example is provided by the Gold and Silversmiths Guild of Australia, which was established in 1988 as a voluntary organization for jewellers. Its website states:

> The Gold and Silversmiths Guild of Australia was formed in 1988 by a group of jewellers concerned that work produced in Australia should be marked as such.... [O]ur members firmly believe that work produced in Australia should be appropriately marked. The first requirement of prospective members is that they have their own Maker's Mark. Our members are all individuals passionately involved in their work and find it difficult to understand why a person involved in this or any other creative activity would not mark their own creations. The Guild accepts the time-honoured practice of jewellers and gold and silversmiths to personally mark their work as desirable, from a position of personal pride, and from the customer confidence point of view. These members' marks are struck on fine silver touch plates for posterity, again an old tradition. They will be an integral part of the history of this industry in Australia.[106]

Members are entitled to use the Guild Mark, which the Gold and Silversmiths Guild of Australia has registered as a device mark entitled 'Kangaroo's Head in Diamond'.[107]

With respect to the use of this mark, the Guild's website states:

> Acceptance as a member entitles you to the use of the Guild mark. This mark is registered in various forms, and therefore protected and can not be used by anybody not a current member of the Guild, each punch is numbered and issued to a member on joining.
> Its use is subjected to strict rules and may be summarised as such:

[106] Available at http://www.gsga.org.au/index.php?option=com_content&view=article&id=11&Itemid=11 [accessed 7 June 2010].

[107] Australian registered trademark 708452, granted to the Gold & Silversmiths Guild of Australia from 13 May 1996.

- The Guild Mark can only be used on metals meeting the Standards now currently set by the Guild.
- The Guild Mark cannot be used unless accompanied by the member's mark.
- The Guild Mark cannot be used unless accompanied by the appropriate metal purity mark.
- The use of the Guild Mark remains optional; all productions need not be marked.
- The use of the Date punch is optional, however if it is used it must be accompanied by the Guild Mark.

> The Guild system of marking uses a date mark which members purchase each year, commencing on January 1st. The mark exhibits the same letter as that used by, The Worshipful company of Goldsmiths – Guildhall in Britain, but within the shape of the diamond border.[108]

The Guild has thus employed the trademark system as a de facto guild mark system. It gains exclusive rights to use the Guild Mark as a trademark, and thus has legal standing to sue those who infringe its rights. In effect, it licenses use of its trademark to Guild members, who must comply with strict conditions as a term of their contract of membership.[109]

In addition to de facto protection through the use of trademarks, intellectual property's trademark doctrine has also developed a specific system that protects guild marks and modern equivalents such as the names, logos, and slogans of professional organizations and industry groups.

[108] Available at http://www.gsga.org.au/index.php?option=com_content&view=article&id=11&Itemid=11 [accessed 7 June 2010].

[109] These conditions can be found on the Gold and Silversmiths Guild of Australia website: http://www.gsga.org.au/index.php?option=com_content&view=article&id=8&Itemid=8 [accessed 7 June 2010].

'RULES RELATING TO GUILD AND DATE MARKS

1. The Guild Mark must be used only in conjunction with a Member's Makers Mark currently registered on the Guild's Touch Plate.
2. The Guild Mark must always be accompanied by a metal purity mark.
3. The Guild Mark can only be applied to Gold, Silver, Platinum or Palladium and their alloys as set out in the Standards for the "Composition and Marking of Precious Metals". (Res. 30.4.03.)

5.5.1.a Guild Marks as Intellectual Property (Collective Trademarks)

Modern equivalents to guild marks can be found within intellectual property's trademark system in the form of 'collective trademarks'.[110] These are a special type of trademark registered by an association for use on the goods and/or services of its members to distinguish the products of members from those of other traders.[111] Examples of modern Australian collective trademarks are owned by the Industry Funds Forum and the United Grand Lodge of Queensland, and each may be used only by members of the registered proprietors in accordance with their rules.

Collective trademarks therefore function in the same way as guild marks, and guild marks have arguably been brought within the intellectual property family in this manner. Each creates its own objects of regulation and, while these objects may be one and the same, the systems

4. The Guild Mark can be struck only on a Member's own work, or works produced under a Member's direct control in supervised workshop conditions. A Member's Punch is not transferable except after written application and only by direct authority of the National Council. (Res. 30.4.03.)
5. The Guild Mark must be struck directly onto a Member's work; it cannot be moulded, stamped or reproduced in any way on a piece of work.
6. The Guild Mark may be used on articles which are:
   a) individually made, OR
   b) reproduced by casting, stamping or other form of reproduction, provided that, in the case of reproduced work, the Member takes responsibility for the quality of the material and work not wrought by the Member.
7. A Member's recognised staff, subject to the conditions of Rule 4, may strike the Guild Mark.
8. The Guild Mark must not be applied to products which are an assemblage of commercially available components.'

[110] Collective trademarks are recognized by international intellectual property treaties. For example, Art. 7*bis* of the *Paris Convention for the Protection of Industrial Property* (1883, as amended) provides for signatory states 'to accept for filing and to protect collective marks belonging to associations the existence of which is not contrary to the law of the country of origin, even if such organisations do not possess an industrial or commercial establishment.'

[111] See the discussion about early collective trademarks in the United States in 'The Collective Trademark: Invitation to Abuse' (1959) 68 *Yale Law Journal* 528–541.

operate in parallel with one another. Although collective trademarks function in a different way than ordinary trademarks,[112] the trademark system has arguably been sufficiently flexible to incorporate into itself an older type of workers' mark, and one that predated and probably influenced the development of the trademark system. Like heraldry, guilds and their marks preserve traditions that have existed for centuries. Meanwhile, the mainstream intellectual property system provides a practical way for guilds (and their modern equivalents, such as professional organizations) to protect their trading symbols with collective trademarks and their legally enforceable monopoly rights.

5.5.2. Hallmarks

Hallmarks are another form of workers' mark and, in many ways, they echo the experience of guild marks. In some respects, hallmarks can be seen as a subset of guild marks (eg, the example of the Gold and Silversmiths Guild of Australia just given would also fall within the discussion of hallmarks), although the function of a hallmark was broader. Guild marks indicate registration with or recognition by an industry organization, as do hallmarks. However, hallmarks have the additional function of guaranteeing the quality of the metal product on which they appear.

Regulation of the manufacture of goods from gold, silver, and platinum with a system of 'hallmarks' can be traced back to the thirteenth and fourteenth centuries, and in some jurisdictions it came to be covered by specific legislation that operated (and, in some places, continues to operate) alongside trademark laws. Although hallmarking systems bear many similarities to trademark law, they are not generally included within the 'intellectual property' rubric. They arguably form another part of intellectual property's extended family or ancestry.

[112] The term 'ordinary' is adopted here to distinguish what would normally be referred to as 'standard' trademarks from collective and certification trademarks. It is used instead of 'standard' to avoid confusion with trading 'standards', which are discussed later at §5.5.3.

5.5.2.a Traditional Hallmarking

Early European hallmarking traditions developed in many jurisdictions. In Britain, laws concerning required standards for gold and silver date from 1238,[113] and the first statute covering hallmarking was set forth in 1300 when King Edward I passed a law stating that no silver or gold was to be sold until its quality had been tested at the headquarters of the Goldsmiths' Company. A mark depicting a lion's head (known as the 'King's Mark') was to be applied to the silver or gold that met the required standard.[114] Thus, a 'hallmark' was originally the sign applied to silver that had been tested for purity by the Worshipful Company of Goldsmiths, a medieval guild established under Royal Charter in 1327. Official standards were set, nominating the correct proportions of silver and copper, and the Goldsmiths' Company became responsible for policing those standards. Testing by an assay office[115] became obligatory in response to fraud by silversmiths who mixed less silver with more copper (the alloy needed as a base for silver, which is too soft if moulded by itself) than required to meet metal purity rules.

A statute of Edward III in 1363 required every goldsmith to use an individual mark (known as the 'maker's mark') to be applied to items of craftsmanship, making it easier to track and punish those who sold sub-standard silver. In the early 1400s, the King's Mark was also adapted slightly to indicate at which office of the Goldsmiths' Company the metal was being tested. A series of rules and laws was applied through the centuries,[116] developing into a quite standardized set of regulations and procedures.

[113] Judith Banister (ed.), *English Silver Hall Marks* (London: W. Foulsham, 2004) at 7.

[114] John Bly, *Discovering Hallmarks on English Silver* (Princes Risborough, Buckinghamshire: Shire Publications, 2002) at 3.

[115] Assay offices are institutions established to test the purity (metallurgical content) of metals. A list of the assay offices of members of the *Convention on the Control and Marking of Articles of Precious Metals* (1972) can be found at the official Convention website: http://www.hallmarkingconvention.org/assay-offices.php [accessed 2 June 2010].

[116] For example, the 'sterling standard' for silver was reintroduced in 1720 (having earlier been abandoned) with the king's head being used as a hallmark to indicate that required taxes had been paid. It was therefore known as the 'Duty Mark'. Bly, above n. 114 at 11.

5.5.2.b Modern Hallmarking

Hallmarking persists as an organized and relatively standardized system that operates in many modern jurisdictions. In some places, such as Australia,[117] hallmarking operates by the force of convention and/or the underpinning of trademark law. In others, such as the United Kingdom, it is backed by the force of specific law.

In the United Kingdom, the *Hallmarking Act* 1973 provides for assay offices to test the purity of silver, gold, platinum and palladium items weighing more than a specific weight, and to 'hallmark' those that meet certain standards. These are marked with a sponsor's mark (also known as a 'maker's mark'), the mark of the inspecting assay office, and the standard of fineness. Other marks can be added, such as the lion passant for sterling silver and a date mark. For example, the item bearing the hallmarks depicted in Figure 5E was hallmarked at the Birmingham Assay Office in the United Kingdom. The marks '925' and the 'lion passant' indicate that it is made of sterling silver (ie, silver that comprises a minimum millesimal fineness of 925). By way of comparison, an item marked with the signs in Figure 5F would be made of 18-carat gold and likewise

Figure 5E. Example of Silver Hallmark from Birmingham Assay Office (UK)

Image kindly provided by the Birmingham Assay Office, UK

[117] See the discussion of the Gold and Silversmiths Guild of Australia at §5.5.1.

Figure 5F. Detail of Silver Hallmark from Birmingham Assay Office (UK)

Images kindly provided by the Birmingham Assay Office, UK (all rights reserved)

hallmarked by the Birmingham Assay Office. Each of these examples contains a sponsor's mark (ie, 'SAO'), fineness mark (ie, '925' or '750'), and the assay office mark (in these examples, an anchor represents the Birmingham Assay Office). The date stamp is an optional sign indicating the year in which the assay office tested the metal. In Figure 5E, the letter 'm' indicates that it was made in the year 2011. In Figure 5F, the common control mark indicates where the metal was tested in accordance with international convention.

Similar systems operate elsewhere, some mandated by government, others voluntarily. Internationally, hallmarks are regulated according to the *Convention on the Control and Marking of Articles of Precious Metals* (1972).[118] Goods exported from one member state need not be re-hallmarked prior to importation to the other member state if they have been marked with the Convention Common Control Mark, the national Assay Office Mark of the exporting member, a responsibility mark indicating the manufacturer, and a fineness mark indicating the metal's purity. However, only nineteen countries have acceded to this treaty.[119] Another international organization, the International Association of Assay Offices (IAAO),[120] operates as a hub for the exchange of information and technical cooperation between assay offices, and particularly

[118] Also known as the '*Hallmarking Convention*' or '*Vienna Convention*'.

[119] See details on the website of the *Hallmarking Convention*: http://www.hallmarkingconvention.org/accession-dates.php [accessed 2 June 2010].

[120] The IAAO website is http://www.theiaao.com/ [accessed 2 June 2010].

as a liaison for European law-making. It has forty-seven members from thirty-seven countries, and works closely with Convention members. Modern hallmarking systems thus vary among jurisdictions. Where they exist, they tend to follow a familiar scheme. Elsewhere, intellectual property's trademark doctrine can provide de facto protection.

Where a governmental regulatory system has not been adopted specifically with respect to hallmarks, it seems quite common for the trademark system to be co-opted to protect monopolies over hallmarks. The earlier discussion[121] of the way in which the Gold and Silversmiths Guild of Australia has used the trademark system to protect its Guild Mark in the absence of a formal system to protect guild marks or hallmarks in Australia provides a good example of an industry body providing a private, non-governmental, de facto hallmark system. The weakness of the system is that not all smiths and jewellers working with the relevant metals are required to comply. However, those who do adopt hallmarks and register them as trademarks can obtain the ability to monopolize those marks when used as a trademark. Laws prohibiting misleading and deceptive trading conduct reinforce this system, providing a deterrent against unaffiliated traders adopting or otherwise misusing the marks.

Another example of a jurisdiction without an assay office system to regulate the use of hallmarks is the United States. Nor does the United States require the hallmarking of precious metals; however, a trader engraving a claim of metal quality (such as gold or silver purity) on an item must also engrave its maker's mark – known within hallmarking practice as its 'trademark' – alongside the claim. In practice, these maker's marks are often registered as trademarks, and thus function as trademarks in both the hallmark and trademark sense of the terms.

An example of this in practice can be seen in the markings used by the US jewellery and silverware company Tiffany & Co. Figure 5G is the example of a mark placed on a Tiffany & Co. silver coffeepot circa

[121] See the discussion of the Gold and Silversmiths Guild of Australia at §5.5.1.

Figure 5G. Tiffany & Co. Hallmark ('trademark'& 'maker's mark') (US)

Photograph © 2012 Museum of Fine Arts, Boston.

1858–1873. Together, the words 'Tiffany & Co.' in conjunction with the gothic 'M' symbol and other markings constitute a hallmark.

As used in Figure 5G, the words 'Tiffany & Co.' are known in hallmarking parlance as the 'trademark' – the mark of the trader – while the gothic 'M' is the 'maker's mark', signifying Edward C. Moore, the silversmith who had designed the item on which the hallmark appeared. As can be seen by comparing the Tiffany & Co. hallmark in Figure 5G with Tiffany & Co.'s registered US trademark depicted in Figure 5H,[122] the company's hallmark 'trademark' is almost identical to its ordinary trademark, which

[122] US registered trademark 0023572, registered 5 September 1893. Details available at USPTO TESS Database: http://tess2.uspto.gov/bin/showfield?f=doc&state=4001:9s27 6u.8.143 [accessed 18 June 2010].

TIFFANY & CO.

Figure 5H. Tiffany & Co. Registered Trademark (US)

Trademark used with kind permission of Tiffany & Co. (all rights reserved)

is registered for use with respect to 'Bronzes, Silver and Plated Ware, and Ornamental Articles in Metal'.[123] Thus, even in the absence of a formal hallmarking or assay office system in the United States, any unaffiliated person who applies the Tiffany & Co. mark to metals or jewellery without authorization would be likely to infringe the company's trademark rights. As such, intellectual property's trademark law offers a de facto means of protection to hallmarks in the United States in a manner similar to that discussed with respect to guild marks.

Thus, hallmarks seem to be another example of an intellectual property–like system that pre-dates modern intellectual property law and can be identified as one of intellectual property's ancestors. It also lives on beside intellectual property law in some places, while in others it has essentially been subsumed within intellectual property law's trademark doctrine. Yet hallmarking itself is not considered to be part of modern intellectual property's 'family'. It has not specifically been brought within the mantle of the World Intellectual Property Organization or the World Trade Organization's intellectual property trade negotiations and treaties, and 'hallmarks' are not regulated as such by state intellectual property bureaucracies.

In this sense, hallmarks are another example of an intellectual property–like doctrine that displays versions of the core criteria – that is, an ideational object is put into an original documented form by a creator – but that is not recognized as 'intellectual property'.

[123] Ibid.

Perhaps the reason for this is historical: in the absence of a formal hallmarking regime, the custom of using hallmarks as trademarks offers de facto protection. Perhaps this renders unnecessary a separate system for registering hallmark 'trademarks' and 'maker's marks' (which could likewise be registered as trademarks by individual craftspeople). To the extent that hallmarks are indicators of metal quality, their function is descriptive and not shielded by trademark law, but protection can be found under consumer protection law that prohibits false and misleading advertising and/or by legislation governing the use of trading 'standards'.[124] From this perspective, it could be argued that hallmarks have indeed been drawn within the intellectual property system – albeit de facto and without fanfare – through the practice of registering them as trademarks. If so, formal hallmarking systems that remain in contemporary commercial conditions may reflect a desire to preserve age-old customs in a mature industry, but those traditions should be distinguished from the intellectual property–like aspects of hallmarking, which do indeed seem to have been brought within the intellectual property system through their use of trademarks. As such, perhaps the intellectual property–like functions of a hallmarking regime are superfluous in a commercial context that offers trademark and passing off protection. If so, there is no need for the legal department of intellectual property to draw hallmarking within its fold de jure, as the task has already been accomplished by trademark law.

Those jurisdictions in which a formal hallmarking system operates separately but in parallel with the trademark system are perhaps adhering to legal traditions that have functioned long and adequately, and that seem in no particular need of change or streamlining. In those places, a dual layer of protection is given to hallmarks, and traders would presumably welcome the ability to protect their marks under both systems.

[124] See the later discussion at §5.5.3.

5.5.3. Standards

'Standards' are arguably another form of workers' marks that display similarities to intellectual property doctrines but that operate outside the intellectual property law system. Their history is not as ancient as that of guild marks or hallmarks. However, like those systems, functions of standards are also replicated within intellectual property law.

Standards are published documents detailing agreed-upon specifications and/or procedures according to which something will be done or made. They are administered by institutions that appoint expert technical committees to create the norms that are then approved as 'standards'. They are intended to create consensus about the nature of products and services, increasing consistency, reliability, quality, and safety, and enhancing consumer knowledge. The earliest and perhaps most fundamental examples of standards were those for weights and measures. With time, standards developed for industrial safety, occupational health and safety, consumer safety, and quality measures for myriad products and services.

To the extent that goods and services marked as complying with standards give accurate information about the products and their sources, they function somewhat like some intellectual property doctrines. Yet, while the minimum standards for the composition and/or quality of their goods and/or services is an area of regulation that bears significant similarities to intellectual property's trademark law and the sui generis doctrine of geographical indications, 'standards' is not a doctrine that is typically thought of as falling under the 'intellectual property' rubric.

The main international standards body, the International Organization for Standardization (ISO),[125] is a non-governmental organization based in Geneva, Switzerland. Established in 1947, its members are the national standards bodies of 162 countries, and the organization develops and publishes standards in accordance with which goods and services can

[125] The name 'ISO' is derived from the Greek word *isos*, meaning 'equal'. See ISO website: http://www.iso.org/iso/about/discover-iso_isos-name.htm [accessed 2 June 2010].

be certified.[126] It has established more than 18,000 standards covering numerous industries. Most standards relate to specific products, materials, and processes, establishing minimum safety standards and 'good practice' requirements. Others are generic and can be applied to many industries.[127]

An example of a standard is ISO 10256:2003,[128] which relates to '[h]ead and face protection for use in ice hockey'. The standard indicates minimum performance requirements and methods for testing helmets and face protectors used in ice hockey, thus creating minimum acceptable norms of quality with which manufacturers should conform. A press release put out by ISO explained the benefits of this standard:

> It is intended help manufacturers design equipment capable of protecting players, goalkeepers and referees by distributing and dampening the force of impact and preventing the penetration of objects. The standard is for manufacturers, conformity assessment agencies, users and ice hockey associations.[129]

[126] For further information about the ISO, see Jack Latimer (ed.), *Friendship Among Equals: Recollections from ISO's First Fifty Years* (Geneva: ISO Central Secretariat, 1997).

[127] For example, ISO9000 standards indicate 'quality management' (which covers 'what the organization does to fulfil: the customer's quality requirements, and applicable regulatory requirements, while aiming to enhance customer satisfaction, and achieve continual improvement of its performance in pursuit of these objectives'), and ISO14000 standards indicate 'environmental management' (which covers what the organization does to 'minimize harmful effects on the environment caused by its activities, and to achieve continual improvement of its environmental performance'). See http://www.iso.org/iso/iso_catalogue/management_standards/iso_9000_iso_14000.htm [accessed 2 June 2010].

[128] The abstract for this standard reads: 'ISO 10256:2003 specifies performance requirements and test methods for head and face protection for use in ice hockey. Perfarmance [*sic*] requirements and test methods, where appropriate, are given for the following: construction; shock absorption; puck-impact resistance; penetration; retention-system properties; field of vision; marking and information. The head and face protection is intended for use by players, goalkeepers and certain functionaries (e.g. referees).' This abstract can be found at the ISO catalogue available at the ISO website: http://www.iso.org/iso/iso_catalogue/catalogue_tc/catalogue_detail.htm?csnumber=28672 [accessed 2 June 2010].

[129] Elizabeth Gasiorowski-Denis, 'They Shoot, They Score! ISO Standard Gives Ice Hockey Better Play with Protective Equipment', ISO Press Release, Ref. 885, available

In addition to addressing safety concerns, sports-related standards may help to create a level playing field for sporting competition. For example, the abstract for ISO 378:1980, which is related to 'Gymnastics Equipment – Parallel Bars', states that it '[s]pecifies the functional and safety requirements for parallel bars for use in competition and training, *in order to permit a true comparison of performance*. Lays down dimensions, material, execution and design.'[130]

In setting out the standards with which products must comply, standards organizations create specifications that take a documented form. While the standards may describe industry best practice, they are original to the extent that they have not previously been established in this form and published as a 'standard'. Standards thus exhibit a version of the core criteria that are common to intellectual property doctrines, yet standards are not themselves considered to be an intellectual property doctrine.[131]

Perhaps one reason that standards have not been drawn within the department of intellectual property relates to the fact that the ISO system is extra-legal, in that its standards are not legislative, ISO cannot regulate their use, and ISO has no authority to enforce compliance. Individual countries may choose to require compliance with ISO standards by legislating accordingly, but the ISO system itself has no legal force. As a department of law, perhaps intellectual property has not concerned itself with standards because of their extra-legal nature.

ISO is not the only standards regulation body. The European Committee for Standardization (CEN)[132] operates similarly to, and

at the ISO website: http://www.iso.org/iso/pressrelease.htm?refid=Ref885 [accessed 7 June 2010].

130 Available at the ISO website: http://www.iso.org/iso/iso_catalogue/catalogue_tc/catalogue_detail.htm?csnumber=4359 [accessed 7 June 2010] (emphasis added).

131 Note, as an aside, that the documents evidencing the standards would probably qualify for copyright protection.

132 CEN's membership comprises thirty-one member states: the EU countries, Croatia, and the three European Free Trade Association countries. See further membership details at CEN's website: http://www.cen.eu/cen/Members/Pages/default.aspx [accessed 2 June 2010].

coordinates its work with, ISO under the provisions of the *Agreement on Technical Cooperation between ISO and CEN* (known as the *Vienna Agreement*) (1991).[133] However, CEN's European standards must be implemented as national standards throughout the territories of its European members, harmonizing standards within those jurisdictions.

Many other jurisdictions have their own standards organizations. For example, the non-governmental organization Standards Australia has developed more than seven thousand 'Australian Standards',[134] some of which have been adopted in Australian legislation.[135] In the United Kingdom, the National Standards Body is known as BSI Group and produces 'British Standards' under Royal Charter. BSI Group gives licenses to use the 'Kitemark' certification trademark[136] with respect to goods and/or services that meet relevant standards for their industries.

5.5.3.a Standards as Intellectual Property (Certification Trademarks)

In many ways, standards operate very much like 'certification marks', which provide a parallel system of standards registration within intellectual

[133] Formally, the *Agreement on Technical Cooperation between ISO and CEN* (1991); passed as ISO Council resolution 18/1990 and CEN General Assembly resolution 3/1990.

[134] See the Standards Australia website: http://www.standards.org.au/DevelopingStandards/BuyingaStandard.aspx [accessed 2 June 2010]. Note that AUSTRALIAN STANDARDS is itself a registered Australian trademark.

[135] For example, the *Interpretation of Legislation Act* 1984 (Victoria), s.38AA(1) states: 'In an Act or subordinate instrument, a reference consisting of the words "Australian Standard" or the letters "AS" followed in either case by a number or a number accompanied by a reference to a calendar year is a reference to the standard so numbered published by or on behalf of Standards Australia.' The *Road Safety (Traffic Management) Regulations* 2009 (Victoria) s.18 state: '*Parking signs must conform with Australian Standard* A traffic control device erected, displayed or placed under this Part that is a traffic sign for the control of stopping or parking of vehicles in accordance with Part 12 of the Road Rules must conform with AS 1742.11–1999.'

[136] UK registered trademark 1523922; Community Trade Mark E3361998. Details available, respectively, at Intellectual Property Office (UK) website, http://www.ipo.gov.uk/domestic?domesticnum=1523922, and http://www.ipo.gov.uk/ohim?ohimnum=E336198 [accessed 4 June 2010].

property's trademark doctrine. Certification marks are used by traders to indicate that their goods and/or services meet particular standards, such as accuracy, composition, and/or quality. Each certification mark may be used only by traders who comply with rules that are first established in conjunction with the mark's registration. As such, certification marks function as a guarantee of standards, thus bridging a gap between 'intellectual property' and consumer protection law.

In Australia, for example, certification marks are registered by the national trademark registry office, IP Australia, but the rules for their use must first be approved by the national consumer protection agency, the Australian Competition and Consumer Commission (ACCC).[137] These rules list the standards that an applicant's accredited goods and/or services must meet for use with the certification trademark, as well as additional standards or requirements that users must meet while using the certification mark. Examples of Australian certification marks are the Aboriginal 'Label of Authenticity' certification mark referred to earlier[138] and the WOOLMARK, which certifies that wool is pure new wool.[139] A

[137] The process for registration is summarized in Australian Competition and Consumer Commission, *Certification Trade Marks: The Role of the ACCC* (Canberra: Australian Competition and Consumer Commission, 1998) at 5: 'Businesses wishing to register a CTM must first apply to the Registrar of Trade Marks. Along with their CTM application they must provide a set of rules on how to use the CTM. These rules must be filed with the registrar with the application or as soon as possible thereafter.... The registrar assesses CTM applications against general trade mark requirements. If an application complies with these requirements, the registrar sends it, along with the CTM rules, to the ACCC for consideration. If the ACCC is satisfied that the test set out in the Trade Marks Act (see below) has been complied with, it returns the trade mark application and the CTM rules to the registrar. The registrar then completes the registration process.'

[138] See the earlier discussion at §5.2.2.c.

[139] Australian trademark registration 765983 (http://pericles.ipaustralia.gov.au/atmoss/falcon_details.show_tm_details?p_tm_number=765983&p_search_no=1&p_ExtDisp=D&p_detail=DETAILED&p_rec_no=2&p_rec_all=4 [accessed 2 June 2010]), registered to Australian Merino Pty Ltd, a subsidiary of Australian Wool Innovation Limited (AWI). AWI offers services to its licensees. See, eg, the AWI website: http://www.wool.com/Design-and-Market_Woolmark_The-Brand_Trust-Woolmark.htm [accessed 2 June 2010].

familiar certification trademark in the United Kingdom is BSI Group's Kitemark trademark, which signifies 'British Standards'.

An interesting aspect of the use of certification marks by organizations such as BSI Group is that they apply classic intellectual property law as part of the business model by which they conduct their activities. Those activities coincide with those of trademark law's certification marks, and the core criteria are present. However, 'standards' is not itself considered to be a doctrine falling within the department of intellectual property law in its own right.

Ordinary trademarks,[140] as opposed to certification trademarks, can also be used by organizations establishing a private regime of standards certification. These do not require the registration of approved standards with which goods and/or services with respect to which the trademark is used must comply, and they thus offer traders a greater degree of flexibility in administering their standards.

An example of an ordinary trademark that operates like a collective trademark is the FAIRTRADE mark of the European Fairtrade Foundation. The Foundation's website advises: 'As a certification label the FAIRTRADE Mark may be used only in direct relation to products that are certified in accordance with Fairtrade standards.'[141]

When they demonstrate such similarities to trademark law's certification marks and are sometimes registered as ordinary trademarks, it is interesting that standards are not treated as part of intellectual property law. They do exhibit versions of the core criteria but, rather like the guild marks and hallmarks discussed earlier, it seems as though standards systems operate alongside intellectual property law, sometimes overlapping but remaining doctrinally independent. It is as though standards systems underpin some of their functions with the legal force of trademark law – particularly collective trademarks – and in doing so they are de facto

[140] See above n. 112 for an explanation of the use of this terminology in this chapter.

[141] Website of the Fairtrade Foundation: http://www.fairtrade.org.uk/business_services/use_of_the_fairtrade_mark.aspx [accessed 2 June 2010].

drawn within the department intellectual property law. Yet the function of standards differs from the function of a trademark to the extent that standards are descriptive of features of goods and services that are common within industries, while trademarks are indicative of particular traders. The two doctrines thus remain apart, trademarks in the department of intellectual property law, and standards in the department of consumer protection or trade/competition regulation.

5.5.4. Conclusion

These examples of doctrines whose objects of regulation share distinct similarities with intellectual property objects but are not included within the intellectual property rubric help to cast light on the nature of 'intellectual property'. In each case, practical – and customary, even if not always legally explicit – systems for the regulation of intangible objects such as signs, symbols, information, and trading reputation have been established, yet they have not been treated by the legal system as 'intellectual property'.

In some cases, these intellectual property–like systems are arguably outside the department of intellectual property because they are not structured around the core criteria, even though they may have helped to create a backdrop against which conceptual patterns for intellectual property regulation were established in the minds of law-makers. For example, heraldry and systems for marking animals with brands and earmarks influenced modern trademark laws. While they may not always have been consciously considered by those who would go on to draft the awards of royal privileges, the decrees, the court decisions that formed early intellectual property laws, or the statutes, judgements, and international agreements that are the sources of modern intellectual property laws, these systems nonetheless constructed an intellectual and conceptual legacy that would influence later developments. However, to the extent that they lack the core criteria, it is understandable why these doctrines are not treated as 'intellectual property' even when they live on in modern times. These examples would therefore tend to lend support to the proposition laid out in earlier chapters that the core criteria are a definitional feature of 'intellectual property'. They would suggest that the framework set out earlier does indeed add explanatory force to the nature of 'intellectual property'.

Other intellectual property–like doctrines are more problematic. They were generally customary precursors of modern intellectual property law and, even where they live on today as intellectual property's extended family, their regulatory functions are replicated within classic doctrines of intellectual property law. Depending on one's perspective, these doctrines may or may not support the conclusion that the framework laid out in Chapters 3 and 4 establishes the skeletal structure of intellectual property doctrines.

On the one hand, it could be argued that their structural similarities to intellectual property doctrines should have led to these doctrines being identified as 'intellectual property', and intellectual property law's failure to do so indicates that something more than the structure laid out in Chapters 3 and 4 is necessary for intellectual propertization.

On the other hand, each of these non–intellectual property doctrines arguably has an intellectual property equivalent. Their non–intellectual property status could therefore be explained by the conclusion that their objects of regulation have indeed been intellectual propertized, even though that process has required the non–intellectual property doctrine to rely on its intellectual property relatives to some extent. Perhaps these non–intellectual property doctrines have retained their extra-legal form outside intellectual property law in order to afford additional regulatory authority, or even just to keep old traditions alive, yet this explanation still leaves unanswered questions.

However, these two explanations are not mutually exclusive. Both would allow for the following conclusions:

1. The core criteria of intellectual property may also be found in non–intellectual property doctrines.

2. Additional information may be required to explain why some doctrines that display the core criteria of intellectual propertization are regarded as 'intellectual property' and others are not.

The remainder of this chapter offers a suggestion as to what that additional information might be. In doing so, it draws a link between the structure of intellectual property outlined in earlier chapters and the political reasons for intellectual propertization that have otherwise been left outside the scope of this investigation.

5.6. Refining the Definition of 'Intellectual Property'

Thus far, this volume has focused on the structure of intellectual property doctrines rather than the reasons for their creation. While this may be artificial from an empirical perspective, as an investigative device it has the advantage of providing insight untainted (as much as is possible in a post-modern world) by politics and rhetoric. It has produced a theory of the construction of intellectual property that seems to be reflected in the structure of the traditional forms of intellectual property's classic doctrines, and that is unlikely to be found in departments of law that are quite distinct from intellectual property. This structure is somewhat supported also by an examination of intellectual property–like doctrines, some of which can be distinguished from 'intellectual property' on the basis that they lack one or more of the core criteria. What is more problematic is the situation in which intellectual property–like doctrines that do display the core criteria are not themselves regarded as 'intellectual property', even as their regulatory functions are emulated by classic intellectual property doctrines. This would seem to suggest that something more than identification of an appropriate metaphysical structure may sometimes be needed before a doctrine will be recognized as falling within the department of intellectual property law.

Previous chapters have argued that the objects regulated by intellectual property laws are ideational in nature, as are the boundaries that demarcate them. To draw an analogy with real property, they are ideational pastures around which abstract conceptual fences are placed through the tool of legal definition. The department of 'intellectual property' thus contains a collection of legal doctrines that each define into existence intellectual property objects to which are attached rights that legally regulate the way in which society at large may use documented forms of those abstract intellectual property objects. In this sense, 'intellectual property' is like a cluster of legal definitions.

Beyond identifying the nature of these definitional concepts (which this study has suggested to be an 'ideational object', evidenced by a 'documented form', created by applying conceptions of 'originality' and 'creatorship', and with which certain 'rights' are associated) through a process of breaking down their constituent concepts into other concepts, 'intellectual property' is therefore difficult to itself characterize or define in its own terms (ie, from an intra-departmental perspective). The risk in trying to do so is attempting to prove too much with the structural definition proposed in this book, leading to a tendency to produce anomalous results with respect to intellectual property–like doctrines that the metaphysical theory does not explain. This suggests that an additional perspective may be in order to refine the theory and allow the definitional task to be completed in what might be called (to borrow a term from Ronald Dworkin)[142] 'hard cases', those in which the absence or presence of any of the core criteria does not seem determinative of whether the doctrine is considered to be 'intellectual property'.

[142] Ronald Dworkin, *Taking Rights Seriously* (London: Duckworth, 1978) at 81 defines 'hard cases' as those where 'a particular lawsuit cannot be brought under a clear rule of law, laid down by some institution in advance.' The term is adopted here to describe those 'cases' of intellectual property–like doctrines that have been created not as a result of the intention of law makers to establish a new intellectual property doctrine, but independently of the department of intellectual property law. Where such a doctrine displays the core criteria, the question may arise at some point: Is this doctrine within intellectual property? Or, if not, why not? These are hard cases to decide if there is no established institution to determine what is and is not intellectual property.

5.6.1. Definition in Context

Concern about how to characterize something that is simply a legal designation or a cluster of legal designations evokes the considerations that H. L. A. Hart discussed in his well-known essay about jurisprudential definition.[143] Hart sought to develop a method of defining conceptual words such as 'corporation', 'rights', and 'duty' that did not have counterparts with which they could be compared in the physical world but that nevertheless suggested meaning.[144] He was, in effect, talking about intangibles, incorporeal objects, or choses in action, each of which is a term commonly used to describe intellectual property.

Hart concluded that when one is trying to define concepts it is unhelpful to ask, for example, what is a right, or what is a corporate body?[145] The problem he identified is that the answers to such questions fall into three categories, none of which provides useful definitions. The answers usually suggest that

1. the word stands for a variant of something with which we are familiar;
2. the word stands for a fiction; and/or
3. the word stands for 'something different from other things just in that we cannot touch it, hear it, see it, feel it.'[146]

[143] H. L. A. Hart, "Definition and Theory in Jurisprudence" (1954) 70 *Law Quarterly Review* 37–60.

[144] Ibid. at 38: 'The first efforts to define words like "corporation" "rights" or "duty" reveal that these do not have the straightforward connection with counterparts in the world of fact which most ordinary words have and to which we appeal in our definition of ordinary words. There is nothing which simply "corresponds" to these legal words and when we try to define them we find that the expressions we tender in our definition specifying kinds of persons, things, qualities, events, and processes, material or psychological, are never precisely the equivalent of these legal words though often connected with them in some way.'

[145] Ibid. at 39. That is, they stand for something intangible or incorporeal, such as intellectual property.

[146] Ibid.

These criticisms are similar to the problematic types of definition summarized in Chapter 2. Just as the definitions explored in that chapter fail to provide more than a superficial, instrumental definition of intellectual property, Hart would likely have found equally unhelpful the question 'what is intellectual property?' The reason he would probably have offered for this lack of a robust and philosophically coherent definition is found in the type of word that 'intellectual property' is when considered from the perspective of its linguistic and legal function.

The resolution of this problem offered earlier was to examine the metaphysics of intellectual property's doctrines and thus produce a structural definition based on the way in which classic intellectual property doctrines function. Testing this approach suggests that it is a solid but sometimes incomplete solution. In situations where the metaphysical definition does not provide a convincing match with what would empirically appear to function outside the department of intellectual property law, Hart's proposal may allow the definitional puzzle to be fully resolved.

Hart argued that conceptual words such as 'right' and 'corporate body' – or 'intellectual property' – describe nothing but a distinct function (they are therefore 'operative' rather than 'descriptive' words),[147] and he thus proposed that in order to determine the significance or function of such words, one should look at the context in which they are used[148] to allude to a specific conclusion of law.[149]

Applying Hart's approach leads us to ask: What is different about the context of signs that leads to the outcome that they are not intellectual propertized when regulated as workers' marks (ie, by doctrines

[147] Ibid. at 45. It could be suggested that they are the building blocks of performative utterances, such as those discussed in Chapter 3, §3.5.2.

[148] Ibid. at 42: 'It is obvious that the use of these sentences silently assumes a special and very complicated setting, namely the existence of a legal system with all that this implies by way of general obedience, the operation of the sanctions of the system, and the general likelihood that this will continue.' Hart was referring to the words 'right' and 'duty', but his argument applies equally to intellectual property.

[149] Hart says such expressions have 'meaning only as part of a sentence the function of which as a whole is to draw a conclusion of law from a specific kind of legal rule' (ibid. at 43).

such as guild marks, hallmarks, and standards), but they are intellectual propertized when regulated by the parallel and overlapping doctrine of trademark law (whether as standard, collective, or certification marks)? Bearing in mind that it may be exactly the same mark being treated differently – as an 'intellectual property object', on the one hand, and not as an 'intellectual property object', on the other – the answer must surely be as follows: as the two doctrines that each regulate with respect to the identical documented form do so simultaneously, and do so in the same context, it is something outside the regulatory doctrine itself that is the additional factor determining whether an object is or is not intellectual propertized. Identical documented forms thus serve different functions in different contexts,[150] and the context can help explain the reason for this in a given situation.

Using the example of a corporation, Hart suggested an external method of explaining the meaning of abstract legal terms by examining their role in context. He recommended:

> If we put aside the question 'What is a corporation?' and ask instead 'Under what types of conditions does the law ascribe liabilities to corporations?' this is likely to clarify the actual working of a legal system and bring out the precise issues at stake when judges, who are supposed not to legislate, make some new extension to corporate bodies of rules worked out for individuals.[151]

Focusing on the function of 'intellectual property', the conditions under which intellectual property law-making occurs and the function(s) that intellectual property laws play, this requires a conceptual shift that results in a way of thinking of intellectual property as a legal mechanism for ordering society. According to this more sociological[152] or regulatory

[150] An analogy could be drawn here between 'words' and 'performative utterances', a distinction that was introduced in Chapter 3, §3.5.2.

[151] Hart, above n. 143 at 56.

[152] Sociological approaches to law focus on its status as a social system. In this sense, law is produced by society, operates in society, and in turn influences society. Sociological jurisprudence examines how that occurs.

perspective,[153] no human description or categorization of things is meaningful unless put in context and placed against the backdrop of the circumstances in which it is occurring.[154] The shift of attention is therefore from the internal workings of intellectual property law to the environment in which intellectual property law functions.

This approach is compatible with the aforementioned view of Richard Rorty that the meaning of language can be understood only in its context,[155] and also with J. E. Penner's suggestion that, as property is a creation of its environment, it is helpful to act like ecologists and examine how property behaves in that environment.[156] Penner suggests that the best way of doing so is to classify according to function. Immanuel Kant's

[153] 'Regulatory' is a term with various possible meanings. It is used here in a slightly broader sense than that suggested by Matthew D. Adler, 'Regulatory Theory', in Dennis Patterson (ed.), *A Companion to Philosophy of Law and Legal Theory* (Oxford: Wiley-Blackwell, 2010), 590–606 at 592, who, after noting that '[d]efining "regulation" proves to be very difficult' (at 591), defines the term to mean 'nontax, noncriminal, public law: legal directives (of some sort) that are issued by governmental bodies; that are enforced by governmental bodies, rather than by private litigants; that are principally enforced through sanctions or incentives other than criminal penalties; and that are not taxes.... The definition is jury-rigged, meant to capture most of the cases commonly counted as regulation, and exclude most that are not. A better definition, like any good piece of conceptual analysis, would do that reasonably well, but would also illuminate the similarities between those items that fall within it.' The sense in which the term is used in this book is broader to the extent that it includes regulation by non-governmental bodies (ie, extra-legal regulation), which may or may not be backed by the force of law.

For discussions about the regulatory approach to law, see Julia Black, 'Regulatory Conversations' (2002) 29:1 *Journal of Law and Society* 163–196; Julia Black, 'Critical Reflections on Regulation' (2002) 27 *Australasian Journal of Legal Philosophy* 1–35.

For a notable application of regulatory theory to intellectual property law in its commercial context, see John Braithwaite and Peter Drahos, *Global Business Regulation* (Cambridge: Cambridge University Press, 2000). See also Peter Drahos, 'The Regulation of Public Goods' (2004) 7:23 *Journal of International Economic Law* 321–339.

[154] Richard Rorty, 'Texts and Lumps', in *Objectivity, Relativism and Truth: Philosophical Papers*, Vol. 1 (New York: Cambridge University Press, 1991), 78–92; Richard Rorty, 'Introduction: Pragmatism as Anti-Representationalism', in John P. Murphy, *Pragramatisim from Peirce to Davidson* (Boulder: Westview Press, 1990), 1–6 at 3.

[155] Ibid.

[156] J. E. Penner, *The Idea of Property in Law* (Oxford: Oxford University Press, 1997/2000) at 3.

suggestion that we cannot know a thing itself so we need to know its categories[157] can also be applied to this approach to suggest that, although we cannot know the abstract nature and boundaries of ideational objects and intellectual property objects themselves, we can understand them by examining how the law categorizes them. Their legal categories accord with their context and function. Contextual approaches like these allow us to add a layer of sophistication to the metaphysical approach offered earlier once a doctrine or object's fundamental intellectual property–like structure has been established. As well as considering the internal structure of intellectual property, they add an external perspective, thus providing an extra dimension to the definition.

Like the metaphysical methodology adopted earlier, a contextual approach is also useful because it bypasses the context of subjective, rhetorical, normative, and politically motivated claims in favour of analysing brute facts about empirical functions (albeit functions that can be interpreted subjectively). These facts are the conditions in which intellectual propertization occurs and in which intellectual property law operates. They might involve a political, social, economic, cultural, or religious context, or a combination of these, or some other sort of environment. For the purposes of defining a doctrine as 'intellectual property', it is arguably irrelevant what the environment is. What matters is the regulatory function that the doctrines play in it, and why they have or have not been embraced by the department of intellectual property law.

What might a contextual approach to defining 'intellectual property' tell us that would allow meaningful distinctions to be drawn between 'intellectual property' doctrines and the intellectual property–like doctrines discussed earlier in this chapter? The answer in each case would depend on a specific analysis of the history and politics of each of the intellectual property–like doctrines to ascertain what function(s) these doctrines play.

[157] Immanuel Kant, *Critique of Pure Reason*, ed. and trans. by Paul Guyer and Allen W. Wood (Cambridge: Cambridge University Press, 1999).

Some intellectual property-like doctrines may remain separate from the department of intellectual property because their governing bodies have resisted interference in their governance from external authorities, including state and international organizations. Particularly where legal force is already given to these doctrines' internal functions by one or more legal doctrines such as trademark law, contract, competition law, and/or consumer law, those responsible for administering intellectual property–like doctrines may see no additional benefit – and perhaps perceive disadvantages – in the loss of autonomy that would be likely to accompany absorption into the department of intellectual property law.

Some intellectual property–like doctrines may remain separate from intellectual property because they are widely regarded as obsolete and there is not the political will to draw them under the intellectual property mantle. This is particularly the case when the doctrine exhibits intellectual property–like functions that are already protected by intellectual property doctrines (such as trademark or copyright law) and the intellectual property–like doctrine is popularly regarded as little more than a cultural relic to be retained – if at all – simply to preserve tradition, but not for any formal regulatory purpose. Such circumstances would create little impetus for law-makers to intellectual propertize the intellectual property–like doctrine.

There may also be myriad other reasons why intellectual property–like doctrines remain outside the department of intellectual property law. These could range from a doctrine's perceived lack of importance by those negotiating the conditions and international legal framework of trade (the importance of this cannot be underestimated in a context in which international trade imperatives provide a key incentive for intellectual property law reform) to administrative concerns. For example, governments may prefer to leave some regulatory functions to be administered privately, thus avoiding the bureaucratic costs associated with administering intellectual property systems. Even personal and political considerations of individual law-makers or their advisors could affect such outcomes.

Hart's approach coincides also with that of Ludwig Wittgenstein, mentioned at the start of this chapter. Wittgenstein suggests that the meaning of a word is often tied to its use in language, and he uses the analogy of a piece in a game. The meaning of a piece is the part it plays in the game, and it is therefore the game that gives it meaning. Similarly, the meaning of a word is the part it plays in language, and the meaning of a legal term is understood by the role it plays in the law.[158] Where regulatory doctrines perform the same role, they arguably exhibit what Wittgenstein described as a 'family resemblance'.[159] Noting such resemblance is the primary task of a metaphysical analysis. Identifying its meaning, and explaining and criticizing its role – why it exists in a particular context, what role it is intended to play, what task it is expected to achieve – are the secondary tasks performed by political (and normative) accounts of intellectual property. From this perspective, the meaning of 'intellectual property' is the role it plays in law. In practice, this is likely to mean the role(s) that acknowledged doctrines of intellectual property play in a society's legal system. Comparisons can then be drawn with the roles that intellectual property–like doctrines play in their social, cultural, or economic contexts.

This chapter thus concludes that political reasons and normative justifications for intellectual propertization do have a place in the definitional analysis of intellectual property, but it is a secondary, explanatory role that adds clarity after the primary structural analysis has been concluded. For example, while the metaphysical approach enables us to determine family resemblance, it does not necessarily identify whether such a resemblance comes about as a result of nature or nurture. When resemblances more closely resemble those shared by kinsfolk living together in the

[158] See Ludwig Wittgenstein, *Philosophical Investigations*, trans. G. E. M. Anscombe (Oxford: Blackwell, 2003) at 27^e,§66ff.

[159] Ibid. at 27^e–28^e, §67, as referred to earlier: 'I can think of no better expression to characterize these similarities than "family resemblances"; for the various resemblances between members of a family: build, features, colour of eyes, gait, temperament, etc., etc. overlap and criss-cross in the same way. – And I shall say: "games" form a family.'

same environment than those shared by blood relatives with a common genetic heritage, a contextual analysis that takes into account the environment – particularly the political environment – of intellectual propertization is likely to add a useful explanatory dimension to the definition of 'intellectual property'.

Many accounts of intellectual property and its doctrines have been written, and from many perspectives. There are black-letter texts focusing on the development of the law through cases and statutes,[160] analytical and critical histories,[161] political analyses[162] and political economy

[160] See, eg, in the United Kingdom: Lionel Bently and Brad Sherman, *Intellectual Property Law* (Oxford: Oxford University Press, 2008); William Cornish and David Llewelyn, *Intellectual Property: Patents, Copyrights, Trademarks and Allied Rights* (London: Sweet & Maxwell, 2007); Jeremy Phillips, *Trade Mark Law: A Practical Anatomy* (Oxford: Oxford University Press, 2003). In the United States: Frank I. Schechter, *The Historical Foundations of the Law Relating to Trade-Marks* (Union, NJ: Lawbook Exchange, 1999; originally published New York: Columbia University Press, 1925); Roger E. Schechter and John R. Thomas, *Intellectual Property: The Law of Copyrights, Patents and Trademarks* (St. Paul, MN: West, 2003). In Australia: Sam Ricketson, Megan Richardson, and Mark Davison, *Intellectual Property: Cases, Materials and Commentary* (Sydney: LexisNexis Butterworths, 2009); Jill McKeough, Andrew Stewart, and Philip Griffith, *Intellectual Property in Australia* (Sydney: Butterworths, 2004).

[161] See, eg, Sherman and Bently, above n. 7; Christopher May and Susan K. Sell, *Intellectual Property Rights: A Critical History* (Boulder, CO: Lynne Rienner, 2005); Mark Rose, *Authors and Owners: The Invention of Copyright* (Cambridge, MA: Harvard University Press, 1993); Deazley, above n. 7; Paul K. Saint-Amour, *The Copywrights: Intellectual Property and the Literary Imagination* (Ithaca, NY: Cornell University Press, 2003).

[162] See, eg, Susan K. Sell, *Private Power, Public Law: The Globalization of Intellectual Property Rights* (Cambridge: Cambridge University Press, 2003); Peter Drahos and Ruth Mayne (eds.), *Global Intellectual Property Rights: Knowledge, Access and Development* (New York: Palgrave Macmillan, 2002); Keith E. Maskus (ed.), *The WTO, Intellectual Property Rights and the Knowledge Economy* (Cheltenham: Edward Elgar, 2005); Carlos María Correa, *Intellectual Property Rights, the WTO and Developing Countries: The TRIPS Agreement and Policy Options* (London: Zed, 2000); Alexandra George (ed.), *Globalization And Intellectual Property* (Aldershot: Ashgate, 2006); Susan K. Sell, *Power and Ideas: North–South Politics of Intellectual Property and Antitrust* (Albany: State University of New York Press, 1998).

analyses,[163] economic analyses,[164] cultural analyses,[165] and so on, not to mention the many micro-analyses of intellectual propertization that appear in the written decisions of courts of numerous jurisdictions. Just as these writings document and comment upon the political pressures – often backed by normative justifications – that have led to the intellectual propertization of objects of regulation by current intellectual property doctrines, similar analyses could be made of intellectual property–like doctrines. Such investigations appear likely to uncover a political context in each case that helps to explain why doctrines that would otherwise seem at home in the department of intellectual property law have been left outside its jurisdiction.

[163] See, eg, Christopher May, *The Global Political Economy of Intellectual Property Rights: The New Enclosures* (London: Routledge, 2009, 2nd ed.); Meir Perez Pugatch, *The International Political Economy of Intellectual Property Rights* (Cheltenham: Edward Elgar, 2004); YiJun Tian, *Re-thinking Intellectual Property: The Political Economy of Copyright Protection in the Digital Era* (Abingdon: Routledge-Cavendish, 2008).

[164] See, eg, Roger D. Blair and Thomas F. Cotter, *Intellectual Property: Economic and Legal Dimensions of Rights and Remedies* (New York: Cambridge University Press, 2005); Michael McAleer and Les Oxley (eds.), *Economic and Legal Issues in Intellectual Property* (Oxford: Wiley-Blackwell, 2007); William M. Landes and Richard A. Posner, *The Economic Structure of Intellectual Property Law* (Cambridge, MA: Belknap Press of Harvard University Press, 2003); Gregory K. Leonard and Lauren J. Stiroh (eds.), *Economic Approaches to Intellectual Property Policy, Litigation, and Management* (New York: NERA Economic Consulting, 2005); Robert P. Merges, *Economics of Intellectual Property Law*, Vols. 1 and 2 (Cheltenham: Edward Elgar, 2008).

[165] See, eg, Rosemary J. Coombe, *The Cultural Life of Intellectual Properties: Authorship, Appropriation, and the Law* (Durham, NC: Duke University Press, 1998); Michael F. Brown, *Who Owns Native Culture?* (Cambridge, MA: Harvard University Press, 2004); Lawrence Lessig, *Free Culture: How Big Media Uses Technology and the Law to Lock Down Culture and Control Creativity* (New York: Penguin, 2005); Siva Vaidhyanathan, *Copyrights and Copywrongs: The Rise of Intellectual Property and How It Threatens Creativity* (New York: New York University Press, 2003); Joanna Demers, *Steal This Music: How Intellectual Property Law Affects Musical Creativity* (Athens: University of Georgia Press, 2006); Bruce Ziff, *Borrowed Power: Essays on Cultural Appropriation* (New Brunswick, NJ: Rutgers University Press, 1997); Paul Goldstein, *Copyright's Highway: From Gutenberg to the Celestial Jukebox* (Stanford, CA: Stanford Law and Politics, 2003).

6 Concluding Remarks

THESE CONCLUDING REMARKS RECAP THE MAIN THEMES addressed throughout the book. This chapter suggests how the research findings may contribute to the literature, and it speculates about possible extensions of this research.

6.1. This Study

The primary aim of this book has been to explore ways of filling a gap in the literature left by the dominance of political, normative, and doctrinal treatments of intellectual property law that base their analyses on assumptions about what intellectual property is and that do not investigate the issue further.

With this in mind, and by working within the 'applied legal philosophy' tradition that investigates legal issues using tools of philosophy and theory, this research has asked: How can legal philosophy explain 'intellectual property'? In particular, how is 'intellectual property' constructed within the legal system? This book has hypothesized that intellectual property is a conceptual legal construct that itself comprises other conceptual legal constructs, such as 'creatorship' and 'originality'. It is constructed within the legal system to allow for the regulation of certain conceptual things – 'intellectual property objects' – which are evidenced in 'documented forms', to which rights have been applied. This argument will be recounted in a brief recap of the line of reasoning and the principal themes.

6.2. Brief Recap of the Argument

Early chapters of this book pointed to the contingent nature of intellectual property and flaws in the standard definitions of intellectual property. While those definitions may have functional purposes, they do not disclose much about the nature of intellectual property.

Further analysis indicated that intellectual property is an institutional fact that is constructed by society through mechanisms such as 'performative utterances' and using core concepts as tools with which to build intellectual property objects. Law-makers choose the form that intellectual property law takes, and thus the form of intellectual property objects. Nevertheless, they arguably build these objects using a structure that is typical of intellectual property doctrines (as opposed to finding them in a state of nature and then regulating them). These are useful and important insights that help to expose popular assumptions and fallacies, and that help to elucidate the nature of intellectual property.

However, occasionally, part of an intellectual property doctrine may lack one of the core criteria, or a doctrine lacking one or more of the core criteria may be grouped under the umbrella of intellectual property law. Moreover, as became evident in Chapter 5, not all legal and customary regulatory doctrines that share these characteristics are categorized as 'intellectual property'. Thus, the presence of the core criteria does not necessarily indicate that something is intellectual property. Focusing only on the structure of 'intellectual property' may not always offer a complete picture, as other areas of law and customary regulation may share these characteristics but not be regarded by the legal system as intellectual property. The research thus concludes that an additional dimension of the investigation may help to explain why intellectual property has evolved in its current forms. Chapter 5 proposed that the extra dimension is a contextual analysis of the environment in which intellectual propertization occurs.

6.3. Themes

The study suggests that, by obtaining a deeper understanding of the way in which intellectual property law – including objects of intellectual property regulation, and the rights by which human behaviour with respect to intellectual property objects is regulated – is constructed by legal systems, we can build firmer foundations on which to base doctrinal, normative, and political discussions about intellectual property law and intellectual propertization. This is explored through several themes.

6.3.1. The Symbolic but Unsettled Nature of 'Intellectual Property'

The discussion began by drawing analogies between the emperor's new clothes (adapted from Hans Christian Andersen's fairy tale) and intellectual property. The initial purpose of recounting this story was to set the scene for the analysis of intellectual property law that follows by challenging readers to question common understandings about intellectual property law. In this sense, the book opened with a 'debunking' exercise whose purpose was to point to illusions and false conceptual assumptions about the nature of intellectual property law, so as to provide a more objective environment from which to start observing the legally constructed nature of 'intellectual property'.

The significance of borrowing the literary device of a fairy tale grew as the nature of intellectual property became clearer with the progression of the research. Just as fairy tales are loaded with meaning and subtext, so too does the way in which intellectual property law and its objects of regulation are constructed reflect the privileging of certain interests. This was demonstrated, for example, by the discussion in Chapter 4 that indicated the difference between intellectual property's application of a notion of the 'Romantic author' and notions of creatorship used in other parts of society. Intellectual property's conceptions of originality are similarly distant from many social understandings of how the old gives rise to the new (also discussed in Chapter 4).

The parallels with critiques of the literary genre of the fairy tale should therefore not go unmentioned, for it has been said that literary fairy tales are

> socially symbolical acts and narrative strategies formed to take part in civilized discourses about morality and behavior in particular societies and cultures. They are constantly rearranged and transformed to suit changes in tastes and values, and they assume mythic proportions when they are frozen in an ideological constellation that makes it seem that there are universal absolutes that are divine and should not be changed.[1]

Much the same could be said about 'intellectual property'. As Chapters 1 and 2 indicated, much of the discourse surrounding intellectual property law is socially symbolic. Much of it is tied to narratives about normative justifications for intellectual property doctrines and their regulations, and these in turn are often employed in political debate and rhetoric about intellectual propertization. As with literary fairy tales, the imperatives and values associated with intellectual property law and its various doctrines are constantly shifting in response to social attitudes, economic conditions, and technological developments. The term 'intellectual property' does not describe universal absolutes, either in the legal doctrines or in their objects of regulation. Intellectual property law reflects ideology, but it is a shifting creed. Just as fairy tales are often perceived as morally neutral, the ideologically loaded nature of intellectual property law's doctrines and the construction of their rules and objects of regulation are sometimes overlooked.

Against this backdrop, this study showed that objects of intellectual property law are not 'brute facts' to be found in a state of nature and then

[1] Jack David Zipes, *Fairy Tale as Myth/Myth as Fairy Tale* (Lexington: University Press of Kentucky, 1994) at 19.

regulated. Rather, they are constructed by the legal system's department of intellectual property law using conceptual tools such as 'originality' and 'creatorship', following a framework typical of intellectual property doctrines.

6.3.2. Definitions of Intellectual Property

The analysis in Chapter 2 sought to offer a deeper explanation of intellectual property than is normally found in the introductory 'definitional' section of textbooks and monographs addressing other aspects of intellectual property laws' operation and consequences.

Rather than relying upon the explanations – generally justifications – for intellectual property that are commonly found in the literature, this study commenced with an investigation of intellectual property as a legal concept, the language of intellectual property, and the ways in which those responsible for making and influencing the law (governments, judges, and stakeholders, such as the proprietors of large intellectual property portfolios) use the language of intellectual property to create and expand the discursive possibilities offered by the sphere of intellectual property, often to advantage chosen interests. Standard definitions of intellectual property were surveyed and analysed, being categorized as definition by enumeration, definition as a type of 'property', stipulative definition, and intuitive definition. While each of these has practical utility, each also lacks intellectual rigour.

The criticism of the common methods of defining 'intellectual property' established a need for a more precise and comprehensive definition of the concept. This was proffered by the metaphysical theory suggested in later chapters.

6.3.3. The Constructed and Self-Referential Nature of Intellectual Property

Having concluded that the definitions ordinarily used in relation to 'intellectual property' offer inadequate explanations of the term and its meaning, the study investigated intellectual property's metaphysical structure. Chapter 3 explored how intellectual property is made, what its constitutive elements are, and how these elements relate to one another.

It proposed a theory of intellectual property that explains how objects of intellectual property regulation are legal constructs being defined into existence by, and then regulated by, the legal department of intellectual property. It suggests that this process of legal construction and regulation occurs, first, with the rules of an intellectual property doctrine being established to create objects of regulation by identifying an ideational object that is evidenced in a documented form and whose boundaries are defined by application of conceptions of 'creatorship' and 'originality'. These constructs are 'intellectual property objects'. Second, 'rights' are associated with the intellectual property objects, privileging proprietors and affecting the ways in which people behave with respect to those intellectual property objects. It was proposed that this structure is typical of doctrines of intellectual property law and, to the extent that jurisprudential definition should allow the identification of an area of law, this methodology offers a way of filling the gap left by the definitions surveyed earlier.

As the exploration of intellectual property's core criteria – the ideational object, the documented form, and the conceptual duo of creatorship/originality by which the 'intellectual property object' is defined – demonstrated in Chapter 4, the notions adopted within intellectual property law are not always aligned with those found in other social systems.

6.3.4. Refining the Theory: Intellectual Property in Context

The book's other main theme is the contingency of intellectual property in a social, political, economic, or other context.

Chapter 5 tested conclusions drawn during the earlier examination of the metaphysical structure of intellectual property laws against intellectual property–like laws and regulations, reaching the subsequent conclusion that the metaphysics of intellectual property gives only a partial explanation of its form. As that chapter identified, not every regulatory regime that displays the core criteria falls within the ambit of 'intellectual property', and not even each doctrine fitting this definition qualifies as intellectual property law. At this point, it may therefore be relevant to consider other influences – including the political context, which may include reference to normative justifications for intellectual propertization – that might have had an impact on whether intellectual propertization of a particular object or regulation, or of a doctrine of law, had occurred.

Thus, even though the approach taken throughout this book was preliminary to the political or normative analytical approaches more common to discussions about intellectual property law, links with those approaches became clear and are important. As Mark Van Hoecke notes: 'Reality partly determines theory. Theory partly creates reality. This is a continuous dialectical interaction without real synthesis: it is an open-ended process.'[2] Politics, political theory, and law are entwined, and intellectual property law is enmeshed in the web they create. Rather than maintaining an artificial distinction between the metaphysical analysis conducted throughout much of this volume, a method of synthesizing and utilizing the respective strengths of these differing theoretical approaches was therefore proposed.

6.4. Contribution to the Literature

The topic addressed by this analysis was large, and the project ambitious. The concluding remarks should perhaps match that ambition with grand claims about the research findings and their contribution to the literature. However, these reflections will be somewhat more modest.

This study has taken several innovative approaches leading to sometimes unexpected conclusions. These include the following:

- Chapter 2 critiqued the standard definitional techniques used in describing 'intellectual property', offering a systematic analysis of the flaws in existing definitions of the concept.

[2] Mark Van Hoecke, *Law as Communication* (Oxford: Hart, 2002) at 15.

- Chapter 3 identified a metaphysical framework around which intellectual property doctrines are constructed, expanding on this in Chapter 4. This, too, was unlike other approaches typically taken in the intellectual property literature.
- Chapter 5 contrasted intellectual property doctrines with intellectual property–like regulatory regimes. The purpose of this analysis was to test the theoretical structure proffered in previous chapters, but the methodology adopted to do so involved indentifying new patterns, parallels, and connections between intellectual property doctrines and other regulatory regimes that perform similar functions. This approach is similarly unusual in the context of the literature concerning intellectual property law.

Thus, new (even 'original', in the sense critiqued in Chapter 4) methods of analysis have been offered in this book, leading to fresh and interesting conclusions. It is hoped that these approaches may perhaps open new directions of discussion about the nature of 'intellectual property', both the body of law and the objects of regulation that it creates. It is also hoped that dialogue on these issues will ultimately enrich the political, normative, and doctrinal research that rests on an implicit notion – if not a more explicit definition – of 'intellectual property' and that some of these approaches may spark debate and discussion in the intellectual property literature, as well as interest in further research of this nature.

6.5. Directions for Future Research

This study raises possibilities for further research in at least two areas of investigation.

First, are there additional core criteria of intellectual property? Or are there perhaps other characteristics that are neither necessary nor sufficient to a finding of 'intellectual property' but whose presence increases the likelihood that an intellectual property object will be identified? The analysis in Chapter 5 could give rise to the identification of common features that help create an environment conducive to intellectual propertization. Perhaps the only addition to the core criteria also needed to explain the distinction between intellectual property and intellectual property–like objects is that the former are created by the legal system, whereas the latter occur in other social systems. Or perhaps another explanation exists. Recurring themes in intellectual property theory that are not addressed in any detail in this volume are the commercial context that typifies intellectual property law-making, and the communicative nature of the objects that it regulates. Perhaps future studies could fruitfully examine, for example, whether 'a commercial context' involving regulation of 'communicative objects' are two common environmental features conducive to intellectual propertization.

Another line of enquiry might be to extend the analysis made herein to investigate how intellectual property law is distinguished from legal departments that seem quite distinct. This book has focused mainly on an 'internal' analysis of intellectual property law and related doctrines demonstrating a 'family resemblance' to intellectual property in order to consider how intellectual property's rules operate together to create 'intellectual property' doctrines and why some doctrines that seem to share intellectual property's core criteria are nonetheless excluded from its immediate family. While this line of enquiry was adopted here for the reasons given in Chapter 5, a fruitful area for future analysis and extension of this avenue of research may be to compare and contrast intellectual property with other departments of law – such as tort, contract, and/or criminal law – to explore whether the differing ways in which various other legal departments define their objects of regulation shed new light on the construction of intellectual property law. It may be that looking beyond intellectual property law and its extended family would help to explain intellectual property even further, perhaps reinforcing the conclusions made within this study and giving them greater explanatory force.

6.6. Likely Implications of This Research for Intellectual Property Law

It is hard to predict the likely implications of the research on intellectual property law and theory.

Intellectual property scholars can be quite cynical, and to some observers the notion that intellectual property is a legal construct may seem almost trite. In this context, a perceptive and thought-provoking comment by Jeremy Phillips and Alison Firth is worth quoting at length:

> [S]ince it is man, and man alone, who has required that his inventions be protected from unauthorised emulation by others, it is worth pausing to enquire why this is so. The lawyer who has been educated within the great human rights traditions of the civil law of continental Europe would hold an invention to be an appropriate subject of property by virtue of the fact that it has been created by the skill and labour of an individual. Such a right might be accorded him along with his other natural rights such as freedom of association, liberty or equality, by virtue of his essential humanity. The common lawyer of the Anglo-American tradition would probably disagree and say that property in an invention was not a natural right to which all are inherently entitled so much as a right which exists only to the extent that a deliberate legal act has made it so, and which should only exist to the extent that it confers a practical advantage or use on one party which outweighs the detriment of it to others. Which of these positions is correct is a matter of personal taste and of jurisprudential speculation; the former is little more than an unverifiable assertion, while the latter pursues an understanding of law by abandoning the pursuit of any higher morality.... The rotation of the earth around its axis does not, however, depend upon the resolution of this issue.[3]

Yet, while the rotation of the earth on its axis may not ride on this issue, the shape of the intellectual property laws that dramatically affect the lives

[3] Jeremy Phillips and Alison Firth, *Introduction to Intellectual Property Law* (London: Butterworths, 1995) at 24–25 (notes omitted).

of the millions of people living on the earth do in fact rest on conclusions drawn about this issue. As Jessica Litman has noted:

> When you turn on your computer, you needn't pay a royalty to Microsoft or Apple® for the use of the operating-system program that makes the computer work. We take this for granted, but it isn't natural law. It is the result of a complicated legal bargain that allocates the different benefits that flow from works of authorship to writers, to publishers, and to the public at large in a way intended to promote the progress of science and useful arts. There's no particular reason why we had to choose this system.[4]

Indeed, a strong case can be made for the need for much greater discussion about how and why intellectual property laws are constructed as they are. From a metaphysical perspective (as opposed to the aforementioned political and normative perspectives), this is all too often overlooked in the literature.

With so much riding on intellectual property laws, it is arguably important that conclusions about these issues are based on informed understandings of the subject matter, and that norms be built from a base of understanding rather than intuitions or politically motivated rhetoric or 'spin'. Thus, even if a theoretical work concerning the construction of intellectual property law is unlikely to end up on the best-seller lists, and even if it might be slow to influence political and normative discussions about intellectual propertization, it remains important.

It remains to be seen what impact the somewhat unusual approach (at least in the context of intellectual property law, although it is acknowledged that such approaches are more common in research concerning other areas of law) taken throughout this book might have. However, it is hoped that, by offering a more philosophically rigorous definition and contributing to a better understanding of the construction, constitution, and rhetorical discourse of 'intellectual property', the theory put forward in this study will ultimately enrich normative and political discussions about intellectual propertization.

[4] Jessica Litman, *Digital Copyright* (Amherst, NY: Prometheus, 2001) at 16.

Appendix

Normative Approaches to Intellectual Propertization

The following points briefly summarize common 'normative' approaches to intellectual property law-making. They are the justifications often given for intellectual propertization, and they are either rights-based or teleological (ie, they focus on the goals to be achieved by the law rather than political or structural reasons for regulation) in nature. They fall into three broad sub-categories: rights-based justifications, economic justifications, and consequentialist justifications. These justifications tend to overlap to some extent, and it is usually suggested that they operate in conjunction with one another. Short lists of relevant readings are provided to assist the reader seeking more information about any of the theories.

A1 Rights-Based Justifications

Rights-based justifications suggest that creators of intellectual property are entitled to property in the works they produce as a matter of natural right (ie, by virtue of being human rather than because of any secondary benefit that they may produce).

A1a Labour Theory ('Lockean Theory')

Labour theory is generally attributed to the philosophy of John Locke, *Second Treatise of Government*.[1] Locke writes:

[1] John Locke, *Second Treatise of Government*, ed. P. Laslett (Cambridge: Cambridge University Press, 1970).

> Though the Earth, and all inferior Creatures be common to all Men, yet every Man has a *Property* in his own *Person*. This no Body had any Right to but himself. The *Labour* of his Body, and the *Work* of his Hands, we may say, are properly his. Whatsoever then he removes out of the State that Nature hath provided, and left it in, he hath mixed his *Labour* with, and joyned to it something that is his own, and thereby makes it his *Property*. It being by him removed from the common state Nature placed it in, it hath by this *labour* something annexed to it, that excludes the common right of other Men. For this *Labour* being the unquestionable Property of the Labourer, no Man but he can have a right to what that is once joyned to, at least where there is enough, and as good left in common for others.[2]

From this is drawn the conclusion that, if somebody mixes his or her labour with material from the state of nature ('the commons'), that person is the owner of the creative result. The resulting property is often described as being owned by 'natural right'.

Empirical examples of labour theory in intellectual property doctrines include copyright's 'sweat of the brow' principle, which rewards property rights in return for the expenditure of labour, effort, or capital.[3] This principle was rejected in relation to compilations in the US copyright case of *Feist Publications, Inc. v Rural Telephone Service Co.* (1991)[4] and the Australian copyright case *IceTV Pty Ltd v Nine Network Australia Pty Ltd* (2009).[5] However, it remains a relevant consideration in copyright law generally and is strongly evident in patent theory.[6]

[2] Ibid., chap. V, §27.

[3] The UK case of *Walter v Lane* (1900) AC 539 is an example of this principle applied.

[4] *Feist Publications, Inc. v Rural Telephone Service Co.* (1991) 499 U.S. 340.

[5] *IceTV Pty Ltd v Nine Network Australia Pty Ltd* (2009) 239 CLR 458.

[6] For examples of cases clearly implementing labour theory, see *Doodeward v Spence* (1908) 6 C.L.R. 406 (Australia) and *Moore v Regents of University of California* 215 Cal.App.3d 709 (1988); affirmed in part, reversed in part, 51 Cal.3d 120, 793 P.2d 479 (1990) (US). See also discussion in Alexandra George, 'Is "Property" Necessary? On Owning the Human Body and Its Parts' (2004) 10 *Res Publica* 15–42.

- Peter Drahos, *A Philosophy of Intellectual Property* (Aldershot: Ashgate, 1996), chap. 3: 'Locke, Labour and the Intellectual Commons' at 41–72.
- Adam D. Moore, *Intellectual Property and Information Control: Philosophic Foundations and Contemporary Issues* (New Brunswick, NJ: Transaction, 2004), chap. 5: 'Toward a Lockean Theory of Intellectual Property' at 103–119.
- Robert Nozick, *Anarchy, State and Utopia* (New York: Basic Books, 1974) at 178–182.

A1b Desert Theory

A variation on labour theory is the theory from desert, which suggests that a person who creates a work deserves to own it, as does a person who invests in creating a work. Similarly, the creator may deserve to be recognized as such.

- Lawrence C. Becker, 'Deserving to Own Intellectual Property' (1992–1993) 68 *Chicago-Kent Law Review* 609–630.
- Gillian Davies, *Copyright and the Public Interest* (London: Thomson-Sweet & Maxwell, 2002) at 14.
- Michael Spence, *Intellectual Property* (Oxford: Oxford University Press, 2007) at 47–49.

A1c Personality Theory

Personality theory suggests that a person must not be alienated from the work that she or he has produced, as that work is an expression of self and to separate it from its creator is to detract from the creator's personhood.

This theory is often associated with Hegel's *Elements on the Philosophy of Right* (1820),[7] which argued that a creator's personality is incomplete unless she or he owns the products of her or his labour. Immanuel Kant, *Critique of Practical Reason and Other Works on the Theory of Ethics* (1781)[8] argued along similar lines.

An example of personality theory reflected in practice in intellectual property law is copyright's 'moral rights' doctrine. This allows a creator to be attributed as such and/or to object to the derogatory treatment of his or her work, even if that work has been sold to another person.

- Alan Brudner, 'Hegel and the Crisis of Private Law' (1989) 10 *Cardozo Law Review* 949–1000.
- Edward J. Damich, 'The Right of Personality: A Common-Law Basis for the Protection of the Moral Rights of Authors' (1998) 23:1 *Georgia Law Review* 1–96.
- Peter Drahos, *A Philosophy of Intellectual Property* (Aldershot: Ashgate, 1996), chap. 4: 'Hegel: The Spirit of Intellectual Property' at 73–94.
- Justin Hughes, 'The Philosophy of Intellectual Property' (1988–1989) 77 *Georgetown Law Journal* 287–366.
- Neil Weinstock Netanel, 'Alienability Restrictions and the Enhancement of Author Autonomy in United States and Continental Copyright Law' (1994) 12 *Cardozo Arts and Entertainment Law Journal* 1–78.
- Jeanne L. Schroeder, *Unnatural Rights: Hegel and Intellectual Property* (Working Paper No. 80, Benjamin N. Cardozo School of Law, Jacob Burns Institute for Advanced Legal Studies, 2004).

[7] Georg Wilhelm Friedrich Hegel, *Elements on the Philosophy of Right*, ed. Allen W. Wood, trans. H. B. Nisbet (Cambridge: Cambridge University Press, 1991).

[8] Immanuel Kant, *Critique of Practical Reason and Other Works on the Theory of Ethics* (Barnes and Noble Publishing, 2004; first published 1788).

A2 Economic Justifications

Economic justifications for intellectual propertization can also be dubbed 'efficiency' arguments. They argue that the law must intervene to prevent market failure.

A2a To Counter Free-Riding / Incentive to Create

This economic justification suggests that, without intellectual property laws to regulate markets, market failure will occur when 'public goods' such as ideational objects and their documented forms are released into society.

Public goods are non-excludable, meaning that once they are offered it is difficult to prevent anyone in society from using them (unless laws are introduced to prohibit such use). They are also non-rival, meaning that they can be used freely by anyone without others' ability to use them being diminished. Thus, free-riding – using goods freely without paying compensation for doing so – is likely to occur unless laws intervene to prohibit this.

The theory is that people are unlikely to invest labour, effort, money, or other resources into producing ideational objects and their documented forms if they get no compensation for doing so because everyone else can free-ride once those goods are produced. This would lead to market failure. As society would be poorer overall without these goods, intellectual property laws are introduced to correct the market by providing incentives for people to create them. In this sense, intellectual property laws are instrumental in nature.

- William M. Landes and Richard A. Posner, 'An Economic Analysis of Copyright Law' (1989) 18:2 *Journal of Legal Studies* 325–363.
- William M. Landes and Richard A. Posner, *The Economic Structure of Intellectual Property Law* (Cambridge, MA: Belknap Press of

(*continued*)

Harvard University Press, 2003), chap. 1: 'The Economic Theory of Property' at 11–36.
- Roger D. Blair and Thomas F. Cotter, *Intellectual Property: Economic and Legal Dimensions of Rights and Remedies* (New York: Cambridge University Press, 2005), chap. 2: 'The Law and Economics of IPRs' at 7–41.

A2b To Counter Information Asymmetry

Information asymmetry is the result of one person in a transaction having more information than others. It can lead to consumers being misled and/or result in consumers making purchasing decisions that are not fully informed. The result is inefficiencies in the market.

Intellectual property doctrines like passing off and trademark law increase the knowledge that consumers receive about goods and services. They allow traders to label their goods and services with indicators of source and/or quality that help consumers distinguish between products in the marketplace. They therefore reduce the likelihood of market failure due to information asymmetries.

- Joseph Feller, Patrick Finnegan, Jeremy Hayes, and Philip O'Reilly, 'Institutionalising Information Asymmetry: Governance Structures for Open Innovation' (2009) 22:4 *Information Technology & People* 297–316.
- James S. Ang, Yingmei Cheng, and Chaopeng Wu, *Does Enforcement of Intellectual Property Rights Matter? Evidence from Financing and Investment Choices in the High Tech Industry* (March 10, 2009), FSU College of Law, Law, Business & Economics Paper No. 09-12, http://ssrn.com/abstract=1357045 [accessed 12 June 2010].

A3 Consequentialist Justifications

Consequentialist justifications argue that intellectual property exists to produce socially beneficial results. The reasoning is as follows:

If x, then y

where

x = intellectual property laws, and
y = a socially desirable outcome.

A3a Utilitarian Theory

Utilitarian theories bear similarities to Jeremy Bentham's notion of the 'greatest happiness for the greatest number'.[9] Few would seek to justify intellectual property laws on purely utilitarian grounds, but utilitarianism is often offered to boost the appeal of other justifications. For example, economic justifications may be put forward in their own right and because they would seem to be in the interests of the majority of people in society.

A3b Instrumentalist Theory

Instrumental arguments for intellectual property rights suggest that providing a reward for labour also functions as a stimulus to creativity. In this sense, intellectual property laws are put forward as a means to an end, rather than an end in themselves (cf. rights-based justifications for intellectual propertization).

- Peter Drahos, *A Philosophy of Intellectual Property* (Aldershot: Ashgate, 1996), chap. 9: 'Intellectual Property: For Instrumentalism, Against Proprietarianism' at 199–228.
- Scott M. Martin, 'The Mythology of the Public Domain: Exploring the Myths Behind Attacks on the Duration of Copyright Protection' (2002–2003) 36 *Loyola of Los Angeles Law Review* 253–322.

[9] Jeremy Bentham, *An Introduction to the Principles of Morals and Legislation* (Oxford: Clarendon Press,1907; first published 1789), chap. 1.

A3c Social Planning Theory

Social planning theory[10] suggests that intellectual property laws help to foster a vibrant, democratic, pluralist, and fair society. As such a society does not arise naturally, governments must implement intellectual property laws to encourage such outcomes. Neil Netanel captures this argument eloquently:

> Copyright is a limited proprietary entitlement through which the state deliberately and selectively employs market institutions to support a democratic civil society. Copyright law provides this support in two fundamental ways. First, through its production function, copyright encourages creative expression on a wide array of political, social, and aesthetic issues. The activity of creating and communicating such expression and the expression itself constitute vital components of a democratic civil society. Second, through its structural function, copyright serves to further the democratic character of public discourse. By according authors and their assigns a proprietary entitlement, copyright fosters the development of an independent sector for the creation and dissemination of original expression, a sector composed of creators and publishers who earn financial support for their activities by reaching paying audiences rather than by depending on state or elite largess. No less importantly, by limiting the scope of that proprietary entitlement, copyright constrains owner control over expression, seeking to preserve rich possibilities for critical exchange and diverse reformulation of existing works.[11]

- Neil Weinstock Netanel, 'Copyright and a Democratic Civil Society' (1996) 106:2 *Yale Law Journal* 283–388.

(*continued*)

[10] The term is coined by William Fisher, 'Theories of Intellectual Property', in Stephen R. Munzer (ed.), *New Essays in the Legal and Political Theory of Property* (New York: Cambridge University Press, 2001) 168–199 at 173.

[11] Neil Weinstock Netanel, 'Copyright and a Democratic Civil Society' (1996) 106:2 *Yale Law Journal* 283–388 at 347.

- Neil Weinstock Netanel, 'Asserting Copyright's Democratic Principles in the Global Arena' (1998) 51 *Vanderbilt Law Review* 217–330.
- Gregory S. Alexander, *Commodity and Propriety* (Chicago: University of Chicago Press, 1997) at 1.
- William Fisher, 'Theories of Intellectual Property', in Stephen R. Munzer (ed.), *New Essays in the Legal and Political Theory of Property* (New York: Cambridge University Press, 2001) 168–199.

Bibliography

Aaker, David A., *Building Strong Brands* (London: Simon & Schuster, 2002).

Abbott, Alison, 'Dispute over First Authorship Lands Researchers in Dock' (2002) 419 *Nature* 4.

Abbott, Frederick M., "Protecting First World Assets in the Third World: Intellectual Property Negotiations in the GATT Multilateral Framework" (1989) 22 *Vanderbilt Journal of Transnational Law* 689–746.

Abrahamson, Scott, 'Seen One, Seen Them All? Making Sense of the Copyright Merger Doctrine' (1998) 45 *UCLA Law Review* 1125–1166.

Adams, Douglas, *Mostly Harmless* (New York: Ballantine, 1992).

Adams, John Norman and Michael Edenborough, 'The Duration of Copyright in the United Kingdom after the 1995 Regulations' (1996) 18:11 *European Intellectual Property Review* 590–596.

Adewopo, Adebambo, 'The Global Intellectual Property System and Sub-Saharan Africa: A Prognostic Reflection' (2002) 22 *University of Toledo Law Review* 749–771.

Adler, Matthew D., 'Regulatory Theory', in Dennis Patterson (ed.), *A Companion to Philosophy of Law and Legal Theory* (Oxford: Wiley-Blackwell, 2010), 590–606.

Afori, Orit Fischman, 'Reconceptualizing Property In Designs' (2008) 25 *Cardozo Arts and Entertainment Law Journal* 1106–1178.

Aitkin, Douglas, *The Culting of Brands: When Customers Become True Believers* (New York: Portfolio, Penguin, 2004).

Alberstat, Philip, 'Copyright Extension in the United States: The Mouse that Roared' (1999) 10:3 *Entertainment Law Review* 61–63.

Alexander, Gregory S., *Commodity and Propriety* (Chicago: University of Chicago Press, 1997).

Alford, William P., *To Steal a Book Is an Elegant Offense: Intellectual Property Law in Chinese Civilization* (Stanford, CA: Stanford University Press, 1997).

Altvater, Elmar and Kazimiera Prunskienê, *Intellectual Property Rights in Central and Eastern Europe: The Creation of Favourable Legal and Market Preconditions* (Amsterdam: IOS Press / Tokyo: Ohmsha, 1998).

American Heraldry Society website: http://www.americanheraldry.org/pages/index.php?n=Registration.Domestic [accessed 7 June 2010].

American Medical Association, *American Medical Association Manual of Style: A Guide for Authors and Editors* (Oxford: Oxford University Press, 2007).

Andersen, Hans Christian, 'The Emperor's New Suit', *Fairy Tales of Hans Christian Andersen* (1837).

Ang, James S., Yingmei Cheng, and Chaopeng Wu, *Does Enforcement of Intellectual Property Rights Matter? Evidence from Financing and Investment Choices in the High Tech Industry* (March 10, 2009), FSU College of Law, Law, Business & Economics Paper No. 09-12, http://ssrn.com/abstract=1357045 [accessed 12 June 2010].

Angell, Marcia, *The Truth About the Drug Companies: How They Deceive Us and What to Do About It* (New York: Random House, 2005).

Anker, Kirsten J., 'Possessing Star Qualities: Celebrity Identity as Property' (2002) 11 *Griffith Law Review* 147–168.

Annas, Marianna, 'The Label of Authenticity: A Certification Trade Mark for Goods and Services of Indigenous Origin' (1997) 3:90 *Aboriginal Law Bulletin* 4.

Aoki, Keith, 'Neocolonialism, Anticommons Property, and Biopiracy in the (Not-So-Brave) New World Order of International Intellectual Property Protection' (1998–1999) 6 *Indiana Journal of Global Legal Studies* 11–58.

Arewa, Olufunmilayo B., 'From J. C. Bach to Hip Hop: Musical Borrowing, Copyright and Cultural Context' (2005–2006) 84 *North Carolina Law Review* 547–645.

Arundell, Thomas, *Historical Reminiscences of the City of London and Its Livery Companies* (London: Richard Bentley, 1869).

Arup, Christopher, 'The United States–Australia Free Trade Agreement: The Intellectual Property Chapter' (2004) 15:4 *Australian Intellectual Property Journal* 205–226.

Asch, S. E., 'Opinions and Social Pressure' (1955) 193:5 *Scientific American* 31–35.

Ashton, Dore, *Picasso on Art: A Selection of Views* (London: Thames & Hudson, 1972).

Ashton, Gordon and Adrian Ward, *Mental Handicap and the Law* (London: Sweet & Maxwell, 1992).

Associated Press and France 24, 'Picasso et les maîtres' (8 October 2008), available at http://royalandco.wordpress.com/2008/10/08/picasso-et-les-maitres/ [accessed 15 May 2010].

Astor, Hilary and Christine M. Chinkin, *Dispute Resolution in Australia* (Sydney: Butterworths, 1992).

ATLAS Collaboration, The, G. Aad, E. Abat, J. Abdallah, et al., 'The ATLAS Experiment at the CERN Large Hadron Collider' (2008) *Journal of Instrumentation* 3, http://www.iop.org/EJ/abstract/1748–0221/3/08/S08003 [online journal, accessed 24 January 2010].

Austin, J. L., *How to Do Things with Words: The William James Lectures Delivered at Harvard University in 1955* (Oxford: Oxford University Press, 1975).

Australian Competition and Consumer Commission, *Certification Trade Marks: The Role of the ACCC* (Canberra: Australian Competition and Consumer Commission, 1998).

'Authorship' (letter to the editor) (1997) 315 *British Medical Journal* 744.

'Authorship Without Authorization' (editorial) (2004) 3:11 *Nature Materials* 743.

AWI website: http://www.wool.com/Design-and-Market_Woolmark_The-Brand_Trust-Woolmark.htm [accessed 2 June 2010].

Ayer, A. J., *The Concept of a Person and Other Essays* (London: Macmillan, 1964) at 82–128.

Babiskin, Lisa M., 'Oh, Pretty Parody: *Music, Inc*' (1994) 8 *Harvard Journal of Law & Technology* 193–230.

Baggott, Jim, *A Beginner's Guide to Reality* (London: Penguin, 2005).

Baker, Susannah L., 'It's All Fun and Games Until Somebody Declares Bankruptcy: A Debtor's Right to Season Ticket Holder Status' (1997) 14 *Emory Bankruptcy Developments Journal* 159–198.

Baldwin, Shawn K., '"To Promote the Progress of Science and Useful Arts": A Role for Federal Regulation of Intellectual Property as Collateral' (1995) 143 *University of Pennsylvania Law Review* 1701–1738.

Banham, Andrew and Stephen Cretney, *Children: The Modern Law* (Bristol: Jordan, 1993)

Banister, Judith (ed.), *English Silver Hall Marks* (London: W. Foulsham, 2004).

Bard, Robert L., *Copyright Duration: Duration, Term Extension, the European Union and the Making of Copyright Policy* (San Francisco: Austin & Winfield, 1999).

Barendt, Eric, Laurnce Lustgarten, Kenneth Norrie, and Hugh Stephenson, *Libel and the Media: The Chilling Effect* (New York: Oxford University Press, 1997).

Barker, Robert, *A Decree of Star Chamber Concerning Printing made July 11, 1637* (reprinted by Grolier Club, from the 1st ed. by Robert Barker, 1637).

Barrington, Shaun, *Harley-Davidson, an Illustrated History* (Castle Hill, Sydney: Lifetime Distributors, 1994).

Barron, Anne, 'No Other Law? Author-ity, Property and Aboriginal Art', in Lionel Bently and Spyros Maniatis (eds.), *Intellectual Property and Ethics* (London: Sweet & Maxwell, 1998), 39–87.

Barry, Nicholas, *An Introduction to Roman Law* (Oxford: Clarendon Press, 1969).

Barthes, Roland, 'The Death of the Author', in Stephen Heath (ed. and trans.), *Image-Music-Text* (New York: Hill & Wang, 1977), 142–148.

Barzel, Yoram, *Economic Analysis of Property Rights* (Cambridge: Cambridge University Press, 1997).

Baudrillard, Jean, *Simulacra and Simulation* (Ann Arbor: University of Michigan Press, 1981).

Becker, Lawrence C., 'Deserving to Own Intellectual Property' (1992–1993) 68 *Chicago-Kent Law Review* 609–630.

Beebe, Barton, 'The Semiotic Analysis of Trademark Law' (2004) 51 *UCLA Law Review* 621–704.

Beier, Friedrich-Karl and Joseph Strauss, 'The Patent System and Its Information Function: Yesterday and Today' (1977) 5 *International Review of Industrial Property* 387–406.

Bennett, Andrew, *The Author* (London: Routledge, 2005).

Bennett, Michelle and Jocelyn Harewood, *Vanuatu* (Melbourne: Lonely Planet, 2003).

Benos, Dale J., Jorge Fabres, John Farmer, Jessica P. Gutierrez, Kristin Hennessy, David Kosek, Joo Hyoung Lee, Dragos Olteanu, Tara Russell,

Faheem Shaikh, and Kai Wang, 'Ethics and Scientific Publication' (2005) 29 *Advances in Physiology Education* 59–74.

Bentham, Jeremy, *An Introduction to the Principles of Morals and Legislation* (Oxford: Clarendon Press, 1907; first published 1789).

Bently, Lionel, 'Copyright and the Death of the Author in Literature and Law' (1994) 57:6 *Modern Law Review* 973–986.

Bently, Lionel, 'R. v the Author: From Death Penalty to Community Service' (2008) 32:1 *Columbia Journal of Law and the Arts* 1–109.

Bently, Lionel, 'Requiem for Registration? Reflection on the History of the United Kingdom Registered Design System', in Alison Firth (ed.), *The Prehistory and Development of Intellectual Property Systems* (London: Sweet & Maxwell, 1997), 3–46.

Bently, Lionel and Spyros Maniatis (eds.), *Intellectual Property and Ethics* (London: Sweet & Maxwell, 1998).

Bently, Lionel and Brad Sherman, *Intellectual Property Law* (Oxford: Oxford University Press, 2001).

Berger, Peter L. and Thomas Luckmann, *The Social Construction of Reality: A Treatise in the Sociology of Knowledge* (London: Penguin, 1991)

Bergman, Bryan, 'Into the Grey: The Unclear Laws of Digital Sampling' (2005) 27 *Hastings Communications and Entertainment Law Journal (Comm/Ent)* 619–652.

Berlin, Isaiah, 'Two Concepts of Liberty', in Henry Hardy (ed.), *Isaiah Berlin, Liberty, Incorporating 'Four Essays on Liberty'* (Oxford: Oxford University Press, 2002), 177.

Bessen, James and Michael J. Meurer, *Patent Failure: How Judges, Bureaucrats, and Lawyers Put Innovators at Risk* (Princeton, NJ: Princeton University Press, 2008).

Bettig, Ronald V., *Copyrighting Culture: The Political Economy of Intellectual Property* (Boulder, CO: Westview Press, 1996).

Bhopal, Raj, Judith Rankin, Elaine McColl, Lois Thomas, Eileen Kaner, Rosie Stacy, Pauline Pearson, Brian Vernon, and Helen Rodgers, 'The Vexed Question of Authorship: Views of Researchers in a British Medical Faculty' (1997) 314 *British Medical Journal* 1009.

Bix, Brian, *Jurisprudence: Theory and Context* (London: Sweet & Maxwell, 1999).

Black, Julia, 'Critical Reflections on Regulation' (2002) 27 *Australasian Journal of Legal Philosophy* 1–35.

Black, Julia, 'Regulatory Conversations' (2002) 29:1 *Journal of Law and Society* 163–196.

Black, Max (ed.), *The Importance of Language* (Englewood Cliffs, NJ: Prentice Hall, 1962).

Blackett, Tom, *Trademarks* (London: Macmillan Press, 1998).

Blackett, Tom, 'What Is a Brand?' in Rita Clifton and John Simmons (eds.), *Brands and Branding* (New York: Profile, 2003), 13–25.

Blair, Roger D. and Thomas F. Cotter, *Intellectual Property: Economic and Legal Dimensions of Rights and Remedies* (New York: Cambridge University Press, 2005).

Blass, Thomas (ed.), *Obedience to Authority: Current Perspectives on the Milgram Paradigm* (London: Lawrence Erlbaum, 2000).

Blossom, John, *Content Nation: Surviving and Thriving as Social Media Changes Our Work, Our Lives, and Our Future* (Indianapolis: Wiley, 2009).

Bly, John, *Discovering Hallmarks on English Silver* (Princes Risborough, Buckinghamshire: Shire Publications, 2002).

Bollier, David, *Brand Name Bullies: The Quest to Own and Control Culture* (Hoboken, NJ: Wiley, 2005).

Bolton, M. B., 'Idea', in Jaegwon Kim and Ernest Sosa (eds.), *A Companion to Metaphysics* (Oxford: Blackwell, 1995), 225–227.

Boyd, Steven S., 'Deriving Originality in Derivative Works: Considering the Quantum of Originality Needed to Attain Copyright Protection in a Derivative Work' (1999–2000) 40 *Santa Clara Law Review* 325–378.

Boyle, James, 'Forward: The Opposite of Property' (2003) 66 *Law and Contemporary Problems* 1–32.

Boyle, James, 'The Second Enclosure Movement and the Construction of the Public Domain' (2003) 66 *Law and Contemporary Problems* 33–74.

Boyle, James, *Shamans, Software and Spleens: Law and the Construction of the Information Society* (Cambridge, MA: Harvard University Press, 1997).

Bracha, Oren, 'The Ideology of Authorship Revisited: Authors, Markets and Liberal Values in Early American Copyright' (2008) 118 *Yale Law Journal* 186–271.

Bradley, A. Jane, "Intellectual Property Rights, Investment, and Trade in Services in the Uruguay Round: Laying the Foundations" (1987) 23 *Stanford Journal of International Law* 57–98.

Braga, Carlos Alberto Primo, 'The Economics of Intellectual Property Rights and the GATT: A View from the South', (1989) 22 *Vanderbilt Journal of Transnational Law* 243–264.

Braithwaite, John and Peter Drahos, *Global Business Regulation* (Cambridge: Cambridge University Press, 2000).

Braudy, Leo, *The Frenzy of Renown: Fame and Its History* (New York: Oxford University Press, 1986).

A Brief Guide to Liturgical Copyright: Liturgical Texts for Local Use: Copyright Information (London: Church House, 1994).

Britton, Karen Gerhardt, *Bale o' Cotton: The Mechanical Art of Cotton Ginning* (College Station: Texas A&M University Press, 1993).

Brontsema, Robin, 'A Queer Revolution: Reconceptualizing the Debate over Linguistic Reclamation' (2004) 17 *Colorado Research in Linguistics*, http://www.colorado.edu/ling/CRIL/Volume17_Issue1/paper_BRONTSEMA.pdf. [online journal, accessed 3 October 2006].

Brooke-Little, J. P., *Boutell's Heraldry* (London: Frederick Warne, 1970).

Brown, Hank and David Miller, 'Copyright Term Extension: Sapping American Creativity' (1996) 44:2 *Journal of the Copyright Society of the USA* 94–102.

Brown, Jeffrey H., '"They Don't Make Music the Way they Used To": The Legal Implications of "Sampling" in Contemporary Music' (1992) *Wisconsin Law Review* 1941–1992.

Brown, Michael F., *Who Owns Native Culture?* (Cambridge, MA: Harvard University Press, 2004).

Brudner, Alan, 'Hegel and the Crisis of Private Law' (1989) 10 *Cardozo Law Reveiw* 949–1000.

Brunet, E., 'Questioning the Quality of Alternative Dispute Resolution' (1987–88) 62 *Tulane Law Review* 1–56 at 14.

Buckland, Andrew, 'Rap, Parody, and Fair Use: *Luther R Campbell aka Luke Skywalker, et al v Acuff-Rose Music, Inc*' (1995) 17 *Sydney Law Review* 599–610.

Buckle, Stephen, *Natural Law and the Theory of Property: Grotius to Hume* (Oxford: Clarendon Press, 1991).

Burk, Dan L., 'Copyright and Feminism in Digital Media' (2006) 14 *American University Journal of Gender, Social Policy & the Law* 519–550.

Burr, Vivien, *An Introduction to Social Constructionism* (London: Routledge, 1995).

California Department of Food and Agriculture website: (http://www.cdfa.ca.gov/ahfss/Livestock_ID/Brand_Registration_Info.html#Cattle [accessed 4 June 2010].

Cane, Peter and Mark Tushnet (eds.), *Oxford Handbook of Legal Studies* (Oxford: Oxford University Press, 2003).

Carr, Cecil Thomas, *Select Charters of Trading Companies, A.D. 1530–1707*. Publications of the Seldon Society 28 (London: Bernard Quaritch, 1913).

Carroll, Lewis, 'Through the Looking-Glass', in *The Complete Works of Lewis Carroll* (London: Nonesuch Press, 1939).

Carter, J. W., Patricia Lane, Gregory J. Tolhurst, and Elisabeth M. Peden, *Helmore Commercial Law and Personal Property in New South Wales* (Sydney: Law Book Company, 1992, 10th ed.).

Carter, James H., 'They Know It When They See It: Copyright and Aesthetics in the Second Circuit' (1991) 65 *St John's Law Review* 773–794.

Carter, Stephen L., 'Does It Matter Whether Intellectual Property Is Property?' (1003) 68 *Chicago-Kent Law Review* 715–723.

CEN website: http://www.cen.eu/cen/Members/Pages/default.aspx [accessed 2 June 2010].

Chalmers, Robert, 'Evergreen or Deciduous: Australian Trends in Relation to the Evergreening of Patents' (2006) 30 *Melbourne University Law Review* 29–61.

Chandler, Daniel, *Semiotics: The Basics* (London: Routledge, 2002).

Chandler, Daniel, *Semiotics for Beginners* (published online: http://www.aber.ac.uk/media/Documents/S4B/semiotic.html [accessed 6 June 2010]).

Chapman, James, 'Holidaying Blair in Conflict of Interest over Copyright Law' (30 July 2006) *The Mail on Sunday* (UK), http://www.mailonsunday.co.uk/pages/live/articles/news/news.html?in_article_id=398339&in_page_id=1770 [accessed 19 September 2006].

CIA – The World Factbook website: http://www.odci.gov/cia/publications/factbookgeos/xx.html [accessed 3 October 2005].

'Cliff Richard Calls for Music Copyright Change' (19 April 2006) *Reuters*.

Clifton, Rita and John Simmons (eds.), *Brands and Branding* (New York: Profile, 2003).

Clifton, Tony, 'A Hot Commodity with a 30,000-Year Lineage' (24 April 2003) *New York Times*, http://www.nytimes.com/2003/04/24/arts/a-hot-commodity-with-a-30000-year-lineage.html [accessed 15 May 2010].

Clinton, Robert, 'The Rights of Indigenous Peoples as Collective Group Rights' (1990) 32 *Arizona Law Review* 739–747.

Coles, Peter, 'Copyright Duration: The European Community Adopts "Three Score Years and Ten"' (1996) 18:7 *European Intellectual Property Review* 379–383.

'The Collective Trademark: Invitation to Abuse' (1959) 68 *Yale Law Journal* 528–541.

College of Arms (UK) website: http://www.college-of-arms.gov.uk/About/08.htm#a [accessed 14 June 2010].

Collins, A. S., *The Profession of Letters: A Study of the Relation of Author to Patron, Publisher, and Public, 1780–1832* (London: Routledge, 1928).

Collins, Hugh, *Regulating Contracts* (Oxford: Oxford University Press, 1999).

Convention on the Control and Marking of Articles of Precious Metals (1972) website: http://www.hallmarkingconvention.org/assay-offices.php [accessed 2 June 2010].

Conway, Danielle M., 'Indigenizing Intellectual Property Law: Customary Law, Legal Pluralism, and the Protection of Indigenous Peoples' Rights, Identity, and Resources', (2008–2009) 15 *Texas Wesleyan Law Review* 207–256.

Coombe, Rosemary J., *The Cultural Life of Intellectual Properties: Authorship, Appropriation, and the Law* (Durham, NC: Duke University Press, 1998).

Copyright Law Review Committee, *Report on Moral Rights* (Canberra: Australian Government Publishing Service, 1988).

Cornish, W. R., *Intellectual Property: Patents, Copyright, Trade Marks and Allied Rights* (London: Sweet & Maxwell, 1981).

Cornish, William and David Llewelyn, *Intellectual Property: Patents, Copyrights, Trademarks and Allied Rights* (London: Sweet & Maxwell, 2007).

Correa, Carlos María, *Intellectual Property Rights, the WTO and Developing Countries: The TRIPS Agreement and Policy Options* (London: Zed, 2000).

Cotter, Thomas F. and Angela M. Mirabole, 'Written on the Body: Intellectual Property Rights in Tattoos, Makeup, and Other Body Art' (2002–2003) 10 *UCLA Entertainment Law Review* 97–138.

Council of Science Editors Editorial Policy Committee, *White Paper on Promoting Integrity in Scientific Journal Publications, 2009 Update* (2009), http://www.councilscienceeditors.org/editorial_policies/whitepaper/entire_whitepaper.pdf [accessed 23 January 2010].

Cowling, Elizabeth, 'Competition and Collaboration: Picasso and the Old Masters', in Johanna Stephenson (ed.), *Picasso: Challenging the Past* (London: National Gallery, 2009), 11–25.

Cox, Noel, 'The Intellectual Property Law and the Protection of Armorial Bearings' (2001) 12 *Australian Intellectual Property Journal* 143–152.

CPA Australia website: http://www.cpaaustralia.com.au/cps/rde/xchg/cpa-site/hs.xsl/become-types-cpa.html [accessed 4 June 2010].

Creighton, W. B., W. J. Ford, and R. J. Mitchell, *Labour Law: Text and Materials* (Sydney: Law Book Company, 1993).

Crews, Kenneth D., 'Harmonization and the Goals of Copyright: Property Rights or Cultural Progress?' (1998) 6 *Indiana Journal of Global Legal Studies* 117–138.

Cruz, Amaury, 'What's the Big Idea Behind the Idea–Expression Dichotomy? Modern Ramifications of the Tree of Porphyry in Copyright Law' (1990) 18 *Florida State University Law Review* 221–250.

CSE Recommendations for Group-Author Articles in Scientific Journals and Bibliometric Databases; available at CSE website: http://www.councilofscienceeditors.org/publications/group_authorship.pdf [accessed 24 January 2010].

Daes, Erica-Irene, *Study on the Protection of the Cultural and Intellectual Property of Indigenous Peoples*, E/CN.4/Sub.2/1993/28 (United Nations, Commission on Human Rights, Sub-Commission on Prevention of Discrimination and Protection of Minorities) (28 July 1993).

Daes, Erica-Irene, 'Intellectual Property and Indigenous Peoples' (2001) 95 *American Society of International Law Proceedings* 143–150.

Dahl, Robert A., *Modern Political Analysis* (Englewood Cliffs, NJ: Prentice-Hall International, 1984).

Damich, Edward J., 'The Right of Personality: A Common-Law Basis for the Protection of the Moral Rights of Authors' (1998) 23:1 *Georgia Law Review* 1–96.

Dauber, Kenneth, *The Idea of Authorship in America: Democratic Poetics from Franklin to Melville* (Madison: University of Wisconsin Press, 1990).

Davenport, Neil, *The United Kingdom Patent System: A Brief History* (Homewell, Havant, Hampshire: Kenneth Mason, 1979).

Davidoff, Frank, 'Who's the Author? Problems with Biomedical Authorship and Some Possible Solutions', Report to the Council of Biology Editors (now Council of Science Editors) from the Task Force on Authorship (February 2000); available at Council of Science Editors website: http://www.councilofscienceeditors.org/publications/v23n4p111–119.pdf [accessed 24 January 2010].

Davies, Gillian, *Copyright and the Public Interest* (London: Thomson-Sweet & Maxwell, 2002).

Davis, Hugh, 'Old Rockers Band Together to Keep Royalties Coming in from their Hits' (29 March 2006) *The Telegraph* (UK), http://www.telegraph.co.uk/news/main.jhtml?xml=/news/2006/03/29/nroyal29.xm [accessed 19 September 2006].

Davison, Peter, 'King James's Book of Bounty: From Manuscript to Print', in *The Library: The Transactions of the Bibliographical Society* (Oxford: Oxford University Press, 1973).

Day, Aidan, *Romanticism* (New York: Routledge, 1996).

de la Torre, Carlos Ruiz, 'Digital Music Sampling and Copyright Law: Can the Interests of Copyright Owners and Sampling Artists Be Reconciled?' (2005) 7 *Vanderbilt Journal of Entertainment Law & Practice* 401–410.

Deane, Phyllis, *The First Industrial Revolution* (Cambridge: Cambridge University Press, 1979).

Deazley, Ronan, 'The Life of an Author: Samuel Egerton Brydges and the Copyright Act 1814' (2006–2007) 23 *Georgia State University Law Review* 809–846.

Deazley, Ronan, *Rethinking Copyright: History, Theory, Language* (Cheltenham: Edward Elgar, 2008).

Deazley, Ronan, Martin Kretschmer, and Lionel Bently (eds.), *Privilege and Property: Essays on the History of Copyright* (Cambridge: Open Book, 2010).

Delius, Christoph, Matthias Gatzemeier, Deniz Sertcan, and Kathleen Wünscher, *The Story of Philosophy: From Antiquity to the Present* (Cologne: Könemann, 2000).

Demers, Joanna, *Steal This Music: How Intellectual Property Law Affects Musical Creativity* (Athens: University of Georgia Press, 2006).

Dicey, A. V., *An Introduction to the Study of the Law of the Constitution* (London: Macmillan, 1959, 10th ed.).

Donson, Fiona J. L., *Legal Intimidation* (London: Free Association, 2000).

Dougherty, Terence, 'Group Rights to Cultural Survival: Intellectual Property Rights in Native American Cultural Symbols' (1998) 29 *Columbia Human Rights Law Review* 355–399.

Douglas, Mary, *The World of Goods: Towards an Anthropology of Consumption* (New York: Routledge, 1996).

Drahos, Peter, *Developing Countries and International Intellectual Property Standard-Setting*, Study Paper 8 (Commission on Intellectual Property Rights).

Drahos, Peter, *Information Feudalism: Who Owns the Knowledge Economy?* (London: Earthscan, 2002).

Drahos, Peter, *A Philosophy of Intellectual Property* (Aldershot: Ashgate, 1996).

Drahos, Peter, 'The Regulation of Public Goods' (2004) 7:23 *Journal of International Economic Law* 321–339.

Drahos, Peter and John Braithwaite, *Global Business Regulation* (Cambridge: Cambridge University Press, 2000).

Drahos, Peter and Ruth Mayne (eds.), *Global Intellectual Property Rights: Knowledge, Access and Development* (New York: Palgrave Macmillan, 2002).

Dworkin, Ronald, *Law's Empire* (London: Fontana Press, 1986).

Dworkin, Ronald, *Taking Rights Seriously* (London: Duckworth, 1978).

Easterbrook, Frank H., 'Intellectual Property Is Still Property' (1990) 13 *Harvard Journal of Law and Public Policy* 108–118.

Eastwood, S., P. Derish, E. Leash, and S. Ordway, 'Ethical Issues in Biomedical Research: Perceptions and Practices of Postdoctoral Research Fellows Responding to a Survey' (1996) 2 *Science and Engineering Ethics* 89–114.

Eisenstein, Elizabeth L., *The Printing Revolution in Early Modern Europe* (Cambridge: Cambridge University Press, 2005).

Elliott, Catherine and Frances Quinn, *English Legal System* (Harlow: Pearson Education, 2002).

Elliott, Tim, 'Spirits Cannot Rest So Far from Home' (13 March 2010), *Sydney Morning Herald*, http://www.smh.com.au/national/spirits-cannot-rest-so-far-from-home-20100312-q45t.html [accessed 30 May 2010].

Erenkrantz, Justin R., 'The Mask and the Mirror', http://www.erenkrantz.com/Words/TheMaskAndTheMirror.shtml [accessed 15 May 2010].

Fairtrade Foundation website: http://www.fairtrade.org.uk/business_services/use_of_the_fairtrade_mark.aspx [accessed 2 June 2010].

Feather, John, 'From Rights in Copies to Copyright: The Recognition of Authors' Rights in English Law and Practice in the Sixteenth and Seventeenth Centuries', in Martha Woodmansee and Peter Jaszi (eds.), *The Construction of Authorship: Textual Appropriation in Law and Literature* (Durham, NC: Duke University Press, 1994), 191–209.

Feinberg, Joel, *The Moral Limits of the Criminal Law: Harm to Self*, Vol. 3 (Oxford: Oxford University Press, 1986).

Feller, Joseph, Patrick Finnegan, Jeremy Hayes, and Philip O'Reilly, 'Institutionalising Information Asymmetry: Governance Structures for Open Innovation' (2009) 22:4 *Information Technology & People* 297–316.

Ferguson, Niall, *Empire: How Britain Made the Modern World* (London: Penguin, 2004).

Fergusson, Rosalind, *The Penguin Dictionary of Proverbs* (Harmondsworth: Penguin, 1983).

Firth, Alison, 'Introduction', in Alison Firth (ed.), *The Prehistory and Development of Intellectual Property Systems* (London: Sweet & Maxwell, 1997), v–vi.

Firth, Alison, (ed.), *The Prehistory and Development of Intellectual Property Systems* (London: Sweet & Maxwell, 1997).

Firth, C. H. and R. S. Rait (eds.), *Acts and Ordinances of the Interregnum, 1642–1660* (London: HMSO, 1911; 3 vols.), Vol. 1 at 184–187 (Ordinance passed 14 June 1963) [L.J., vi., 96–97; Husband, pp. 213–216].

Fish, Stanley, *Is There a Text in This Class? The Authority of Interpretive Communities* (Cambridge, MA: Harvard University Press, 1980).

Fisher, William, 'Theories of Intellectual Property', in Stephen R. Munzer (ed.), *New Essays in the Legal and Political Theory of Property* (New York: Cambridge University Press, 2001),168–199.

Flanagin, Annette, Lisa A. Carey, Phil B. Fontanarosa, et al., 'Prevalence of Articles with Honorary Authors and Ghost Authors in Peer-Reviewed Medical Journals' (1998) 280:3 *Journal of the American Medical Association* 222–224.

Forer, Lois G., *A Chilling Effect: The Mounting Threat of Libel and Invasion of Privacy Actions to the First Amendment* (New York: W. W. Norton, 1987).

Foster, Patrick, 'Musicians Celebrate Victory as Go-ahead Given for Copyright to be Extended to 95 Years' (13 February 2009) *Times*, http://entertainment.timesonline.co.uk/tol/arts_and_entertainment/music/article5720510.ece [accessed 16 January 2010].

Foucault, Michel, *The Archaeology of Knowledge*,trans. A. M. Sheridan Smith (London: Routledge, 2002).

Foucault, Michel, *The Foucault Reader*, ed. Paul Rabinow (New York: Pantheon, 1984).

Foucault, Michel, *Les mots et les choses* (Paris: Éditions Gallimard, 1966).

Foucault, Michel, *The Order of Things: An Archaeology of the Human Sciences* (London: Routledge Classics, 1989).

Foucault, Michel, 'What Is an Author?' in *The Foucault Reader*, ed. Paul Rabinow (New York: Pantheon, 1984), 101–120.

Frankel, Susy, 'WTO Application of "the Customary Rules of Interpretation of Public International Law" to Intellectual Property' (2006) 46 *Virginia Journal of International Law* 365–432.

Freeman, Michael (ed.), *Alternative Dispute Resolution* (Aldershot: Dartmouth, 1995).

Fuller, Lon L. 'The Forms and Limits of Adjudication' (1978) 92 *Harvard Law Review* 353–409.

Fuller, Lon L. *Legal Fictions* (Stanford, CA: Stanford University Press, 1967).

Fysh, Michael, *Russell-Clarke on Copyright in Industrial Designs* (London: Sweet & Maxwell, 1974).

Gaither, Ronald, 'The Chillin' Effect of Section 506: The Battle over Digital Sampling in Rap Music' (2001) 3 *Vanderbilt Journal of Entertainment Law & Practice* 195–209.

Galassi, Susan Grace, 'Picasso's 'Old Master' Period', in Johanna Stephenson (ed.), *Picasso: Challenging the Past* (London: National Gallery, 2009), 109–139.

Gallie, W. B., 'Essentially Contested Concepts', in Max Black (ed.), *The Importance of Language* (Englewood Cliffs, NJ: Prentice Hall, 1962), 121–146; first published in (1956) 56 *Proceedings of the Aristotelian Society* 167.

Garon, Jon M., 'Normative Copyright: A Conceptual Framework for Copyright Philosophy and Ethics' (2003) 88 *Cornell Law Review* 1278–1360.

Gasiorowski-Denis, Elizabeth, 'They Shoot, They Score! ISO Standard Gives Ice Hockey Better Play with Protective Equipment', *ISO Press Release*, Ref. 885, available at ISO website: http://www.iso.org/iso/pressrelease.htm?refid=Ref885 [accessed 7 June 2010].

Gay, Joshua (ed.), *Free Software, Free Society: Selected Essays of Richard M. Stallman* (Boston: GNU Press, 2002).

Gee, Lim Heng, 'A Study of the Historical Development of the Malaysian Patent System', in Alison Firth (ed.), *The Prehistory and Development of Intellectual Property Systems* (London: Sweet & Maxwell, 1997), 81–121.

George, Alexandra, (ed.), *Globalization and Intellectual Property* (Aldershot: Ashgate, 2006).

George, Alexandra, 'Brand Rules: When Branding Lore Meets Trade Mark Law' (2006) 13:3 *Journal of Brand Management* 215–232.

George, Alexandra, 'The Difficulty of Defining "Property"' (2005) 25:4 *Oxford Journal of Legal Studies* 793–813.

George, Alexandra, 'The (In)Justice of Globalisation by Intellectual Propertisation' (2007) 93 *Archiv für Rechts- und Sozialphilosophie* 17–31.

George, Alexandra, 'Is "Property" Necessary? On Owning the Human Body and Its Parts' (2004) 10 *Res Publica* 15–42.

George, Alexandra, 'Propertizing the Immaterial: The Commodification of Valuable Intangibles', in Rachel Moffat and Eugene de Klerk (eds.), *Material Worlds* (Cambridge: Cambridge Scholars Press, 2007), 134–147.

George, Alexandra, 'What Is "Intellectual Property"? Standard Definitional Methods and Their Flaws', in Tomasz Gizbert-Studnicki and Mateusz Klinowski (eds.), *Law, Liberty, Morality and Rights* (Warsaw: Wolters Kluwer Polska-Oficyna, 2010), 164–175.

George, Andrew G. A., 'The Law of Arms in Queensland' (2008) 49 *Heraldry News* 3–6.

George, Robert P., *In Defense of Natural Law* (Oxford: Clarendon Press, 1999).

GNU Project website: http://www.gnu.org/gnu/manifesto.html [accessed 8 December 2008].

Godden, Geoffrey A., *Encyclopaedia of English Pottery and Porcelain Marks* (London: Herbert Jenkins, 1964).

Gold and Silversmiths Guild of Australia website: http://www.gsga.org.au/ [accessed 16 June 2010].

Goldman, Robert and Stephen Papson, *Nike Culture: The Sign of the Swoosh* (London: Sage, 1998).

Goldstein, Paul, *Copyright's Highway: The Law and Lore of Copyright from Gutenberg to the Celestial Jukebox* (New York: Hill & Wang, 1994).

Goldstein, Paul, *Copyright's Highway: From Gutenberg to the Celestial Jukebox* (Stanford, CA: Stanford Law and Politics, 2003).

Golvan, Colin, 'The Protection of *At the Waterhole* by John Bulun Bulun: Aboriginal Art and the Recognition of Private and Communal Rights', in Andrew T. Kenyon, Megan Richardson, and Sam Ricketson (eds.), *Landmarks in Australian Intellectual Property Law* (Melbourne: Cambridge University Press, 2009), 191–208.

Gordon, Wendy J., 'Intellectual Property Law', in Peter Cane and Mark Tushnet (eds.), *Oxford Handbook of Legal Studies* (Oxford: Oxford University Press, 2003), 617–646.

Gower, Andrew, *Gowers Review of Intellectual Property* (London: HM Treasury, 2006).

Grant, Francis J. (ed.), *The Manual of Heraldry: A Concise Description of the Several Terms Used, and Containing a Dictionary of Every Designation in the Science* (Edinburgh: John Grant, 1929).

Graveson, R. H., *Status in the Common Law* (London: Athlone Press, 1953).

Gray, Wood, Richard Hofstadter, and Keith W. Olson, *An Outline of American History* (United States Information Agency).

Greene, Mott, 'The Demise of the Lone Author' (2007) 450 *Nature* 1165.

Greenfield, Jeanette, *The Return of Cultural Treasures* (Cambridge: Cambridge University Press, 1995).

Grubb, Philip W., *Patents for Chemicals, Pharmaceuticals and Biotechnology: Fundamentals of Global Law, Practice and Strategy* (Oxford: Oxford University Press, 2004).

Guellec, Dominique and Bruno van Pottelsberghe de la Potterie, *The Economics of the European Patent System: IP Policy for Innovation and Competition*, trans. Luigi Sordelli (Oxford: Oxford University Press, 2007).

Guest, Anthony Gordon (ed), *Oxford Essays in Jurisprudence* (Oxford: Oxford University Press, 1961).

GUSTO Investigators, The, 'An International Randomized Trial Comparing Four Thrombolytic Strategies for Acute Myocardial Infarction' (1993) 329:10 *New England Journal of Medicine* 673–682.

Hacking, Ian, *The Social Construction of What?* (Cambridge, MA: Harvard University Press, 2000).

Haemmerli, Alice, 'Whose Who? The Case for a Kantian Right of Publicity' (1999) 49 *Duke Law Journal* 383–492.

Hahn, Melissa, 'Digital Music Sampling and Copyright Policy: A Bittersweet Symphony? Assessing the Continued Legality of Music Sampling in the United Kingdom, the Netherlands, and the United States' (2006) 34 *Georgia Journal of International and Comparative Law* 713–742.

Halbert, Debora J., *Resisting Intellectual Property* (London: Routledge, 2005).

Hallmarking Convention website: http://www.hallmarkingconvention.org/accession-dates.php [accessed 2 June 2010].

Halvey, John K., 'A Rose by Any Other Name: Computer Programs and the Idea–Expression Distinction' (1985) 34 *Emory Law Journal* 741–776.

Hanks, Peter and Bryan Keon-Cohen (eds.), *Aborigines and the Law* (Sydney: George Allen & Unwin, 1984).

Hansard (17 May 2006), Column 332WH, http://www.publications.parliament.uk/pa/cm200506/cmhansrd/cm060517/halltext/60517h0061.htm [accessed 19 September 2006].

Harden, Ian and Norman Lewis, *The Noble Lie: The British Constitution and the Rule of Law* (London: Hutchinson, 1986).

Hardie, Martin, 'The Bulun Bulun Case: John Bulun Bulun & Anor v R & T Textiles Pty Ltd' (1988) *Indigenous Law Bulletin* 87; (1998) 4:16 *Indigenous Law Bulletin* 24, http://www.austlii.edu.au/au/journals/ILB/1998/87.html [accessed 12 May 2010].

Hardin, Garrett, 'The Tragedy of the Commons' (1968) 162 *Science* 1243–1248.

Harley Owners Group website: http://www.harley-davidson.com/wcm/Content/Pages/HOG/HOG.jsp?locale=en_US [accessed 23 January 2010].

Harris, J. W., *Property and Justice* (Oxford: Oxford University Press, 1996).

Hart, H. L. A., "Definition and Theory in Jurisprudence" (1954) 70 *Law Quarterly Review* 37–60.

Haslam, John, *Medical Jurisprudence as It Relates to Insanity* (New York: Garland, 1979; rpt. of 1817 ed.).

Hazlitt, W. Care, *The Livery Companies of the City of London: Their Origin, Character, Development, and Social and Political Importance* (London: Swan Sonnenschein, 1892).

Hegel, Georg Wilhelm Friedrich, *Elements on the Philosophy of Right*, ed. Allen W. Wood, trans. H. B. Nisbet (Cambridge: Cambridge University Press, 1991).

Helberger, Natali, 'Never Forever: Why Extending the Term of Protection for Sound Recordings Is a Bad Idea' (2008) 30:5 *European Intellectual Property Review* 174–181.

Heller, Michael A., 'The Tragedy of the Anticommons: The Transition from Marx to Markets' (1998) 111 *Harvard Law Review* 621–688.

Heller, Michael A., *The Gridlock Economy: How Too Much Ownership Wrecks Markets, Stops Innovation, and Costs Lives* (New York: Perseus, 2010).

'Hells Angel Member Not in Criminal Organization' (27 March 2008) *CTV News*, http://www.ctv.ca/servlet/ArticleNews/story/CTVNews/20080327/

hellsangels_guilty_080327/20080327?hub=CTVNewsAt11 [accessed 23 January 2010].

'Hells Angels Criminal Organization, Judge Rules' (1 July 2005) *CBC News*, http://www.cbc.ca/canada/story/2005/07/01/bikers-ruling.html [accessed 23 January 2010].

Hertz, Richard, 'Legal Protection for Indigenous Cultures: Sacred Sites and Communal Rights', (1993) 79:3 *Virginia Law Review* 691–716.

Hirstein, William, *On Searle* (Belmont, CA: Wadsworth, Thompson Learning, 2001).

Hogan, Patrick Colm, *The Culture of Conformism: Understanding Social Consent* (Durham, NC: Duke University Press, 2001).

Honoré, Anthony M., 'Ownership', in Anthony Gordon Guest (ed.), *Oxford Essays in Jurisprudence* (Oxford: Oxford University Press, 1961), 107–147.

Honoré, Tony, 'Rights of Exclusion and Immunities against Divesting' (1960) 34 *Tulane Law Review* 453–468.

Hopwood, Graham, *Handbook of Art* (Melbourne: Graham Hopwood, 1971).

Horton, Richard and Richard Smith, 'Time to Redefine Authorship' (1996) 312 *British Medical Journal* 723.

Hovey, Craig, *The Patent Process: A Guide to Intellectual Property for the Information Age* (New York: Wiley, 2002).

Hughes, Ann, *The Causes of the English Civil War* (London: MacMillan Press, 1998).

Hughes, Justin, 'The Philosophy of Intellectual Property' (1988–1989) 77 *Georgetown Law Journal* 287–366.

Hulme, E. Wyndham, 'On the Consideration of the Patent Grant, Past and Present' (1897) 51 *Law Quarterly Review* 313–318.

Humphry, Alison, 'An Opportunity Lost for Aboriginal Self-Determination: Australia's Compliance With ILO 169' (1995) 2:1 *Murdoch University Electronic Journal of Law*, http://www.murdoch.edu.au/elaw/issues/v2n1/humphry21.html [accessed 7 June 2010].

Hunter, Dan, 'Culture War' (2005) 83 *Texas Law Review* 1105–1136.

Hurowitz, Richard, 'Surviving Copyright Infringement: Fair Use of Protected Works in "Biopics"' (1997–1998) 22 *Columbia Journal of Law & theArts* 247–268.

IAAO website: http://www.theiaao.com/ [accessed 2 June 2010].

'Information for Authors', *The Lancet* (January 2010), http://download.thelancet.com/flatcontentassets/authors/lancet-information-for-authors.pdf [accessed 24 January 2010].

International Committee of Medical Journal Editors, *Uniform Requirements for Manuscripts Submitted to Biomedical Journals: Writing and Editing for Biomedical Publication* (October 2008).

IP Australia, ATMOSS database website (for trademark searches): http://pericles.ipaustralia.gov.au/atmoss/falcon.application_start [accessed 16 June 2010].

ISO Website: http://www.iso.org/iso/about/discover-iso_isos-name.htm [accessed 2 June 2010].

Jacobson, Nels, 'Faith, Hope & Parody: *Campbell v Acuff-Rose*, "Oh, Pretty Woman," and Parodists' Rights' (1994) 31 *Houston Law Review* 955–1026.

Jamar, Steven D., 'The Protection of Intellectual Property Under Islamic Law' (1992) 21 *Capital University Law Review* 1079–1106

Janke, Terri, 'Indigenous Arts Certification Mark', Case Study 8 in *Minding Culture: Case-Studies on Intellectual Property and Traditional Cultural Expressions* (Geneva: World Intellectual Property Organization, 2003), http://www.wipo.int/tk/en/studies/cultural/minding-culture/studies/indigenousarts.pdf [accessed 14 June 2010].

Janke, Terri, *Minding Culture: Case-Studies on Intellectual Property and Traditional Cultural Expressions* (Geneva: World Intellectual Property Organization, 2003), http://www.wipo.int/tk/en/studies/cultural/minding-culture/studies [accessed 14 June 2010].

Janke, Terri, *Our Culture: Our Future: Report on Australian Indigenous Cultural and Intellectual Property Rights* (Sydney: Michael Frankel, 1998).

Janke, Terri, 'Use of Trade Marks to Protect Traditional Cultural Expressions', Case Study 2 in *Minding Culture: Case-Studies on Intellectual Property and Traditional Cultural Expressions* (Geneva: World Intellectual Property Organization, 2003), http://www.wipo.int/export/sites/www/tk/en/studies/cultural/minding-culture/studies/trademarks.pdf [accessed 14 June 2010].

Janke, Terri, *Writing Up Indigenous Research: Authorship, Copyright and Indigenous Knowledge Systems* (Sydney: Terri Janke, 2009).

Janson, Jonathan, 'A Brief Overview of the Dutch Art Market in the 17th c', http://www.essentialvermeer.com/dutch-painters/dutch_art/ecnmcs_dtchart.html [accessed 15 May 2010].

Jary, David, 'The McDonaldization of Sport and Leisure', in Barry Smart (ed.), *Resisting McDonaldization* (London: Sage, 1999), 116–134.

Jaszi, Peter, 'On the Author Effect: Contemporary Copyright and Collective Creativity', in Martha Woodmansee and Peter Jaszi (eds.), *The Construction of Authorship: Textual Appropriation in Law and Literature* (Durham, NC: Duke University Press, 1994), 29–56.

Johnson, E. Scott, 'Protecting Distinctive Sounds: The Challenge of Digital Sampling' (1987) 2 *Journal of Law & Technology* 273.

Jones, Peter W., 'Indigenous Peoples and Intellectual Property Rights' (1996) 4 *Waikato Law Review* 117–140.

Jones, Richard H., 'The Myth of the Idea/Expression Dichotomy in Copyright Law' (1990) 10:3 *Pace Law Review* 551–607.

Jordan, Brenda G. and Victoria Louise Weston, *Copying the Master and Stealing His Secrets: Talent and Training in Japanese Painting* (Honolulu: University of Hawaii Press, 2003).

Kahn, Joseph, 'Sane Chinese Put in Asylum, Doctors Say' (16 March 2006) *New York Times*.

Kant, Immanuel, *Critique of Practical Reason and Other Works on the Theory of Ethics* (Barnes and Noble Publishing, 2004; first published 1788).

Kant, Immanuel, *Critique of Pure Reason*, ed. and trans. Paul Guyer and Allen W. Wood (Cambridge: Cambridge University Press, 1999).

Kelsen, Hans, *Introduction to the Problems of Legal Theory* (Oxford: Clarendon Press, 1992).

Kenyon, Andrew T., Megan Richardson, and Sam Ricketson (eds.), *Landmarks in Australian Intellectual Property Law* (Melbourne: Cambridge University Press, 2009).

Khan, Ali, 'Islam as Intellectual Property' (2000–2001) 31 *Cumberland Law Review* 631–684.

Kim, Jaegwon and Ernest Sosa (eds.), *A Companion to Metaphysics* (Oxford: Blackwell, 1995).

King, Michael and Chris Thornhill (eds.), *Luhmann on Law and Politics: Critical Appraisals and Applications* (Oxford: Hart, 2006).

Kline, Scott M. and Matthew C. Floyd, 'Managing Confidential Relationships in Intellectual Property Transactions: Use Restrictions, Residual Knowledge Clauses, and Trade Secrets' (2006) 25 *Review of Litigation* 311–348.

Kramsch, Claire, *Language and Culture* (Oxford: Oxford University Press, 1998).

Krausse, Anna C., *The Story of Painting: From the Renaissance to the Present* (Cologne: Könemann, 1995).

Kravis, Randy S., 'Does a Song by Any Other Name Still Sound as Sweet? Digital Sampling and Its Copyright Implications' (1993) 43 *American University Law Review* 231–276.

Kready, Laura Fry, *A Study of Fairy Tale*s (Forgotten Books, 2008; originally published 1916).

Krygier, Martin, 'Thinking Like a Lawyer', in Wojciech Sadurski (ed.), *Ethical Dimensions of Legal Theory* (Amsterdam: Rodolpi, 1991), 67–90.

Kuruk, Paul, 'Role of Customary Law under Sui Generis Frameworks of Intellectual Property Rights in Traditional and Indigenous Knowledge', (2007) 17 *Indiana International and Comparative Law Review* 67–118.

Laddie, Hugh, Peter Prescott, and Mary Vitoria, *The Modern Law of Copyright and Designs*, Vol. 1 (London: Butterworths, 1995).

Lakoff, George, *Don't Think of an Elephant: Know Your Values and Frame the Debate* (White River Junction, VT: Chelsea Green, 2004).

Lakwete, Angela, *Inventing the Cotton Gin: Machine and Myth in Antebellum America* (Baltimore: Johns Hopkins University Press, 2005).

The Lancet website: http://www.download.thelancet.com/flatcontentassets/authors/icmje.pdf [accessed 24 January 2010].

Landes, William M. and Richard A. Posner, 'An Economic Analysis of Copyright Law', (1989) 18:2 *Journal of Legal Studies* 325–363.

Landes, William M. and Richard A. Posner, *The Economic Structure of Intellectual Property Law* (Cambridge, MA: Belknap Press of Harvard University Press, 2003).

Lange, David, 'Recognizing the Public Domain' (1981) 44 *Law and Contemporary Problems* 147–178.

Landes, William M. and Richard A. Posner, 'Reimagining the Public Domain' (2003) 66 *Law and Contemporary Problems* 463–483.

Lange, David L. and H. Jefferson Powell, *No Law: Intellectual Property in the Image of an Absolute First Amendment* (Stanford, CA: Stanford Law Books, 2009).

Latimer, Jack (ed.), *Friendship Among Equals: Recollections from ISO's First Fifty Years* (Geneva: ISO Central Secretariat, 1997).

Lemley, Mark A., 'Property, Intellectual Property, and Free Riding' (2004–2005) 83 *Texas Law Review* 1031–1076.

Lemley, Mark A., 'Romantic Authorship and the Rhetoric of Property' (1997) 75 *Texas Law Review* 873–906.

Lenderman, Max, *Experience the Message: How Experiential Marketing Is Changing the Brand World* (Toronto: McClelland & Stewart, 2007).

Leonard, Gregory K. and Lauren J. Stiroh (eds.), *Economic Approaches to Intellectual Property Policy, Litigation, and Management* (New York: NERA Economic Consulting, 2005).

Lessig, Lawrence, *Free Culture: How Big Media Uses Technology and the Law to Lock Down Culture and Control Creativity* (New York: Penguin, 2005).

Lewis, Nicholas B., 'Shades of Grey: Can the Copyright Fair Use Defense Adapt to New Re-Contextualized Forms of Music and Art?' (2005) 55 *American University Law Review* 267–306.

Libling, D. F., 'The Concept of Property: Property in Intangibles' (1978) 94 *Law Quarterly Review* 538.

Lide, E. Casey, 'ADR and Cyberspace: The Role of Alternative Dispute Resolution in Online Commerce, Intellectual Property and Defamation' (1996) *Ohio State Journal on Dispute Resolution* 192–222.

Litman, Jessica, 'After Feist' (1992) 17 *University of Dayton Law Review* 607–616.

Litman, Jessica, *Digital Copyright* (Amherst, NY: Prometheus, 2001).

Litman, Jessica, 'The Politics of Intellectual Property' (2009) 27 *Cardozo Arts and Entertainment Law Journal* 313–320.

Litman, Jessica, 'The Public Domain' (1990) 39 *Emory Law Journal* 965–1024.

Locke, John, *Second Treatise of Government*, ed. P. Laslett (Cambridge: Cambridge University Press, 1970).

Loughlan, Patricia, 'Qualitative Standards for the Protection of Literary and Artistic Works', in Alice Ehr-Soon Tay and Conita S. Leung (eds.), *Australian Law and Legal Thinkers in the 1990s: A Collection of 32 Australian Reports to the XIVth International Congress of Comparative Law* (Athens 31 July–6 August 1994), 263.

Loughlan, Patricia, '"You Wouldn't Steal a Car …": Intellectual Property and the Language of Theft' (2007) 29 *European Intellectual Property Review* 401–405.

Loveland, Ian, *Constitutional Law: A Critical Introduction* (London: Butterworths, 1996).

Luhmann, Niklas, *Social Systems* (Stanford, CA: Stanford University Press, 1996).

Lury, Giles, *Brandwatching: Lifting the Lid on Branding* (Dublin: Blackhall, 2001).

MacCormick, Neil, 'Law as Institutional Fact', in Neil MacCormick and Ota Weinberger, *An Institutional Theory of Law: New Approaches to Legal Positivism* (Dordrecht: D. Reidel, 1986), 49–76.

MacCormick, Neil and Zenon Bankowski, 'Speech Acts, Legal Institutions, and Real Laws', in Neil MacCormick and Peter Birks (eds.), *The Legal Mind: Essays for Tony Honoré* (Oxford: Oxford University Press, 1986),121–133.

MacCormick, Neil and Peter Birks (eds.), *The Legal Mind: Essays for Tony Honoré* (Oxford: Oxford University Press, 1986).

MacCormick, Neil and Ota Weinberger, *An Institutional Theory of Law: New Approaches to Legal Positivism* (Dordrecht: D. Reidel, 1986).

Macpherson, C. B., 'Human Rights as Property Rights' (1977) 24 *Dissent* 72–77.

Maddock, Kenneth, 'Aboriginal Customary Law', in Peter Hanks and Bryan Keon-Cohen (eds.), *Aborigines and the Law* (Sydney: George Allen & Unwin, 1984), 212–237.

Madow, Michael, 'Private Ownership of Public Image: Popular Culture and Publicity Rights', (1993) 81 *California Law Review* 127–240.

Magee, Bryan, *The Story of Philosophy* (London: Dorling Kindersley, 1998).

Malkan, Jeffrey, 'What Is a Copy?' (2005) 23 *Cardozo Arts and Entertainment Law Journal* 419–463.

Marcus, Caroline, 'Stop Me if My Tag Is Showing' (17 May 2009) *Sydney Morning Herald*, http://www.smh.com.au/lifestyle/lifematters/stop-me-if-my-tag-is-showing-20090516-b6pk.html [accessed 31 January 2010].

Martin, Scott M., 'The Mythology of the Public Domain: Exploring the Myths Behind Attacks on the Duration of Copyright Protection' (2002–2003) 36 *Loyola of Los Angeles Law Review* 253–322.

Marx, Karl, *Early Writings*, ed. and trans. T. Bottomore (London: Watts, 1963).

Maskus, Keith E. (ed.), *The WTO, Intellectual Property Rights and the Knowledge Economy* (Cheltenham: Edward Elgar, 2005).

May, Christopher, *The Global Political Economy of Intellectual Property Rights: The New Enclosures* (London: Routledge, 2009, 2nd ed.).

May, Christopher and Susan K. Sell, *Intellectual Property Rights: A Critical History* (Boulder, CO: Lynne Rienner, 2005).

McAleer, Michael and Les Oxley (eds.), *Economic and Legal Issues in Intellectual Property* (Oxford: Wiley-Blackwell, 2007).

McCardle, Meredith, 'Fan Fiction, Fandom, and Fanfare: What's All the Fuss?' (2003) 9 *Boston University Journal of Science and Technology Law* 443–468, Part IIIE.

McCarl, Bruce A., 'Citations and Individuals: First Authorship Across the Alphabet' (1993) 15:2 *Review of Agricultural Economics*, 307–312.

McIntyre, Greg, *Aboriginal Customary Law: Can It be Recognised?* Background paper (Perth: Law Reform Commission of Western Australia, 2005).

McKeough, Jill, Andrew Stewart, and Philip Griffith, *Intellectual Property in Australia* (Sydney: Butterworths, 2004).

McLeod, Kembrew and Rudolf Kuenzli (eds), *Cutting Across Media: Appropriation Art, Interventionist Collage, and Copyright Law* (Durham, NC: Duke University Press, 2011).

McRae, Heather, Garth Nettheim, Laura Beacroft, Luke McNamara, and Shelley Wright, *Indigenous Legal Issues: Commentary and Materials* (Sydney: Law Book Company, 2003).

McRae, Heather, Garth Nettheim, Thalia Anthony, Laura Beacroft, Sean Brennan, Megan Davis, and Terri Janke, *Indigenous Legal Issues: Commentary and Materials* (Sydney: Law Book Company, 2009; 4th ed.).

McSherry, Corynne, *Who Owns Academic Work? Battling for Control of Intellectual Property* (Cambridge, MA: Harvard University Press, 2001).

Meltzer, F., *Hot Property: The Stakes and Claims of Literary Originality* (Chicago: University of Chicago Press, 1994).

Merges, Robert P., 'Battle of Lateralisms: Intellectual Property and Trade' (1990) 8 *Boston University International Law Journal* 239–246.

Merges, Robert P., *Economics of Intellectual Property Law*, Vols. 1 and 2 (Cheltenham: Edward Elgar, 2008).

Merthyr Tydfil County Borough Council Trading Standards Service, Wales, website: http://www.merthyr.gov.uk/tradingstandards/services_contents.html [accessed 25 May 2006].

Metz, Lance, 'Review of the Textile Industry of South-West England: A Social Archaeology, by Marilyn Palmer and Peter Neaverson' (2006) 32:2 *Journal for Industrial Archaeology* 69.

Michael, Mike, 'A Paradigm Shift? Connections with Other Critiques of Social Constructionism', in David J. Nightingale and John Crosby (eds.), *Social Constructionist Psychology: A Critical Analysis of Theory and Practice* (Birmingham: Open University Press, 1999), 52–66.

Miller, Karl, *Authors* (Oxford: Clarendon Press, 1989).

Moffat, Rachel and Eugene de Klerk (eds.), *Material Worlds* (Cambridge: Cambridge Scholars Press, 2007).

Moles, Robert N., *Definition and Rule in Legal Theory: A Reassessment of H. L. A. Hart and the Positivist Tradition* (Oxford: Basil Blackwell, 1987).

Mollerup, Per, *Marks of Excellence: The History and Taxonomy of Trademarks* (London: Phaidon, 1998).

Moore, Adam D., *Intellectual Property and Information Control: Philosophic Foundations and Contemporary Issues* (New Brunswick, NJ: Transaction, 2004).

Moore, Christopher, 'Creative Choices: Changes to Australian Copyright Law and the Future of the Public Domain' (2005) 114 *Media International Australia* 710–82.

Morely, Tim, 'Copyright Term Extension in the EC: Harmonization or Headache?' (1992) 24 *Copyright World* 10–17.

Morris, A.I. and Barry Quest, *Design: The Modern Law and Practice* (London: Butterworths, 1987).

Moustakas, John, 'Group Rights in Cultural Property: Justifying Strict Inalienability' (1990) 74 *Cornell Law Review* 1179–1227.

Munzer, Stephen R. (ed.), *New Essays in the Legal and Political Theory of Property* (New York: Cambridge University Press, 2001).

Murphy, Howard, *Aboriginal Art* (London: Phaidon Press, 1998).

Murphy, John P. and Ana R. Murphy, *Pragmatism from Peirce to Davidson* (Boulder, CO: Westview Press, 1990).

Murphy, Kim, 'Speak Out? Are You Crazy?' (30 May 2006) *Los Angeles Times*.

Murphy, Tim, Simon Roberts, and Tatiana Flessas, *Understanding Property Law* (London: Sweet & Maxwell, 2004).

Museu Picasso de Barcelona website: http://www.museupicasso.bcn.es/en/ [accessed 15 May 2010].

Nard, Craig Allen and Andrew P. Morriss, 'Constitutionalizing Patents: From Venice to Philadelphia' (August 2004) *Case Research Paper Series in Legal Studies*, Working Paper 04–12.

Nathan, David (ed.), 'Aboriginal and Torres Strait Islander Languages', *World Wide Web Virtual Library*, http://www.dnathan.com/VL/austLang.htm [accessed 30 May 2010].

National Institutes of Health, Office of the Director, *Guidelines for the Conduct of Research in the Intramural Research Programs at NIH* (Committee on Scientific Conduct and Ethics, National Institutes of Health, Office of the

Director: May 2007), http://www1.od.nih.gov/oir/sourcebook/ethic-conduct/Conduct%20Research%206–11–07.pdf [accessed 24 January 2010].

Netanel, Neil Weinstock, 'Alienability Restrictions and the Enhancement of Author Autonomy in United states and Continental Copyright Law' (1994) 12 *Cardozo Arts and Entertainment Law Journal* 1–78.

Netanel, Neil Weinstock, 'Asserting Copyright's Democratic Principles in the Global Arena', (1998) 51 *Vanderbilt Law Review* 217–330.

Netanel, Neil Weinstock, 'Copyright and a Democratic Civil Society' (1996) 106:2 *Yale Law Journal* 283–388.

Newman, Jon O., 'New Lyrics for an Old Melody: The Idea/Expression Dichotomy in the Computer Age' (1999) 17 *Cardozo Arts and Entertainment Law Journal* 691–703.

Newsome, Matthew A. C., 'Restricted Tartans and Copyright' (April 2007) *Scottish Banner*, http://www.albanach.org/restricted.htm [accessed 14 June 2010].

Nicholas, Barry, *An Introduction to Roman Law* (Oxford: Clarendon Press, 1969).

Nightingale, David J. and John Crosby (eds.), *Social Constructionist Psychology: A Critical Analysis of Theory and Practice* (Birmingham: Open University Press, 1999).

Nimmer, M. B., P. Marcus, D. A. Myers, and D. Nimmer, *Cases and Materials on Copyright and Other Aspects of Entertainment Litigation Including Unfair Competition, Defamation, Privacy* (St. Paul, MN: West, 1991).

Nowell-Smith, Simon, *International Copyright Law and the Publisher in the Reign of Queen Victoria* (Oxford: Clarendon Press, 1968).

Nozick, Robert, *Anarchy, State and Utopia* (New York: Basic Books, 1974).

Obaldia, Irma De, 'Western Intellectual Property and Indigenous Cultures: The Case of the Panamanian Indigenous Intellectual Property Law' (2005) 23 *Boston University International Law Journal* 337–394.

Oddi, Samuel A., 'TRIPS: Natural Rights and a "Polite Form of Economic Imperialism" ', (1996) 29 *Vanderbilt Journal of Transnational Law* 415–470.

Office of the United States Trade Representative, 'Special 301 Report Finds Progress and Need for Significant Improvements', Press release (Washington, DC, 29 April 2005).

Office of the United States Trade Representative, *2004 Special 301 Report: Executive Summary* (Washington, DC, 2005).

Ogden, C. K., *Bentham's Theory of Fictions* (London: Kegan Paul, Trench, Trubner, 1932).

Olins, Wally, *On B®and* (London: Thames & Hudson, 2004).

Online Encyclopedia of Silver Marks, Hallmarks Makers' and Marks website, 'Tiffany Silvery Marks and Dates': http://www.925–1000.com/Tiffany_Date_Code.html [accessed 7 June 2010].

Ono, Shoen, *Overview of Japanese Trademark Law* (Yuhikaku, 1999).

Panesar, Sukhninder, *General Principles of Property Law* (Harlow: Pearson Education, 2001).

Pastoureau, Michael, *Heraldry: Its Origins and Meaning*, trans. Francisca Garvie (London: Thames & Hudson, 1997).

Patterson, Dennis, *Law and Truth* (Oxford: Oxford University Press, 1996).

Patterson, Dennis, (ed.), *A Companion to Philosophy of Law and Legal Theory* (Oxford: Wiley-Blackwell, 2010).

Patterson, Lyman Ray, *Copyright in Historical Perspective* (Nashville: Vanderbilt University Press, 1968).

Patterson, Dennis, 'Free Speech, Copyright, and Fair Use' (1987) 40 *Vanderbilt Law Review* 1–66.

Patterson, L. Ray et al., 'Regents Guide to Understanding Copyright and Educational Fair Use' (1997) 5 *Journal of Intellectual Property Law* 243–305.

Penner, J. E., *The Idea of Property in Law* (Oxford: Oxford University Press, 1997).

Pettit, D. Bradley, 'Can an Attorney Defer Recognition of a Fee Income in a Case Involving a Structured Settlement?' (1996) 70 *Florida Bar Journal* 36.

Petty, Ross D., 'Of Tartans and Trademarks' (2004) 94 *Trademark Reporter* 859–880.

Philbrick, Francis S., 'Changing Conceptions of Property Law' (1938) 86 *University of Pennsylvania Law Review* 691–732.

Phillips, Jeremy, *Trade Mark Law: A Practical Anatomy* (Oxford: Oxford University Press, 2003).

Phillips, Jeremy and Alison Firth, *Introduction to Intellectual Property Law* (London: Butterworths, 1995).

Pigeon-Bormans, Anne and Pierre Lautier, 'Photographies of Picasso's Work Protected by Copyright' (6 September 2004), http://www.avocats-publishing.com/Photographies-of-PICASSO-S-WORK, the website of

Paris intellectual property law firm Avocats en propriété intellectuelle [accessed 15 May 2010].

Pine, L. G., *The Story of Heraldry* (London: Country Life, 1952).

Pollock, Frederick, *Pollock on Torts* (1923, 13th ed.).

Porter, Brian E. and Mark B. Robinson, *Protected Persons and Their Property in New South Wales* (Sydney: Law Book Company, 1987).

'Portraits of Picasso' (18 October 1996) *The Atlantic Online*, http://www.theatlantic.com/past/docs/unbound/flashbks/picasso/picasso.htm [accessed 10 May 2010].

Posey, Darrell A. and Graham Dutfield, *Beyond Intellectual Property: Toward Traditional Resource Rights for Indigenous Peoples and Local Communities* (Ottawa: International Development Research Centre, 1996).

Posner, Richard A., 'Do We Have Too Many Intellectual Property Rights?' (2005) 9 *Marquette Intellectual Property Law Review* 173–185 (presented at the Eighth Annual Honorable Helen Wilson Nies Memorial Lecture in Intellectual Property Law, Marquette University Law School, 28 March 2005).

Pound, Roscoe, *Social Control Through Law* (New Haven, CT: Transaction, 1942).

Powerhouse Museum (Sydney) website, Harley Davison Exhibition: http://www.powerhousemuseum.com/previous/harley_legend.asp [accessed 18 January 2010].

Proctor, Charles, *Mann on the Legal Aspect of Money* (Oxford: Oxford University Press, 2005).

Pugatch, Meir Perez, *The International Political Economy Of Intellectual Property Rights* (Cheltenham: Edward Elgar, 2004).

Puri, Kamal, 'The Term of Copyright Protection: Is It Too Long in the Wake of New Technologies?' (1990) 12 *European Intellectual Property Review* 12–20.

Puri, Kanwal K., *Industrial Design Law in Australia and New Zealand* (Sydney: Butterworths, 1986).

Putnam, George, 'Literary Property: An Historical Sketch', in George Putnam(ed.), *The Question of Copyright* (New York: Knickerbocker, 1896).

Putnam, George, (ed.), *The Question of Copyright* (New York: Knickerbocker, 1896), 351–411.

Queensland Primary Industries and Fisheries Brands Office website: http://www.dpi.qld.gov.au/4790_5223.htm [accessed 4 June 2010].

Rahmatian, Andreas, 'The Gowers Review on Copyright Term Extension' (2007) 29:9 *European Intellectual Property Review* 353–356.

Rawlings, Gertrude Burford, *The Story of Books* (New York: D. Appleton, 1901).

Rawls, John, *Political Liberalism* (New York: Columbia University Press, 1996).

Raz, Joseph, *The Authority of Law: Essays on Law and Morality* (Oxford: Clarendon Press, 1979).

Read, Donald, *The Power of News: The History of Reuters, 1849–1989* (Oxford: Oxford University Press, 1999).

Reichman, J. H., 'Electronic Information Tools: The Outer Edge of World Intellectual Property Law' (1992) 17 *University of Dayton Law Review* 797–838.

Reichman, J. H., 'The Globalization of Private Knowledge Goods and the Privatization of Global Public Goods' (2004) 7:2 *Journal of International Economic Law* 279–320.

Rennie, Drummond and Annette Flanagin,' Authorship! Authorship! Guests, Ghosts, Grafters, and the Two-Sided Coin' (1994) 271:6 *Journal of the American Medical Association* 469–471.

Rennie, Drummond, Annette Flanagin, and Veronica Yank, 'The Contributions of Authors' (2000) 284 *Journal of the American Medical Association* 89–91.

Ricketson, S., 'The Concept of Originality in Anglo-Australian Copyright Law' (1992) 39:4 *Journal of the Copyright Society of the USA* 265–288.

Ricketson, S., 'Confidential Information: A New Proprietary Interest?' (1977) 11 *Melbourne University Law Review* 223–245.

Ricketson, Sam, Megan Richardson, and Mark Davison, *Intellectual Property: Cases, Materials and Commentary* (Sydney: LexisNexis Butterworths, 2009).

Riding, Alan, 'A Family Feud over a Picasso (On Wheels); A New Car's Logo Divides the Heirs of a Lucrative Name' (19 April 1999) *New York Times*, http://www.nytimes.com/1999/04/19/arts/family-feud-over-picasso-wheels-new-car-s-logo-divides-heirs-lucrative-name.html?pagewanted=all [accessed 15 May 2010].

Ries, Al and Laura Ries, *The Origin of Brands: How Product Evolution Creates Endless Possibilities for New Brands* (New York: HarperCollins, 2004).

Riesenberg, Don and George D. Lundberg, 'The Order of Authorship: Who's on First?' (1990) 264:14 *Journal of the American Medical Association* 1857.

Riley, Angel R., 'Recovering Collectivity: Group Rights to Intellectual Property in Indigenous Communities' (2000) 18 *Cardozo Arts and Entertainment Law Journal* 175–225.

Rimmer, Matthew, 'Australian Icons: Authenticity Marks and Identity Politics' (2004) 3 *Indigenous Law Journal* 139–179.

Rimmer, Matthew, 'Robbery Under Arms: Copyright Law and the Australia–United States Free Trade Agreement' (2006) 11(3) *First Monday*: http://firstmonday.org/htbin/cgiwrap/bin/ojs/index.php/fm/article/view/1316/1236 [online Journal, accessed 15 January 2010]; also available at SSRN: http://ssrn.com/abstract=855805 [accessed 15 January 2010].

Roberts, R. J., 'Is Information Property?' (1987) 3 *Intellectual Property Journal* 209–215.

Robinson, Richard, *Definition* (Oxford: Clarendon Press, 1968).

Rockman, Howard B., *Intellectual Property Law for Engineers and Scientists* (Hoboken, NJ: Wiley-IEEE, 2004).

Rodrigues, Jr., Edson Beas, and Bryan Murphy, 'Brazil's Prior Consent Law: A Dialogue between Brazil and the United States over Where the TRIPS Agreement Currently Sets the Balance Between the Protection of Pharmaceutical Patents and Access to Medicines' (2006) 16 *Albany Law Journal of Science & Technology* 423–456.

Rogers, Edward S., "The Social Value of Trade-marks and Brands" (1947) 37 *Trade Mark Bulletin* 249–254.

Rohrbacher, Blake, 'More Equal Than Others: Defending Property-Contract Parity in Bankruptcy' (2005) 114 *Yale Law Journal* 1099–1132.

Romaine, Suzane (ed.), *Language in Australia* (Cambridge: Cambridge University Press, 1991).

Rorty, Richard, 'Introduction: Pragmatism as Anti-Representationalism', in John P. Murphy and Ana R. Murphy, *Pragmatism: From Peirce to Davidson* (Boulder, CO: Westview Press, 1990), 1–6.

Rorty, Richard, *Objectivity, Relativism and Truth: Philosophical Papers*, Vol. 1 (New York: Cambridge University Press, 1991).

Rorty, Richard, "Texts and Lumps", in *Objectivity, Relativism and Truth: Philosophical Papers*, Vol. 1 (Cambridge: Cambridge University Press, 1991).

Rose, Mark, 'The Author as Proprietor: *Donaldson v Becket* and the Genealogy of Modern Authorship' (1988) 23 *Representations* 51–85.

Rose, Mark, *Authors and Owners: The Invention of Copyright* (Cambridge, MA: Harvard University Press, 1993).

Rose, Mark, 'Copyright and Its Metaphors' (2002–2003) *UCLA Law Review* 1–16.

Ross, Hamish, *Law as a Social Institution* (Oxford: Hart, 2001).

Ross, Joseph S., Kevin P. Hill, David S. Egilman, and Harlan M. Krumholz, 'Guest Authorship and Ghostwriting in Publications Related to Rofecoxib: A Case Study of Industry Documents from Rofecoxib Litigation' (2008) 299:15 *Journal of the American Medical Association* 1800–1812, http://www.councilofscienceeditors.org/publications/v23n4p111-119.pdf [accessed 24 January 2010].

Rothman, Jennifer E., 'The Questionable Use of Custom in Intellectual Property' (2007) 93 *Virginia Law Review* 1899–1982.

Royal Society of Medicine website: http://www.pnas.org/site/misc/iforc.shtml#ii [accessed 23 January 2010].

Ruston, Gerald, 'On the Origin of Trademarks' (1955) 45 *Trade-Mark Reporter* 127–144.

Sadurski, Wojciech, *Freedom of Speech and Its Limits* (Dordrecht: Kluwer Academic, 1999).

Sadurski, Wojciech, (ed.), *Ethical Dimensions of Legal Theory* (Amsterdam: Rodolpi, 1991).

Sainsbury, Maree, *Moral Rights and Their Application in Australia* (Sydney: Federation Press, 2003).

Saint-Amour, Paul K., *The Copywrights: Intellectual Property and the Literary Imagination* (Ithaca, NY: Cornell University Press, 2003).

St. Clair, William, 'Metaphors of Intellectual Property', in Ronan Deazley, Martin Kretschmer, and Lionel Bently (eds.), *Privilege and Property: Essays on the History of Copyright* (Cambridge: Open Book, 2010), 369–395.

Salter, Brent, *Copyright, Collaboration and the Future of Dramatic Authorship* (Strawberry Hills, Sydney: Currency House, 2009).

Samuels, Edward, 'The Idea–Expression Dichotomy in Copyright Law' (1989) 56 *Tennessee Law Review* 321–463.

Sanderson, John, *'But the People's Creatures': The Philosophical Basis of the English Civil War* (Manchester: Manchester University Press, 1989).

Sapherstein, Michael P., 'The Trademark Registrability of the Harley-Davidson Roar: A Multimedia Analysis' (1998) *Boston College Intellectual Property and Technology Forum*. http://www.bc.edu/bc_org/avp/law/st_org/iptf/articles/content/1998101101.html [online journal, accessed 23 January 2010].

Saunders, David, *Authorship and Copyright* (London: Routledge, 1992).

Scafidi, Susan, 'Intellectual Property and Cultural Products' (2001) 81 *Boston University Law Review* 793–842.

Schaffner, Derek J., 'The Digital Millennium Copyright Act: Overextension of Copyright Protection and the Unintended Chilling Effects on Fair Use, Free Speech and Innovation' (2004) 14 *Cornell Journal of Law and Public Policy* 145–169.

Schechter, Frank I., *The Historical Foundations of the Law Relating to Trade-Mark Law* (Union, NJ: Lawbook Exchange, 1999; originally published New York: Columbia University Press, 1925).

Schechter, Roger E. and John R. Thomas, *Intellectual Property: The Law of Copyrights, Patents and Trademarks* (St. Paul, MN: West, 2003).

Schiller, Arthur, 'Trade Secrets and the Roman Law: The Actio Servi Corrupti' (1930) 30 *Columbia Law Review* 837–845.

Schmitt, Bernd, *Experiential Marketing: How to Get Customers to Sense, Feel, Think, Act, and Relate to your Company and Brands* (New York: Free Press, 1999).

Schonning, Peter, 'Survey of the Term of Protection of Authors' Rights' (2000) 11:4 *Entertainment Law Review* 59–72.

Schroeder, Jeanne L., *Unnatural Rights: Hegel and Intellectual Property* (Working Paper No. 80, Benjamin N. Cardozo School of Law, Jacob Burns Institute for Advanced Legal Studies, 2004).

Schwoerer, Lois G., 'Liberty of the Press and Public Opinion: 1660–1695', in J.R. Jones (ed.), *Liberty Secured? Britain Before and After 1688* (Stanford, CA: Stanford University Press, 1992), 199–230.

Searle, John R., *The Construction of Social Reality* (London: Penguin, 1996).

Self, Henry, 'Digital Sampling: A Cultural Perspective' (2001–2002) 9 *UCLA Entertainment Law Review* 347–360.

Sell, Susan K., 'Industry Strategies for Intellectual Property and Trade: The Quest for TRIPS, and Post-TRIPS Strategies' (2002) 79 *Cardozo Journal of International and Comparative Law* 79–108.

Sell, Susan K., *Power and Ideas: North–South Politics of Intellectual Property and Antitrust* (Albany: State University of New York Press, 1998).

Sell, Susan K., *Private Power, Public Law: The Globalization of Intellectual Property Rights* (Cambridge: Cambridge University Press, 2003).

Seltzer, Leon E., *Exemptions and Fair Use in Copyright: The Exclusive Rights Tensions in the 1976 Copyright Act* (Cambridge, MA: Harvard University Press, 1978).

Seville, Catherine, 'From Pirates to Eagles: America's Changing View of Copyright' (2007) 29:10 *European Intellectual Property Review* 406–410.

Shakespeare, William, *The Complete Works of William Shakespeare* (Cambridge: Cambridge University Press, 1987).

Shauer, Frederick, 'Social Foundations of the Law of Defamation: A Comparative Analysis' (1980) 1 *Journal of Media Law and Practice* 3–23.

Sheffield Assay Office website: http://www.assayoffice.co.uk/Services/UK_Hallmarks.asp [accessed 4 June 2010].

Sheikh, Aziz, 'Publication Ethics and the Research Assessment Exercise: Reflections on the Troubled Question of Authorship' (2000) 26 *Journal of Medical Ethics* 422–426.

Sherman, Brad and Lionel Bently, *The Making of Modern Intellectual Property Law: The British Experience, 1760–1911* (Cambridge: Cambridge University Press, 1999).

Sherman, Brad and Alain Strowel (eds.), *Of Authors and Origins* (Oxford: Clarendon Press, 1994).

Shiner, Roger A., 'Law and Its Normativity', in Dennis Patterson (ed.), *A Companion to Philosophy of Law and Legal Theory* (Oxford: Wiley-Blackwell, 2010), 417–445.

Shiva, Vandana, *Plunder or Protect? Understanding Intellectual Property Rights* (London: Zed, 2001).

Sinclair, M.B.W., 'Plugs, Holes, Filters, and Goals: An Analysis of Legislative Attitudes' (1996–1997) 41 *New York Law School Law Review* 237–284.

Smart, Barry (ed.), *Resisting McDonaldization* (London: Sage, 1999).

Smilansky, Shaz, *Experiential Marketing: A Practical Guide to Interactive Brand Experiences* (London: Kogan Page, 2009).

Smith, Richard, 'Authorship: Time for a Paradigm Shift?' (editorial) (1997) 314 *British Medical Journal* 992.

Smith, Richard, 'Authorship Is Dying; Long Live Contributorship' (1997) 315 *British Medical Journal* 696, http://resources.bmj.com/bmj/authors/article-submission/authorship-contributorship [accessed 24 January 2010].

Smith, Shaun, 'Brand Experience', in Rita Clifton and John Simmons, *Brands and Branding* (Princeton, NJ: Bloomberg Press, 2004).

Sobota, Katharina, 'Don't Mention the Norm' (1991) IV:10 *International Journal for the Semiotics of Law* 45–60.

Somoano, M. Leah, '*Bridgeport Music, Inc. v. Dimension Films:* Has Unlicensed Digital Sampling of Copyrighted Sound Recordings Come to an End?' (2006) 21 *Berkeley Technology Law Journal* 289–310.

Spence, Michael, *Intellectual Property* (Oxford: Oxford University Press, 2007).

Stallman, Richard (author) and Joshua Gay (ed.), *Free Software, Free Society: Selected Essays of Richard M. Stallman* (Boston: GNU Press, 2002).

Stallman, Richard (author) and Joshua Gay, 'Did You Say "Intellectual Property"? It's a Seductive Mirage' (2004), available at *GNU* website, http://www.gnu.org/philosophy/not-ipr.xhtml [accessed 5 September 2006].

Standards Australia website: http://www.standards.org.au/DevelopingStandards/BuyingaStandard.aspx [accessed 2 June 2010].

Stassinopoulos Huffington, Arianna, *Picasso: Creator and Destroyer* (New York: Avon, 1989).

Stationers' and Newspaper Makers'Company website: http://www.stationers.org/copyright.php [accessed 8 June 2009].

Stephen, James Fitzjames, *A History of the Criminal Law of England* (1883; rpt. London: Routledge, 1996).

Stephenson, Johanna (ed.), *Picasso: Challenging the Past* (London: National Gallery, 2009).

Strickland, Carol, *The Annotated Mona Lisa: A Crash Course in Art History from Prehistoric to Post-Modern* (Kansas City: Andrews McMeel, 1992).

Sundara Rajan, Mira T., *Copyright and Creative Freedom: A Study of Post-Socialist Law Reform* (London: Routledge, 2006).

Sykes, J. B. (ed.), *The Concise Oxford Dictionary of Current English* (Oxford: Clarendon Press, 1976, 6th ed.).

Szasz, Thomas, *Insanity: The Idea and Its Consequences* (New York: Wiley, 1987).

Tan, David, 'Beyond Trademark Law: What the Right of Publicity Can Learn from Cultural Studies' (2008) 25 *Cardozo Arts and Entertainment Law Journal* 914–994.

Tay, Alice Ehr-Soon and Conita S. Leung (eds.), *Australian Law and Legal Thinkers in the 1990s: A Collection of 32 Australian Reports to the XIVth International Congress of Comparative Law* (Athens, 31 July–6 August 1994).

Teubner, Gunther, *Law as an Autopoietic System* (Oxford: Blackwell, 1993).

Thomas, Mark, 'Information as Property: Humanism or Economic Rationalism in the Millenium?' (1998) 14 *Queensland University of Technology Law Journal* 203–213.

Thorley, Simon, Richard Miller, Guy Burkill, Collin Birss, and Douglas Campbell, *Terrell on the Law of Patents* (London: Sweet & Maxwell, 2006).

Trees, Kathryn, *Contemporary Issues Facing Customary Law and the General Legal System: Roebourne – A Case Study*, Background Paper No. 6 (Perth: Law Reform Commission of Western Australia, 2004).

Tscharntke, Teja, Michael E. Hochberg, Tatyana A. Rand, Vincent H. Resh, and Jochen Krauss, 'Author Sequence and Credit for Contributions in Multiauthored Publications' (2007) 5:1 *Public Library of Science Biology (PLoS Biology)* 13–14.

Turnbull, Paul, 'Theft in the Name of Science', (2008) 21 *Griffith Review*, http://www.griffithreview.com/images/stories/edition_articles/ed21_pdfs/turnbull_ed21.pdf [accessed 30 May 2010].

Tushnet, Rebecca, 'Payment in Credit: Copyright Law and Subcultural Creativity' (2007) *70 Law & Contemporary Problems* 135–174.

Tye, Michael, 'Image/Imagination', in Jaegwon Kim and Ernest Sosa (eds.), *A Companion to Metaphysics* (Oxford: Blackwell, 1995), 234–235.

Tyler, Tom R., 'Compliance with Intellectual Property Laws: A Psychological Perspective' (1996–1997) 29 *New York University Journal of International Law and Politics* 219–235.

Tyler, Tom R., *Why People Obey the Law* (Princeton, NJ: Princeton University Press, 2006).

Underkuffler, Laura S., *The Idea of Property: Its Meaning and Power* (Oxford: Oxford University Press, 2003).

United Nations website, Member States: http://www.un.org/News/Press/docs/2006/org1469.doc.htm [accessed 13 April 2009].

United Nations website, United Nations Member States, *Press Release* ORG/1469 (3 July 2006): http://www.un.org/News/Press/docs/2006/org1469.doc.htm [accessed 30 September 2011].

United States of America, H R Report No. 94–1476, 94th Congress, 2d Session (1976).

University of Sydney website, the 'University of Sydney's Coat of Arms': http://sydney.edu.au/heraldry/coat_of_arms/index.shtml [accessed 16 June 2010].

Upton, Nicholas, *Doctorum sui temporis Maecenas* (early 15th century).

Vaidhyanathan, Siva, *Copyrights and Copywrongs: The Rise of Intellectual Property and How It Threatens Creativity* (New York: New York University Press, 2003).

Van Hoecke, Mark, *Law as Communication* (Oxford: Hart, 2002).

Vaver, David, 'Does the Public Understand Intellectual Property Law? Do Lawyers?' *University of Oxford Faculty of Law Legal Studies Research Paper Series*, Working Paper No. 23/2006 (May 2006).

Vincent, Laurence, *Legendary Brands: Unleashing the Power of Storytelling to Create a Winning Market Strategy* (Chicago: Dearborn Trade, 2002).

Wager, Elizabeth, 'Bye Bye By-line, Hello Contributors' (2006) 99 *Journal of the Royal Society of Medicine* 542–543.

Waldron, Jeremy, *Liberal Rights: Collected Papers, 1981–1991* (New York: Cambridge University Press, 1993).

Waldron, Jeremy, *The Right to Private Property* (Oxford: Clarendon Press, 1988).

Walsh, Michael, 'Overview of Indigenous Languages of Australia', in Suzane Romaine (ed.), *Language in Australia* (Cambridge: Cambridge University Press, 1991) 27–48.

Watson, Alan, 'Trade Secrets and Roman Law: The Myth Exploded' (1996) 11 *Tulane European and Civil Law Forum* 19–29.

Wedderburn, K. W., *The Worker and the Law* (Harmondsworth: Penguin, 1986).

Weinand, Peter, 'Copyright Term Harmonisation in the European Union' (1994) 40 *Copyright World* 24–28.

Westfall, David and David Landau, 'Publicity Rights as Property Rights' (2005) 23 *Cardozo Arts and Entertainment Law Journal* 71–123.

Wheeler, John, *The English Legal System* (Harlow: Pearson Education, 2002).

Wilf, Steven, 'Who Authors Trademarks?' (1999) 17 *Cardozo Arts and Entertainment Law Journal* 1–46.

Williams, S. G., 'Existence', in Jaegwon Kim and Ernest Sosa (eds.), *A Companion to Metaphysics* (Oxford: Blackwell, 1995), 145–150.

Wipperfürth, Alex, *Brand Hijack: Marketing Without Marketing* (New York: Portfolio, Penguin, 2005).

Wiseman, Leanne, 'The Protection of Indigenous Art and Culture in Australia: The Labels of Authenticity'(2001) 23 *European Intellectual Property Review* 14–25.

Wittgenstein, Ludwig, *Philosophical Investigations*, trans. G. E. M. Anscombe (Oxford: Blackwell, 2003).

Woodmansee, Martha, *The Author, Art, and the Market: Rereading the History of Aesthetics* (New York: Columbia University Press, 1994).

Woodmansee, Martha, 'On the Author Effect: Recovering Collectivity' (2000) 10 *Cardozo Arts and Entertainment Law Journal* 279–292.

Woodmansee, Martha and Peter Jaszi (eds.), *The Construction of Authorship: Textual Appropriation in Law and Literature* (Durham, NC: Duke University Press, 1994).

World Intellectual Property Organization, *Introduction to Intellectual Property Theory and Practice* (London: Kluwer Law International, 1997).

World Intellectual Property Organization website, Traditional Knowledge, Genetic Resources and Traditional Cultural Expressions/Folklore: http://www.wipo.int/tk/en [accessed 8 June 2010].

World Intellectual Property Organization website, Treaties and Contracting Parties: http://www.wipo.int/treaties/en/ShowResults.jsp?country_id=ALL&start_year=ANY&end_year=ANY&search_what=C&treaty_id=15&treaty_id=2 [accessed 18 January 2009].

World Trade Organization website, membership list: http://www.wto.org/english/theWTO_e/whatis_e/tif_e/org6_e.htm [accessed 18 January 2009].

Yen, Alfred C., 'A First Amendment Perspective on the Idea/Expression Dichotomy and Copyright in a Work's "Total Concept and Feel"' (1989) 38 *Emory Law Journal* 393–436.

Yi Jun Tian, *Re-thinking Intellectual Property: The Political Economy of Copyright Protection in the Digital Era* (Abingdon: Routledge-Cavendish, 2008).

Yu, Peter K., 'Cultural Relics, Intellectual Property, and Intangible Heritage' (2008) 81 *Temple Law Review* 433–506.

Yurkowski, Rachel A., 'Is *Hyde Park* Hiding the Truth? An Analysis of the Public Interest Defence to Copyright Infringement' (2001) 32:4 *Victoria University of Wellington Law Review* 1053–1086.

Zheng Chengsi, 'Intellectual Property and Information Property' (1989) 9 *European Intellectual Property Review* 327–329.

Ziff, Bruce, *Borrowed Power: Essays on Cultural Appropriation* (New Brunswick, NJ: Rutgers University Press, 1997).

Zimbabwe Ministry for Justice and Legal Affairs website, Department of Deeds, Companies, Trade Marks, Patents and Industrial Designs: http://www.justice.gov.zw/index.php?option=com_content&view=article&id=51%3Adepartment-of-deeds-companies-trade-marks-patents-and-industrial-designs&catid=35%3Adepartments&Itemid=55 [accessed 7 June 2010].

Zimmerman, Diane Leenheer, 'Fitting Publicity Rights into Intellectual Property and Free Speech Theory: Sam, You Made the Pants Too Long!'

(1999–2000) 10 *DePaul-LCA Journal of Art and Entertainment Law* 283–314.

Zimmerman, Diane Leenheer, 'It's an Original!(?): In Pursuit of Copyright's Elusive Essence' (2004–2005) 28 *Columbia Journal of Law and the Arts* 187–212.

Zipes, Jack David, *Fairy Tale as Myth/Myth as Fairy Tale* (Lexington: University Press of Kentucky, 1994).

Zolotykh, Natalia, 'The Use and Regulation of Intellectual Property Rights in Russia', in Elmar Altvater and Kazimiera Prunskienê (eds.), *Intellectual Property Rights in Central and Eastern Europe: The Creation of Favourable Legal and Market Preconditions* (Amsterdam: IOS Press//Tokyo: Ohmsha, 1998), 138–146.

FILMOGRAPHY

Great White (1980). Originally released in Italian as *L' Ultimo squalo*. Directed by Enzo G. Castellari.

Harley Davidson and the Marlboro Man (1991). Directed by Simon Wincer.

Jaws (1975). Directed by Steven Spielberg.

Surviving Picasso (2006). Directed by James Ivory.

Wild Hogs (2007). Directed by Walt Becker.

Index

CPSIA information can be obtained at www.ICGtesting.com
Printed in the USA
LVOW13s0041211213

366092LV00012B/349/P

9 781107 691773